AIRCRAFT *VERSUS* AIRCRAFT

AIRCRAFT VERSUS AIRCRAFT

THE ILLUSTRATED STORY OF FIGHTER PILOT COMBAT SINCE 1914

NORMAN FRANKS

Crescent Books
New York

Aircraft versus Aircraft was conceived, edited and designed by Grub Street Copyright © 1986 by Grub Street

Text copyright © 1986 by Norman Franks Color artwork by Peter Endsleigh Castle and Terry Hadler

This 1990 edition published by Crescent Books, distributed by Crown Publishers, Inc, 225 Park Avenue South, New York, New York 10003

Franks, Norman L. R. Aircraft versus Aircraft: the illustrated story of fighter pilot combat since 1914.

Includes index
1. Fighter plane combat–History. 2. Fighter pilots. I. Title.
UG700. F73.
1986 358,4'14 86-905

h q f e d c b a

Printed in Italy by Stige

ACKNOWLEDGEMENTS

I'd like to give especial thanks to the following:

Air Vice Marshal H A C Bird-Wilson CBE DSO DFC AFC
Group Captain D E Gillam DSO DFC AFC
Group Captain J B Wray DFC
Wing Commander G J Gray DFC
Wing Commander P H M Richey DFC LdH
Wing Commander J E Storrar DFC AFC
Squadron Leader G G A Davies DFC
Squadron Leader R F Noble DFC
Squadron Leader A H Smith DFC
Squadron Leader D W A Stones DFC
Flight Lieutenant M S Allen DFC
Flight Lieutenant V C Fittall DFC
Flight Lieutenant A Mc Peart DFC
Major Douglas K Evans USAF Rtd

CONTENTS

CHAPTER ONE

THE FIRST ENCOUNTERS

THE TRUE HISTORY OF AVIATION is only as old as the 20th century, but Man's struggle to master the secrets of flight stretches back over the centuries to Leonardo da Vinci and beyond.

In the 18th century balloons provided part of the answer. On November 21, 1783 the first manned flight took place in Paris. Louis XVI and Marie Antoinette were among the crowd who watched as Pilâtre de Rozier and Marquis D'Arlandes floated into the sky in the second balloon built by the Montgolfier brothers. Later that year, on 1 December, a hydrogen-filled balloon designed and flown by Jacques Alexandre César Charles, flew 27 miles before returning to earth. In 1785 the Frenchman Jean-Pierre Blanchard and the American John Jeffries crossed the English Channel in a balloon.

The first military aviators were not far behind them. In 1794 the French Revolutionary armies experimented with tethered balloons as a means of observing the movements of the enemy and directing operations. At Maubeuge the gallant Captain Coutelle, commanding the Company of Aérostiers in the Artillery Service, ascended above the French lines 'to examine the works of the enemy, his positions and his forces'. Five days later the enemy found his range with a cunningly concealed 17 pdr and two near-misses brought the balloon and Captain Coutelle swiftly down to earth. Undaunted, Coutelle rose above the battle-field at Fleurus, on June 26, 1794, signaling information to his commander, General Jourdan.

In the 19th century the distance covered by record-breaking balloon flights rapidly increased. In November 1836 the giant British 'Vauxhall' balloon flew from London to Weiburg in Germany, covering a distance of 480 miles in 18 hours. The Alps were crossed in September 1849 when the Frenchman François Arban flew from Marseilles to Turin. Ten years later, in the United States, John Wise in just under 20 hours flew from St Louis to New York, a distance of 812 miles.

In spite of these successes balloons remained essentially uncontrollable, at the mercy of the wind and air currents. Only powered flight could provide the pilot with a choice of direction. In 1852 the French engineer Henri Giffard fitted a balloon with a 3 hp steam engine, which drove a propeller, and a primitive rudder. This was the first step in the path of development which led to the massive dirigible of 1909, Zeppelin 1, the prototype of the airships which carried out the first air raid on London on the night of January 19, 1915.

Left: Two-seat Bleriot monoplane. The extra weight of an observer, machine-gun and ammunition seriously affected aircraft performances, but in order to attack or defend, the machine-gun had to be taken aloft and fitted in the best position possible: here a Lewis gun is fitted on on improvized angle bracket.
Right: Virtually all kinds of aircraft at the beginning of WW1 were unarmed observation types, and like this German pre-war Taube (Dove) type two-seater, were also monoplanes. Only as air fighting developed did the airmen set about arming their machines.

Graf Ferdinand von Zeppelin's interest in aerial warfare had first been aroused when he ascended in a Union Army observation balloon during the American Civil War. He completed his first giant rigid military airship – LZ1 – in 1900. It was twice the length of a modern Boeing 747 Jumbo Jet. Less spectacular but ultimately more decisive were the parallel developments taking place in the powered, manned flight of heavier-than-air machines.

On December 17, 1903, at Kill Devil Hill, Kitty Hawk, North Carolina, Orville and Wilbur Wright took it in turns to pilot their Flyer I in four sustained flights. The fourth and longest flight lasted 59 seconds and covered a distance of 852 ft. Modern aviation had been born.

On October 15, 1905 the Wrights' Flyer III recorded a flight of just over 24 miles in 28 minutes. Two weeks later they approached the US War Department with an offer to build a military aircraft. The offer was turned down by the sceptical American military. The Wright brothers received an equally unenthusiastic response from the British War Office and Admiralty, who between 1906 and 1909 rejected a number of proposals put to them by the aviation pioneers.

Despite the failure of their military initiative, the Wrights' achievements stimulated a spate of activity by European designers and aviators. The French led the field, and in 1908 Wilbur Wright sailed to France to give a series of demonstration flights at a racecourse near Le Mans. In the same year an officer in the French Army, Captain Dorand, designed and built the first aircraft intended specifically for military use. In common with a number of eccentric machines of 1908 – among them the Roshon Multiplane and Alexander Graham Bell's Cygnet II – Dorand's unorthodox aircraft never left the ground.

Infinitely greater success attended the flight on July 25 of Louis Blériot's Type XI monoplane. Taking off from Les Baraques, near Calais, at 4.41 am, Blériot landed heavily 76 minutes later at Northfall Meadow near Dover, thereby winning the £1000 prize offered by the London *Daily Mail* for the first aviator to cross the Channel in either direction. Like many an aviation pioneer, Blériot enjoyed a measure of good luck. His engine began to overheat when he was still well out to sea and he was saved from disaster by a cooling squall of rain.

A month after Blériot's triumph came the first great Aviation Week held at Reims. This in turn led to a series of air-racing competitions, including the Circuit of Europe race of 1911 and the celebrated seaplane races sponsored by the French industrialist Jacques Schneider, the first of which was flown in 1913.

In the years leading up to World War I the French aero industry was entirely self-sufficient. Aircraft were being built in dozens of small factories and workshops around Paris. In 1913 not a single airframe was imported into France, while at the same time 285 aircraft were exported along with 100 tons of spares. In that year French aviators held the world records for speed, distance over a closed circuit, and height. In August Adolphe Pégoud made the first parachute descent from an aircraft in Europe. A month later he demonstrated the first elementary aerobatics, maneuvers which in a short time would become part of the wartime training of fighter pilots.

Blériot's flight had destroyed the image of the airplane as an object of curiosity, the plaything of daredevils with more money than sense. The military began to take an interest in heavier-than-air machines. In France airplanes took part in the Grandes Manoeuvres of September, 1910. By the end of the year there were 39 French military pilots and 29 military aircraft, of Blériot, Breguet, Farman, Voisin and Antoinette design, operating under the aegis of the newly created Inspectorate of Military Aeronautics.

In Germany in the summer of 1910 the training of volunteer officer pilots began at Döberitz. In that fall seven airplanes were purchased for the Army. Battle was now joined between proponents of the Zeppelin arm and their heavier-than-air rivals. In 1912 the significant decision was made to abandon plans for a fleet of battlefield reconnaissance airships in favor of airplanes. In the fall of that year the Döberitz establishment was expanded into a Fliegertruppe. A year later four Flieger Bataillone, each consisting of three companies, were set up in garrison towns across Germany. The Bavarian army followed suit with a Flieger Kompanie consisting of two companies.

In the United States the US Army had had second thoughts about the Wright brothers' offer. At the beginning of August 1908, after a series of trials at Fort Myer in Virginia, the Army took delivery of a Wright Flyer, designating it Model A. The *Washington Evening Star* greeted the purchase with a grander designation – 'Aeroplane No. 1, Heavier-than-Air Division, United States Aerial Fleet'. The Model A was to remain the 'Aerial Fleet's' only airplane until March 1911 when the US Congress made available the first $25 000 of a $125 000 appropriation to buy more aircraft.

AIRPLANES GO TO WAR

That year saw the introduction of military airplanes to a theatre of war. On September 29 Italy had declared war on Turkey after a dispute over the Italian occupation of Cyrenaica and Tripolitania. Three weeks later, on October 22, Captain Carlo Piazza, commander of the Italian expeditionary force's airplane section, piloted his Blériot XI on the first operational flight undertaken by a military aircraft, carrying out a reconnaissance of Turkish positions between Tripoli and Azizzia.

The campaign saw a number of significant 'firsts'. Also out on reconnaissance duties on October 22 was Captain Moizo, piloting a Nieuport. His aircraft was holed in several places by enemy groundfire, thus securing him a niche in the history of aerial warfare as the first pilot to sustain damage in action. Four days later the energetic Captain Piazza, accompanied by Lieutenant Gavotti in an Etrich Taube, directed fire from the battleship *Carlo Alberto* on to Turkish positions. Their flimsy aircraft bucketed about in the sky in the shock waves of the battleship's shells whistling beneath them, an ordeal which was soon to become all too familiar to aircrew on the Western Front.

To Lieutenant Gavotti went the honour of the first bombing sortie on active service. On November 1 he dropped four 4.5 lb Cipelli bombs on Turkish positions at Ain Zara and Taguira. Gavotti carried the bombs in a leather bag and the detonators in his pocket. Circling over the Turkish positions, he placed the bombs on his knees, fitted them with detonators and dropped

The BE2c, the standard RFC observation and reconnaissance aircraft between 1914-16. It carried an observer/gunner in the forward cockpit, surrounded and hampered by wires and struts.

them over the side of his Etrich Taube. Not to be outdone, the pace-setting Piazza undertook the first air drop of propaganda leaflets on January 10, 1912. On February 24 and 25 he brought back the first wartime reconnaissance photographs taken from an airplane.

In Britain military flying began in 1878 with the building of a balloon at the Woolwich Arsenal. The Balloon Section was incorporated into the Royal Engineers in 1890 and saw action in the Boer War, directing the fire of British artillery at Magersfontein and during the battle of Lombard's Kop. In 1894 a balloon factory had been established in South Farnborough, in the heart of 'Army country'. It moved to a bigger site in 1905 and, growing in importance, was in 1912 designated the Royal Aircraft Factory.

The Army's first dirigible, 'Nulli Secundus', flew for the first time in September 1907. Simultaneously experiments with heavier-than-air machines were being conducted at Farnborough by the flamboyant American aviation pioneer William Cody. On October 16, 1908 Cody's giant bamboo-constructed 'Army Aeroplane No. 1' staggered 1390 feet across Laffan's Plain. This development brought the Army to realize that they had spent £2500 on heavier-than-air experiments and funds were immediately cut off. It was not until October 1910 that the Balloon Section of the Royal Engineers was provided with funds to 'afford opportunities for aeroplaning'.

The Army finally acquired some heavier-than-air machines after the April 1911 expansion of the Balloon Section of the Royal Engineers into an Air Battalion comprising a Headquarters at South Farnborough, No. 1 (Airship) Company, also at Farnborough, and No. 2 (Aeroplane) Company at Larkhill on Salisbury Plain. By the summer Britain's first air force had assembled: six Bristol Boxkite biplanes, one Henri Farman, a heavily modified Louis Wright biplane and a Blériot XI monoplane privately owned by Lieutenant B A Cammell.

Senior officers were singularly unimpressed and General Nicholson, the Chief of the Imperial General Staff, remained of the opinion that aviation was a useless and expensive fad advocated by a few cranks. Nevertheless, at the beginning of 1912 the Committee of Imperial Defence recommended the establishment of a 'Flying Corps' with separate Military and Naval Wings serviced by a Central Flying School. In the wake of the Committee's proposals came the foundation of the Royal Flying Corps on April 13, 1912. From the start, however, interservice rivalries kept the Military and Naval Wings apart. The Navy, which had

already set up its own flying school at Eastchurch, went its own way, experimenting with aircraft produced by domestic and foreign manufacturers and testing machine-guns, bombing and the dropping of torpedoes. The Army remained wedded to the reconnaissance role of the airplane and continued with the docile, inherently stable machines produced by the Royal Aircraft Factory. Separation was complete in July 1914 when the RFC's Military Wing was renamed the Royal Flying Corps and the Naval Wing became the Royal Naval Air Service.

1914 – THE TRIALS BEGIN

In the summer of 1914 the moment arrived for the European powers to put their infant air forces to the test. On July 28, a month after the assassination at Sarajevo of the Archduke Franz Ferdinand by Slav nationalists, Austria-Hungary declared war on Serbia. Two days later the Tsar ordered a general mobilization of the Russian armed forces. German mobilization followed on the afternoon of August 1, four hours after the expiration of their ultimatum to St Petersburg. Simultaneously the telegraph flashed mobilization orders through France. The inbuilt, unstoppable momentum generated by the execution of these gigantic military plans was about to engulf the continent in war. On August 3, Germany declared war on France – on the false pretext that French aeroplanes had bombed Nuremberg – and advance German units moved into Luxembourg. By midnight Britain had been drawn into the war; between August 12 and 17 the bulk of the British Expeditionary Force crossed the Channel to France.

The great German deployment preliminary to the execution of the Schlieffen Plan – the swinging left hook aimed through Belgium at Paris – involved seven armies and 1.5 million men. In comparison with the millions of troops on the move the opposing air forces were tiny. On the outbreak of war the RFC had five squadrons, with three more planned. On August 11 the first RFC personnel embarked for France at Southampton. Ahead of them flew Lieutenant H D Harvey-Kelly of No. 2 Squadron, whose BE2b, No. 347, became the first RFC aircraft to land in France. Nearly three years later Harvey-Kelly was to die in aerial combat with a German pilot who went on to become one of the greatest aces of the war – Freiherr Manfred von Richthofen.

In the days following his cross-Channel flight Harvey-Kelly was joined by the rest of the RFC's contingent of 63 aircraft: Nos 2 and 4 Squadrons, equipped with BE2s, No. 3 with Blériot monoplanes and Farman biplanes, and No. 5 with

Farmans, Avro 504 biplanes and Factory-built BE8s. Flying over the Channel – crossed for the first time by Blériot only five years before – the pilots improvised lifebelts out of motorcar inner tubes. All the RFC aircraft were unarmed but the pilots had been given orders that if a Zeppelin was spotted they were, regardless of their own safety, to ram it. Flying to Dover on the first leg of his journey, Captain (later Air Chief Marshal Sir) Philip Joubert de la Ferté of No. 3 Squadron was 'proceeding peacefully twenty miles north of Portsmouth at about 3000 feet, when my mechanic gripped my shoulder and shouted in my ear, "Zeppelin, sir!" Shuddering with fright, I looked over my shoulder and saw one of the Spit forts lifting its head above the morning mist. In this light it looked just like an airship – but I had a lot to say to the mechanic when we landed.'

On August 17 the RFC moved their headquarters from Amiens to Maubeuge, 11 miles southwest of Mons, near the spot where 120 years before Captain Coutelle had undertaken the first aerial reconnaissance. The move was made in an assortment of hastily commandeered transport vehicles, one of which – No. 5 Squadron's bomb lorry – still bore the livery of a famous sauce manufacturer.

At the end of the month the ten aircraft of Squadron Commander C R Samson's Eastchurch Wing of the RNAS flew into Ostend. Coming in to land, they were fired on by a unit of Royal Marines, a fate which had also befallen two airplanes of the RFC's No. 3 Squadron flying up the road to Mons, where they were shot at by their own troops. Shield-shaped Union Jacks were hurriedly painted on the underside of the British airplanes' wings. Later they were replaced by the colored roundels used by the Allied air forces, while the German aircraft displayed the familiar black crosses.

In August 1914 the heavier-than-air component of the German Imperial Air Service comprised 246 aircraft (half of them Etrich Taube types), 254 pilots and 271 observers. This broke down into 33 Feldflieger Abteilungen (field flight sections) of six airplanes each, and eight Festungflieger Abteilungen (fortress flight sections) of four airplanes each. The latter were tasked with protecting fortress towns along Germany's frontiers. The Feldflieger Abteilungen were under the direct operational control of the Army, one being allotted to each individual Army headquarters and one to each Army Corps. Britain's principal ally, France, could muster some 138 frontline aircraft in her Army's Service D'Aviation Militaire (comprising 21 escadrilles of two-seaters, each with six aircraft, and four single-seater escadrilles, each with three Blériot monoplanes for liaison with the cavalry), but her preeminence in the aero-industry provided her with the base to increase the frontline strength to 801 airplanes by the end of 1914. At this stage the Germans possessed 575 aircraft and the British 133.

AIRCRAFT SEEK A ROLE
During the early weeks of the war the airplane was still only tolerated by a suspicious army and its role was seen solely in terms of Army and Corps HQ reconnaissance and artillery cooperation. Initial experience was not encouraging. The RFC's first reconnaissance flight from Maubeuge was flown by Captain Joubert de la Ferté and Captain Mappleback in a BE2a. They lost their way and their roundabout trip via Tournai and Cambrai – where they had to ask for directions – took eight hours. Clearly the airmen on both sides needed time to learn to 'see' from the air. Nevertheless, it was an air reconnaissance report on September 3 which alerted General Galliéni to von Kluck's exposed flank on the Marne as he moved obliquely past the defences of Paris.

The air forces on the Western Front were now demonstrating their value, but their size and organization still lagged behind their potential. The battles of the opening months of the war raged across large tracts of France and Belgium, too great an area to be covered comprehensively by the air forces at the disposal of the Allies and the Germans. At squadron level it was impossible to operate as a unit because the pilots had received no formation training. In any event, the assortment of aircraft at commanders' disposal – with their very different rates of performance – presented a further obstacle. Pilots on both sides therefore continued to fly lone sorties.

From the beginning encounters occurred as both sides went about their reconnaissance duties. In the words of the RFC Manual of June 1914. 'It is not to be expected that aircraft will be able to carry out their duties undisturbed. In war, advantages must be fought for and the importance of aerial reconnaissance is so great that each side will strive to prevent the other side making use of it'. There was also the problem of aiming and firing any sort of gun as in many aircraft the crew was surrounded by a mass of support and control wires. There were wooden struts, large biplane wings and for the most part a large wooden propeller on the front. Any misshooting by either pilot or observer could cause untold damage to their own airplane.

As the air war developed the armory and Armament Officer became an important part of any squadron. Here RFC crews collect their machine-guns and ammo drums. Like many Armament Officers, this Lieutenant from a Scottish Regt has been seconded from the army.

HOW TO ATTACK?

These drawbacks prompted a search for alternatives which verged on the bizarre. Steel darts, or flechettes, were among the proposals, along with a small bomb fixed to a grapnel trailed beneath a fast scout airplane and detonated electronically from the cockpit.* This suggestion was made in an anonymous RFC report of 1915 which also included a discussion of the merits in aerial combat of the blunderbuss: 'A heavy and scattering charge of grape- and chain-shot fired from a smooth-bore weapon something like a large blunderbuss affords a pilot a better chance of bringing down a hostile aeroplane by aiming his own than when aiming a single bullet in this manner ... the pattern should not be less than 20 ft wide at 50 yds range; this means a cone of dispersion of about 8 degrees from the moment of leaving the muzzle.'

*Note: This remarkable method of attack was successfully employed against an Albatros two-seater by the Russian ace Staff Captain Alexander A Kazakov on March 18, 1915. Kazakov's grapnel mechanism jammed as he unreeled it and he finished the job by ramming the Albatros with his undercarriage.

German aviators were spared a 'whiff of grapeshot'. Aircrew persisted with pistols, rifles and carbines despite the difficulty the pilot faced in putting himself and his unstable machine into a position where he or his observer could get a clear shot at an opponent. Nor was his prey likely to oblige him by flying a straight course. He would be weaving about, or trying to get in a shot himself. These first clashes, employing the most rudimentary tactics, marked the beginning of air combat.

On August 22, 1914 a hostile aircraft suddenly appeared over Maubeuge. Six RFC aircraft took off in 'pursuit' but the German got away. One Farman that was in the chase was still climbing hard and had reached only 1000 feet half an hour after the Albatros had flown off. The pilot of the Farman was 2nd Lieutenant L A Strange of 6 Squadron and his struggle to climb had been impeded by the weight of a Lewis machine-gun he had fixed to his aircraft. On landing he was ordered to remove this weighty item from the Farman and in future to carry only a rifle.

Three days later the RFC had its first success. Three aircraft of 2 Squadron, one of them piloted by Lieutenant Harvey-Kelly, pursued and harassed a German two-seater, eventually forcing it down. Harvey-Kelly landed near by and accompanied by his observer chased the crew into a wood. The Germans made good their escape and the two RFC flyers returned to the German machine, set light to it, then flew back to their base. On the same day another enemy aircraft was forced down and captured. By September 7 the RFC had accounted for five hostile machines.

The French also scored some successes. On October 5 Pilot Sergeant Joseph Frantz and his mechanic Corporal Quenault of Escadrille VB24 shot down an Aviatik B-type two-seater with a Hotchkiss machine-gun mounted on the nose of their Voisin 'chicken coop'. The Germans carried only sidearms in the early days but as the number of encounters and air fights increased (they could hardly be called combats at this stage), they began to consider heavier defensive and offensive firepower.

Machine-guns provided the inescapable answer and Allied and German pilots began to fit them to their sturdier machines. The RFC adopted the gas-operated Lewis gun, which had undergone successful air-firing tests in the United States in 1912. At 27 lb the Lewis was just under

half the weight of the Vickers and by 1915 BSA were turning out large quantities of the US-designed weapon. It was adapted for use in the air by replacing the stock with a spade grip and later by discarding its aluminum cooling fins and jacket. Cooled by the draft of the slipstream and enjoying the advantage of the dust-free aerial environment, the Lewis gun functioned more efficiently aloft than in the mud of the trenches below.

The French adopted the Hotchkiss, another aircooled machine-gun, whose strip feed was replaced by a drum feed to provide a flexible observer's weapon. The Germans chose the lightweight Parabellum, a modification of the watercooled Maxim. The Parabellum dispensed with the water jacket, replacing it with a perforated casing which allowed a steady flow of slipstream air. With its pistol grip and stock and drum magazine, the *leichte* MG'14 became a serviceable observer's weapon weighing almost 18 lb less than the standard Maxim.

The land battles of the opening weeks of World War 1 might for a fleeting moment have been recognized by Frederick the Great, Napoleon or von Moltke. In August 1914 British regimental

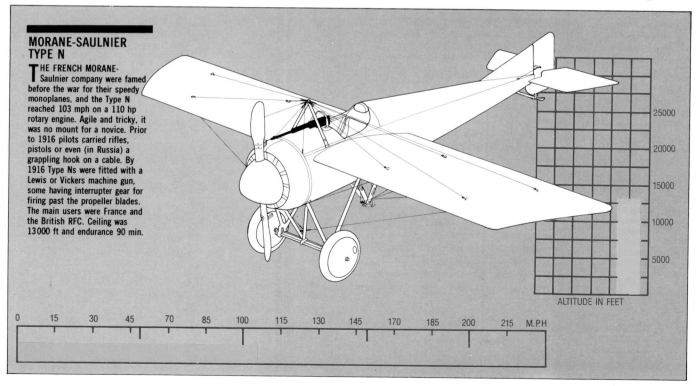

MORANE-SAULNIER TYPE N

THE FRENCH MORANE-Saulnier company were famed before the war for their speedy monoplanes, and the Type N reached 103 mph on a 110 hp rotary engine. Agile and tricky, it was no mount for a novice. Prior to 1916 pilots carried rifles, pistols or even (in Russia) a grappling hook on a cable. By 1916 Type Ns were fitted with a Lewis or Vickers machine gun, some having interrupter gear for firing past the propeller blades. The main users were France and the British RFC. Ceiling was 13000 ft and endurance 90 min.

25000
20000
15000
10000
5000
ALTITUDE IN FEET

0   15   30   45   70   85   100   115   130   145   170   185   200   215   M.P.H

Right: The Morane type N 'Bullet'. Like the aircraft used by the Frenchman Roland Garros in 1915, this RFC machine has deflector plates rivetted on both propeller blades.

ROLAND GARROS

THE PILOT WHO AS MUCH AS ANY other put the machine-gun in the air was a pre-war French aviator, named Roland Garros. Born in October 1888, Garros became a pilot in 1909 and the following year flew in America in the Statue of Liberty Air Race. In 1911 he won the Paris to Rome air race as well as the Paris to Madrid race.

When the war began in August 1914, he immediately joined Escadrille MS23, flying Morane-Saulnier monoplane single-seat aircraft. He flew alongside such other early notables as Eugene Gilbert, Marc Pourpe, Armand Pinsard and Jules Vedrines. Their first duties were observation and reconnaissance missions but each experimented with some form of offensive armament. It was Garros who was the first to mount a machine-gun to the front of his Morane, set to fire through the twin blades of the propeller. His first success came on April 1, 1915 – an Albatros two-seater. This victory was followed on April 11 by an Aviatik two-seater shot down in flames, then he destroyed an LVG near Dunkirk on April 12. Victory number four, another Aviatik, fell with a dead crew on April 14, and two days later down went number five, an Albatros. However, his success was short-lived, for he was forced to land inside the German lines on April 19 when his engine gave out while on a bombing sortie. Taken prisoner, he spent three years in captivity, but escaped in 1918. Garros returned to operational flying, but everything had changed. The war in the air was now a deadly game at speeds that had been unthinkable in 1915. On October 5, 1918, just over a month before WW1 ended, Garros was shot down in combat with a Fokker DVII. So died the first great ace of the war.

officers had been ordered to sharpen their swords as they went to war. Cavalry swept across the battlefields and French infantry went into action in the red trousers which proved a death warrant for tens of thousands, mown down by the concentrated firepower of rifle and machine-gun. After the Schlieffen Plan broke down outside Paris, the Allies and the Germans, each striving to envelop the other's western flank, moved in a series of sidesteps towards the Belgian coast in what became known as 'the race to the sea'. As winter approached the war of movement ground to a halt. The front stabilized and then congealed into a vast trench system which stretched 475 miles from the North Sea to the Swiss border. In 1914 the British Army considered 250000 sandbags a month to be sufficient for all its needs. By May 1915 they were asking for six million.

Allied and German armies now faced each other across a few hundred yards of 'no-man's-land'. Rolls of barbed wire, breastworks, traversing machine-gun positions, snipers and supporting artillery fire made the trenches highly dangerous. For almost 3½ years, apart from occasional limited successes, the 'lines' remained static. Battles came and went, a few yards would be taken here, a few lost there. When any major success did occur – as at Cambrai in 1917 – it took the victors so much by surprise that they were quite unprepared to exploit the breakthrough with the essential support.

THE FIGHTING PILOT

By the spring of 1915 barbed wire and the machine-gun had banished cavalry from the battlefield. Traditionally the cavalry, when they were not attacking the enemy, were the eyes of the army. They could ride round the enemy positions, circle a hill or high ground, or look at the enemy's rear areas. The advent of static trench warfare rang down the curtain on centuries of military history. Now the cavalry were superseded by the airplane, which could overfly barbed-wire entanglements, trenches and machine-guns. Now it was the airplane's task to look behind the enemy lines. Moreover, the airplane could penetrate further to reconnoiter the enemy's lines of supply, his dumps, road and rail systems, returning with verbal and photographic reports. It remained to find the tools for the job. The airmen were still feeling their way. There were no instruction manuals, no grizzled veterans of aerial combat to hand down their knowledge. Each day brought fresh situations and new problems. Not all aircraft carried machine-guns. Those without preferred speed to fighting as a means of escape.

Gradually two distinct types of aircraft developed – the 'workers' and the 'fighters'.

At the same time the more aggressive pilots on both sides were seeking to exploit the improved performance and reliability of the aircraft which were now in service by looking for action. These were the men who would write the air-combat manuals – if they lived long enough.

Even the most aggressive fighting pilot was limited by his equipment. He could still be frustrated by an indifferent engine, or hampered by weight of gun and ammunition. As a new generation of more robust aircraft became available, pilots began to develop the first principles of fighter combat technology and tactics. It was agreed that the best way to attack another aircraft was to aim one's own airplane at it, but the difficulty was that the propeller prevented forward fire. The problem elicited a variety of solutions.

By March 1915 the RFC had eight squadrons in France with a total of 85 airplanes covering twelve different types. Of these, only four were single-seaters, three were Martinsyde SIs, and one an SE2A, plus one FB5 fighting biplane two-seater, of which more later. The French had single-seaters, three were Martinsyde S1s, and being the most famous. It was in a Morane that the Frenchman Roland Garros made history in the annals of air combat.

A celebrated prewar airman, Garros had been posted to Escadrille MS26, based at Le Bourget, during the winter of 1914. During this period he was seconded to the Morane Saulnier aircraft company's airfield at Villacoublay, where he

Top: The Vickers FB5 'Gunbus', – a 'Pusher'type – carried an observer in the front cockpit, had a clear field of fire, but was always vulnerable to rear attack. **Above**: The BE9 had the observer's cockpit in front of the whirling blades. This machine, No. 1700, was attached to 16 Squadron RFC for trials in 1915 but was not a success.

assisted Raymond Saulnier with his experiments to develop a synchronization device for a machine-gun-armed tractor aircraft. Saulnier's experiments made little headway as the Hotchkiss machine-gun used with the interrupter gear displayed a tendency to foul the propeller when the synchronization broke down. To protect the propeller Saulnier fixed metal deflectors to the blades.

Eventually the synchronization tests were abandoned, but Garros decided to concentrate on the deflector blades. He commissioned Panhard to construct heavier armored deflectors mounted on a specially designed Chauvière airscrew waisted at its inner ends. Garros' mechanic Jules Hué designed a bracing system for the deflectors and scooped out their inner faces into a channel shape, the better to clear the 8-mm solid copper bullets fired by the machine-gun. After successful air-firing trials Garros flew north in his Hotchkiss-armed Morane monoplane to rejoin his squadron at Dunkirk. On 5 February 1915, the Morane Saulnier Company was granted French patent No. 477.530 for the design of an armored airscrew fitted with a firearm. The French military remained unimpressed and an order for 10 similarly armed Morane Type Ns was cancelled. Garros' first success came on April 1. The Germans took little notice of the apparently unarmed Morane Type N, especially when it pointed its nose directly at them. Within seconds Garros had emptied three Hotchkiss strip magazines into an Albatros two-seater, killing its crew and sending it down in flames.

Garros had been the first to record a kill in what was to become the conventional method of air attack. Two weeks later he scored his second victory. On 19 April, however, over Cambrai Garros' Morane was hit by ground fire and forced

LANOE GEORGE HAWKER

SON OF A DISTINGUISHED military family, Hawker was born in December 1890, and upon leaving school joined the Royal Engineers, but transferred to the RFC before the war, having qualified as a pilot privately at Hendon. He was sent to France with 6 Squadron in October 1914 and for his early bombing and reconnaissance flights won the DSO. In 1915 the ever-inventive Hawker fitted a Lewis gun to his Bristol Scout set to fire from its position by the cockpit. He also flew an FE2 two-seater in which he gained his first two successes forcing down two-seaters on June 21 and 23. Flying the Bristol on July 25, he fought a number of combats destroying two Albatros C-types and forcing another to land, a feat which brought him the award of the Victoria Cross. Flying the FE and also the Bristol, he was continually engaged in air fighting patrols, forcing down another Albatros two-seater on July 31, an Aviatik on August 2, then an Aviatik and a Fokker Eindekker scout on August 11. His last victory was another German scout which crashed on September 7.

He was Britain's first successful air fighter, and the first to be rewarded with the highest gallantry award for air combat. His other reward was to be given command in September 1915 of the RFC's first fighting squadron – No. 24 – to be equipped totally with single-seat scouts, the DH2 pusher-type biplane. On November 23 he flew a patrol which ran into Albatros DII scouts of Jagdstaffel 2, meeting the rising ace Manfred von Richthofen. After a classic duel, Hawker finally had to make a run for his own lines and was shot down by the German – Richthofen's 11th official victory. Hawker was buried by his crashed DH2.

to land. He glided down near Ingelmunster and in the time remaining to him before capture made desperate attempts to set fire to his aircraft.

But the Morane stubbornly refused to go up in flames. Garros was taken prisoner and his aircraft – badly scorched but with the mechanism all in one piece – was transported to Iseghem for examination by German technical officers. The secret was out but it would be a while before the Germans capitalized on it.

On the British side several flyers attempted to overcome the difficulties of firing a machine-gun at a hostile machine. Lieutenant Louis Strange, who in the previous August had been ordered to remove a machine-gun from his Farman, was one of them. No. 6 Squadron with whom he flew had received a Martinsyde Scout. This aircraft had a gun mounted on the top wing, fixed to fire over the propeller. To reload the gun – it was drum-fed – the pilot had to stand, hold the control stick between his knees and reach up. Strange began to fly this machine on scouting missions, or as escort to the squadron's two-seaters.

Another member of 6 Squadron was Captain Lanoe Hawker. An aggressive, fearless pilot whose motto was 'Attack Everything!', Hawker had won the DSO in April 1915 for a bombing raid in a BE2c on the Zeppelin shed at Gontrode near Ghent. Converting to a single-seater Bristol C Scout (No. 1611), Hawker lashed a single-shot hunting rifle and then a Lewis gun to the port side of the fuselage, just under the cockpit. The Lewis gun was set to fire at an angle, enabling the bullets to pass outside the arc of the propeller. The gunsight was fixed to the port rear center-section strut and it required all of Hawker's considerable skill as a pilot to master the technique of flying the Bristol crabwise in order to get in a shot.

On the evening of July 25, Hawker flew a lone offensive patrol (OP) and using this tactic attacked three separate German two-seaters in his Bristol Scout. The first – an Aviatik C-type – he sent down in a spin. Later he forced another Aviatik down to land, then shot down an Albatros in flames near Zillebecke. For this and for many actions over previous months, Hawker was awarded the Victoria Cross. It was the third awarded to an airman, but the first specifically for air combat.

Another solution to the problems of firing a machine-gun along the line of flight was the removal of the propeller from the line of fire. The engine was taken from the front of the airplane and located behind the pilot in the 'pusher' position. This left the crew in a forward nacelle covering a field of fire from left to right of 180

degrees. The first pusher type, the two-seater Vickers FB5 (Fighting Biplane), reached France in the summer of 1915. Called the Vickers 'Gunbus', the FB5 was the first RFC airplane designed as a fighter. It also became the first type to equip an entire squadron when in July 1915 No. 11 Squadron, RFC, flying FB5s, arrived in France. The FB5 remained in service for only a few months, as it was no match for the faster, more heavily armed Fokkers which appeared on the Western Front later in the year.

The Vickers 'Gunbus' was followed by a number of 'pusher' types. The two-seater FE2b went into service in the summer of 1915. The last production model of the FE2 series – the FE2d, powered with a 250 hp Rolls-Royce MkII (Eagle) engine – arrived on the Western Front in July 1916 and remained in service until the following summer. The single-seater DH2, designed by Geoffrey de Havilland, was delivered in February 1916 to No. 24 Squadron, the first squadron to be equipped entirely with single-seater fighters.

The 'pusher' enjoyed a modest degree of success, but one of the type's principal drawbacks was inherent in its design. With the engine behind the pilot, the 'pusher' was vulnerable to bullets from an opponent firing in what was becoming the customary way, from behind. To fire backwards over the top wing the observer in an FE2d had to stand on his seat, with only his feet and ankles below the rim of the cockpit. This maneuver had to be accomplished without the benefit of a parachute. Landing a 'pusher' was also more hazardous than in a tractor type. The heavy engine could go only one way if a pilot nosed forward into the ground – in the same direction straight through the cockpit.

By mid-1915 most reconnaissance aircraft of both sides carried a machine-gun in the observer's cockpit used for defense. Occasionally the pilot would fix a gun to the top wing to fire forward or rig up a mounting like Hawker's 'angle-off' gun. As early as May 1915 a Martinsyde S1 had been adapted with an overwing Lewis gun fired by a flexible Bowden cable, but the device encountered the recurring problem of the high-viscosity oil freezing and causing the weapon to jam. As air fighting increased, units on both sides began to take more defensive measures. When the two-seaters did their reconnaissance or artillery spotting, the more nimble of the single-seater scouts would escort them and be their protectors. This in turn developed into close escort flights as well as offensive patrols to combat not only enemy reconnaissance aircraft, but also the opposing scout types. The air war was escalating.

WESTERN FRONT OCTOBER 26, 1915

FB5 VERSUS **ALBATROS CI**

The first aircraft to serve on the Western Front in 1914 had severe difficulty even carrying a machine-gun and ammunition, and it was some time before effective methods of mounting the guns for use in combat were devised. Generally, the first method was to provide the observer, usually in the rear cockpit, with a trainable gun, though pusher aircraft such as the FB5 were sometimes fitted with a fixed forward-firing gun to supplement the gun used by the observer from his nose position.

Meanwhile, the pilots were starting to explore the possibilities of aerial fighting, and gradually certain fundamental principles emerged. Most important was the need for surprise, to give the opponent as little time as possible for evasive maneuvers; allied to this was the need to get as close as possible to give the maximum chance of fire being effective; and always it was vital to exploit any weaknesses in the opponent's aircraft while maximizing the advantages of one's own.

The first RFC unit to be given aerial combat as a specific task was B Flight of No. 5 Sqn, which began to use the FB5 in April 1915; an encounter between its commander, Capt Robert Lorraine, and an Albatros CI in October of that year encapsulated all the first principles.

TIMETABLE

1 Lorraine and Lubbock, at 1000 ft over Houthem, see two Albatros CIs, 4 miles away and much higher.
2 Lorraine starts climbing gradually to 9000 ft; Lubbock is already briefed to wait for the order before opening fire, while Lorraine gets as close as possible.
3 Closing with the German, Lorraine pretends to climb above him.
4 The Albatros opens fire at a range of about 400 yards, climbing to meet the FB5.
5 After almost standing his aircraft on its tail to lure the Albatros on, Lorraine dives steeply, firing with both guns and passing just under the German fighter.
6 Lorraine's upper wing and his opponent's undercarriage pass only 5 ft apart.
7 Turning toward his opponent, Lorraine follows the Albatros into a dive; he opens fire again, but both guns jam.
8 Lorraine continues to dive, so steeply that Lubbock is almost thrown out.
9 Lubbock manages to unjam the guns, and the FB5 continues to follow the Albatros.
10 Before Lorraine can regain a firing position he sees the Albatros crash behind the Allied lines: Gerold is dead, shot through the stomach; Bucholz is slightly wounded.

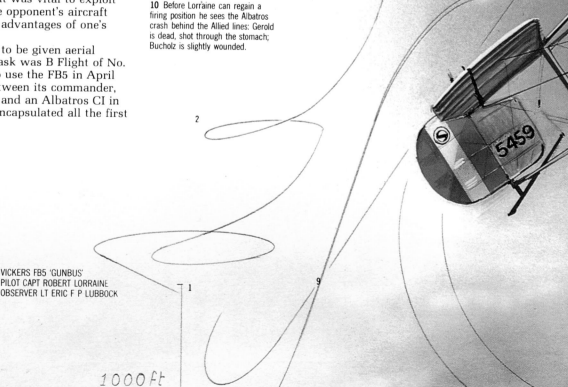

VICKERS FB5 'GUNBUS'
PILOT CAPT ROBERT LORRAINE
OBSERVER LT ERIC F P LUBBOCK

1000ft

ALBATROS CI
PILOT UNTEROFFIZIER GEROLD
OBSERVER LEUTNANT BUCHOLZ

CHAPTER TWO

THE AIR FIGHTER IS BORN

I N 1915 THE EUROPEAN CONFLICT spread across the world. Fronts had been opened up in German East Africa and the Near East. On April 25 an Anglo-French expeditionary force, which included Australian and New Zealand divisions, landed on the Gallipoli peninsula in an attempt to knock Turkey out of the war. For the first time Britain's civilian population found themselves in the front line when on January 19 Zeppelins L3 and L4 bombed King's Lynn and Great Yarmouth; four people were killed and sixteen injured. From the Sudan to St Omer aircraft were on active service, but it was on the Western Front that the next chapter in the history of aerial combat would be written.

Above the trenches and shellpocked no-man's-land flew increasing numbers of Allied and German aircraft. The armies of both sides had begun to fire at them as they crossed the lines, so height became more important. Height also conferred an advantage in combat, a factor quickly grasped by pilots and recognized as crucial. Diving on an opponent from above and behind increased the element of surprise and added speed during the attack whilst leaving enough in hand for the pilot to regain height after it. A sharp lookout was now more than ever vital to a pilot's survival and the paramount rule was never to let an enemy 'get on your tail'. The continual scanning of the sky thus involved could be exhausting. The Canadian ace Raymond Collishaw, who arrived in France with No. 3 Wing RNAS in the summer of 1916, recalled:

'W*HILE IN THE AIR YOU CONSTANTLY turned your head, first to one side and then to the other, making sure that nothing was on your tail. This, by the way, was the reason for the traditional silk scarves worn by the fighter pilots. In an open cockpit, into which you were strapped, you needed something around your neck and silk did not chafe as you turned your head about. I recall one of the pilots of Naval Three who had received a new white silk scarf from a girl in England. In a matter of a month or two he had worn it out.'*

While pilots were establishing the basic rules of fighter tactics, aircraft designers were still searching for a reliable way of synchronizing a stream of bullets through the propeller blades of a tractor aircraft – 'the inevitable device', as Anthony Fokker called it. Raymond Saulnier had not been the only designer to experiment with an interrupter gear. Before the outbreak of war

L. V. G. Doppeldecker
System Schneider.
Schulmaschine.

Left: Front view of a Fokker EIV with a 150 hp Le Rhone engine. This model was specially built for Max Immelmann, to carry three Spandau machine-guns. It proved unsuccessful. Not only was the Fokker Eindekker fast becoming obsolete by early 1916, but the extra weight of the guns badly affected performance.

Above: An LVG B-type German observation machine, encountered by all the early aces of WW1. It was unarmed, and crews soon carried rifles and automatic pistols for self-defense. The later C-types carried a Parabellum machine-gun in the observer's cockpit and later the pilot had a forward-firing Spandau machine-gun.

experiments had been carried out in Russia by Lieutenant Poplavko, in Britain by two brothers named Edwards and in Germany by Franz Schneider, Chief Designer of the LVG Company. Schneider patented his interrupter gear in July 1913 and later fitted a machine-gun to the prototype LVG EV1 two-seater monoplane. In 1915 the machine was sent to the front for tests, but it was lost and Schneider's interrupter gear was temporarily forgotten.

BIRTH OF THE FIGHTER
It fell to the talented young Dutch designer Anthony Fokker - who was making airplanes for the Germans after being turned down by the British and the French - to examine Roland Garros' captured Morane Type N. He immediately saw that the triangular steel wedges fitted by Jules Hué were a dangerous device for the pilot. The impact of the bullets could shatter the propeller or ricochet back into the fragile airplane. The alarming vibrations set up when the bullets hit the deflectors might in time shake loose

the engine mounting. At his Schwerin works Fokker confronted the difficulty: '*THE technical problem was to shoot between the propeller blades, which passed a given point 2400 times a minute, because the two-bladed propeller revolved 1200 times a minute. This meant that the pilot must not pull the trigger or fire the gun as long as one of the blades was directly in front of the muzzle. Once the problem was stated, its solution came to me in a flash.*'

It took Fokker less than three days to design a simple engine-driven system of cams and push-rods which operated the trigger of a Parabellum machine-gun once during each revolution of the propeller. In effect, the propeller fired the gun. Finally, Fokker fixed a wooden disc to the propeller to see the bullets' path in relation to the propeller. He found that the bullets pierced the disc within a short distance of each other, well out of line of either blade. The bullet pattern revealed how much time there was between the striking of the cam (which was linked with the trigger of the machine-gun) and the actual firing of the bullet.

Fokker installed the synchronization system and a lightened Parabellum 1MG'14 in one of his M5K/MG monoplanes, flew it to Berlin and gave an air-firing demonstration for the German General Staff. Once again the military reacted cautiously to a technical breakthrough. Major Thomsen, chief of the *Idflieg* (the Army Air Force Inspectorate) promised Fokker an Iron Cross if he could bring down an enemy machine in combat. With his monoplane (designated EI) he was despatched to General von Heeringen's headquarters in the Fifth Army sector opposite Verdun. Kitted out in the field-grey tunic of a lieutenant in the German Army, he began to fly over the lines in search of a live target. But Fokker lacked the killer instinct of the true fighter pilot and balked at the prospect of picking off 'cold meat'. The first pilot to shoot down an enemy airplane with a synchronized machine-gun was Kurt Wintgens of the Bavarian reconnaissance section Feldflieger Abteilung 6b (F1.Abt 6b). A French Morane single-seater had been harassing the sector of front covered by F1.Abt 6b and Wintgens finally located it in the late afternoon of July 1. Wintgens was below the French pilot, who was flying at 7000 ft. The Frenchman dived to attack but Wintgens slipped the EI out of the way and as the Morane passed by attacked and shot it down. As the Morane had gone down over the French lines, Wintgens' claim was not upheld by the German High Command. Two weeks later he scored a confirmed victory over his own lines.

The EI monoplane, or Eindecker as it became known, was the first modern fighter. It was light, maneuverable, climbed well and could be dived at a steep angle without shedding its wings. Powered by an 80 hp Oberursel engine, it had a

top speed of 83 mph (at 5–6000 ft) and a ceiling of 11 500 ft. The EI entered service in June 1915, to be replaced in September by the more powerful EII and then the EIII, the main production model.

Initially the RFC was spared the full weight of the Eindecker. Its potential was not fully grasped at first and it was assigned either singly or in pairs to escort two-seaters. Pilots were ordered not to fly offensive patrols over the Allied lines for fear of yielding up the secret of Fokker's synchronization mechanism. Supply was slow and by the end of October 1915 there were only 55 Eindecker types on the Western Front. By the end of the year the number had crept up to 86.

Nevertheless this period rapidly became known as that of the 'The Fokker Scourge'. Improved tactics and organization made up for the relatively small numbers of Eindeckers, and by the fall of 1915 they had gained undeniable mastery in the skies over the Western Front. Groups of four Eindeckers began to fly together in Kampfeinsitzer Kommandos (KEKs) – forerunners of the permanent Jagdstaffeln units which were to emerge in 1916. To compensate for the Eindecker's indifferent endurance (1½ hours at 80 mph) the KEKs were directed to intercept incoming hostile aircraft by a primitive 'early warning' system provided by forward anti-aircraft batteries. Such was the devastating effect of the Eindeckers on Allied spotter aircraft that on January 14, 1916 RFC HQ ordered that reconnaissance aircraft were always to be escorted by at least three combat aircraft flying in close formation, and that a mission was to be abandoned if one of the escorts became detached. The war in the air had entered a new phase. For the first time one side held the initiative, gaining that vital element which was to be disputed by future warring generations – air supremacy.

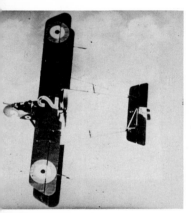

Above: Most successful of the early RFC fighter-types was another 'Pusher', the Airco DH2. Armed with a Lewis gun in the pilot's forward protruding cockpit, it helped defeat the Fokker Scourge of 1915-16.
Right: Morane Biplane (No. 5137) used by 3 Squadron RFC until shot down by Immelmann on March 2, 1916.

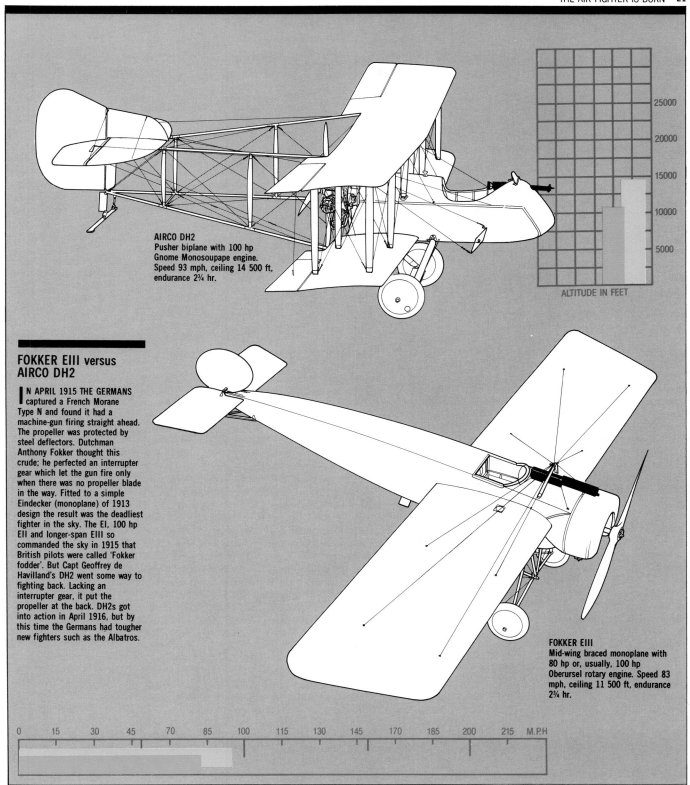

AIRCO DH2
Pusher biplane with 100 hp
Gnome Monosoupape engine.
Speed 93 mph, ceiling 14 500 ft,
endurance 2¾ hr.

25000

20000

15000

10000

5000

ALTITUDE IN FEET

FOKKER EIII versus AIRCO DH2

IN APRIL 1915 THE GERMANS captured a French Morane Type N and found it had a machine-gun firing straight ahead. The propeller was protected by steel deflectors. Dutchman Anthony Fokker thought this crude; he perfected an interrupter gear which let the gun fire only when there was no propeller blade in the way. Fitted to a simple Eindecker (monoplane) of 1913 design the result was the deadliest fighter in the sky. The EI, 100 hp EII and longer-span EIII so commanded the sky in 1915 that British pilots were called 'Fokker fodder'. But Capt Geoffrey de Havilland's DH2 went some way to fighting back. Lacking an interrupter gear, it put the propeller at the back. DH2s got into action in April 1916, but by this time the Germans had tougher new fighters such as the Albatros.

FOKKER EIII
Mid-wing braced monoplane with
80 hp or, usually, 100 hp
Oberursel rotary engine. Speed 83
mph, ceiling 11 500 ft, endurance
2¾ hr.

0   15   30   45   70   85   100   115   130   145   170   185   200   215   M.P.H

IMMELMANN'S TURN

The KEKs provided the proving ground for aces like Mulzer, Lörzer and Parschau. The most famous of them all was Max Immelmann, who flew in F1. Abt 62 with his friend and rival Oswald Boelcke. Initially Immelmann was overshadowed by Boelcke, who had scored his first victory on July 4 piloting a two-seater Albatros CI, one of the first C Class armed aircraft with a Parabellum machine-gun for the observer. When Boelcke moved on to a new EIII, Immelmann inherited the Albatros. But it was in F1.Abt 62's second EIII that Immelmann scored his first victory on August 1, taking off in pursuit of ten RFC BE2cs which had bombed the unit's airfield at Douai, and forcing down a straggler as it headed for the safety of the British lines. Much has been written about the 'Immelmann Turn' – supposedly devised by Immelmann during his

first weeks in the Eindecker – but in his own letters to his family, in which he describes his successes, nothing is specifically mentioned and one wonders if this celebrated maneuver was merely a journalistic fantasy. Immelmann, like his contemporaries on both sides of the lines, was always improvising and learning; maybe on one occasion he put his nimble Fokker into a steep climb, stall-turned at the top, then twisted down onto his opponent for a second attack. The maneuver worked at that moment. He would not have needed to use his turn every time he attacked an Allied plane. If he made his normal approach, with his superior machine the likely result was either a quick kill, or a chase that usually ended in his favour.

Immelmann writes of a circling turn when he cut inside his opponent and opened fire – Victory No 3, September 21. Then came a pursuit, firing bursts of 20–30 rounds – but it took 400 rounds before the plane (a BE2c) fell – October 10, No 4. On October 26, came No 5 – a Gunbus – '... I took up pursuit, hiding behind his tail all the time.' In fact the two-man crew in this 11 Squadron FB5 did not even see him until his gun opened fire; with the pusher type it was difficult to have a clear rear view. Immelmann's tactic was simply to close in below and behind in the FB5's blind spot. Another BE2c on November 7 went down without seeing the German. The 7th victory on December 15, a Morane Parasol, came after a long chase when Immelmann gradually moved up from below to an attacking position and despatched the two men from 3 Squadron RFC with 150 rounds. Immelmann's only ploy on this occasion was a feint attack which caused the British pilot to fly southeast for a while rather than due west and the safety of the British lines.

The German's first victory of 1916 came on January 12 – another Gunbus of 11 Squadron. The pilot saw him and, with the pusher's usual tactic, turned to face the Fokker head-on. Immelmann and the FB5 went into a turning circle until he got behind the pusher and sent it down in flames to force-land. When he landed beside his conquest, the observer was dead, but the RFC pilot said when questioned that he and his brother pilots were well aware of the name of Immelmann. The 12th victory was another pusher type – an FE2b, on March 29. Immelmann was fully aware of the sort of airplane it was even though he called it a Farman. So he '... adopted (my) tactics accordingly', which was to get well behind the pusher even though it placed him in front of two others, but they were some distance away and above.

On April 25 Immelmann met two of the new

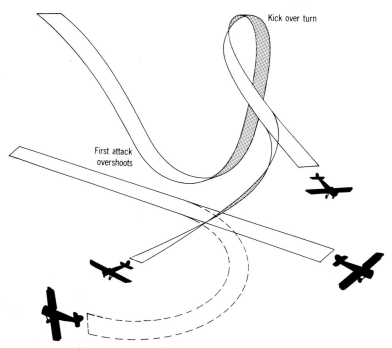

Kick over turn

First attack overshoots

THE IMMELMANN TURN

Attributed to the German ace Max Immelmann, the maneuver began with the growing tendency of pilots to dive on an opponent from an above-and-behind position. If the initial attack did not inflict fatal damage on the target aircraft, the pilot would pull up. At the top of his climb, he would stall-turn and as he began to drop to the right, he would rudder sideways. This would then put him in a good position to dive again on the opponent from the same direction. If the target aircraft had made a turn to either the left or the right, the attacking aircraft would still hold position to cut inside the turns.

DH2 pusher scouts flown by Captain J O Andrews and Lieutenant S E Cowan, both future 'aces', of 24 Squadron (commanded by Lanoe Hawker VC). Immelmann later admitted to being outfought by the two British machines. 'The two worked splendidly together...', he wrote '... and put eleven shots into my machine ...' and he only saved himself by '...a nosedive of 1000 metres'.

His 15th victory was a classic case of a hunter becoming the hunted. On the evening of May 16 he saw a lone Bristol Scout (of 11 Squadron, RFC) chasing two LVG two-seaters. The British pilot made the fundamental error of not keeping a sharp look-out. Concentrating too much on his pursuit, he unwittingly allowed Immelmann to dive on his machine, take careful aim and fire 15–20 rounds from each gun. The EIII was now carrying two machine-guns, and for a brief period Immelmann experimented with an EIV with three machine-guns. But the aircraft proved to be both heavy and unreliable and so Immelmann reverted to the EIII.

Immelmann's last victories came on the day of his own death – 18 June. He shot down two FE2b pushers but in the second combat that evening, over Lens, he died. The Germans say his Fokker fell apart and he was killed in the crash – possibly he wrecked his propeller when his synchronization gear failed (it had happened twice before to Immelmann) – or perhaps Corporal J Waller, Lieutenant G R McCubbin's observer, shot Immelmann down as the RFC claimed, perhaps even shot off the German ace's propeller! Certainly McCubbin had put his FE in a good position from where Waller was able to fire into the Fokker as it flew in front of him after Immelmann had just crippled another FE, which became the German's 17th victory. Max Immelmann passed into aviation history, very much a product of his time. Certainly he learnt his lessons well, pursued, harried, crept up unseen and finally fired. If his aim was sure only a few rounds secured victory; sometimes it took all or almost all of his ammunition. Almost always the kill was made from behind, either in a straight dive, pursuit or circling turn. Such tactics ensured that the job was done at minimum cost and risk.

Many a fighter pilot has come to grief through ignorance of his opponent's capabilities. Recognition of enemy types is a vital factor in aerial combat. Many of Immelmann's victories were two-seat observation aircraft which were 'easy meat' for a Fokker pilot. Some of the FB5s or FE2bs put up a fight and of course the two DH2s nearly got him.

A pilot had to sum up an opponent quickly, and not assume from its position that it could not, for the moment, harm him. When the Nieuport 11 (the famous Bébé) appeared on the Western Front in the summer of 1915, it might have fooled some German pilots. Initially, the Nieuport was equipped with a Lewis gun installed on the upper wing and fixed to fire forward and down over the propeller with the use of a Bowden cable. Later it could be pulled down by the pilot and fired upwards. This also made it easier for the pilot to change the ammunition drum on this gun.

If an unwary German saw it below him, he might have assumed that he had a moment or two to decide on an attacking move, only to find the

Max Immelmann, who usually operated over the Lille area, consequently becoming known as the 'Eagle of Lille'. He was perhaps the best-known of the early German aces of WW1 and gained 17 official victories before his death in combat.

WESTERN FRONT JANUARY 12, 1916

FOKKER EIII VERSUS FB5

The name of the German ace Max Immelmann has survived to this day not so much because he was one of the first successful German fighter pilots but on account of a maneuver attributed to him. Immelmann was among the first pilots to fly the new Fokker EIII, with its machine-gun arranged to fire through the arc of the propeller and an interrupter gear to prevent it hitting the blades; the maneuver bearing his name was used by the Fokker pilots, and subsequently by their Allied counterparts, to reverse positions with an opponent on their tail.

TIMETABLE

1 Heading for the front line soon after first light, Immelmann sees the bursts of AA shells between Arras and Bapaume, indicating the presence of enemy aircraft. The accompanying Fokker turns away to the south, then Immelmann sees a Vickers FB5 'Gunbus' heading east.
2 Realizing that the danger from the pusher Gunbus lies with the gunner in front, Immelmann decides to get into the FB5's blind spot below its tail: diving steeply from head-on, he sees the observer kneeling to fire his gun, but is not hit.

3 The Gunbus tries to turn to bring its gun to bear.
4 Immelmann manages to stay behind the Gunbus and follows it round as the British pilot continues to turn.
5 Finally Immelmann's fire finds its mark: the gasoline tank is holed, pouring fuel over the engine and bursting into flames.
6 The Gunbus glides down to land and Immelmann follows: the observer is dead, and the wounded pilot tells his conqueror that he had panicked and managed only a short burst; it is the German's eighth victory.

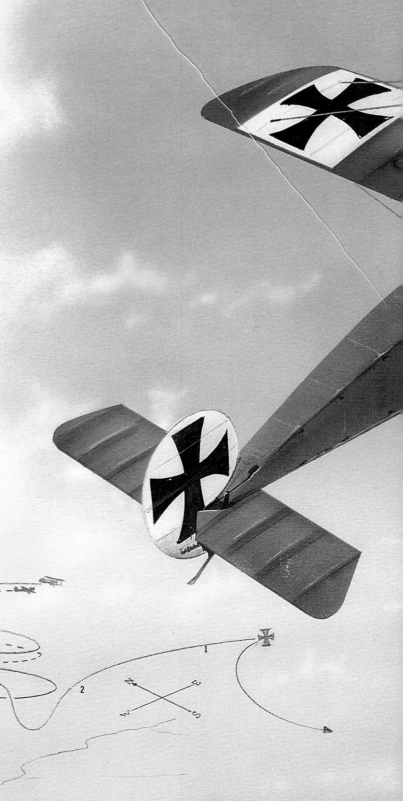

Nieuport's top gun stitching a line of bullet holes in his undersides. For his part the Nieuport pilot's tactic was to attempt to edge up behind and below the German aircraft and fire upwards before being seen. The pilot and/or observer in the German aircraft would be more likely to watch for a rear attack, probably from above but perhaps from dead astern. The sun, too, was the danger area. It did not take long for air fighters to exploit the use of the sun to cover their approach, provided always that it was shining and that it was in a favorable position relative to the target aircraft.

While Germany had Boelcke and Immelmann, the RFC had its rising stars although 'officially' it did not flaunt its pilots' achievements. The popular press, however, did. One of the exponents of the Nieuport Scout was Albert Ball.

Ball, not yet 20 years of age when Immelmann died, had joined the RFC in October 1915, being seconded from the Army like so many of the pilots of WW1. Gaining his 'wings' he was sent to a two-seater squadron, No. 13, flying BE2c at Savy airfield. He flew these until May when he was sent to fly single-seat Nieuport Scouts with No.11 Squadron which was still flying the Gunbus but had a few Nieuports and Bristol Scouts on its strength. By the end of May, Ball had been involved in a number of air fights and by July had been the winner of nine battles. He then went to 8 Squadron flying BE2cs, then returned to 11 Squadron and his Nieuport, in August. That same month he was sent to 60 Squadron which also flew Nieuports.

Ball used the tactics of most RFC Nieuport pilots: to secure an attacking position beneath the enemy aircraft and fire the top-wing Lewis gun up into it. On the evening of July 2 Ball destroyed two German airplanes. The second, an Aviatik two-seater, was attacked in just this manner, from below: '*I DIVED UNDER THE HOSTILE machine, pulling gun down and firing ¾ of a drum directly overhead into the hostile machine, which then side-slipped to earth.'*

In the evening of August 22 he destroyed two Roland two-seaters in one air fight with several Rolands while flying on escort duty.

'... [*I] GOT UNDER THE MACHINE EMPTY-ing drum, machine turned and went down steeply with fire and smoke coming out of fuselage ... three machines that were left fired at the Nieuport. Nieuport got level with the nearest machine and put a drum in with bursts of 5 to 10*

shots, machine went down quite out of control and fell in a village, landing on top of houses.'

To achieve these results, Ball's Nieuport was rigged to be tail-heavy, making the aircraft more stable and leaving Ball free to aim, fire and reload his Lewis machine-gun with both hands.

Ball and the other aces of the mid-1916 period flew alone, as much out of necessity as personal preference. Despite the number of machines the belligerents could now put up in the air – Germany 4856, France 4990, Britain 1741 – there were still no large formations darkening the skies over the Western Front. The single-seat scouts were still part of some two-seater squadrons. With perhaps three or four to a squadron, they had to operate alone in order to spread the workload. This was soon to change as scouts came together in units to operate as squadrons. By then pilots like Ball had become used to fighting alone. It was what they did best, and it took a brave man to suggest change when they were getting the results which were so important to overall morale.

DICTA BOELCKE

As well as helping to organize the formation of the new Jastas, Boelcke was asked to put down on paper a set of rules for air fighting, from the experience he personally had gained. Called the *Dicta Boelcke* these rules were issued to all fighting units.

During the Second World War, the German fighter pilots had these same rules printed out in booklet form, as after 23 years Boelcke's basic principles still applied. They were:

1. *Always try to secure an advantageous position before attacking. Climb before and during the approach in order to surprise the enemy from above, and dive on him swiftly from the rear when the moment to attack is at hand.*
2. *Try to place yourself between the sun and the enemy. This puts the glare of the sun in the enemy's eyes and makes it difficult to see you and impossible for him to shoot with any accuracy.*
3. *Do not fire the machine guns until the enemy is within range and you have him squarely within your sights.*
4. *Attack when the enemy least expects it or when he is preoccupied with other duties such as observation, photography, or bombing.*
5. *Never turn your back and try to run away from an enemy fighter. If you are surprised*

Oswald Boelcke, Germany's 'father of the fighting pilots' of WW1. He personally shot down 40 Allied aircraft but more importantly he carefully studied fighting tactics and persuaded his superiors to form fighting squadrons – Jastas – to combat the French and British. He died leading just such a squadron, Jasta 2, which then became known as 'Jasta Boelcke'.

by an attack on your tail, turn and face the enemy with your guns.

6. *Keep your eye on the enemy and do not let him deceive you with tricks. If your opponent appears damaged, follow him down until he crashes to be sure he is not faking.*

7. *Foolish acts of bravery only bring death. The Jasta must fight as a unit with close teamwork between all pilots. The signal of its leaders must be obeyed.*

With the exception of Rule 6 [only valid for the period when lone pilots fought each other, and quickly obsolete when larger numbers of aircraft were in the skies] Boelcke's fighting rules gave the basic fighting tactics for all air combats.

THE ACES EMERGE

While Albert Ball was still feeling his way on the BE2cs, the 25-year-old German ace Oswald Boelcke was writing a comprehensive report on the organization, tactics and aircraft at the front. The ideas he outlined in the winter of 1915 were crystallized in the air fighting over Verdun, which began at the end of February 1916. Although he had flown and fought alone over Verdun, Boelcke saw clearly that, with the increasing number of aircraft coming into service, the way forward lay in the organization of specific fighting units. Boelcke's immense prestige – he was awarded the Pour Le Mérite in January 1916 – and his technical brilliance ensured him a direct line of communication with the High Command. In the summer of 1916 Boelcke's ideas were accepted and August saw the formation of the first seven Jagdstaffeln ('hunting flights', usually shortened to Jasta) followed by eight more in September. By the end of 1916 the number of Jastas had grown to 33. Four of the new Jastas – each consisting of up to 12 aircraft – were immediately thrown into action after the British launched their offensive on the Somme at the beginning of July. Jasta 2, commanded by Boelcke, arrived at Bertincourt, in Second Army's sector, at the end of August. On September 2, piloting a Fokker DIII on Jasta 2's first operational flight, Boelcke scored his 20th victory, shooting down a DH2 which was escorting a BE2c on a reconnaissance flight. While the Jasta underwent a short, intensive period of training, Boelcke continued to fly alone, taking off early in the morning on a patrol which 'almost daily brought him an Englishman for breakfast'. The author of this laconic remark was a young Lieutenant who had been singled out by Boelcke during a tour of the Eastern Front – Manfred von Richthofen.

On September 17 Richthofen was one of the four pilots who accompanied Boelcke on Jasta 2's first offensive patrol. Flying the new Albatros DIs and DIIIs and Halberstadt DIIs, Jasta 2 mounted devastating formation sweeps over its sector, putting every available pilot and machine into the air. In the process they regained the air superiority held first by the Eindeckers and then relinquished to the Nieuport XIs and the DH2s. Jasta 2's supremacy was confirmed on November 23 by von Richthofen's victory over the commander of No. 24 Squadron, the pugnacious Major Lanoe Hawker. Hawker had joined the squadron's 'A' flight, led by Captain J O Andrews, in a patrol over the German lines. Five DIIs of Jasta 2 lured the patrol eastward and ever deeper into enemy territory. Two of the patrol's DH2s were forced to turn for home with engine trouble before the trap was sprung. When the attack came, Andrews' machine was hit and he was forced to break off the engagement and limp back to the British lines. Hawker was left on his own, but characteristically pressed on, making straight for the DII piloted by von Richthofen. In the dogfight which followed, the DII's advantage in speed and climb were matched against the obsolescent DH2's superior turning circle. The contest turned into a deadly turning duel with both aircraft steadily circling downwards at close to stalling speed. Von Richthofen has left us a detailed account of the outcome: '*S*O IT WENT, both of us flying like madmen in a circle, with engines running full out at 3,000-m altitude. First left, then right, each intent on getting above and behind the other. I was soon acutely aware that I was not dealing with a beginner, for he did not dream of breaking off the fight. He had a very maneuvrable crate, but mine climbed better, and I finally succeeded in coming in above and behind him ... The circles that we made about each other were so narrow that I estimated them to be not further than 80 to 100 m. I had time to view my opponent. I peered perpendicularly at him in his cockpit and could observe every movement of his head ... he finally had to decide whether to land on our side or fly back to his own lines. Naturally he attempted the latter, after trying in vain to evade me through looping and such tricks. As he did so my first bullets flew by his ears, for prior to that I had not fired a shot. At about 100 m altitude he tried to escape towards the Front by flying zigzag, making his plane a difficult target to hit. It was now the given moment for me. I followed him from 50 down to 30 m altitude, firing steadily. About 50 m behind our lines he plunged down with a shot through the head.'*

Adjutant Dudley L Hill with his Nieuport 17 Scout of the Lafayette Escadrille (N124). This Nieuport carries both a wing-mounted as well as cowling-mounted machine-guns. Hill flew with the Lafayette for two years and then with the United States Air Service (USAS) until the end of WW1.

In the two months leading up to Christmas 1916 Jasta 2 accounted for 76 British aircraft for the loss of seven of its own machines. By then its begetter, Oswald Boelcke, was dead, killed on October 28, 1916 after he had gained a total of 40 victories. Ironically he collided with one of his own men, his Albatros breaking up in the air. This occurred a month before Richthofen's duel with Hawker. But the Jastas had taken firm root. In the summer of 1917 they were to be concentrated into fighter wings (Jagdeschwaden), each of them consisting of three or four Jastas. These were often moved from one part of the front to another, achieving a formidable concentration of air power. Their nomadic existence prompted the Allies to nickname them 'circuses', a term which grew in currency when their pilots began to fly highly decorated aircraft. The most famous circus of them all was Jagdeschwader 1, formed on July 26 by the amalgamation of Jastas 4, 6, 10 and 11 and led by von Richthofen. The fighting at Verdun had vindicated the French system of escadrilles de chasse and had produced a number of pilots whose aggression, individuality and killer instinct marked them out from the rest.

One of them was Jean Navarre of Escadrille N67, who on October 25, 1915 had scored the first French double victory of the war, shooting down two German aircraft behind the French lines. Flying over Verdun in his Nieuport 11, he scored another 10 victories before being shot down and severely wounded. Like Albert Ball, Navarre fought alone, approaching an enemy until he was a few feet below him and then standing up in the cockpit of his highly unstable Nieuport to direct a stream of fire from his wing-mounted Lewis gun into the belly of his prey. With the French undertaking large-scale offensive patrols in the skies above the battlefield, Navarre was already a figure from the past.

Two other Frenchmen, Charles Nungesser and Georges Guynemer, were making names for themselves in the French Air Service. Both men flew the Morane and then the Nieuport, and both were aggressive fighters. Nungesser went on to become France's third ranking 'ace' with 45 victories, although he was wounded more than a dozen times and, had at one time or another, broken every major bone in his body.

Guynemer, one of the greatest heroes of France, became a pilot with Escadrille N3. N3, N26, N73 and N103 were formed into a Group called Les Cigognes – the Storks. In part this was an élite fighting unit; to be assigned to the Storks Group was to join the most famous of the French fighting units.

Within the French Air Service was formed one Escadrille that captured the imagination of many people then and later, although it has to be said that historians found it an emotive subject to exploit. Basically the embryo squadron was formed by the French to accommodate a number of American flyers who had either been living or working in France, or who quickly went to her aid when the war began. With America being neutral until 1917, these volunteers had to join the French Foreign Legion and then transfer to France's Aviation Section. Despite innumerable problems of setting up this squadron (even choosing a name for it was not easy) it at last became a reality and was sent to the Front in April 1916 to be called eventually the Lafayette Escadrille – officially N 124.

This unit also flew the Nieuport Scout, on the Vosges Sector, at the time a relatively quiet part of the front. It too carried out escort or patrol flights, more often than not lone operations. It was on one such mission that it gained its first combat success, in many ways unique.

Kiffin Rockwell, with the French rank of Sergent, crossed the lines looking for Germans, but engine trouble forced him to turn for home. Then he saw below him a German two-seater observation aircraft flying above the French lines. As Rockwell dived on it, its rear gunner, easily seeing him, opened fire on the diving Nieuport. The gunner's burst slammed in to the American's machine, but Rockwell kept on diving until he was just 25 yards from the German, then fired. Rockwell had only a second to aim before he had to swerve to avoid a collision and his gun fired just four rounds, which was later confirmed by the squadron armorer. Yet thôse four bullets hit the observer, the pilot and the engine. Both of the crew were seen collapsed in their seats and smoke poured from the engine as the two-seater fell to earth in the German trench area.

It had been Rockwell's first combat, the first time he had seen a German aircraft in the air and the first time he had fired his machine-gun. He had been lucky - lucky to score a kill with just four bullets, but lucky too that the German observer had not hit him or a vital part of his Nieuport. Attacking a two-seater from above and

RAOUL LUFBERY

THE HERO OF THE AMERICAN volunteer force that flew with the French Air Service in Squadron N124 – the Lafayette Escadrille – was born in France of an American father and a French mother. In China in 1911 he became mechanic to the French aviator Marc Pourpe. In 1914 Pourpe joined the French Air Service when war began. Following him, Lufbery (because of his American citizenship) had to join via the Foreign Legion. Pourpe was soon killed in action and, determined to avenge him, Lufbery became a pilot, and by 1915 was flying bombing and observation duties. Lufbery joined other American flyers in the Lafayette Squadron. His first victories came on August 3, 1916 when he shot down two two-seaters over Fort Vaux, followed by an Aviatik on August 8. By the end of the year his score stood at five giving him 'ace' status. Flying Nieuports and later SPADs during 1917, Lufbery brought his score of official victories to 17.

In 1918 he transferred to the American Air Service, being attached to the 94th Aero Squadron as teacher and advisor on fighter tactics, giving his experience to the new American pilots. The 94th flew Nieuport 28 Scouts, and began war patrols over the front in April, although Lufbery was not allowed to fly in combat. On May 19, however, he took off after a two-seater that flew near the airfield. He was seen to attack, then swerve away as though trying to clear a gun jam. As he resumed his attack, his fighter suddenly burst into flames and began to fall. Rather than die a slow death by burning, the ace of the Lafayette chose to jump to his death, a tragic end for this American who became a French hero.

VICTORIES CLAIMED BY THE AMERICAN LAFAYETTE ESCADRILLE

Date	Pilot	Aircraft Destroyed
1916		
May 18	Kiffin Rockwell	Two-seater
May 22	Bert Hall	Aviatik
May 24	Bill Thaw	Fokker EIII
Jul 21	Charles Nungesser (French)	Aviatik
Jul 23	Bert Hall	Fokker EIII
Jul 27	Lt. de Laage (French)	Two-seater
Jul 27	Kiffin Rockwell	EA
Jul 31	Raoul Lufbery	Two-seater
Aug 3	Raoul Lufbery	Two-seater
Aug 3	Raoul Lufbery	Two-seater
Aug 8	Raoul Lufbery	Aviatik
Aug ?	Norman Prince	Kite Balloon
Aug 23	Norman Prince	Aviatik
Sep 9	Kiffin Rockwell	Two-seater
Sep 9	Norman Prince	Fokker EIII
Oct ?	Norman Prince	Fokker EIII
Oct 12	Lt de Laage (French)	Fokker EIII
Oct 12	Raoul Lufbery	Roland CII
Oct 12	Didier Masson	Fokker EIII
Oct 12	Norman Prince	Fokker EIII
Dec 27	Raoul Lufbery	Two-seater
1917		
Jan 25	Raoul Lufbery	Two-seater
Apl 8	Lt de Laage (French)	Scout
Apl 8	Lt de Laage (French)	Scout
Apl 13	Raoul Lufbery	Two-seater
Apl 24	Raoul Lufbery	EA
Apl 26	Charles Johnson	Albatros DIII
Apl 26	Willis Haviland	Albatros DIII
Apl 28	Bill Thaw	Two-seater
Jun 12	Raoul Lufbery	Two-seater
Aug 18	Walter Lovell	Albatros DV
Sep 4	Edwin Parsons	Two-seater
Sep 19	David Peterson	Albatros DV
Sep 22	Raoul Lufbery	Two-seater
Oct 16	Raoul Lufbery	Two-seater
Oct 24	Raoul Lufbery	Two-seater
Oct 24	Raoul Lufbery	Two-seater
Oct 27	Bill Thaw	Albatros DV
Dec 3	Bill Thaw	Rumpler C
Dec 4	Raoul Lufbery	Two-seater
Dec 4	Raoul Lufbery	EA
Dec 4	Kenneth Marr	Two-seater
1918		
Jan 1	James N Hall	Albatros DV

behind was always a danger. An observer with a cool head and a good eye had a fair chance of hitting a fast approaching target as it grew in his sights. He too could be the first to be hit when the scout opened fire, so he had a vested interest in being quicker and on target. As the scout pilot learnt his trade he soon came to realize that attacking a two-seater needed care, strategy and

The FE2b used the combination of a clear forward field of fire for its observer with provision for a fixed forward firing gun for the pilot. To overcome the vulnerability to rear attacks, the observer also had a Lewis gun on a tripod in order to fire back over the top wing. The FE2b's success lasted until the summer of 1917 when it was relegated to night bombing.

patience. A pilot had to try to surprise the two-seater, to see if, perhaps, the observer was busy looking at the ground, using a camera, etc., or perhaps maneuver directly above the hostile plane, then dive vertically. The observer and pilot were sometimes less likely to look directly overhead. Alternatively the scout pilot would try to get below and behind, keeping the tail and elevators between him and the observer. The fighter could then either fire upwards in a quick zoom, or, if the scout had a pull-down gun, the pilot could fire upwards with it.

Meanwhile, the Lafayette Escadrille gradually improved its skill and by the end of 1916 had scored 20 confirmed successes.

KEEPING THE SCORE

What constituted a confirmed success? It had become important to know how many aircraft each side shot down and equally important to confirm successes. One could debate however, why it was so important to know how many airplanes an individual pilot destroyed. For instance, say a pilot shoots down six enemy aircraft in four months of war flying. Let us say too he killed four enemy flyers. How is that achievement compared to that of a soldier behind a machine-gun in a trench who helps to stem an attack and kills (although he would not know it), say, 60 enemy soldiers. He may do that several times over many months! Who has, in respect of numbers, achieved more for his side in winning the war? History may recall the pilot with six victories, but does it know of Private 'X', who fought no less courageously and put 200 of his country's enemies out of action? This is a simplified view but an interesting line of thought.

It therefore became the norm for a pilot, if he had been successful in an air fight, to put in a report and hope that it would be confirmed. Perhaps another pilot saw it, or front-line troops watched the action and saw an enemy plane fall. The wreckage may have fallen on the victorious pilot's side of the lines. This was not unknown, but rarer for the British, French and Belgian flyers than for the Germans. The reason for this was simple. Almost from the beginning the Allied Air Forces took the challenge to the Germans. Their

Presented By Residents in The PUNJAB

plan was always to fly and patrol over the German side of the lines. The Germans, therefore, while they still sent two-seaters over the Allied side to fly reconnaissance missions – rarely if ever escorted by scouts, and relying more on clouds and height – usually patrolled only on their side. The German scouts, then, had only to wait for the British or French to come to them. If they shot down an Allied airplane, its wreckage was usually located and a victory claim verified. Thus the Germans were able to confirm their pilots' successes more easily.

The Allied pilots had more difficulty, resulting in a system of what were loosely termed 'victories'. During WW1 a 'victory' did not necessarily mean an enemy aircraft destroyed. After WW2 when a victory had that meaning, it became confusing to relate the two systems. In the main, detailed interest in WW1 flying did not really start until the 1950s. The many books that were published in the 1930s were written by the men who had been 'there', and at that time there was no need to define victories and, of course, absolutely no reason to make any comparison.

A WW1 scout pilot who returned from a successful engagement on the other side of the lines might claim to have destroyed a German aircraft. He had seen it crash, seen it go down in flames, or seen it fall earthwards, and perhaps its pilot had been thrown out. Hopefully, as mentioned before, someone else had seen it and would be able to confirm, to corroborate, his 'claim'.

As air-fighting was rarely so clear cut, there was another victory claim: the 'out of control'. Flying at height, speed, above cloud or haze, near rain squalls, a pilot was often, especially after 1916, not absolutely certain of his kill. If he attacked a German airplane which then began to spin earthwards from 15 000 ft, it was impossible to know whether it actually crashed. The victorious pilot would, if he was wise, not follow it down. A battle might still be raging about him; he might be short of fuel and need to start back to his side of the lines and not have time to see if his enemy had in fact crashed. He would be able to report only that he believed he had shot down a German aircraft. If this too was borne out by another flyer or the army in the front lines, then his 'out-of-control victory' would also be confirmed. In WW2 this would be the equivalent of the 'probable' claim. The difference was that in WW1, his out-of-control/probable would be added to a pilot's individual score. Thus the six victories of our earlier mythical pilot might comprise four destroyed and two 'out of control'.

As the air-war escalated in 1917–18, these were generally the two main types of victory. In 1916 particularly, the RFC had another – the 'forced-to-land'. With the battles of 1915–16 being often isolated encounters between two, or perhaps no more than five or six aircraft, it was, perhaps, a little more leisurely, more gentlemanly.

If a British single-seater pilot got the upper hand in a fight, – bearing in mind that 95% of these fights were on the German side of the lines – the German pilot had an easy way out: he could spiral down and land. Of course, the British pilot had no way of knowing if the German had just landed, had his aeroplane damaged, or if the pilot (and/or observer) had been wounded. Once the German had landed he was immune from any further depredation from his 'victor' – the war was still fairly gentlemanly at this stage. One could sneak up and shoot him in the back in the air, but one did not hit a man when he was down. Later, certainly, but not in 1916! If, then, the opponent had landed, it was a moral victory for the British pilot. That the German might be mortally wounded, injured, or just had his aircraft damaged would be unknown. In 1916, therefore, pilots had such scores credited to their names. Albert Ball had several 'forced-to-land' victories in his accepted 47 'victories': not, therefore, 47 enemy aircraft destroyed, but something like 23 destroyed, two out of control and 21 forced to land, plus one balloon. Balloons were also counted in a pilot's score. A kite balloon, used by both sides for observation purposes, became an aerial victory if seen to be deflated or sent down in a ball of flames.

By 1917–18 the war had become less gentlemanly. A damaged aeroplane might still land, but three things might influence a pilot to get well clear of the air battle before doing so, or indeed try to get home. One, he might be shot up on the way down by another pilot, there being any number of enemy aircraft in the battle area. Two, he might be shot up on the ground. Three, his victor might not let him gently spiral down but try to make sure of his kill. So, by 1918, victories were either destroyed aircraft or balloons, plus those aircraft seen to go down, and, in the opinion of the witnesses, 'out of control' (and likely to crash).

It is not difficult to visualize that a pilot in trouble might put his aircraft in a spin in the hope that his opponent would think him wounded or damaged and leave him alone. Once out and away from danger he would right his machine and fly home a wiser and still living man. More often than not, however, the attacker knew if he had hit the other plane with a damaging burst, may even have seen the pilot jerk back as he was hit, or slump down in his tiny cockpit and fall over the control column while the aircraft flicked into a screaming nosedive or helpless spin.

During 1917–18 the RFC/RAF (and until April 1918 the RNAS) received weekly communiqués printed by HQ in France and issued to all units. They were called 'Comic Cuts' by the flyers in the field, but read nevertheless. The purpose of these communiqués was to report the progress of the air war and to disseminate other intelligence of interest. They also mentioned the majority of successful combats, naming the pilot or observer/gunner involved. Some amateur historians believe that only if a British victory was mentioned in the communiqué was it made 'official'. This is not so. Some reports of combats failed to reach headquarters in time to meet the weekly printing deadline, for instance. By the second half of 1918, with the increased frequency of combats, listing of enemy victories outgrew the limited space available. Out-of-control victories were therefore omitted. This, to some, seemed to indicate that out-of-control victories were no longer recognized. Again this is not so, and an analysis of pilots' victory scores for the period clearly supports this. The French and Germans had similar communiqués, although a victory mentioned here *did* make it official.

In WW2 victories were more clearly defined – they were either destroyed, probably destroyed or damaged. Only the destroyed – if confirmed – were allowed in a pilot or gunner's score. The probables and damaged were acknowledged in his combat record and sometimes mentioned in a citation for a decoration. The definition of a victory, therefore, was very different in WW1 from WW2.

NEW MACHINES

The year 1916 had seen a general escalation in air combat above the Western Front. Both sides now had interrupter gears to allow machine-guns to fire through the propeller of tractor-engined aircraft: However, the RFC's pusher types had begun to defeat the Fokkers. New fighting squadrons arriving in France were equipped totally with scouts, 24 Sqdn as already mentioned, with DH2s, 29 Sqdn with Nieuports, 27 Sqdn with Martinsyde Scouts, 70 Sqdn with a two-seater Sopwith 1½-Strutter aircraft plus other FE2d squadrons. The new Sopwith Pup Scouts were also equipping some RFC and RNAS squadrons, carrying a single Vickers machine-gun located right in front of the pilot and firing through the propeller. The main scout in France

with RNAS squadrons was the Sopwith Triplane, a very successful type with the Naval flyers. These new types wrested air superiority from the Germans during and after the great Somme battles that began in July 1916.

The Germans too were receiving new scout types. The new Jastas were being equipped with a Fokker biplane, the DII, which was not a success although a number of the rising 'aces' did fly them. The Halberstadt DI also arrived but both of these new scouts failed to establish themselves positively. But the Albatros DI (later the DII) did begin to wrest air supremacy from the DH2s and Nieuports. Although the DI was a heavy aeroplane, it was maneuvrable, had speed in attack and could fly away from trouble if necessary. At first they joined with the Fokker DIIIs and Halberstadt DIIs, but these were gradually superseded by the Albatros Scout. With two Spandau machine-guns firing through the propeller it, plus the later DIII and DV types, dominated the war zone until early 1918.

AIRSHIP ATTACK

Because of Germany's total war policy she had to attack England, and aircraft were the only means by which to do this. Airplanes had made isolated bomb raids on England since the early days of the war but it was to be the airship that began to strike fear and apprehension into the hearts of British civilians.

Very vulnerable to adverse weather conditions, the German airships, known universally as Zeppelins, although the Zeppelin and Schulz-Lanz companies both built airships for Germany, had the capability in moderate to good weather – at night – to range over England, largely to the east and south east of the country.

Despite their size and supposed vulnerability to damage from ground and air defenses, they proved hard to attack and destroy. At first, Britain's air defense squadrons, both RFC and RNAS, did not possess aircraft with the capabilities to do them any great harm. When the airships appeared, the Home Defence units would send up those aircraft available but night flying was itself in its infancy and the pilot going aloft above a darkened England had virtually no aids, certainly no radio, or radar. Once in the air he either saw the airship or, more usually, saw absolutely nothing except the odd searchlight looking in vain for the night raider. Consequently, in the early months of the war, it was easier to attack the airship's bases than try to catch them in the air.

However, the first airship was shot down on

These 'Public Warning' leaflets appeared in numbers in the large cities of Britain during the Great War. Best-known of the German types was the Taube (Dove). These were monoplanes with graceful, swept-back wings just like the wings of a dove. Any number of these flew over England in the early days of the war, but later came the huge airships and Gotha bombers that rained death and destruction on the civilian population.

June 7, 1915. Three had raided England on the previous evening and the RNAS at Furnes, Belgium, were alerted. Two Henri Farmans were sent off to bomb the Zeppelin base at Evere, while two Morane Parasols flew to try an interception. It was 1 am when one of the pilots (Flight Sub Lieutenant R A Warneford) spotted an airship over Dixmude. He pursued it for 45 minutes, gradually catching up the Zeppelin near Bruges. Warneford came under fire from the airship's defenses, and he banked away to try to climb above the huge enemy. The Zeppelin turned to join combat with the Morane with its machine-gunners, as Warneford struggled to get above to use his six 20 lb Hales bombs, his only armament. The airship then turned away, as Warneford reached 10 000 ft. Switching off his engine, he started a diving attack from above, closing in to 150 ft above the Zeppelin. He began releasing his bombs as he swooped above the airship from the stern to the front. An explosion erupted in the forward section of the airship and soon afterwards it plummeted to the ground in flames. The gallant Warneford was awarded the VC but sadly he died in an aeroplane crash ten days later.

Warneford's victory had been an airship on its way home from England. The next one to be destroyed fell to a pilot over England. Lt William Leefe-Robinson was with No. 39 Home Defence Squadron, at Sutton's Farm, Essex (later known as RAF Hornchurch). His first encounter with an airship came on the night of April 25–26 1916 when he found a Zeppelin (LZ97) over London. Robinson had struggled up in his BE2d that took nearly an hour to reach 10 000 ft. When he reached 8000 ft he saw the Zeppelin way above him and opened fire from his position. The airship released part of its ballast and almost contemptuously rose upwards and disappeared from view.

After a further four fruitless months success came on the night of September 2–3. London was the target for no fewer than 16 airships – the Germans' greatest air effort of the war in airship warfare. Robinson and Lt Fred Sowrey took off in their BEs just after 11 pm, Robinson taking 53 minutes to reach his patrol height of 10 000 ft. The dark sky was almost cloudless and for an hour Robinson patrolled his assigned air 'lane' but saw nothing.

Then an airship was illuminated by searchlights over the east of London, Robinson having reached 13 000 ft. He managed to maintain this height (200 ft above the airship's), but then the Zeppelin was lost in cloud. Robinson then saw explosions on the ground, flew in the general direction and found an airship again in search-

lights and decided to gather all speed in a dive from 12 000 ft. Anti-aircraft shells were exploding well below the huge gas-bag as Robinson levelled out 800 ft below it and opened fire with his Lewis gun into the massive target. In two attacks he emptied two drums but saw no result. Firing his third and last drum, he saw a glow and then the airship erupted in flames. The SL11 (a Schulz-Lanz airship, not a Zeppelin design) fell in flames, forcing Robinson to move quickly out of the way. Robinson too was rewarded with the Victoria Cross.

There were, therefore, two methods of destroying airships at this stage of the war when flying fragile, under-powered and lightly armed aircraft. One tactic was to drop small bombs on the airship, while the other, very much like the Western Front fighter pilots, was to dive below the airship, using the speed to stay with the target, and fire upwards with a Lewis gun. In this case the gun, fixed to fire upwards, was placed immediately in front of the pilot's (rear) cockpit. The front cockpit of these 'night-fighter' BE2ds were covered in.

CHAPTER THREE

NEW SCOUTS, NEW TACTICS

B Y THE END OF 1916 THE AIR WAR had become a particularly deadly business. Air fighting had developed apace on both sides of the lines in France. Each had synchronized machine-guns, engines and airframes were fairly reliable, and suitable tactics had evolved. However, the type of tactics adopted depended as much on what each side could achieve with its equipment, just as much as the necessity to combat the opposition's own tactics. In some cases it was not so much a case of bettering an opponent, as being satisfied to stay alive. If a pilot knew he was inferior in performance, maneuverability or armament, he would try to improvize to survive.

Those in command on the ground as well as the various squadron and flight commanders, soon learnt how to pursue a course of minimal casualties – if allowed through circumstance to do so. It was obvious that the slower two-seaters on Corps work (army support, reconnaissance, artillery observation, and so on) or bombing enemy store dumps, railway stations and troop concentrations, needed protection. Reliability in equipment, and an increase in the numbers of aircraft meant that the skies were busier than hitherto. The scouts now flew to protect the slower aircraft as well as to seek out hostile aircraft and the new year of 1917 saw the air war escalate beyond the imagination of the flyers of the previous two years.

On the German side, the Albatros Scouts (introduced in 1916) were dominating the air war. They were fast, nimble and, with twin Spandau machine-guns, heavily armed. German pilots were not keen to dive them full out as they tended to shed their top wing. They were also heavy in a turn but otherwise the Jastas successfully maintained air superiority on their side of the lines.

The British, ever the innovators, were still adapting some of their aircraft to perform above their designed capability. But there were several new types on the drawing-boards, some even being produced. However, things were destined to get worse for the British before they ever began to improve.

The winter of 1916–17 kept the war in limbo, but the coming of spring changed all that. The Somme offensive of 1916 was replaced in the spring of 1917 by the Battle of Arras. To support it the RFC, and some of the RNAS squadrons in France supporting it, would fill the sky with its aircraft. Total control of the air would be required, but with the Jastas in command it would be hard to achieve.

Left: Albatros DIII scout – the new breed of fighting scouts with which the Germans reclaimed air superiority in the spring of 1917. This particular DIII – painted black with white crosses, was flown by Lieutenant Joachim von Bertrab of Jasta 30 who gained six victories before falling to Edward Mannock of 40 Squadron on August 12, 1917. He was wounded and landed inside Allied lines to become a prisoner.

Above: Sopwith Pup. A delight to fly, it helped to bridge the gap between the now out-dated 'Pusher' types and the new generation of scouts, the Camel and SE5. Armed with a single Vickers gun firing through the propeller it was more maneuverable than the Albatros Scouts but could not out-climb them. This Pup was used by 46 Squadron in 1917.

The battle began on April 9. It was expected to last until early May but had to be prolonged. The French had opened an offensive on the Aisne, in Champagne, but had been bloodily repulsed. The Arras battle therefore was continued to help support their flank.

In the air battle the Germans with their fighting Jastas had a field day. By the time May came the RFC had suffered tremendous casualties. The Albatros and Halberstadt scouts were given innumerable targets, the most they'd ever had so far. This in part was why this period became known as 'Bloody April' by the RFC.

On March 31 1917, nine days before the Battle began, the RFC in France consisted of 23 Corps and bombing squadrons, 22 scouting squadrons (single- and two-seater), plus four Naval single-seat scout squadrons, one attached to each of four RFC Brigades. On the Arras Battle front itself, the RFC had 25 squadrons, totalling 365 airplanes of which about a third were scouts. On the opposing side, the Germans had 195 aircraft, half of which were scouts. However, what the Germans lacked in numbers they made up for in superior machines. The Albatros and Halberstadt scouts were far better than the RFC types.

By the time the battle opened on Easter Monday, the Germans had already shot down 75 British aircraft in the preceding five days, 44 of them falling on April 6 alone. By the end of April, the RFC and RNAS had lost over 150 aircraft and 316 airmen, the French and Belgians 200 aircraft. The British claimed over 260 German airplanes shot down by RFC aircraft, the Germans listing nearly 370 lost along the whole front.

There is little doubt that the Nieuport was still the best fighting scout aircraft on the Allied side, still better than even the new Sopwith Pup, but

obviously the British Government was not happy about relying on a French airplane with which to fight the Germans. Nevertheless, the Pup was steady and relatively easy to maneuver and dubbed a 'nice' machine by many of its pilots. Sixty-six Squadron, equipped with Pups, arrived in France in March 1917. Its senior flight commander was Captain J O Andrews, MC, who had flown alongside Hawker in 24 Sqdn the previous year. He was a superb scout pilot with the good eyesight essential for spotting the enemy first and being a successful air fighter.

The Pup pilots quickly found – if they lived long enough – that they could turn inside an Albatros although it could outclimb a Pup, especially above 14 000 ft. Its speed was greater than the Sopwith's and if the German pilot needed to take the risk he could certainly outdive the British machine. The RFC pilot, therefore, needed to surprise the Albatros pilot, use height to overcome his disadvantage in level flight, then lure the Albatros pilot into a close duel where his better turn gave him the advantage. The Pup pilot was equally aware that if he did not beat his opponent, he would be hard pressed to regain the safety of his own lines.

GERMAN ADVANTAGES

This was why the RFC and RNAS flyers were always at a disadvantage. They eventually had to return across the front lines to gain friendly territory. The German scouts, almost always patrolling behind their lines, had several advantages. They could choose the moment of battle, decide when to engage or when to break off action. The Germans could stay longer in the air, for they need take off only when front-line observers telephoned back to say British, or French, aircraft were approaching. And of course, they did not have to conserve fuel to get home. If they were damaged or outfought they could go down and land, whereas Allied pilots obliged to land could only expect to face captivity in a German prisoner of war camp.

Even the forces of nature were against the Allied flyers. The predominant wind blew from west to east. This helped them to fly across the lines, but it was against them when they tried to fly back, perhaps damaged, low on petrol or even wounded – or all three!

The German Jasta pilot had time to climb to a good height, often flying inland in order to return from the east and be well above the Allied machines. Numbers were also important. Because of the RFC system, they were generally out numbered.

NIEUPORT 17 versus ALBATROS DIII

BY THE TIME THE ALLIES had at last got the the upper hand of the Fokker monoplanes in the late spring of 1916 there were newer and much better German fighters to contend with. Best of all were the Albatros series. After 1915 practically every German warplane had a heavy but reliable six-cylinder inline engine, and these gave enough power for the new Albatros scouts to have two machine guns without loss of performance. The DIII, which entered service in early 1917, soon showed it was a close match for anything the Allies could put against it. Yet the very fact that its designers had been told to copy the Nieuport shows the worth of these small and light French machines. Amazingly agile, their main unusual feature was an extremely small lower wing. There was no magic in this arrangement, though the Albatros copied it, and the only real advantage was improved pilot view. Many of the greatest Allied aces chose to fly a Nieuport, but the Nieuport 17 was one of the low-power scouts which became sluggish if fitted with two guns.

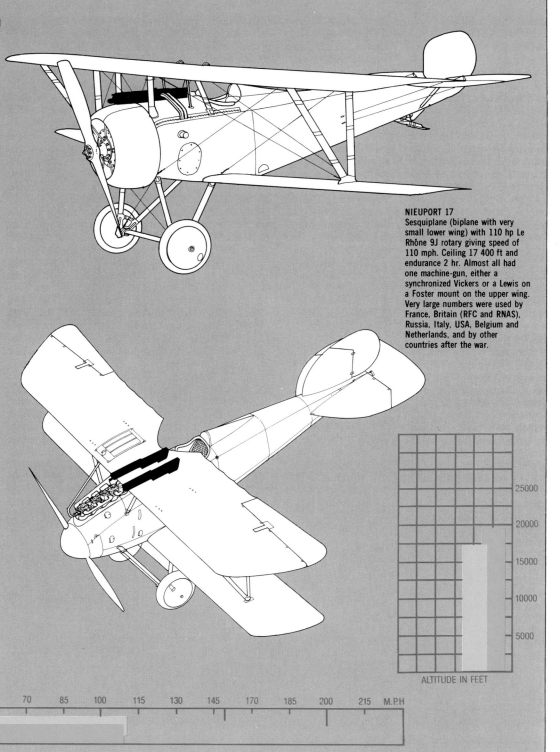

NIEUPORT 17
Sesquiplane (biplane with very small lower wing) with 110 hp Le Rhône 9J rotary giving speed of 110 mph. Ceiling 17 400 ft and endurance 2 hr. Almost all had one machine-gun, either a synchronized Vickers or a Lewis on a Foster mount on the upper wing. Very large numbers were used by France, Britain (RFC and RNAS), Russia, Italy, USA, Belgium and Netherlands, and by other countries after the war.

ALBATROS DIII
Streamlined biplane with 160/175 hp water-cooled Mercedes DIIIa engine giving a speed of 109 mph. Ceiling 18 000 ft and endurance 2 hr. A notable feature was the beautifully shaped fuselage, with plywood skin. Armament was two synchronized 7.92 mm Spandau machine-guns. These formidable fighters were built in Austria as well as in Germany.

25000

20000

15000

10000

5000

ALTITUDE IN FEET

0   15   30   45   70   85   100   115   130   145   170   185   200   215   M.P.H

An RFC Squadron comprised three flights of six aircraft (18 in all). In order to have a workable roster on days when there was no special operation going on, 'A' Flight might take the morning patrol, 'B' the afternoon one, while 'C' Flight rested. The next day 'B' and 'C' Flights flew the patrols while 'A' rested – and so on. Normally each patrol was just five aircraft, which allowed for leave or sickness of one pilot in that flight. Only rarely would two flights join company; during an offensive, or for some special operation, there might be a whole squadron 'show' when a maximum effort would be called for.

Generally, however, just five scouts would fly into 'Hunland', as the British flyers called the enemy side of the lines. This number would be reduced by one or even two if engine troubles forced anyone back: rarely would a patrol have to be cancelled. There is any number of recorded cases of patrols being flown by just two pilots – or even one, provided he was experienced enough to fly alone.

The Germans therefore usually had more machines aloft. They did not patrol in the same way as their Allied counterparts. The RFC were protecting Corps or bombing aircraft, either directly or in general support, by patrols designed to engage German scouts that otherwise might find the two-seaters.

A Jasta comprised at first six aircraft, then 12. Later the unit size increased to 14, and by the end of the war, was 21. Serviceability made these set numbers vary, but in the mid-war years a typical Jasta patrol strength might be perhaps seven or eight. As 1917 progressed it became usual for Jastas to fly together, thereby doubling the patrol strength. In June came the first Jagdeschwader, which placed Jastas 4, 6, 10 and 11 together. While this did not mean that the new unit could put up between 30 and 40 scouts at one time, it certainly increased the number of fighting aircraft. Its first commander was the redoubtable Manfred von Richthofen, who by June 1917 boasted a personal victory tally of 54. Patrols at Jasta strength were still flown, but if Allied activity increased, von Richthofen could lead any number of aircraft towards the battle area. Once in sight of the British, the group would generally split up and its pilots make individual attacks. Von Richthofen, after all, had no in-flight control over his pilots. There was no radio communication then, and hand signals or wing-waggling gave only very limited instructions to those few pilots near enough to see them.

The formation of Jagdeschwader 1 came at a time when overall the Germans on the Western Front were outnumbered 2 to 1 in the air, but because of the small patrol units employed by the British and French, this superiority was not always apparent in actual air actions.

In the race for superiority, there were new aircraft reaching the front in mid-1917. A new two-seat aircraft, the Bristol Fighter, arrived in April, just in time for the Arras offensive, equipping 48 Squadron, commanded by Major W Leefe Robinson VC, who had shot down the first German airship over England. The Bristol Fighter was a new concept, with the pilot having a machine-gun firing through the propeller and an observer/gunner with a Lewis gun in his rear cockpit. (Stronger gunners later carried two Lewis guns, the extra fire-power compensating for a slight loss in performance, but they were rather heavy for the gunner to manipulate.)

On the squadron's first patrol, on April 5, the six Bristol Fighters ran into Jasta 11, led by von Richthofen. The Bristols closed up, relying on the combined fire from the rear gunners to protect them from the nimble Albatros Scouts. In the ensuing fight, the Bristols' guns froze, and four of new type were shot down, Robinson being in one of them. He was taken prisoner.

Von Richthofen himself dismissed the new British aircraft as an airplane not to be feared. He was wrong. Because the lubricating oil in the new guns had frozen and because the pilots kept in close formation, the Albatros pilots were able to dispose of four of them in quick succession. Later pilots of the Bristol, which by the war's end equipped a number of squadrons and special flights, developed a more fluid and more aggressive set of tactics. With its speed and maneuverability it could dogfight any German single-seater. The pilot also had the advantage of a gunner to protect his rear while he concentrated on an attack. Some of the top-scoring 'aces' flew Bristol Fighters – a type which remained in RAF service till 1931.

Another new type was the SE5, a single-seater that equipped another new squadron, No. 56. The squadron's senior Flight Commander was Captain Albert Ball DSO MC. The new SE5 had both a Vickers machine-gun set on the engine cowling, firing through the propeller and, as a sort of insurance, a Lewis gun on the top wing that could be fired forward over the propeller arc, or pulled down to fire upwards like the Nieuport. Although the SE5 was a good scouting type that was to remain a front-line fighter for the rest of the war, Albert Ball, although he flew it, preferred a Nieuport. Owing to his standing and prestige in the RFC he was allowed a Nieuport (B 522) for his

Cockpit of a Nieuport 17 with wing-mounted Lewis gun. There are several items of interest visible here. The Bowden cable attached to the gun handle and trigger grip was used to fire the gun from the cockpit. The other cable attached to the bottom of the trigger grip was for the pilot to pull down the gun to replace the ammunition drum (not fitted in this picture). Once pushed back, the gun barrel would catch in the 'V' spring clip on the forward pylon. Note too the cross-wires gun sight, rear view car mirror, and adjustable map case beneath the windscreen. The bead for the 'ring and bead' gun sight can just be seen in front of this windscreen.

RODERIC STANLEY DALLAS

BORN IN JULY 1892, STANLEY Dallas was a Queenslander, who joined the Australian Army in 1913. Soon after war began he tried to transfer to the Royal Flying Corps but was rejected. Determined not to be stopped from flying, he applied to join the Royal Naval Air Service and was accepted in 1915. At the end of that year he joined No. 1 Naval Wing at Dunkirk flying both single- and two-seat aircraft, claiming his first victory on April 23, 1916.

He flew a number of different aircraft, including Nieuport Scouts, and after his first year in France had accounted for about a dozen victories (although Dallas did not keep very accurate records of his personal claims). At the beginning of 1917, 1 Naval Wing became 1 Naval Squadron and began to re-equip with Sopwith Triplanes, and Dallas began to build up an impressive score, many of his victims being Albatros Scouts. By early March 1918 his score had been raised to 27, making a total of 41, and earning him the DSC and bar, followed by the DSO.

When the RFC and the RNAS became the Royal Air Force on April 1, 1918, Dallas was given command of 40 Squadron, a former RFC unit, and changed from flying Sopwith rotary-engined fighters to the in-line-engined SE5. By May 1918, he had brought his score to over 50, making him the top-scoring Australian pilot of WW1.

His luck ran out on the first day of June 1918, flying on a lone patrol along the front. Dallas was on the British side, probably looking for German two-seater observation aircraft, when he was surprised by three Fokker Triplanes of Jasta 14 and shot down by the Staffelführer, Leutnant Hans Werner. Dallas's death gave the German his sixth victory.

personal use while with 56 Squadron. He felt at home in the Nieuport. Having been successful as a 'lone wolf' pilot he needed time to learn how to become a responsible patrol leader. As he was still determined to fly off on his own whenever possible, he wanted the confidence the Nieuport gave him. He knew his Nieuport could outclimb an Albatros Scout in case he needed to get out of trouble and, while it was slower than the Albatros, it was faster in the climb.

Ball, by this time, had some 30 victories in all categories, having had nearly 60 air combats while with 11 and 60 squadrons in 1916. Fifty-six Squadron was not given permission to cross the lines for its first two weeks but it was Ball who shot down the squadron's first victim on the morning of April 23, 1917 – in his Nieuport.

He took off alone and found two Albatros two-seaters over Cambrai at 8000 ft. Ball used the same tactics, diving to secure a position beneath his opponent in order to fire his wing-mounted Lewis gun upwards. His fire sent one Albatros down; he followed, snapping off further bursts, until it crashed upside down near Tilloy. Later that morning he flew out alone in his SE5, and, engaging another two-seater, used his same tactic; this time his gun jammed. Landing at another airfield, he cleared the jam and was back in action before noon.

Still alone, he found five Albatros DIIIs over Cambrai and gave chase. Catching them up he dived on the nearest German and fired 150 rounds (his Vickers gun-belt filled with one tracer round every three bullets) at close range. His target went down, burst into flames and crashed. The other Albatros Scouts sent a few bullets his way but then flew off. Ball then forced a two-seater to land after firing half a Lewis drum from underneath. The German observer was mortally wounded in the neck and died later, on May 15.

By that date Ball had himself been dead a week. In his last days in action, using the SE5 and occasionally his Nieuport, he raised his tally to about 47 'victories'. He died in action on the evening of May 7, falling not in combat but after becoming disorientated in low cloud. So died England's great air hero of that time, recognized by the award of a posthumous Victoria Cross. In the citation to this, his country's highest gallantry medal, it states that Ball had destroyed 43 German aircraft and one balloon. In the context of victories of WW1, 'destroyed' is incorrect. As has already been discussed, victories, whether 44, 47 or any other computed figure, were of all categories: enemy aircraft destroyed (crashed or in flames); 'out of control' [believed crashed, or

forced to land]; pilot landed with a damaged airplane, a wounded observer or himself wounded; or a pilot just getting away from trouble. This last was an important 'victory'. Not only was the survivor morally the winner of an air battle, but he had stopped, however temporarily, the enemy from doing his job and had thereby possibly saved the lives of some Allied soldiers in the battle zones.

SE5 OR CAMEL?

The sister to the SE5 on the Western Front from July 1917 until the end of the war, and perhaps the most famous of all British aircraft to see action during WW1, was the Sopwith Camel.

Developed by the Sopwith Company, following three successful forerunners, the Pup, Triplane and, to an extent the two-seater Sopwith 1½-Strutter, the Camel was a rugged, pugnacious and deadly adversary for the Germans on the Western Front as well as the Austro-Hungarians in Northern Italy. It carried two synchronized Vickers machine-guns mounted on the engine cowling. Unlike the SE5 which had an in-line engine, the Camel, like previous Sopwith designs, had a rotary engine, which went round with the propeller.

The Camel, once mastered, was a good fighting machine, but pilots with faint heart needed extra care. To the unwary it was difficult to fly, as many tyro pilots discovered. Its built-in masses – engine, guns, cockpit/pilot – were all concentrated within the first seven feet of the aeroplane's fuselage. This helped to give the Camel, with the rotary engine's torque, turning capabilities not previously seen in a fighter. The highly sensitive controls responded instantly to a pilot's touch. The experienced pilot welcomed this response and maneuverability, but the new pilot, progressing perhaps from a docile training aircraft, had to be doubly alert, Sir Leslie Hollinghurst, who had flown many Camels in 1917–18 in England, once told me that in a loop, for instance, one had to fly it through the maneuver, whereas with other types one let the aeroplane fly one through it.

It was often this development in aircraft design and performance that subsequently dictated the tactics which pilots employed to survive in combat. Having spoken to or corresponded with a good number of fighter pilots of both World Wars, over the last 20 years or so, I have heard many stories about the methods devised by these pilots to ensure their survival in combat situations. The friendly rivalry between Camel and SE5 pilots regarding the superiority of

Above: SE5A scout of 29 Squadron at the end of WW1. This type carried a wing-mounted Lewis gun and a Vickers gun which fired through the propeller arc, its butt jutting into the pilot's cockpit. The Aldis gun sight can be clearly seen in front of the cockpit.
Right: The Aldis gun sight and the fuselage-mounted Vickers gun can be seen clearly in this picture of an SE5A cockpit. The two triggers on the control column are also clearly shown. The two rings on the fuselage side hold the SE's long exhaust tubes in place.

their machines was echoed in WW2 by Hurricane and Spitfire pilots.

Nevertheless there were essential differences in performance and flexibility of the two aircraft. In 1917 both types were welcome equipment on the Western Front, but gradually the Camel proved itself to be better at lower altitudes, and the SE5 at high. Consequently, Camels were used for ground attack missions from late 1917 until the end of the war. Another fundamental difference between the Camel and the SE5 that pilots discovered was that an SE5 pilot was usually able to break off an action and evade trouble with its greater speed – 132 mph – against the Camel's 118 mph – although the Camel could climb faster and higher. While the SE5 pilot could fly away from trouble, the pilot of the Camel invariably had to fight his way out, using its greater maneuverability.

Sopwith Camels began reaching front-line squadrons in June 1917. The RNAS at Dunkirk began receiving Camels that went to 4 Naval Squadron who had been flying Pups. In the RFC 70 Squadron re-equipped with Camels from their 1½-Strutters. The first Camel victory occurred on June 4 when Flight Commander A M Shook of 4 Naval sent a German aircraft in a steep dive into a dense sea haze. The next day Shook attacked 15 hostile aircraft sending one scout down to crash, a second spinning down 'out of control'.

In 70 Squadron, Captain C Collett shot down the RFC's first Camel kill on June 27. In July 45 Squadron swapped 1½-Strutters for Camels while 6 Naval Squadron got them in August. Yet the RFC in general still struggled on with Nieuports and Sopwith Pups until late in the year.

The late Arthur Gould Lee, with whom I talked on a few occasions, told me in 1968 of some of his experiences while flying Pups in 46 Squadron in 1917. After a period at the front from May to July, where he learned to survive in the air, 46 Squadron was pulled out of the line. It was based at Sutton's Farm to defend London against German Gotha bombers that had raided the City. The Squadron returned to France at the end of August. On their first patrol they ran into Richthofen's Circus, the Germans' DVs completely outclassing their Pups. All they could do was to try to avoid being shot down. Even then three Pups failed to get home and the two survivors reported seeing an all-red German plane

WESTERN FRONT JULY 6, 1917

THE LUFBERY CIRCLE

Bombers and reconnaissance aircraft have always needed defensive tactics to combat the superior performance of opposing fighters. One early and enduring response to the threat was to fly in formation, and by the summer of 1917 over the Western Front even single-seaters of the Allied air forces were regularly using formations to reduce the losses to German Albatros DIII and DV scouts that had reached a peak during 'Bloody April' earlier that year.

Formation flying was made more effective with the adoption of the defensive circle, which involved aircraft under attack flying in a circular pattern, each covering the tail of the one in front. The tactic was frequently referred to as the Lufbery Circle, after the famous Escadrille Lafayette pilot. Although it is unlikely that Lufbery actually invented the technique, American fliers of both world wars habitually referred to it as the 'Lufbery'.

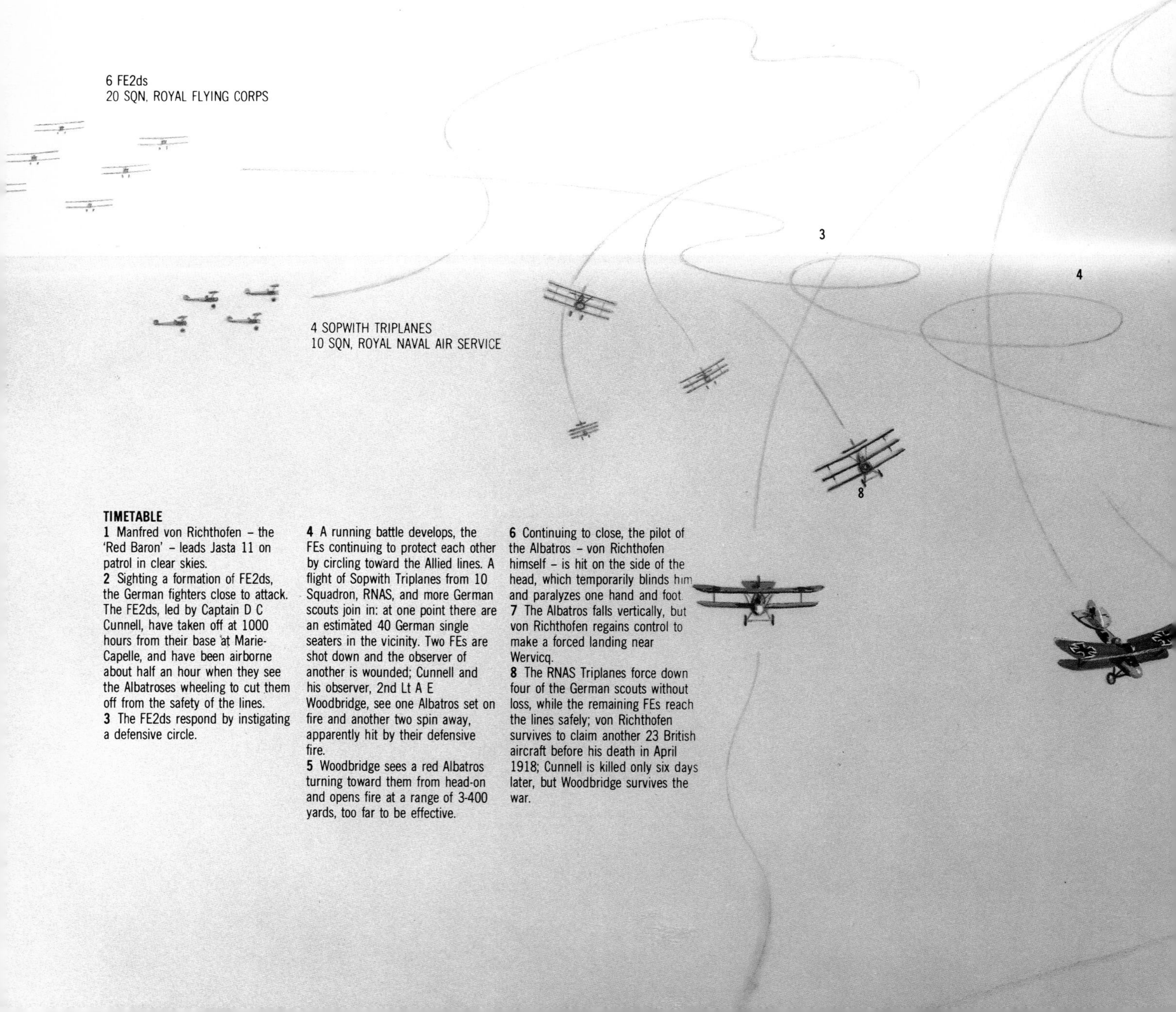

6 FE2ds
20 SQN, ROYAL FLYING CORPS

4 SOPWITH TRIPLANES
10 SQN, ROYAL NAVAL AIR SERVICE

3

4

8

TIMETABLE

1 Manfred von Richthofen – the 'Red Baron' – leads Jasta 11 on patrol in clear skies.
2 Sighting a formation of FE2ds, the German fighters close to attack. The FE2ds, led by Captain D C Cunnell, have taken off at 1000 hours from their base at Marie-Capelle, and have been airborne about half an hour when they see the Albatroses wheeling to cut them off from the safety of the lines.
3 The FE2ds respond by instigating a defensive circle.

4 A running battle develops, the FEs continuing to protect each other by circling toward the Allied lines. A flight of Sopwith Triplanes from 10 Squadron, RNAS, and more German scouts join in: at one point there are an estimated 40 German single seaters in the vicinity. Two FEs are shot down and the observer of another is wounded; Cunnell and his observer, 2nd Lt A E Woodbridge, see one Albatros set on fire and another two spin away, apparently hit by their defensive fire.
5 Woodbridge sees a red Albatros turning toward them from head-on and opens fire at a range of 3-400 yards, too far to be effective.

6 Continuing to close, the pilot of the Albatros – von Richthofen himself – is hit on the side of the head, which temporarily blinds him and paralyzes one hand and foot.
7 The Albatros falls vertically, but von Richthofen regains control to make a forced landing near Wervicq.
8 The RNAS Triplanes force down four of the German scouts without loss, while the remaining FEs reach the lines safely; von Richthofen survives to claim another 23 British aircraft before his death in April 1918; Cunnell is killed only six days later, but Woodbridge survives the war.

6

5

7

GERMAN FRONT LINE

with three wings. Arthur Lee thought the German pilot must have been flying a captured Naval Sopwith Triplane. It was, in fact, Manfred von Richthofen (nicknamed 'The Red Baron') in the new Fokker DR1 Triplane.

THE RED BARON'S TRIPLANE

Anthony Fokker's 'new' design – not actually a new concept, as evidenced by the Sopwith Triplane – reached the front on August 21, 1917, flown in by Fokker himself to Richthofen's Group at Courtrai. Von Richthofen liked the new type from the start and was linked with the Triplane until he was killed in 1918. Kurt Wolff also flew the new aircraft, as did Werner Voss. Both pilots were experienced 'aces' – and indeed several of the leading German pilots took to the Triplane during the fall of 1917. It was nimble, very maneuverable, light on the controls and, although it was slower than either the Camel or SE5, only a brave RFC pilot took on a Triplane. It could turn very quickly, so in a dogfight it would very soon gain the advantage. The British tactic in fighting Triplanes was to dive and zoom – not to get into close action. The first appearance of the Fokker Triplane caused a shocked surprise among the RFC flyers. Like Gould Lee, they thought it was a Sopwith. On September 2 von Richthofen flew one over the front and attacked a British RE8 observation machine. The British crew made not the slightest move to defend themselves, thinking the approaching plane must be a naval fighter. Too late they realized it was hostile, when the Fokker's twin Spandaus set their aircraft ablaze.

Kurt Wolff, the leader of Jasta 11, and victor in 33 air fights, was killed in a Triplane on September 5. He led a patrol of four Albatros DVs but became separated from them over the front. He was spotted and dived upon by some Camels of 10 Naval Squadron. Flight Sub Lieutenant N MacGregor hit the Fokker with a burst from his Vickers guns that damaged the Triplane and set its engine on fire. It fell to earth and blew up on impact.

Just a week later Voss died in a classic lone dogfight with the SE5s of 56 Squadron. In the morning he had claimed his 48th victory. He was due for leave and in fact his two brothers had arrived at the airfield to take him back to Germany. He had first to fly an evening patrol, but failed to return.

Voss had shot down his last 10 victories in his new Fokker between September 3 and 23. On this last evening he flew out with two Albatros pilots. Over the front they saw an air battle in progress between Albatroses, Camels and SPADs while SE5s, Bristol Fighters and RE8s were also in the vicinity. Sixty Squadron's SE5s were among them.

Lieutenant H A Hamersley of this latter unit was attacked by Voss in his silver-colored Triplane when spotted by the nine pilots of 56 Squadron – nine experienced pilots, including James McCudden, Gerald Bowman, Arthur Rhys David, Keith Muspratt, Richard Maybery and R T C Hoidge. In the initial attack McCudden and Rhys David went down on the Fokker from behind. Voss saw the danger, left Hamersley to stagger back across the lines, slammed full rudder and skidded round to face the SEs. One of the other SE5s, flown by V P Cronyn, developed an oil pressure problem and was unable to climb quickly. Voss saw the SE5 in trouble, turned to attack, and fired at it. Cronyn was amazed to see how quickly the Fokker turned but luckily the British pilot had sufficient speed to turn under the German, a maneuver he performed several times; in desperation he resorted to the old method of shaking off a pursuing enemy aircraft. Completing the second revolution of a spin, Cronyn flattened out and found that Voss had gone, although now engaged by the other SEs.

Hoidge shot at one of the Albatros Scouts which dived down but then found the Triplane above him – but his Lewis-gun drum was empty. Flying towards the lines, he changed it, then flew and attacked the Triplane as it flew head-on at McCudden's scout. Voss's fire splattered McCudden's wings. The other Albatros was trying to give cover to the Fokker but was later sent down, leaving Voss surrounded by six SEs, but he was turning, twisting, diving, zooming

Sopwith Triplane used by the Royal Naval Air Service in their squadrons in France, supporting the RFC. A number of Naval aces cut their combat teeth on the Triplane in 1917. With one Vickers machine-gun firing through the propeller, a remarkable rate of roll and a fast climb, it was beloved by those who flew it but only remained in front-line use for seven months. Between May and July 1917, Naval 10 Squadron, led by Raymond Collishaw, shot down 87 German aircraft.

Right: The Red Baron, Manfred von Richthofen is strapped into his Fokker DR1 Triplane. Von Richthofen flew various Triplanes to shoot down 20 of his 80 victories, before his death in action on April 21, 1918.

Below Right: Von Richthofen poses with some of his JG1 pilots. From left to right: Ltn Kurt Kuppers (5), Ltn Heinrich Maushake (7), Ltn Werner Steinhauser (10), Ltn Krefft the Technical Officer, unknown, Ltn von Gluczewski (3), unknown, Ltn Lubbert, unknown, Ltn Bockelmann (3).

with impunity, peppering all the British machines. According to the SE5 pilots Voss had several opportunities to get away, having gained height above them, but each time he continued the combat. There is little doubt that Voss had complete mastery of his aircraft and his environment. He was a superb and fearless fighter pilot in that element. More than once McCudden put himself in a good attacking position, only to find

'... *To my amazement he [Voss] kicked on full rudder without bank, pulled his nose up*

slightly, gave me a burst while he was skidding sideways, and then kicked on opposite rudder before the results of this amazing stunt appeared to have any effect on the controllability of his machine.'

Suddenly, despite all his maneuvers, Voss put his Fokker right in front of Rhys David's SE5. Rhys David opened fire with both his Vickers and Lewis gun. For the first time, Voss kept in a straight line and then went down. Voss had put up a splendid and spectacular fight and had seemed in complete control of the situation, and had probably revelled in the scrap. He fell behind the British lines, and was buried by his enemies.

Another 'ace' to die in September 1917 was the Frenchman Georges Guynemer. He, like Albert Ball, was a loner, and, like Ball was always in the thick of the action. Both pilots would often return victorious but with their machine shot to ribbons. He had 54 victories. When he failed to return, his death, like that of many a great 'ace' of WW1, was shrouded in mystery.

The fall of 1917 saw both sides with some excellent fighting aircraft. The Camel and SE5A were becoming established, the Bristol Fighters were taking over from the FE2b, and the Nieuports and SPADs were being used by both the French and some RFC squadrons. The Belgian Aviation Militaire had been flying Nieuport Scouts and Sopwith Camels, but were re-equipping with the Hanriot HD1. It was a French design supplied to the Belgian and Italian Air Services. The Italians too flew a variety of machines: Nieuports, SPADs, Hanriots and the Ansaldo SVA5. All had machine-guns firing through the propeller arc.

Above: Hanriot HD1 scout usually flown by the Italian ace Silvio Scaroni who scored 26 victories. He was shot down on July 12, 1918 and although he survived, the war ended before he recovered from his wounds.
Above right: Pilots of the Austro-Hungarian Squadron, Flik 55J. The aircraft is a Phonix DII armed with two Schwarzlose machine-guns mounted each side of the engine or inside of the fuselage, their breeches protruding above the instrument panel. It was a fast scout, but slow in the climb and perhaps a little too stable for a fighter. Note the flare pistol fixed on the top wing center section. The middle pilot is Hauptman Jozsef von Meier who scored 10 victories.

By the end of 1917, the Italian Air Service had 15 fighter squadrons, eight equipped with Hanriot HD1s, four with SPADs and three with Nieuports. In addition the Italians had 14 squadrons of Caproni bombers plus 30 reconnaissance and artillery observation squadrons. However diverse the equipment and wherever the front, their object was still to destroy enemy aircraft in order to protect their side's observation and bombing planes. These two-seaters were also far more sophisticated by late 1917, yet no match for a determined single-seater scout.

KNIGHTS OF THE AIR?
WW1 aircraft had no protective armor, no self-sealing fuel tanks, and no parachutes. Once a fighting pilot had survived long enough to become a veteran, and had got over the initial desire to open fire at long range and get in close, he could stay cool long enough to aim at the real target – the pilot. It was not difficult. Most air battles lasted a very short time; rarely more than a few minutes. By late 1917 the lone pilot was almost a thing of the past; the patrol leader was the new champion in the air.

Leading a patrol of any size, the leader would need to see the enemy first, secure a good position from which to attack and hopefully bring the maximum number of guns against a surprised enemy. The leader needed a cool head, to size up a combat situation, to use sun and cloud to advantage, then destroy the maximum enemy for the minimum loss.

Much has been written about the 'Chivalrous Knights of the Air', when dealing with WW1 air warfare. Certainly in the beginning there were many examples of gentlemanly conduct – especially when neither side could do little more than fire a pistol or carbine at each other. On occasion a pilot might not press home an attack if it was obvious that his opponent was out of ammunition or his guns had jammed. Yet the reality was not so gallant. Once the war in the air became serious and the machine-gun began to dominate the air fights, it was kill or be killed. Few pilots had the time, the opportunity or the inclination to put chivalry before the certain destruction of an enemy. For one thing they had seen too many of their friends die ugly, painful deaths. Without parachutes pilots faced death by fire in a contraption of wood, canvas, paint and fuel that burned very easily; fire in the air was usually fatal. If wings or tailplanes broke off it meant a dive or spin to certain death hundreds of feet below. In either case a pilot often chose to jump and end it more cleanly.

In any event, once an attacking pilot had put himself into a favorable position to make an attack – with luck, unobserved – he could aim at the leather-clad figure whose back loomed in the gun-sight. Hitting the pilot was an almost certain guarantee of victory.

On September 4, 1917 Arthur Gould Lee, still flying Pups with 46 Squadron, went to help a British RE8 observation plane being pursued by an Albatros Scout. The German broke off the action and began to fly east, straight and level; obviously he had not seen the Pup. Lee closed in. The German was making the fatal mistake of not looking behind him and not altering course.

Lee got to within ten yards – really close. He saw the pilot clearly. He wore a dark brown flying helmet, with a white strap holding his goggles in place. Lee took careful aim through his Aldis sight, right between the German's shoulder blades. Still he did not look round. It was impossible for Lee to miss: he pressed the trigger and with his first shots the German's head jerked back. The Albatros reared up on its tail as the wounded or dying pilot clutched at and pulled back the 'stick'. Then the Albatros fell over to the left and dropped into a near-vertical dive. Lee followed it down, to make certain of his victory. That was Lee's mistake. To follow a victim down, looking intently for the enemy plane to disintegrate, flame or crash, making sure the other pilot was not shamming, left one open to a surprise attack. It happened now. Lee, while

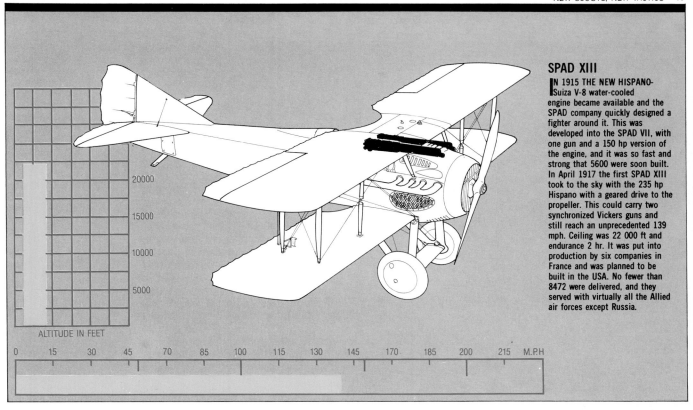

SPAD XIII

IN 1915 THE NEW HISPANO-Suiza V-8 water-cooled engine became available and the SPAD company quickly designed a fighter around it. This was developed into the SPAD VII, with one gun and a 150 hp version of the engine, and it was so fast and strong that 5600 were soon built. In April 1917 the first SPAD XIII took to the sky with the 235 hp Hispano with a geared drive to the propeller. This could carry two synchronized Vickers guns and still reach an unprecedented 139 mph. Ceiling was 22 000 ft and endurance 2 hr. It was put into production by six companies in France and was planned to be built in the USA. No fewer than 8472 were delivered, and they served with virtually all the Allied air forces except Russia.

ALTITUDE IN FEET

20000

15000

10000

5000

0   15   30   45   70   85   100   115   130   145   170   185   200   215   M.P.H

watching his Albatros, was attacked from above and suddenly surprised and surrounded. He was lucky to escape, lucky that the German pilot who led the attack was not a better shot and returned home victorious, unharmed and a little wiser.

Gould Lee's squadron, like other scout units, were given a variety of tasks, all nerve-wracking but none so bad as the Distant Offensive Patrols (DOP). Unlike normal patrols, these DOPs went deep – 15 or more miles behind the front lines. These missions were designed to trap German aircraft who felt safe so far back. They might be scouts, fledgling flyers on pre-operational training flights, or two-seaters beginning or ending their high level penetrations into the Allied rear areas.

ON PATROL

As the Pups flew on they would constantly change position, each pilot ceaselessly quartering the sky. They would tilt the aircraft first to one side then the other to cover all the blind spots. At 15 miles over, they would be hard put to it to fight their way out if attacked. Even at this early stage in the evolution of air warfare, many pilots fitted tiny rear-view mirrors to their aircraft, usually to a center-section wing strut. It covered only a

small rear area and was no real substitute for looking round, first left, then right. The longer a pilot survived at the front the more skilled he became. A novice pilot was invariably 'blind' to what was happening about him; he would return from patrol and, on being questioned by his leader as to what he had seen, would invariably have nothing to report. He would then be astounded to learn the number of aircraft they had been near, both friendly and hostile. It was something that had to be learned. The quicker one saw distant aircraft the more likely one was that to be the hunter – not the hunted – and all the time the patrol would have been battling against the prevailing westerly wind.

Clouds were another danger to any patrol. Enemy planes might lurk there, ready to pounce on any who flew too near, and who silhouetted against cloud, would stand out like flies on a bed sheet. The camouflaged British aircraft would no longer blend in with the landscape below. It mattered less for the gaudily painted German scouts. They invariably chose the battle area and they were over their home ground. In case of trouble, however, the cloud, provided that it was large enough, gave sanctuary, a chance to escape, a chance to survive.

GEORGES GUYNEMER

THE FRAIL FRENCH PILOT WHO became the darling and the hero of France was at the height of his fame when he disappeared over the French lines in September 1917. Guynemer had been turned down by the French Army in 1914 but later succeeded in joining the Air Service, trained as a pilot and in 1915 flew Morane two-seaters. On July 19, he and his observer shot down a German observation aircraft, setting him on the road to become France's leading ace by 1917.

Going on to fly single-seat Nieuports with Escadrille N3, his score steadily rose. He was an aggressive fighter, and his score was soon second on the Allied side only to that of the British ace, Albert Ball. Like Ball, Guynemer would often attack against high odds, fight his way out, and return with his scout shot to ribbons.

In 1917, his Escadrille was re-equipped with SPAD S.VIIs. The squadron was part of the élite Cigognes (Storks) Group. Guynemer often scored double, triple, and on May 25 1917, four victories in a day. His score reached 50. Although he was asked to retire from active flying lest his loss should damage French morale at a time when the French Army was taking heavy casualties at Verdun, he refused. His 54th and final official victory came on September 6, 1917 (his unofficial score was nearer 90). Five days later he failed to return from a flight over the French battle front and although the Germans credited a German two-seater with shooting him down, it is believed his SPAD was hit by ground fire. It crashed in the front lines during a barrage and both Guynemer and his aircraft were obliterated in the shelling.

Sometimes the DOPs were in direct or even indirect support of a bomb raid, but more often than not they were flown in pursuance of the RFCs policy of being 'offensive'. Few pilots, if they really thought about it – and most merely followed orders – could see their value. Occasionally they would surprise an enemy aircraft, but often it meant battling against the elements for an hour or two, with the problem of flying twice through the front-line anti-aircraft barrage, known affectionately in WW1 as 'Archie'.

The Pup pilots of late 1917 were, in any case, more vulnerable in combat with Albatros DIIIs or the new DVs and Fokker Triplanes. If they did get involved in a fight they had not the speed to get away. They would hope to see the enemy first, make a diving attack on him – out of the sun if the patrol leader was wise enough – zoom up to a higher altitude and fly off using the momentum and speed of the diving attack to escape. If a dogfight developed, it was every man for himself, using as little ammunition as possible. With empty gun or guns the hapless pilot could expect no mercy from the less chivalrous pilots of 1917.

Both sides would set traps in the air. With Jastas beginning to be massed in Jagdgeschwadern, two Jastas could fly out together. One at a lower altitude might tempt a British or French patrol to attack it, only to find the higher Jasta, who had been lurking in the sun's glare, diving down, Spandaus blazing.

Von Richthofen and his Jasta leaders would do this, or even when flying in just one formation his plan would be to attack while his back was protected by his pilots. This was sound strategy, strategy developed to the full in WW2 when pilots had radio with which to communicate with each other. In WW1 communication was effected only with wing-waggling, hand signals or Very flares. On the Allied side, leaders and deputy leaders used streamers attached to wing struts or tails for quick identification in the air. The Germans recognized their leaders by their machines color or markings.

Although the lone pilot was almost a feature of the past, there were still flyers of both sides who fought alone between regular patrols. One on the British side was James McCudden, of 56 Squadron, who had been in the Voss fight.

McCudden had progressed through the ranks from mechanic in 1914, to NCO pilot and by 1917 to captain and flight commander in one of the RFC's premier squadrons. Perhaps because of his experience and his determination to better himself and succeed, he put more thought and consideration into his air fighting. Certainly he found the SE5 scout a delight to fly, and once he had mastered the machine came to understand its fighting potential.

As he had earlier flown the now obsolete Sopwith Pup, he knew about being the underdog. Now, however, with an SE5, he no longer had to fight his way out of a tight spot. It was he who could dictate the terms when fighting the Albatros Scouts, or the Fokkers, or the new Pfalz DIII scouts that began to appear on the Western Front towards the end of 1917. Yet he also developed other tactical ideas. The performance of the SE5 encouraged him to take on the high-flying German two-seater reconnaissance and photographic machines.

STALKING THE HIGH-FLYERS

By late 1917 the Germans had four main reconnaissance aircraft: the later versions of the Albatros C-types and LVG, plus the DFW CV and the Rumpler CIV. All four types would fly above 15000 ft, the DFW and Rumpler often encountered – or seen – above 17000 ft. On their incursions to the rear areas of the British or French fronts they were unescorted and unsupported. Their only defense, apart from the experience of the pilot or observer, was the height at which they flew, for few Allied scouts could achieve that without losing valuable performance.

McCudden, however, decided that he could. He worked on his SE5 (helped by his previous experience as a mechanic) to get every ounce of power from the engine and streamlined the SE5 to minimize drag. Later he even fitted a large propeller boss to his aircraft to give a little extra streamlining effect to the blunt nose of the SE5.

Once aloft, he would stalk the German two-seaters. Flying high, he would catch sight of them as they crossed the lines and would let them penetrate well over before making his move. Using sun, cloud or haze he would gradually creep up on his adversary, then swoop down to just below and behind the two-seater – his favorite position for attacking them. In this way he was out of sight of the observer, who was in any event engaged on his primary taks of observing the ground, taking photographs, etc. If the British pilot was spotted and the pilot began to maneuver his aircraft so as to let the observer fire at him, McCudden, in his position, could easily cut inside a turn to remain in the blind spot. All the while he would be firing his Lewis gun or his Vickers. Unlike Ball, he did not necessarily need to pull down the Lewis gun to fire upwards into the two-seater; just stay in position and fire, pulling down the gun only to replace the drum.

One of his first victories over the high flying two-seaters came on October 1, 1917. After chasing a Rumpler which was at 21 000 ft and being unable to get his SE above 19 000 ft, he found another Rumpler a little lower down. Still in the early stages of developing his tactics, he attacked prematurely and despite being hit, the two-seater managed to fly eastwards while the observer was hit and collapsed in his cockpit. Finally McCudden had to leave it gliding back inside German lines with its engine stopped.

McCudden's lone stalking tactics at high altitude could sometimes exact a considerable physical toll. In his memoirs *Flying Fury* he recalled a hunting expedition of February 17 1917:

'*I* HAD BEEN UP ABOUT 40 MINUTES WHEN I saw a Rumpler cross our lines at 17 500 feet. He was above me, for I was at 17 000 feet. I followed him all the way to Arras and then back to Bourlon Wood, where we arrived at about 18 000 and 18 300 respectively, the Rumpler still being above, for by now I had found that this Rumpler had about the best performance of any that I had seen up to that time.*

At Bourlon the Hun turned west again, and I followed him as far as Bapaume, and again back to Bourlon Wood, over which we now arrived at 20 000 feet, with the Rumpler still a little above, for up at 20 000 feet it was impossible to zoom up to an opponent who is 200 feet above. By now the old Hun, realizing that he was still safe, turned once more west and flew back to Peronne and again back to Bourlon, where we now arrived at 21 000 feet, with the Hun still a little higher. Then he started to fly, nose down, east, as apparently he had completed his task.

At last I was able to get a good position, after chasing him for 50 minutes, but on opening fire at close range, both my guns stopped at once, the Vickers owing to a broken belt, and the Lewis because of the intense cold. I could not rectify the Vickers, but after reloading the Lewis it fired fairly well. By now the Hun was diving fairly steeply and presented a very easy target, so I fired another burst from the Lewis, but apart from seeing my tracer bullets enter his fuselage it had no apparent effect.

We were now down to 10 000 feet, west of Cambrai, in a very short time and, seeing many other enemy machines about, I turned away.

I felt very ill indeed. This was not because of the height or the rapidity of my descent, but simply because of the intense cold which I experienced up high. The result was that when I got down to a lower altitude, and could breathe more oxygen, my heart beat more strongly and tried to force my sluggish and cold blood around my veins too quickly ... My word, I did feel ill, and when I got on the ground and the blood returned to my veins I can only describe the feeling as agony.'

Between then and the end of the year, McCudden shot down 19 German two-seaters, several on these special lone stalking shows, including four on December 23 and three on December 28. In the new year of 1918 he added 15 more to his tally including another four in one day, on February 16. At least ten fell inside the British lines, several others very near the lines on the German side. Not all his two-seater kills were on these special patrols but at least 20 were: making McCudden perhaps the most successful stalker of enemy reconnaissance aircraft in the war. Coupled with the fact that he was a strict but equally successful patrol and flight leader, this probably makes him the premier RFC/RAF air fighter of WW1. Unlike other high-scoring aces who were all for attacking anything and everything, McCudden always flew to the rule: 'He who fights and runs away, lives to fight another day.' Often the more 'dashing' pilots, while running up respectable scores, were eventually caught out and shot down. McCudden died in a flying crash in July 1918 when returning to France to command 60 Squadron. One can only guess how many victories this 'thinking' pilot might have achieved had he survived.

Two-seat Brandenburg C1 observation plane of the Austro-Hungarian 'Luftfahrtruppen', being engaged by an Italian Nieuport 17, over Northern Italy, 1917.

CHAPTER FOUR

DAWN OF THE DOGFIGHT

I N MANY WAYS, EVENTS IN 1918, AS far as air fighting and fighting tactics were concerned, were dictated by all that had gone before. By then the war in the air had matured. The issue was clear: it was now a straightforward struggle for victory.

If nothing else it was, in terms of numbers, a year of big air battles. The Allies were pouring men and aircraft into the battle zones, not only in France, but in northern Italy, Palestine and Mesopotamia, the numbers augmented by the continuing build-up of the Americans.

The United States had entered the war in April 1917, but in terms of trained pilots and operational aircraft it was at first non-effective. Its gradual build-up in pilots and airmen soon became a flood. However, aircraft for them to fly had to come from Britain and France. The nucleus of its experienced flyers came from those men who had joined either the British or French air forces before America took up arms. The Lafayette Escadrille of 1916 had grown into a corps – the Lafayette Flying Corps. The Escadrille could take only so many men; others had flown with other French squadrons. There were also a number of Americans with the Royal Flying Corps and, after April 1917, operational pilots in the United States Air Service (USAS) were attached to British squadrons where their acquired experience helped to form the nucleus of USAS squadrons. By early 1918 the USAS were growing stronger. The RFC gave them Camels, the French Nieuport 28s and SPADs.

With considerable misgiving, the Germans realized that the weight of American involvement would soon be felt in France – if not in aircraft, at least in soldiers, guns, ammunition, supplies and money. France and Britain had to be defeated, and there was no time to lose. The Allies knew Germany was building up for a spring offensive and when Russia capitulated in December 1917 men and guns released from the Russian front joined the build-up in the west.

By early 1918 the scout squadrons of the RFC and RNAS were nearly all Camel- and SE5-equipped. The Pups and Triplanes had gone, the last of the Nieuports going. The two squadrons of SPADs were also soon to be replaced. The FE2s were gone, except for night bombing, being wholly replaced by Bristol Fighters.

British bombing squadrons were now all DH4s, DH9s, or Handley Page 0/400s. The BE2s had been replaced in corps squadrons with RE8s or AWFK8s. The main fighter aircraft in the French Air Service was the SPAD SVII, soon to be replaced by the SXIII and the Nieuport 27, while

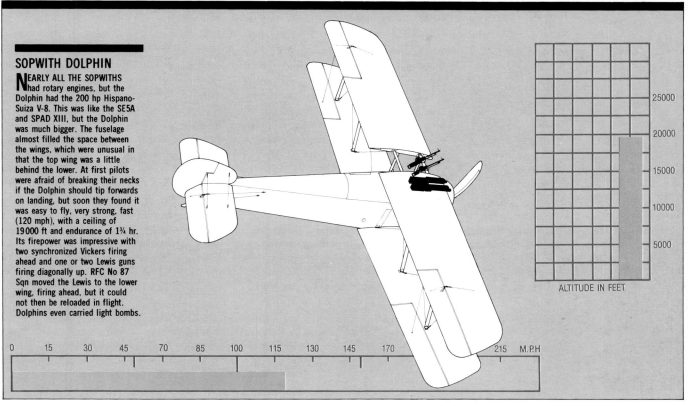

SOPWITH DOLPHIN

NEARLY ALL THE SOPWITHS had rotary engines, but the Dolphin had the 200 hp Hispano-Suiza V-8. This was like the SE5A and SPAD XIII, but the Dolphin was much bigger. The fuselage almost filled the space between the wings, which were unusual in that the top wing was a little behind the lower. At first pilots were afraid of breaking their necks if the Dolphin should tip forwards on landing, but soon they found it was easy to fly, very strong, fast (120 mph), with a ceiling of 19 000 ft and endurance of 1¾ hr. Its firepower was impressive with two synchronized Vickers firing ahead and one or two Lewis guns firing diagonally up. RFC No 87 Sqn moved the Lewis to the lower wing, firing ahead, but it could not then be reloaded in flight. Dolphins even carried light bombs.

ALTITUDE IN FEET
25000 20000 15000 10000 5000

0   15   30   45   70   85   100   115   130   145   170   215   M.P.H

Left: Sopwith 2F1 Camel, perhaps the best known of all British WW1 fighters. Usually armed with twin Vickers machine-guns, this Camel was flown by the RNAS and has a single Vickers gun and a wing-mounted Lewis gun.

the small Belgian contingent had its Hanriot scouts.

On the German side the mainstay of its Jasta aircraft was the Albatros DV, supported by the Pfalz DIII. The Fokker DR1 Triplane was still in evidence, especially in JG1 under von Richthofen. It had gone through a bad patch in the late fall of 1917, the type being temporarily grounded for the wing structure to be strengthened. Although it remained at the front until the summer of 1918, JG1 pilots were its main user. There were also one or two new and interesting types now on the front. The Hannover CLIII was a two-seat escort and close-support aircraft which was not an easy opponent for an Allied pilot. Another was the latest design from Halberstadt, the CLIV. This began to re-equip the Halberstadt CLII units in the spring of 1918 with the expansion of the 'Schlachstaffeln' – ground attack and escort.

It was no surprise that these ground-attack aircraft began reaching the front. Since the middle of 1917 a feature of the air war in France had been aircraft attacking troops and positions on the ground. During the Battle of Cambrai in November 1917, the RFC were very much in evidence in this close-support role, especially the Sopwith Camels. Thereafter this became a

regular feature of the tactics of both sides.

The German offensive on the Western Front opened on March 21 1918. As soon as early morning fog and mist cleared sufficiently for air operations, both sides were fiercely engaged, closely supporting their ground forces and instigating dogfights. It was a hectic affair of low-level air battles, each side trying to stop the other from strafing and bombing the attacking or defending troops.

A new British scout arrived in France as the German offensive began – the latest from the Sopwith stable – named the Sopwith Dolphin. This was a robust aircraft with an unusual back-stagger top wing - that is, the top wing was farther back than the lower. Unlike the usual Sopwith machines, the design had an in-line water-cooled engine instead of an air-cooled rotary one.

The back-stagger wing design was not liked. The DH5 of 1917 had the same wing configuration and had been unpopular. The Dolphin differed also in that the pilot's head was above the top wing. This led to the feeling that if a pilot nosed right over in a crash he would break his neck. In the event there was only one possible mishap of this nature in the four operational squadrons using the Dolphin in France. The machine had a number of other unusual features. The field of vision was far better than in the more conventional fighters, and pilots who flew it in action liked the unrestricted view.

It carried two Vickers machine-guns mounted in front of the pilot. In addition it could carry two Lewis guns on the top wing cross-section. Fixed to fire upwards, these guns were in an easy and convenient position for the pilot to fire and reload. Generally, however, the Lewis guns were discarded, or restricted to just one. The late Air Chief Marshal Sir Leslie Hollinghurst was a young pilot in 87 Squadron in 1918. I remember him telling me how inaccurate the Lewis guns were, and that in the air they tended to swing about a bit. But the Dolphins were fast and maneuverable and could more than hold their own with any German scout.

Eighty-seven Squadron also experimented with additional guns, one located on each of the lower wings set to shoot past the propeller arc. They were fired by pulling a wire from the cockpit but they could not be reloaded once the drum had been emptied. Dolphins lost none of their agility at high level and in the early days were used against high-flying two-seaters. They even experimented with oxygen for those high combats, but once hit by a bullet the oxygen tank, fixed just behind the pilot, exploded quite spectacularly, so, as Hollinghurst told me, they were quickly discarded. There were enough problems without that.

As the last German offensive in France petered out, a new German scout, the Fokker DVII, began to arrive at the front. It was a solid, yet agile, biplane with an in-line engine and twin Spandaus. Although the Albatros, Pfalz and Fokker Triplanes remained in evidence on the Western Front for the rest of 1918, the new Fokker Biplane gradually dominated the air war during the final months of the conflict.

MASSED COMBAT

Meanwhile, those final months saw encounters between varying numbers of scouts, often in huge dogfights. The Allied side, especially on the British front, had at last learnt to use bigger formations to combat the large groups of German scouts. During the whole of the war the Germans were outnumbered. It was their practice to concentrate the units rather than spread their numbers in small patrols as the Allied air forces usually did. By mid 1918, with the RFC and RNAS having united to form the Royal Air Force (April 1, 1918), the various wings were flying Combined Offensive Patrols (COPs). These might be in the form of two, three or even four squadrons, flying patrols, escorts to bombers or raiding German airfields. They would not necessarily be all the same aircraft types. Indeed, to exploit the best qualities in each aircraft type, a COP might consist of Camels at 12 000 ft, SE5s at 18 000 ft and Dolphins at 21 000 ft. Sometimes even Bristol Fighters were in evidence. It was a brave German group that tackled all these but when it did, there developed large air battles that extended at anything from around 20 000 ft right down to ground level.

By this stage, of course, the knowledge was there. There was little new to learn about the basic principles of air tactics and air combat. In WW1 any flying maneuver was called a 'stunt', and three basic stunts were the climbing turn, the half roll and the spin.

The climbing turn, while not always taught as a priority maneuver, enabled a pilot to gain the height over an opponent which was acknowledged as all-important in air fighting. It was not the easiest maneuver to perform, requiring careful manipulation of all three controls: ailerons, elevator and rudder.

The half roll, which could also be used combined with a climbing turn, was the quickest way of getting round, even quicker than a vertical turn when, with the machine held on its wingtip, the elevator was used as the rudder. In a turning fight between two scouts the better pilot (or the better machine) will gradually get above the other and then he will half-roll his machine when he has sufficient height and pull out on the other's tail. The other can do one of two things. If he wants to continue the fight – and he may be forced to – he

Fokker DVII scout that came to the Western Front in the spring of 1918 and very soon dominated the air war over France. Fast, maneuverable, strong and with twin Spandau guns, it equipped the vast majority of Jastas in the last months of the war.

Top: The SPAD scout eventually superceded the Nieuport as France's first-line fighter. It was also used by the Italians and the British. This example, B3508, is a SPAD VII in German markings following its capture in late 1917. It had flown with 19 Squadron and had a single Vickers gun. The Aldis sight and a ring and bead sight are visible.
Above: Sopwith Camel of 43 Squadron in 1918, flown by Captain Henry Woollett MC. The white blotches are special markings for a mission attacking German balloons.

will also half-roll and continue to do so, throwing his adversary off his tail until he is able to make a climbing turn and regain position. Or, instead of half rolling in the first place, he will put his machine into a spin.

In this maneuver, the pilot dived and at the same time rotated around his longitudinal axis. A machine is impossible to hit while it is in a spin, therefore a pilot could always take refuge in one, but if he wanted to spin right down he had to ensure that he was on the right side of the lines. The maneuver was useful for getting down quickly to where, perhaps, some friendly aircraft were, or for escaping into cloud.

The scared novice, always in danger of just diving away from trouble, then became a sitting target for his opponent.

As far as the RAF pilots could discern, the German scouts rarely seemed to have any kind of set formation.

Air Chief Marshal Sir Donald Hardman had flown Dolphins in 19 Squadron in 1918. He later wrote about this phenomenon: '*THE AVERAGE PILOT could detect not only that a formation was hostile, but also what type enemy aircraft it consists of when the formation is only so many specks in the sky, a great distance away, after he has been "out" a few months. It was a constant source of surprise that Germans never flew in any recognized formation but just exactly like a cluster of flies. I am convinced that if they had adopted our method of formation they would have given us a great deal more trouble. The British squadrons flew in three different flights, each having a Flight Commander, a deputy leader, to trap the formation close and to take the Flight Commander's place if he fell out or was shot down, and five pilots. Now supposing "A" flight was flying at 15 000 ft, "B" flight would fly at 16 500 ft or thereabouts and slightly behind and at one side, and the remaining flight would hold a position of another 1500 ft, above "B" slightly behind and the opposite side to "B" of "A".*

'*The numerous advantages of this formation are at once obvious even to the novice. The top flight is supposed to be high enough to look after itself, the middle flight is safe because if it is attacked the top one can swoop down and sandwich the attacking enemy aircraft, in any case give them an extremely uncomfortable time for an advantageous position. The bottom flight is*

RAYMOND COLLISHAW

RAY COLLISHAW WAS A Canadian, born in British Columbia in November 1893. He joined the Royal Naval Air Service in 1916, joining 3 Wing which flew Sopwith 1½-Strutters on bombing missions. However, Collishaw was an aggressive flyer and downed his first enemy aircraft on October 12 1916. In February 1917 3 Wing became 3 Naval Squadron, and was equipped with Sopwith Pups. He next joined 10 Naval Squadron flying Triplanes, and moved south to join the RFC's 11 Wing on the Western Front. Collishaw became a deadly exponent of the Sopwith Triplane, and his Canadian flight became one of the most feared over France. Each of their machines bore a name beginning 'Black', Collishaw's being 'Black Maria'.

Towards the end of 1917 the squadron re-equipped with Sopwith Camels but then he joined 13 Naval Squadron, also flying Camels, and with this unit brought his score to 41. By this time he had won the DSO and DSC and he then took command of 3 Naval, also a Camel unit. Squadron commanders were forbidden to fly so Collishaw did not add to his score until mid-1918 when orders were relaxed. Between June and September, by which time 3 Naval had become 203 Squadron RAF, Collishaw accounted for a further 19 enemy aircraft, bringing his score to a round 60. He received a bar to his DSO and the DFC. In addition he was involved in more than 50 air fights that resulted in the forcing-down of German aircraft so his true WW1 score might well have been in the 80s.

In 1919 he took 47 Squadron to South Russia to fight the Bolsheviks, claiming two further air victories. During WW2 he commanded the RAF in the Western Desert and reached the rank of Air Vice-Marshal CB CBE. He died in 1977.

safer still for the same reason.

'On the other hand if the squadron wishes to attack one or both of the lower flights can go down and fight while the remaining unit will sit up above and keep watch also keeping off other enemy aircraft from the flight beneath. Therefore if weather and cloud formation permit it the method is excellent and very successful providing it is kept well by the flight commanders and compact by the deputy leaders.

'The enemy I saw flew in no sort of asemblance of a formation apparently without even a leader, and yet frequently I have noticed them all seemingly working to one and the same end without any visible means of understanding each other, and yet they must have been under one brain because no two pilots think and see the same.'

Donald Hardman also had his views on the German aircraft he met in combat: '*I*T MUST BE remembered that while the Camel and SE5 were on the front, the Germans had five new and completely successful scouts fighting against us, two Albatros', DV and DVa (the latter quite the most beautiful machine ever made), the Pfalz, the Fokker triplane and lastly the Fokker biplane with the 200 horse power Mercedes engine. One wonders, if the war had continued another six months or a year, whether the Dolphins, Camels and SE5s, already hopelessly outclassed, would still have been on active service, or whether the long-promised Snipes and Martinsyde scouts would have really replaced them.

'When I say the enemy scouts were "successful" I do not mean that individually they outclassed our scouts: I mean that they were each in turn used with a certain amount of success.

'The Albatros was a machine that when manipulated skilfully was good at say heights up to about 10 000 ft, where it became heavy and clumsy on turns. It had no special qualities worth noting, being reasonably fast and fairly "splitarse"*at any height, and therefore it was a nice machine to meet in combat as its tactics were limited to its comparatively mediocre performance. I fancy that the Germans clung to it so long because it was such a nice machine to fly, unlikely to catch fire and having a fairly good gliding angle. It had one bay with "V"-shaped struts, a body made of thin matchwood, beautifully streamlined and shaped like a fish, a longish fishtail. The Pfalz unlike the Albatros was not a popular machine with the Hun pilot; it was prone to catch fire, had little glide, and was not so strong as

its predecessor, and therefore, although it actually came on the front later than the Albatros, it disappeared before it.

'However it was rather more splitarse* and had a slightly higher ceiling, 19 000 ft or 20 000 ft. It had one bay with "V"-shaped struts, extensions, a rather deep and narrow fish-shaped body with a square tail.

'It was more or less regarded as "cold meat" by the British pilot and known as the foolish Pfalz fish. The Hun was always rather afraid of them and consequently didn't make the best of them.

'The Fokker Triplane was a splendid machine when used well. It had tactics entirely of its own, and if the Hun had kept to these properly he would have made a greater success of it; I imagine he didn't because repetition grows wearisome and he must constantly obey the machine instead of his own head.

'Now this machine having three planes had a great deal of lift and consequently a lot of resistance; it had a rotary engine and so was very light. Therefore two things are obvious: it had a remarkably good climb, a very good ceiling and was exceptionally slow in the dive, having no weight and a good deal of resistance. Now the Hun, who had just come off the "Albatros" or the "Pfalz", loved diving as both these machines were specially designed for it and so he occasionally forgot himself and tried it with the triplane, whereupon the top plane fell off or the machine broke up all together. Therefore in a fight he must be content to leave chasing out of the question unless it is in the nature of a climb, he must lure the enemy onto him, spin away, stand on his tail and shoot upwards; both of these stunts he could do better than any other machine. In fact he could remain on his tail for a surprising amount of time. Directly he has finished that burst of shooting he must fall over, spin again and repeat, dragging his enemies with him; they will come all right, for none can resist chasing a machine downwards in easy stages.

'Of course, it is essential that a triplane keeps out of a dogfight as he is a fat little target and has not the level speed of his opponent.

'Fortunately it was rarely that one came across a number of these machines in the hands of pilots who realized to the full their value and made use of it.

'They had one bay with one single strut running through slightly extended upper planes and a short square body with a small fan-shaped

---

* 'Splitarse' refers to the effect on the pilot when pulling an aircraft into a tight turn. Also referred to as Split-S.

SOPWITH FI CAMEL
versus FOKKER DrI

DESIGNED BY HERBERT SMITH at the Sopwith works at Kingston, near London, the Camel got into action in July 1917. It got its name from its hump. There was no magic about it, and indeed it was a tricky and dangerous machine to fly. The big rotary engine, combined with the way nearly all the heavy items were grouped in the front 4 ft of the aircraft, gave it strange gyroscopic properties, so that in a tight turn to the right (and it could turn very tightly indeed) the nose tried to go violently downwards, while turning left it tried to climb. Once a pilot had mastered the Camel he could kill anything in the sky. British (RFC and RNAS) Camels alone destroyed over 2800, and others served with Belgium, the USA and Greece. Perhaps the only machine that it could not easily outmaneuver was the Fokker DrI (Dr from dreidecker, meaning triplane). This was actually inspired by the British Sopwith Triplane. Not many of either were made, but Manfred von Richthofen, the greatest ace of the war, loved his scarlet DrI (hence his name 'the Red Baron') and was killed in it on April 21, 1918 – shot down by a Camel.

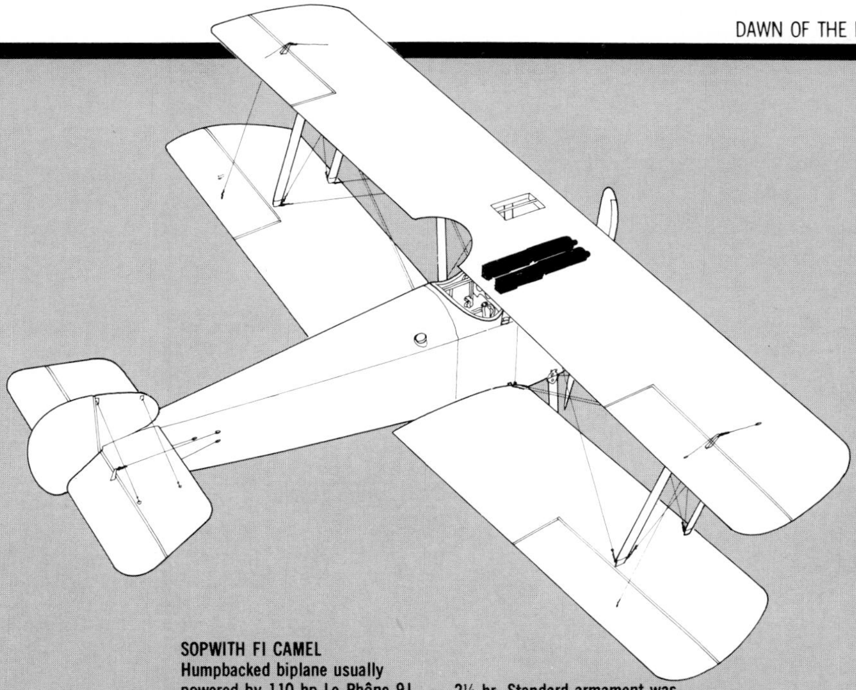

SOPWITH FI CAMEL
Humpbacked biplane usually powered by 110 hp Le Rhône 9J, 130 hp Clerget 9B or 150 hp Bentley BR1 rotary engine, giving speed of from 109 to (with the Bentley) 124 mph. Ceiling was typically 22 000 ft and endurance 2½ hr. Standard armament was two synchronized Vickers machine-guns, but the naval 2F1 'Ship's Camel', and night-fighter versions, had one Vickers and a Lewis on a Foster mount on the upper wing.

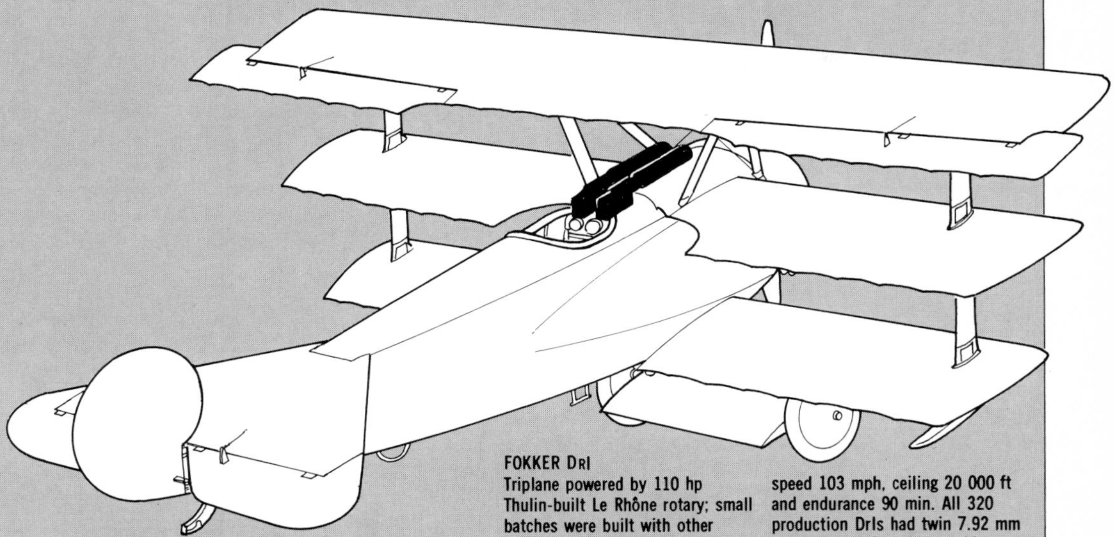

FOKKER DrI
Triplane powered by 110 hp Thulin-built Le Rhône rotary; small batches were built with other rotaries of up to 200 hp and one had a clumsy water-cooled Mercedes inline. Typical maximum speed 103 mph, ceiling 20 000 ft and endurance 90 min. All 320 production DrIs had twin 7.92 mm synchronized Spandau machine-guns.

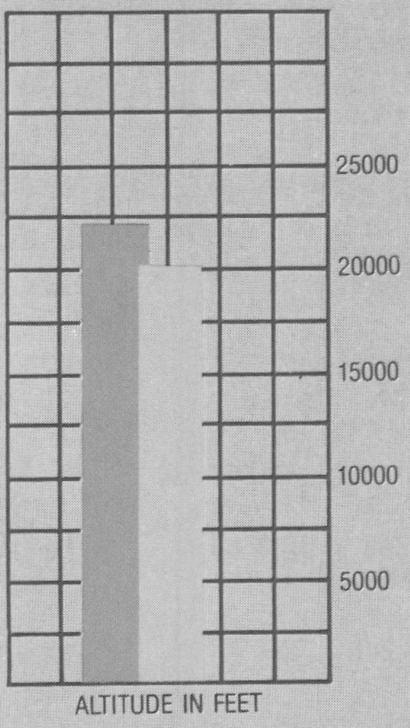

25000

20000

15000

10000

5000

ALTITUDE IN FEET

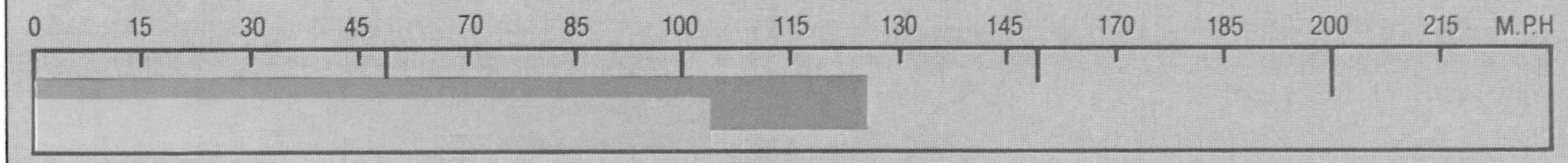

| 0 | 15 | 30 | 45 | 70 | 85 | 100 | 115 | 130 | 145 | 170 | 185 | 200 | 215 | M.P.H |

tail. The planes were very thick in front and tapered off to a point.

Now we come to the Fokker Biplane.

'*This machine prevalent on the front at the end of the war had all the good points of its predecessors and several more, in fact it was as near perfect as any machine during the war.*

'*It could climb up to 20 000 ft at a terrific speed, had a very good speed on the level, could dive almost at any rate, having an extremely high factor of safety. It turned at a lightning speed and would perform any other stunt better than any other machine. We had one machine that was capable of showing fight on equal terms – the Snipe – and as there were only two squadrons of them and many scores of Fokkers the remainder of our machines got a pretty bad time. It had one bay with two struts, a little forward stagger, a good deal of incidence and very little dihedral. It also possessed extensions and a square body with a square tail. The wingtips were square.*'

CAMEL TACTICS

The Sopwith Camel, perhaps the best-remembered of all the WW1 aircraft, had its own tactics.

The pilot had to learn the following:

1. A quick change to an entirely opposite direction by vertically banked or stall turns. This is useful in diving on to an enemy aircraft, especially a two-seater approaching in an opposite direction. Also used to throw an enemy aircraft off your tail.

2. A spin. To do this, shut off engine and put the machine on a bank, kick on bottom rudder and pull in the stick. To come out of it push stick forward and take off rudder. This maneuver is useful in losing height quickly to attack a machine well below you, or in throwing off an enemy aircraft diving on to your tail. In the latter case do not go into a spin unless other methods, such as a stall turn, fail, as a spin always results in loss of height.

3. Vertical dives. Learn to shoot while diving as steeply as possible. You can practice this both on the range and by taking a sight through the Aldis on any ground object and diving as steeply as possible on to it. It is best to do this by shutting off fuel, leaving throttle and fine adjustment where they give normal revs, and to turn on fuel again at the bottom of the dive, or by shutting throttle completely until dive is finished. A vertical dive is most likely to surprise the enemy aircraft you are attacking and offers him a poor target.

4. A roll. To do this, get the machine going at about 70 mph, nose slightly up at angle of about 30 degrees with the ground. Shut off engine. Pull back stick sharply and almost simultaneously kick on full rudder. Take off rudder when upside down and you will come right side up in normal flying position. The war value of this maneuver is not great but it might be used to impress an enemy aircraft when attacking and to offer a poor target.

5. Looping. Put the machine down about 90 mph. Pull the stick back and take off right rudder. When over the vertical cut off engine and pull the stick right back. This maneuver has been used successfully to throw an enemy aircraft off the tail and bring the attacked machine into a position of attack on the tail of the enemy aircraft.

ATTACKING TWO-SEATERS
The natural tendency of the two-seater pilot, when attacked, was to turn sharply in order that his rear gunner could get in a defensive shot past the tail. If the attacking scout also pulled round, it then put itself in a position to be shot at. To counter this, the scout pilot had to turn in the opposite direction and, with his superior speed, turn after the two-seater. The scout kept the target's tail between him and the enemy rear gunner, staying slightly beneath the two-seater for additional cover.

The year of 1918, with its bigger air formations, was essentially a leaders' war. Von Richthofen, in his way, had been a leader since 1917. He fell on April 21, 1918, having gained 80 aerial victories. Those wishing to disparage his victory tally often say he scored against slow and obsolete British aircraft, or that he fought at the head of a formation that always guarded his tail, or that he fought only when the odds or his tactical position favored him.

THE ACES

Von Richthofen was the most successful German air fighter, so let us look at his achievements. Of his 80 victories many were inferior to either his Albatros or his Fokker Triplanes. But should he

Above: Bristol Fighter. This two-seater fighter arrived on the Western Front in April 1917 but was used defensively and was not a success. Once used offensively and flown by a good team of pilot and gunner, it became a formidable opponent. The type remained in RAF service until the 1930s.

Right: Although hardly a scout, this heavily armed RE8 flown by Captain D F Stevenson DSO MC and Lieutenant J Baker MC of 4 Squadron, 1918, was always on the look-out for trouble. It has a wing-mounted Lewis and a Vickers gun on the side of the fuselage for the pilot, while Baker has a single Lewis in his rear cockpit. Note the off-set Aldis sight to the right of the cockpit.

on that account, have refrained from attacking them? Of course not. Yet what of the types not inferior to his? Among his victories were eight Sopwith Camels, three SE5s, four Bristol Fighters, one Sopwith Dolphin, four SPADs, five Nieuport Scouts, plus a number of FE2bs and DH2s, which had a reasonable chance of survival. At least eight of his opponents were minor 'aces', with anything up to 10 victories. That he fought at the head of a group of fighters and chose his time to attack, or chose not to engage, was surely the mark of a good tactician. In his task – to inflict the maximum damage with the minimum loss – he succeeded admirably. He made few mistakes. Only two really stand out. On July 6, 1917 he chased an FE2b too long, was shot down and

wounded. On April 21, 1918 he chased a Camel too long and too far – was shot down and killed. Had he lived to fly a Fokker DVII he might have scored over a hundred victories.

On the Allied side there was the great McCudden, a superb patrol leader. Mick Mannock, another leader, also had a certain amount of 'dash' in his fighting but nevertheless used his flight in 74 Squadron to do the maximum damage. Raymond Collishaw, ex-RNAS, gained 60 victories and had innumerable indecisive combats that undoubtedly led to unrecorded kills in three years of fighting. In Naval 10 he led one of the most successful Flights in France and later, in Camels, led 203 Squadron, RAF.

Donald McLaren of 46 Squadron, with 54 victories, was another able patrol leader; as was John Gilmore of 65 Squadron. There were still a few individualists who would occasionally strike out on their own, but they had the skill and experience to survive – for a while anyway. W G Barker gained many of his 52 victories in Italy, often flying alone or with just one or two fellow pilots. When he later commanded a Bristol Fighter Squadron, he took his personal Camel with him, adding to his score. Beauchamp-Proctor of 84 Squadron could lead successful patrols and hold his own in individual combat. He was also a successful destroyer of kite balloons, shooting down 16 plus 38 aircraft.

JAMES ANDERSON SLATER

BORN IN NOVEMBER 1896, JIMMY Slater joined the Royal Sussex Regiment in 1914 and was later commissioned in the Irish Rifles. In 1915 he transferred to the RFC and flew as an observer with 18 Squadron, and was then accepted for pilot training. Returning to France he joined 1 Squadron, flying Nieuport Scouts and was credited with three victories by May 1917.

Returning to England as an instructor, he was promoted to Captain and joined the newly formed 64 Squadron that flew the DH5 scout with its distinctive back-stagger top wing. Back in France that autumn as a flight commander with 64 he in fact shot down the squadron's first victory on November 30, a DFW two-seater.

The squadron converted to SE5s in 1918 and during the period March to May Slater ran up an impressive score of 20 kills, bringing his total to 24, and winning the MC and bar and the DFC. On six days he scored double victories, most of his opponents being single-seater scouts.

He returned to England to instruct and did not see further combat. After the war he continued as a flying instructor in both England and in the Middle East. He then served with a number of squadrons at home and abroad, before taking up another instructing post at the Central Flying School in England, but was killed in a flying accident the day before his 29th birthday.

ACE PILOTS OF VON RICHTHOFEN'S JAGDGESCHWADER NR. 1

CREDITED WITH FIVE OR MORE COMBAT VICTORIES

Name	Unit	Total
Ltn Hans Adam	Jasta 6	21 Killed Nov 15 1917
Oblt Frhr von Althaus	Jasta 10	9
Offz Stellv. Paul Aue	Jasta 10	10 Wounded Sep 19 1917
Ltn Frhr von Barnekow	Jasta 11	11
Oblt Frhr Oscar von Boenigk	Jasta 4	26 Led Jasta 2 in 1918
Ltn Otto Brauneck	Jasta 11	9 Killed Jul 26 1917
Ltn von Breiten-Landenberg	Jasta 6	5 Wounded Apl 26 1918
Ltn M W B-Bodener	Jasta 6	5 Killed Jul 18 1918
Ltn Karl Deilmann	Jasta 6	6
Oblt Kurt von Doering	Jasta 4	11 JG4 May 1918
Oblt Eduard von Dostler	Jasta 6	26 Killed Aug 21 1917
Ltn Heinz Dreckmann	Jasta 4	11 Killed Jul 30 1918
Ltn Fritz Friedrichs	Jasta 10	21 Killed Jul 15 1918
Vfw Willi Gabriel	Jasta 11	11
Oblt Hermann Goring	—	22 JG1 Cdr 1918
Ltn Justus Grassmann	Jasta 10	10
Ltn Gilbert-W Groos	Jasta 11	6
Oblt Fritz Grosch	Jasta 4	6 Wounded Aug 24 1918
Ltn Siegfried Gussmann	Jasta 11	5
Vfw Aloys Heldmann	Jasta 10	15
Vfw Franz Hemer	Jasta 6	18 Wounded Aug 9 1918
Ltn Johan Janzen	Jasta 6	13 POW Jun 9 1918
Ltn Erich Just	Jasta 11	6
Ltn Hans Kirschstein	Jasta 6	27 Killed Jul 16 1918
Ltn Hans Klein	Jasta 4	22 Wounded Feb 19 1918
Ltn Egon Koepsch	Jasta 4	9
Ltn Wilhelm Kohlbach	Jasta 10	5
Vfw Fritz Krebs	Jasta 6	6 Killed Jul 16 1917
Ltn Kurt Kuppers	Jasta 6	5
Ltn Arthur Laumann	Jasta 10	26
Ltn Erich Loewenhardt	Jasta 10	53 Killed Aug 10 1918
Ltn Heinrich Maushake	Jasta 4	7 Wounded Nov 3 1918
Ltn Eberhardt Mohicke	Jasta 11	9 Wounded Mar 1 1918
Ltn Ulrich Neckel	Jasta 6	30
Ltn Alfred Niederhoff	Jasta 11	7 Killed Jul 28 1917
Ltn Friedrich Noltenius	Jasta 6	20
Ltn Hans von der Osten	Jasta 4	5 To Jasta 11. Wounded Mar 1918
Ltn Victor von Pressintin	Jasta 4	15 Killed May 31 1918
Oblt Wilhelm Reinhard	Jasta 11	20 CO JG1. Died Jul 3 1918
Manfred von Richthofen	—	80 CO JG1. Killed Apl 21 1918
Lothar von Richthofen	Jasta 11	40 Brother
Wolfram von Richthofen	Jasta 11	8 Cousin, later General WW2
Vfw Edgar Scholz	Jasta 11	7 Killed May 2 1918
Fwbl Friedrich Schumacher	Jasta 10	5 Wounded Jul 24 1918
Ltn Werrner Steinhauser	Jasta 11	10 Killed Jun 26 1918
Ltn Ernst Udet	Jasta 4	62 Jasta 4 May 1918
Ltn Werner Voss	Jasta 10	48 Killed Sep 23 1917
Oblt Erich von Wedel	Jasta 11	13
Ltn Hans Weiss	Jasta 11	16 To Jasta 11. Killed May 1918
Ltn Paul Wenzel	Jasta 6	10 Wounded Aug 11 1918
Ltn Richard Wenzel	Jasta 11	12 To Jasta 4
Ltn Kurt Wolff	Jasta 11	33 Killed Sep 15 1917
Ltn Joachim Wolff	Jasta 11	10 Killed May 16 1918
Vfw Kurt Wusthoff	Jasta 4	27 POW Jun 17 1918

There were also the Bristol Fighter 'aces'. Andrew Edward McKeever shot down, or shared with his gunners, 30 victories. John Gurdon scored 27, Bill Staton 26, Alan Hepburn 23. Arthur Atkey and his gunner C G Gass shot down 29 German aircraft between May 7 and June 2, 1918, Atkey having already shot down 6 Germans while flying a DH4 bomber! Another exponent of the Bristol Fighter was Sgt E J Elton. With his gunners he shot down 16 aircraft between February 26 and March 29, 1918. Gone were the days when Bristol Fighter pilots flew their aircraft like two-seaters. Handled like a single-seat scout, with a good man 'in the back', they were deadly.

The French ace of aces was Capitaine René Fonck, who ended the war with 75 'official' victories, while his own estimate was 127! In his book *Mes Combats* he recorded how different his approach to combat was from that of Georges Guynemer. Guynemer, he recalled, faced enemy fire regularly but Fonck thought the strategy dangerous. Fonck always chose the blind spots, although he knew that in doing so he had to open fire from whatever position he found himself in. He would conserve his ammunition, firing perhaps only 6 to 10 bullets at a time. He was, in any event, a superb shot – he excelled at gunnery both in his SPAD, or with rifle or carbine on the ground. His methods succeeded. Besides being economical with his ammunition, his short bursts helped his aim and reduced the chances of his guns jamming. He forced himself to act coolly, with a clear head, to wait, to be patient. When the enemy got nervous or made the slightest error Fonck would pounce. He studied German tactics and used that knowledge to advantage.

For a time both Fonck and Guynemer used the SPAD XII, armed with a 37-mm cannon mounted between the cylinder blocks of the 200-hp geared Hispano-Suiza engine, and firing through the propeller hub. Its breech was in the cockpit, its barrel passing through the hollow airscrew shaft. Guynemer flew it in early July 1917 and gained his 49th, 50th, 51st and 52nd victories with it. The cannon was a single-shot weapon and had to be reloaded by hand during combat. Fumes from the gun made it unpleasant in action, it was a heavy machine, with vibration from the geared H-S engine affecting marksmanship; it was not a machine that was in action for long. Fonck flew the XII long enough to gain 11 kills, seven of which were confirmed. He flew long and hard. He scored his first official victory in August 1916, his 75th official victory ten days before WW1 ended. Twice he shot down six on one day and on August

FOKKER DVII versus ROYAL AIRCRAFT FACTORY SE5A

THE ROYAL AIRCRAFT Factory at Farnborough was the official British center for the design (and also limited production) of military aircraft. Tens of thousands of 'Factory' aeroplanes served with the RFC, and the best was the SE5A scout. Originally flown as the SE5 in November 1916, it was extremely strong, not difficult to fly. The British ace, Albert Ball, had always flown a Nieuport. He thought the SE sluggish, but after its speed and firepower had saved him from death he became a convert. The only fault lay in the engine, which in some forms was very unreliable. Once it got a good engine the SE was the master of all it met, with the exception of the Fokker DVII. This only got into action in the last seven months of the war, but was the best 'Hun' fighter of all.

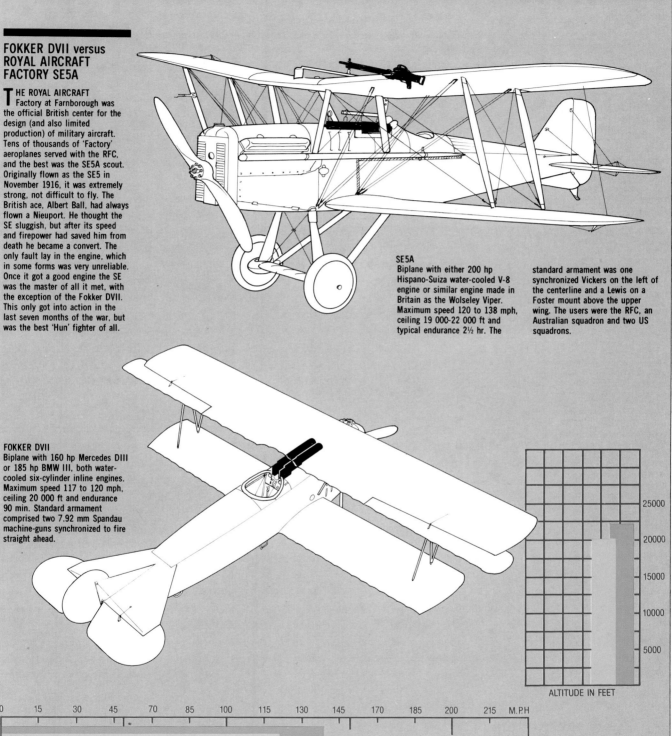

SE5A
Biplane with either 200 hp Hispano-Suiza water-cooled V-8 engine or similar engine made in Britain as the Wolseley Viper. Maximum speed 120 to 138 mph, ceiling 19 000-22 000 ft and typical endurance 2½ hr. The standard armament was one synchronized Vickers on the left of the centerline and a Lewis on a Foster mount above the upper wing. The users were the RFC, an Australian squadron and two US squadrons.

FOKKER DVII
Biplane with 160 hp Mercedes DIII or 185 hp BMW III, both water-cooled six-cylinder inline engines. Maximum speed 117 to 120 mph, ceiling 20 000 ft and endurance 90 min. Standard armament comprised two 7.92 mm Spandau machine-guns synchronized to fire straight ahead.

25000

20000

15000

10000

5000

ALTITUDE IN FEET

0   15   30   45   70   85   100   115   130   145   170   185   200   215   M.P.H

RUDOLF BERTHOLD

BORN IN DITTERSWIND, SOUTH Germany, in March 1891, Berthold first joined the army but transferred to the air service in 1913. He began the war as an observer, winning the Iron Cross, but from early 1915 flew as a pilot, initially on bombing raids over the British front. In September 1915 he was wounded in a fight with a British scout.

At the beginning of 1916 his unit, Fliegerabteilung 23, received its first Fokker monoplanes and began to do battle with the British RFC. Berthold scored his first victory on February 5, 1916. Subsequently, he had to force-land after taking on three British BEs single-handed and later crashed while testing a Pfalz monoplane. In October 1916 he recorded his tenth victory and was awarded Germany's highest decoration, while commanding Jasta 14. In August 1917 he took command of Jasta 18 and in one month shot down 14 British aircraft before himself being shot down and severely wounded in the right arm. Despite being virtually one-armed, he returned to combat as commander of Jagdgeschwader No. II (Jastas 12, 13, 15 and 19). His Fokker DVII was specially modified so that he could fly one-handed, and his score reached 40 by August 1918. Dubbed the 'Iron Knight' for his determination to keep flying despite constant pain, he shot down his final two opponents on August 10, raising his total to 44. Then in a dogfight with Sopwith Camels, he was shot down and crashed, suffering yet more injuries. His combat days were over.

After the war, Berthold joined the Freikorps and later fought against Communists in the Balkans. Returning to Germany, torn by civil war, he was murdered by German Communists on December 15, 1919 at the town of Harburg.

14, 1918 he destroyed three in ten seconds. The three Germans came at him head-on. As he crossed them he fired a burst at each and hit all three. They fell near the city of Roye, burning on the ground, separated by less than 100 meters. These brought his total to 60 victories.

The French too had seen the value of the steep climbing turn which they called the 'chandelle'. In fact both the French and the British flew more or less identical maneuvers. The 'vrille' was a nose-spin to the British, a tailspin to the Americans. Throttle back the engine, put the controls to one side and the aircraft begins to fall in a spin – perhaps useful in 'playing dead' when the enemy thinks he has scored. Then the 'renversement' – more or less an Immelmann turn, or a stall turn. In this, one pulls up sharply without increasing power. As the stall begins, the pilot puts the controls to the side he wishes to turn to and the aircraft slowly stall turns in that direction. By putting on full power the pilot can dive down facing the way he has just come. It was the quickest way of making a 180° turn.

The American Air Service meanwhile was adding to its strength. Most of its squadrons were initially equipped with the Nieuport 28, a version that carried two machine-guns, mounted on the engine cowling but offset on the pilot's left side. It had a tendency to shed its wing fabric in a high-speed turn or pull-up, so the Americans were sometimes less than aggressive, but when they re-equipped with SPADs they were more effective. The SPAD could outclimb the Fokker biplanes, the rest was easy.

Eddie Rickenbacker, a pre-war American racing driver, became the top 'ace' of the USAS with 26 victories. Despite the problems with the Nieuport 28s, Rickenbacker scored 12 of his victories on the type, 14 more on SPADs. He flew with the famous 94th Aero Squadron whose tally in 1918 was 67 German aircraft and balloons.

In September 1918 Rickenbacker was promoted to captain and, on September 25, flew alone towards the front lines. He saw two LVG two-seaters with five Fokkers above and behind and climbed into the sun – out of their vision. High in the sun he throttled back and nosed over, diving into the Fokkers. His first burst knocked out one, which crashed with the pilot dead in the cockpit. Intending to zoom up to regain lost height, he noticed that the Fokkers were in such disarray that he had time to go down on the two recce aircraft. They in turn began to dive when they saw the SPAD. With one eye on the Fokkers above, Rickenbacker fired at the second LVG as they separated, their observers both firing at him.

The American steepened his dive, passing out of the gunner's view, then zoomed up under the LVG. The German pilot turned to afford his rear man a shot at the scout and then the leading LVG came up behind the SPAD, its tracer screaming over Rickenbacker's head. 'Rick' zoomed diagonally out of range, made a 'renversement' (stall turn) and came back at the first LVG. This maneuver was repeated several times, the Fokkers still above and still confused, but the battle was moving deeper into hostile territory. The two LVGs were suddenly flying parallel to each other about 50 yards apart. Putting his SPAD into a side-slip, Rickenbacker got one LVG between himself and the other, opened fire and sent the LVG down in flames. He then pulled away and headed for home, having secured his 8th and 9th victories.

Lieutenant Donald Hudson scored six victories with the American 27th Aero Squadron in 1918. Three of these he shot down on August 1 1918. His combat report records: '*WE WERE attacked by eight Fokker biplane Chasse machines east of Fere-en-Tardenois at 8.10 am. I tried to bank to the left and fell into a spin, when I came out there were four enemy aircraft on my tail. I tried to turn again but fell into another spin. I was followed by the four EA [enemy aircraft] down to 1000 m. As I was coming out of the spin a machine was headed straight at me. I fired and he turned to the left; I turned a little to the left and turned back again being right on his tail. I fired about 20 rounds into him. He fell off slowly on his right wing and went into a spin. I turned on the other machines and went into a spin. When I came out the other machines were climbing up. Just as the fight began I saw an enemy plane fall off on his right wing and spin in exactly the same manner as the machine I shot down. I saw something else fall in flames. A SPAD passed within 20 feet of my right wing, falling on its back. My engine was boiling and I could not climb as my Nourrice was empty and by using the hand pump I could just keep going. Then northeast of the railroad between Fere-en-Tardenois and Spaoney, I encountered a Rumpler biplane at between 100 and 200 m. He passed me on the right and banked up to give his observer a good shot at me. I turned and got on his tail and followed him in a circle firing right into the cockpit. Suddenly his right wing came off and he crashed. I was being fired at by machine guns on the ground and was essing when I noticed another Rumpler under me to my left. I turned down and fired at the observer. He disappeared and the machine crashed just beside*

The American Air Service had no fighting aircraft of its own in WW1, so used French and British machines. A number of squadrons operated with the Nieuport 28 which carried two Vickers machine-guns mounted to the left hand side of the forward fuselage and cowling. The 94th 'Hat-in-the-Ring' Squadron flew them in April 1918. Edward Rickenbacker scored several victories in a Nieuport 28. It was maneuverable and had a fast climb but was not popular as it tended to shed wing fabric in a dive. This example is a post-war civil registered airplane.

the railroad embankment. I circled the machine once to see if either the pilot or the observer got out, but they did not. Confirmation for three requested.'

There were a number of American as well as Dominion pilots with the Royal Flying Corps and Royal Air Force in the war. Two squadrons, the 17th and the 148th, were both with the RAF although manned by American personnel. Lieutenant Field E Kindley was with the 148th and scored the unit's first combat victory on 13th July 1918 – an Albatros DIII scout. *AT 8.57 am I saw an EA below us between Poperinghe and Ypres. An Albatros came out of the clouds between me and my formation. After climbing head-on over him, I half-rolled and shot two bursts of one hundred rounds into him at point blank range. Soon he and another EA were on my tail, diving vertically at me. Of course, I was watching them and when the one I had fired two bursts at tried to come out of his dive, I saw his tail come loose and he went down in a vertical dive with the tailplane hanging to his fuselage. He continued to dive vertically through the clouds and to the best of my knowledge, must have crashed not far from the south east of Ypres. By this time three EA were firing upon me and I maneuvered my way through the clouds back to*

the lines and rejoined my formation.'

Field Kindley went on to shoot down a total of 12 German aircraft, all with the 148th, flying Sopwith Camels. Sadly he did not survive long the peacetime years he had helped to fight for. In 1920 he died in a flying accident at Kelly Field, San Antonio, Texas. Kindley Field airforce base on the island of Bermuda was named after him.

By the summer of 1918 the Royal Air Force had got its fighting tactics down to a fine art. So much had progressed in just four years, so much learnt, so much was now being put into the air war in France.

On August 8 came the huge Allied offensive as the Battle of Amiens opened, followed by other battles culminating in the assault on the German Hindenburg Line on September 27. For Germany it was the beginning of the end. In August the RAF had over 800 aircraft to support the Army's battles, the French over 1100. The Germans had only 365, of which 140 were fighters.

By this late stage of the war the last two major types of scouting aircraft came to the Western Front. For the RAF it was the Sopwith Snipe, for the Germans the Fokker DVIII. The Snipe was to prove the best of the Allied fighters of WW1 but it equipped only two Squadrons before the war ended, No 43 and No 4 AFC Squadrons. Had the war lasted into 1919 many Camel squadrons would have been re-equipped with the Snipe. The

WESTERN FRONT SEPTEMBER 18, 1918

BALLOON ATTACK

The German observation balloons that hung temptingly close to the front lines were not attractive targets: normally protected by large numbers of guns on the ground, and invariably by aircraft patrolling overhead, they were dangerous to attack, and few pilots relished the task. One who did was Frank Luke, in the summer of 1918 a pilot with the 27th Aero Squadron, US Army Air Service.

On his first encounter with the Germans, on August 16, 1918, Luke had detached himself from a squadron patrol, flown off on his own and returned to claim a victory — a claim which the squadron declined to recognize. Teaming up with another pilot who had fallen into disfavor with the squadron, Joe Wehrner, Luke began a personal campaign against German balloons that was to result in the destruction of 20, along with six aircraft, Luke himself claiming 14 of the balloons and four of the aircraft, Wehrner accounting for the remainder.

There were two basic methods for attacking balloons, which when threatened would be hauled down rapidly while the observers parachuted to the ground. The first involved getting well behind the German lines and approaching the balloon low from the east, where the defenders would least expect an attack, then zooming up and opening fire from below, though this meant coming under intensive ground fire just as speed was lost in the climb. The preferred approach was a dive from directly above, fast enough to catch the balloon before it could be hauled down.

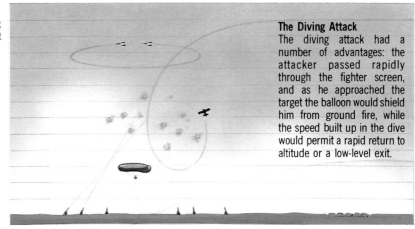

The Diving Attack
The diving attack had a number of advantages: the attacker passed rapidly through the fighter screen, and as he approached the target the balloon would shield him from ground fire, while the speed built up in the dive would permit a rapid return to altitude or a low-level exit.

TIMETABLE
1 Luke and Wehrner have taken off at 1600 hours to look for balloons above St Mihiel; to date Luke has claimed eight balloons destroyed.
2 Seeing two balloons near Labeuville, they climb above cloud to 12 000 ft.
3 As Luke dives on the first balloon, shells from the AA guns on the ground explode around his SPAD.
4 The AA gunners have to cease firing to avoid hitting the balloon, which explodes under Luke's fire.
5 Pulling out of the dive, Luke sees that Wehrner has not attacked the other balloon, and climbs to attack it himself.

6 Diving again, Luke hits the second balloon, which also bursts into flames. He then looks for Wehrner.
7 Wehrner has been engaged by a patrol of Fokker DVIIs: Luke climbs toward the battle and shoots down two of the Fokkers, then breaks away and is making for the lines when he sees a German two-seater which he also shoots down, making five victories in ten minutes. Returning to his base he finds that Wehrner has not survived the encounter with the Fokkers; Luke himself dies shooting it out with German troops after being forced down behind enemy lines on September 29.

3

4

6

GERMAN OBSERVATION BALLOON

LT JOE WEHRNER

TWO SPAD XIIIs,
25TH AERO SQUADRON,
US ARMY AIR SERVICE

1

2

GERMAN FOKKER DVII PATROL

7

LT FRANK LUKE

5

MAJOR ACES OF WW1

BRITISH EMPIRE

Name	Nationality	Total	Date	
Major E Mannock	British	73	1917–18	Killed in action
Major W A Bishop	Canadian	72	1917–18	
Major R Collishaw	Canadian	62	1916–18	
Major J B McCudden	British	57	1916–18	Killed in accident
Capt A W B–Proctor	South African	54	1917–18	
Capt D M MacLaren	Canadian	54	1918	
Major W G Barker	Canadian	52	1916–18	
Major R S Dallas	Australian	51	1916–18	
Capt G E H McElroy	Irish	49	1917–18	Killed in action
Capt A Ball	British	47	1916–17	Killed in action
Capt R A Little	Australian	47	1917–18	Killed in action
Major T H Hazell	Irish	43	1917–18	
Capt P F Fullard	British	42	1917	
Major J Gilmour	British	40	1917–18	
Capt J I T Jones	British	40	1918	
Capt F R McCall	Canadian	37	1917–18	
Capt W G Claxton	Canadian	36	1917–18	
Capt H W Woollett	British	36	1917–18	
Capt S M Kinkead	South African	36	1917–18	
Capt J S T Fall	Canadian	34	1916–18	
Capt W L Jordan	British	34	1917–18	
Capt A C Atkey	Canadian	33	1917–18	
Major G H Bowman	British	32	1917–18	
Major A D Carter	Canadian	31	1917–18	POW
Capt A E McKeever	Canadian	30	1917–18	
Capt A H Cobby	Australian	30	1918	

BELGIAN

Name		Total	Date
Lt Willy Coppens		37	1917–18
Adj Andrew de Meulemeester		11	1917–18
Lt Edmund Thieffry		10	1917–18

FRENCH

Name	Total	Date	
Capt Rene Fonck	75	1917–18	
Capt Georges Guynemer	54	1916–17	Killed in action
Lt Charles Nungesser	45	1916–18	
Capt Georges Madon	41	1917–18	
Lt Maurice Boyau	35	1917–18	Killed in action
Lt Michel Coiffard	34	1917–18	Died of wounds
Lt Jean Bourjade	28	1917–18	
Capt Armand Pinsard	27	1916–18	
Lt Rene Dorme	23	1916–17	Killed in action
Lt Gabriel Guerin	23	1917–18	Killed in action
Lt Claude Haegelen	22	1917–18	
Lt Pierre Marinovitch	22	1917–18	
Capt Aldred Hertaux	21	1916–17	
Capt Albert Deullin	20	1916–18	

ITALIAN

Name		Total	Date	
Major Francesco Baracca		34	1916–18	Killed in action
Lt Silvio Scaroni		26	1917–18	
Lt Col Pier R Piccio		24	1917–18	
Lt Flavio Barachini		21	1917–18	Killed in action
Capt Fulco R di Calabria		20	1916–18	

AMERICAN

Name		Total	Date	
Capt E V Rickenbacker	AEF	26	1918	
Capt W C Lambert	RAF	22	1918	
Capt A T Iaccaci	RAF	18	1918	
Lt F Luke Jr	AEF	18	1918	Killed in action
Capt F W Gillet	RAF	17	1918	
Major R Lufbery	FR/AEF	17	1916–18	Killed in action
Capt H A Kuhlberg	RAF	16	1918	
Capt O J Rose	RAF	16	1918	
Capt C W Warman	RAF	15	1917	
Capt E W Springs	RAF/AEF	15	1918	

Fokker DVIII also came too late to be effective but it was beginning to make its mark as the war ended. In a way it brought the Germans full circle. Its first successful scout was the Fokker monoplane. The Fokker DVIII too was a monoplane.

WING FORMATION

The strength and superiority of the RAF allowed it to develop its own wing formations. The 80th Wing began using its squadrons in combined fighter sweeps in layers, Snipes high up, Bristol Fighters below, and Camels below them. They would penetrate 15–20 miles into enemy territory between Ypres and Arras. They succeeded in clearing the skies of German fighters, but failed to destroy them. In consequence the wing took the war to the German bases, either to destroy the aircraft on the ground, or to destroy their bases and/or force the aircraft up to fight.

The commander of this wing was Colonel L A Strange DSO MC DFC: the same L A Strange who, in 1914, had been ordered to remove a machine-gun from his aircraft as it affected its ability to climb. Strange escorted a DH9 bomber squadron to bomb the German base. Some of his escorting aircraft also carried bombs and, if not engaged by German aircraft, they would in turn make a bombing swoop. His wing formation might look like this:

```
SNIPES
4 AFC Sqdn    BRISTOL FTRS
7/8000 ft     88 Sqdn      CAMELS
              6000 ft      46 Sqdn    SE5s
                           4000 ft    2 AFC Sqdn   DH9s
                                      3000 ft      103 Sqdn
                                                   2000 ft
```

The bombers were given close escort by the SE5s, who were in turn covered by the Camels. The Bristols above covered the others and in turn were covered by the new Sopwith Snipes.

On the occasions when they were engaged by German fighters, it was such an armada that the Germans could engage only the high escort squadrons. To attempt to go for the bombers or

ALEXANDER NORMAN DUDLEY PENTLAND

LIKE R S DALLAS, JERRY Pentland came from Queensland, Australia. He was born in September 1894 and initially served in the Australian Light Horse in Egypt and at Gallipoli in 1914-16. Transferring to the RFC, he flew in France with 16 Squadron on BE2Cs before going on to scouts in 1917, flying SPADs with 19 Squadron. He was a very aggressive air fighter, and when aircraft were not about he would go down to strafe the Germans on the ground. Once on such a flight he had a British artillery shell smash right through his fuselage without either exploding or causing him to crash. In the air he shot down 10 German aircraft in two months and won the MC.

Following a rest and a spell spent helping to train new pilots in England, he became a flight commander with 87 Squadron, one of the new Sopwith Dolphin squadrons forming in the spring of 1918. He went to France with them in April, and in four months accounted for a further 13 German aircraft, to bring his score to 24 (which includes one he shot down when flying BEs in 1916). He received the DFC, but was wounded in combat on August 25 and did not see further action.

After the war he returned to Australia, flying with Australian National Airways in the 1930s, following a brief spell in the RAAF. In WW2, with the rank of Squadron Leader in the RAAF, he ran an air-sea-rescue service in the Pacific, for which he was awarded the AFC.

the lower escorts meant leaving themselves open to attack from above.

The last year of the war saw a number of large dogfights. Right up to the end the German Air Service was in no way defeated despite the superiority of numbers against them. In the final analysis it was the lack of fuel that was their worst enemy. One of the last dogfights occurred on the morning of November 4, one week before the Armistice, south-east of Ghent.

The patrol of seven Camels of 65 Squadron was led by Captain J L M White and included Captain M A Newnham DFC. I corresponded with Group Captain Newnham a few years before his death in 1974 and this battle was mentioned. Newnham claimed 17 victories in WW1 and was in the thick of this fight, which was fought in company with the Camels of 204 Squadron. They were at 12 000 ft when White saw no less than 40 Fokker DVIIs with yellow and green tails. From 16 000 ft they began swooping down on the Camels. Seeing them, White turned his pilots underneath the Fokkers, making their attacking dive too steep to get in telling bursts. Then the mix-up started and, with the Germans having lost the initiative in the opening clash, the encounter developed into a whirling dogfight.

The Camels of 65 Squadron claimed 15 successes, eight destroyed, six out of control and one damaged and driven down; 204 Squadron added two destroyed plus five out of control. Many of the, by now, classic maneuvers were used in this fight, which some say – with 22 Germans shot out of the battle – was the greatest dogfight of the war. John White shot down four, the first two by using the tight turning capabilities of the Camel, the third by keeping his cool and his sights on during a head-on attack, the fourth by hanging on to the tail of a Fokker and forcing it into a spin.

Maurice Newnham stuck to the tail of a Fokker whose pilot was unable to shake off the experienced English pilot, who fired a long burst from 10 yards, right into the cockpit. The Fokker went down in an inverted spin. Newnham then 'zoomed' up beneath another Fokker, firing short bursts into it. The German did a half-roll, Newnham getting on its tail to fire at point-blank range. As the German zoomed up, Newnham, clinging to its tail in a vertical bank, saw the enemy pilot fall forward, his machine going to earth in a vertical nose-dive.

Another pilot half-rolled onto a Fokker's tail, another got behind a Fokker and fired at 10 yards range; yet another had a Fokker zoom up dead ahead, and hammered it at point-blank range,

MAJOR ACES OF WW1

GERMAN

Name	Total	Date	
Rittm Manfred v Richthofen	80	1916–18	Killed in action
Oblt Ernst Udet	62	1917–18	
Oblt Erich Loewenhardt	53	1917–18	Killed in action
Ltn Werner Voss	48	1917	Killed in action
Ltn Fritz Rumey	45	1917–18	Killed in action
Hpt Rudolph Berthold	44	1916–18	
Ltn Paul Baumer	43	1917–18	
Ltn Josef Jacobs	41	1917–18	
Hpt Bruno Loerzer	41	1917–18	
Hpt Oswald Boelcke	40	1916	Killed in action
Ltn Franz Buchner	40	1917–18	
Oblt Lothar v Richthofen	40	1917–18	
Ltn Karl Menckhoff	39	1917–18	POW
Ltn Heinrich Gontermann	39	1917	Died of wounds
Ltn Max v Muller	36	1917–18	Killed in action
Ltn Julius Buckler	35	1916–18	
Ltn Gustav Dorr	35	1918	
Hpt Eduard v Schleich	35	1917–18	
Ltn Josef Veltjens	34	1917–18	
Ltn Otto Koennecke	33	1917–18	
Oblt Kurt Wolff	33	1917	Killed in action
Ltn Heinrich Bongartz	33	1917–18	
Ltn Theo Osterkamp	32	1917–18	
Ltn Emil Thuy	32	1915–18	
Ltn Paul Billik	31	1917–18	
Rittm Karl Bolle	31	1917–18	
Oblt Gotthard Sachsenberg	31	1917–18	
Ltn Karl Allmenroder	30	1917	Killed in action
Ltn Karl Degelow	30	1918	
Ltn Heinrich Kroll	30	1916–18	
Ltn Josef Mai	30	1917–18	
Ltn Ulrich Neckel	30	1918	
Ltn Karl Schaefer	30	1917	Killed in action

AUSTRO-HUNGARIAN

Name	Total	Date	
Hpt Godwin Brumowski	40	1916–18	
Off Stelle Julius Arigi	32	1916–18	
Oblt Frank Linke-Crawford	30	1917–18	Killed in action
Oblt Benno Fiala, Ritt v Fernbrugg	29	1916–18	

while still another attacked a Fokker broadside and put five bursts into it at very close range.

World War 1 ended at 11 am on the 11th day of November 1918. In four years the aeroplane had developed from an immature, unreliable mass of wood, wire and fabric to a mature, fast and deadly killing-machine. It had progressed from being a 'jack of all trades' to covering a variety of specialist functions: air fighting, bombing, reconnaissance artillery-ranging, contact patrols, ground attack, nightfighting, anti-submarine operations, attacking ships, and so on.

The flyers who survived could pass on the lessons learned, the tactics proved in action, how it should be done. But would they have to? Only the future would tell.

CHAPTER FIVE

LESSONS OF THE PAST, TESTING FOR THE FUTURE

N O SOONER HAD THE GREAT War ended than another conflict, which had been rumbling along for some months, flared up in earnest. The Russian Revolution of November 1917 had created in its wake an air war between the Bolsheviks and the White Russians. These counter-revolutionaries in South Russia were supported by Britain and France, and while the French only sent soldiers the RAF sent a squadron to support the Whites. It was commanded by Ray Collishaw DSO DSC DFC, who had ended WW1 with 60 confirmed victories.

The squadron – No. 47 – that had flown in Macedonia in WW1, was divided into three flights. 'A' Flight had DH9s, 'C' Flight DH9As – both two-seat day bombers, while 'B' Flight had Sopwith Camels, and was commanded by Captain S M Kinkead DSC DFC, another former naval 'ace' with 30 victories in WW1. Kinkead's pilots were all flyers who had seen some action towards the end of WW1 and they arrived in Russia as 'volunteers' in the spring of 1919.

While the DH9s flew reconnaissance and bombing missions, Kinkead's handful of 'clapped-out' Camels flew escort sorties to the De Havillands. The Bolshevik forces had a number of aircraft with which to oppose the White Russians. They were flown by Russian pilots, as well as German mercenaries. It must have been strange for the British pilots, for the Bolsheviks had not only German types such as Fokker Triplanes, Fokker DVIIs, Pfalz DIIIs, and Albatros DVs, but also Nieuports and SPADs.

The Camel flight's first victory was scored by an American, Marian Aten, who was to gain five victories in Russia and win the DFC. It was a classic mistake made by the 'Red' pilot who was flying a Nieuport. The Russian dived on the Camel which was at 2000 ft having had engine trouble. The Russian failed to make his attack successfully, and overshot his target, allowing Aten to get onto the diving Nieuport's tail and send it crashing into the banks of the River Volga. The next day, in a raid on a Bolshevik HQ, the DH9s came under attack by a SPAD and a Fokker Triplane, but the escorting Camels shot down the SPAD and drove off the Triplane.

In May 1919, 47 Squadron claimed seven Red aircraft and during a raid on a Bolshevik airfield, several Red aircraft took off to intercept the RAF machines. These included Nieuports, SPADs, an Albatros, a Fokker DVII and even an ancient Sopwith 1½-Strutter! The Fokker shot down two DH9s, but five Red aircraft were shot down.

In August this same Fokker, painted black and

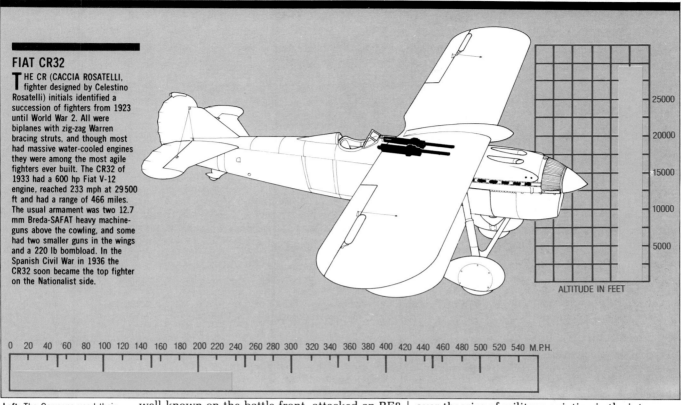

FIAT CR32

THE CR (CACCIA ROSATELLI, fighter designed by Celestino Rosatelli) initials identified a succession of fighters from 1923 until World War 2. All were biplanes with zig-zag Warren bracing struts, and though most had massive water-cooled engines they were among the most agile fighters ever built. The CR32 of 1933 had a 600 hp Fiat V-12 engine, reached 233 mph at 29 500 ft and had a range of 466 miles. The usual armament was two 12.7 mm Breda-SAFAT heavy machine-guns above the cowling, and some had two smaller guns in the wings and a 220 lb bombload. In the Spanish Civil War in 1936 the CR32 soon became the top fighter on the Nationalist side.

25000

20000

15000

10000

5000

ALTITUDE IN FEET

0 20 40 60 80 100 120 140 160 180 200 220 240 260 280 300 320 340 360 380 400 420 440 460 480 500 520 540 M.P.H.

Left: The Germans used their new Me109B, C, and D models in Spain, albeit only in limited numbers, but they proved far superior to most of the Republican aircraft they encountered. In January 1939 the new 109E began to arrive, the aircraft that would see action in the first years of WW2. The E models were coded 6-91 through 6-130. This picture of 6-109 is in the standard markings of J88.

well known on the battle front, attacked an RE8 escorted by Aten and another pilot. In this fight, which also included two Red Nieuports, all three Bolshevik aircraft were shot down. August saw several Red aircraft shot down, and even the redoubtable Ray Collishaw added to his WW1 score by downing an Albatros DV on October 9. (He also added a Red aircraft 'out of control' in September to bring his total 'victories' to 62.)

The tactics employed during this war in Russia were virtually the same as these used during WW1. The RAF crews had all learned their trade in WW1 and the leaders were all successful pilots from that conflict with the necessary skill to survive in air combat. Even some of the two-seater pilots had been scout pilots in 1917–18, so they too knew how to out-fight the Bolsheviks.

That war lasted until the end of 1919 as far as active British (and RAF) involvement was concerned, although aerial activity continued for two more years on other fronts. Siberia saw air actions and then followed the Russo-Polish conflict that continued into 1921.

THEORIES OF AIR WAR

The same year saw the publication of the Italian General Guilio Douhet's *The Command of the Air*, a book which exercised a considerable influence over theories of military aviation in the inter-war years. Douhet had reached the conclusion that the outcome of all future wars would be decided by the exercise of air power. Massive bomber fleets of up to 1000 aircraft would pulverize up to 50 targets a day. Flying a zig-zag course and escorted by heavily armored 'battleplanes', these aerial armadas would pose insuperable problems for the fighter defenses. In the unlikely event of a successful interception they would be outgunned by the 'battleplane' escort and swamped by weight of numbers. Despite Douhet's apocalyptic vision of aerial warfare, the fighter was not banished from the skies. Indeed, it provided the only available means of countering the confident proposition that 'the bomber will always get through'.

By the early 1930s considerable technical advances were being made in aviation. Engine power increased dramatically and the introduction of the supercharger boosted speed at high altitude. The monoplane layout began to come into its own, along with the retractable undercarriage and the enclosed cockpit. The development in the late 1920s of the ground-air radio link went some way towards solving the problems of bomber interception and laid the foundations of the air defense environment of the future. Arma-

JOAQUIN GARCIA-MORATO

J OAQUIN GARCIA-MORATO Y Castano was already an experienced pilot before the Spanish Civil War began, having flown against Arab guerillas in Morocco, and later as a fighter instructor. He joined the Nationalist forces, initially flying Nieuport-Delage 52 fighters in which on August 12 1936 he gained his first victory, a Vickers Vildebeeste. He next flew a German Heinkel 51 in which he shot down his next three opponents, but then switched to the Italian Fiat CR32. In the CR32 he claimed his 5th victory on September 11 before forming his Patrulla Azul (Blue Patrol) of three Fiats. His Blue Patrol grew to become not only a squadron but a group, eventually expanding into two fighter groups.

By the end of 1936 his score was into double figures, including claims over a Hawker Fury, a Potez 540 and a Russian I-15. On January 3, 1937 he shot down two Russian SB2 bombers; these were much faster than his Fiat, but he got them through a high climb and high-speed dive from altitude. By 1938 he was Chief of Operations. Though his time in the air was limited, he still flew whenever and whatever he could, including He51s, Me109Bs, Do17s, He111s and even Ju52s. From time to time he still flew with his old group, shooting down four Republican fighters in the second half of 1938. On December 24 he shot down no fewer than three Polikarpov R-5 attack bombers, bringing his score to 39. His 40th and last victory was over an I-15 on January 19, 1939. He was killed after the war while performing aerobatics in his personal Fiat CR32 for the benefit of newsreel cameras.

ment became more heavy and stressed-skin construction began to appear on new types, although many fighters still relied on fabric covering for most of their airframe, making for easier repair of battle damage and greater simplicity of construction. These crucial developments can be seen in the Hawker Hurricane, which first flew in the autumn of 1935 and entered service with the RAF's No. 111 Squadron at the end of 1937. It was the first operational fighter capable of speeds in excess of 300 mph and the first fighter to be armed with eight 0.303 machine-guns. Despite these advances, the era of the biplane was not quite over. Production of the RAF's Gloster Gladiator biplane continued until 1940 and despite its obsolescence it equipped 13 RAF squadrons on the outbreak of war. The Italian Fiat CR 42 entered service in 1939 and remained in production until 1942.

THE SPANISH CIVIL WAR

In July 1936 another major air war began – in Spain. The military revolt of 1936 produced within a few weeks two contending and relatively well defined sides both of which received substantial foreign aid. The insurgent Nationalists (led by General Franco) were aided by Germany, Italy and Portugal. The government, or Republican, forces received help from the Soviet Union.

At the beginning of the Civil War the only fighter aircraft available in Spain were 36 domestically built Nieuport Delage Ni D.52s, all but seven of which made up the republican interceptor arm. It was not long, however, before both

sides began to receive more modern aircraft.

Towards the end of 1936 the Nationalists were reinforced by German Heinkel 51 biplanes – the advanced guard of the German-manned Condor Legion – and light, maneuverable Italian Fiat CR 32 biplanes. Initially the He 51s were flown by Spanish pilots, but the results were so unsatisfactory that their German 'instructors' began to fly operationally. From the start the CR 32s were flown by Italian volunteer pilots who had joined the Spanish Foreign Legion.

The Soviet Union supplied the Republicans with Polikarpov I-15 biplanes (known as Chatos) and I-16 monoplanes (Ratas). The I-16 fighter, 300 of which were eventually supplied to the Republicans, was the most modern aircraft of the day. Stubby and low-winged, it could reach 280 mph in level flight and climb to 16 400 ft in six minutes. At low speeds and low altitude it was extremely unstable and performed at its best only when flown by the most confident and experienced pilots.

The Spanish Civil war quickly became a testing ground for the modern aircraft of the late 1930s. Small detachments of German and Italian pilots were given the opportunity to test new types in combat. The Italians introduced the Fiat all-metal Gr 50 fighter and the SM 79 bomber. Among the types tested by the Condor Legion were the He111 and Do17 bombers. These sleek, twin-engined aircraft were fast enough to outpace most fighters. Without adequate warning fighters could not gain the height to intercept them. If they found themselves above the bombers, the only hope of inflicting damage lay in a steep dive and a

Above: The Germans evaluated a number of their aircraft in the Spanish Civil War, including the Henschel Hs123 dive-bomber. However, it was in the close support role that it achieved its best success, and the dive-bombing role was taken over by the devastating Ju87 Stuka.
Left: In Spain the Republican's best fighter was the Russian Polikarpov I-16 'Rata' fighter. It had perhaps the fastest rate of roll of any fighter of its day and an outstanding all-round performance. It was a little unstable and tricky to fly, but proved a formidable opponent in Spain, the Far East and later in the early days of the war in Russia. Unhappily, this picture shows one that came second in a dogfight.

short burst of fire before the bombers flew away from the danger.

The He51 proved a failure, easily outclassed by the I-16, and was eventually relegated to ground-attack duties. The Nationalists, both Spanish and Italian, fought on with the robust and maneuverable Fiat CR 32, 127 seeing service in Spain. The Germans replaced their He51s as fighters in December 1936 with the arrival in Spain of their new Messerschmitt 109s, for operational evaluation. These were only prototypes and did not engage in combat, but their performance was encouraging enough for Hugo Sperrle, the commander of Germany's 'Condor Legion', to urge the German Air Ministry to provide a quantity of 109s for the Legion's fighter component – Jagdgruppe 88.

During 1937–8 air fighting increased in intensity with the increased speeds of aircraft bringing in the need for new tactics. Some of the Fiat squadrons flew in vics (sections of three), an accepted flight pattern that had developed over the years of peace. Height was still the significant factor making it necessary to revise an old WW1 tactic. Nationalists or Republicans used the advantage of height in dive and zoom attacks, in order to catch the fast, modern bombers.

The fighters of both sides flew regular escort sorties for their respective bombers, or in on the defensive flying interception missions. On May 13, 1938, for instance, Fiats of Group 3-G-3, escorting bombers, were stepped high above them. The Fiats ran into a large formation of Ratas flying at their level and Chatos below. Seeing the Fiats, the lower Chatos began to dive away, but the Ratas joined combat, and the dogfight began.

Captain José Larios was trying hard to maneuver up and around the I-16s in order to get his sights on one of them, but they were very fast. Larios pulled his Fiat into tight turns, the best tactic against the Rata. As the fight continued, a Rata dived on Larios, but he saw it just in time. He banked hard, pulling the Fiat's nose up to meet it, both fighters firing, then flashing past each other. He banked to fire at another Rata; this too was soon gone. Then a Rata came up from below. Larios pulled onto its tail, fired, and saw his tracer slam into its fuselage. It dived out of control, Larios spiralling with it, snapping off bursts, then he left it to crash down. It was his first victory.

The greatest development in the air war, however, was the arrival, at last in numbers, of the German Me109. By mid-1937 there were two He51 squadrons and one Me109 squadron of some 15 to 20 of the new fighters. At this time one He51 squadron 3/J88 was commanded by Lieutenant Adolf Galland. A future 'ace' of WW2, he had no opportunity to gain victories in Spain, indeed with the inferior He51 he and his pilots had to avoid confrontation with the vastly superior Chatos and Ratas.

The 109s went into action in July 1937. On July 12, Gunther Lützow led his squadron into a formation of Ratas, their appearance being an unpleasant surprise for the Government pilots. The Ratas had from now on to contend with a superior enemy fighter and well trained pilots. However, in this first action one Messerschmitt was shot down. By the end of the year 1/J88 and 2/J88 were both flying 109s.

A number of German pilots had their initial combat experience in Spain. Among these were Lützow, Wolfgang Schellman, Walter Oesau, Wilhelm Bathasar (who shot down four Russian SB-2 Bombers in six minutes on February 7, 1938), Wolfgang Lippert and Herbert Ihlefeld. The greatest, however, was Werner Mölders, who was to influence not only the war in Spain, but also the development of the Luftwaffe's fighter strategy in WW2.

NEW TACTICS
Mölders arrived for his 'tour' in Spain in April 1938 and shot down his first Russian aircraft (an I-16) having closed in to point-blank range before firing. It was the first of his 14 victories in Spain, which made him the top scoring pilot of the Condor Legion. His eventual standing enabled him to dictate a number of changes in the fighter arm. He will be remembered mostly for his development of fighter tactics.

Me109s were not, however, darkening the sky

with masses of aircraft, in comparison, for instance, to the Government forces' total of 13 I-15 and I-16 equipped squadrons. At most only about 60 Me109 models were used in Spain during the period 1937-39. In consequence they were used sparingly, and initially, as in most air forces, they operated in vics of three aircraft. However, the Germans, because of their fewer numbers, began to fly in pairs. And they found that the best way of operating was to fly in line-abreast with about 200 yards between them. In this way by searching the area between, each pilot was able to see and cover the other pilot's blind spots, traditionally the area behind and below the aircraft. Therefore, if an attack took place on one of the pair, the other would warn him and, as he broke away outwards, the second 109 would also break in the same direction. Thus, if the attacking aircraft continued his attack on the turn, he would soon find the second 109 on his tail.

Conversely, if the lead 109 pilot made an attack, his wingman was in an ideal position to protect his leader from the rear. This enabled the leader to concentrate on his attack, knowing his

back was protected by his Number Two. The Germans called this pair the Rötte, and, by increasing this formation with a second pair, two pairs became the Schwarm. The four-man Schwarm doubled the offensive and defensive power of the formation, and each additional pair strengthened the formation still further.

The increasing speed and sophistication of the modern fighter required a new generation of tacticians to develop a fresh approach to aerial combat. The senior officers in most of the world's air forces were all flyers of World War 1 vintage with World War 1 thinking. Because of their conservatism, it was left to brilliant young pilots like Werner Mölders to reshape fighter tactics, just as Boelcke and von Richthofen had done 20 years before.

In Spain one problem initially encountered by Jagdgruppe 88 was the difficulty of changing the direction of a Schwarm during combat. There were 600 yards between the innermost and outermost aircraft, and this meant that a radical change of direction could only be accomplished by a gradual change of course. Mölders overcame this problem by rediscovering the crossover turn, a maneuver developed in World War 1. Much practice was needed before a Schwarm could execute an efficient crossover turn, but a smooth finished product was aided by the distance between the aircraft. Four aircraft in near line abreast, spaced at 200-yard intervals, could cross over much more easily than five or seven flying in a stepped-up vic formation at 30-yard intervals.

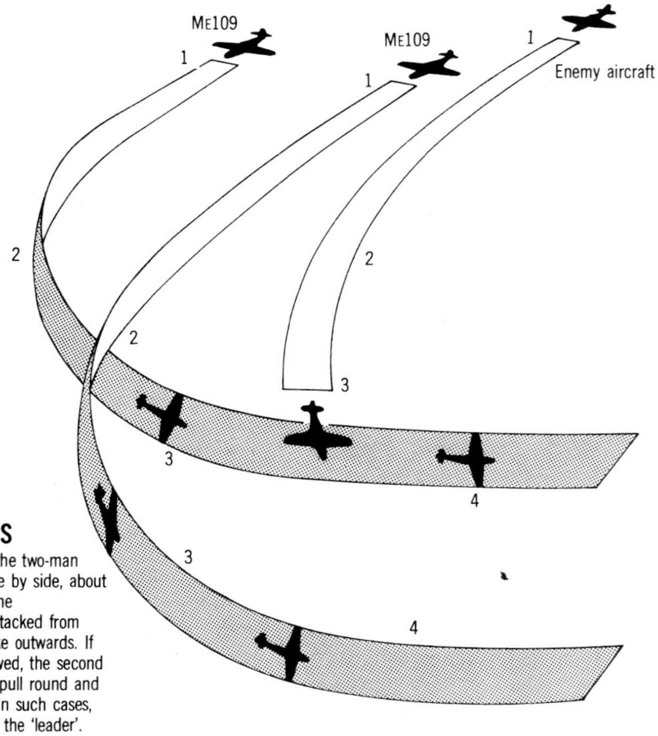

THE HUNTING MESSERSCHMITT

Mölders also helped to develop the 'Frei Jagd' – Free Hunt. Me109s would hunt alone, free from escorting bombers or protecting reconnaissance flights. This was the true role of the fighter pilot, the hunter, seeking his prey.

On August 23, 1938 Mölders led his squadron on a free hunt and found an SB-2 bomber. Despite good defensive fire from the bomber, Mölders closed in, setting the SB-2 on fire, but then he saw Ratas closing in. Pulling his 109 round into a tight turn he passed between two Ratas and dived to ground level and got away. (The SB-2 was later confirmed as destroyed.)

These Messerschmitts were initially the B, C and D Models, but in August 1939 came the E Model. (The 109E would later be prominent in the first year or so of WW2.) However, it was in a 'D' that Mölders went on to gain his final victories in the war before returning to Germany in late 1938. He had gained his 14 kills in less than six months. A hero of Germany and the Luftwaffe, a favorite

ME109 TACTICS

Developed in Spain, the two-man 109 element flew side by side, about 200 yards apart. If one Messerschmitt was attacked from behind, the pilot broke outwards. If the enemy pilot followed, the second 109 pilot could then pull round and behind the attacker. In such cases, neither 109 pilot was the 'leader'. This basic tactic is still used today in modern jet combat.

The tactics adopted by the Me109s in Spain proved invaluable to the Germans in World War 2. Because so few took part in Spain, the Condor Legion pilots flew in pairs rather than threes, which created the two-man 'Rotte' that proved so successful in the first year of WW2, and which was later copied by all of the major combatants.

of Göring, he was in the unique position of being certain that his opinions would be respected. More than just a successful pilot, Mölders was a thinking air tactician, a visionary with the personality of leadership that commanded attention. He studied his opponents' tactics in order to better his own. The Me109 was far better at height, so he would lead his pilots to lure the Republican fighters up to his level. He knew that if the Ratas did get above him, they would attack from the sun then form a circle and stay together for mutual support and also (because, unlike the 109s, they had no radios) keep within visual contact. Mölders countered this tactic by letting one pair of 109s attack while a second pair waited to pounce on any Rata pilot who broke away from the protection of the circle. He judged that the Republicans' tactics were primitive and that they invariably remained on their own side of the front lines and were not too aggressive. Few fighter pilots made such contributions to air fighting.

If the Germans had found the right way to fly and fight, the Spanish pilots had not. Both the Fiat and Russian Rata pilots still fought as individuals once the leader of a formation had led them to the enemy. They found that too many aircraft increased the dangers of collision and often pilots, after an initial clash, were more anxious to avoid hitting other aircraft than to shoot down opponents. The 109s of course had radio and their pilots were able to converse with each other. Other pilots could only dive into the enemy and begin the classic dogfight of 1918 vintage.

Yet dogfights were still successful for pilots who knew the ropes and had the courage to press on. For example, José Larios got a Chato on November 2, 1938 during a dogfight. Following the initial clash between Fiats, Ratas and Chatos, one of the latter came at him head-on, both pilots opening fire. As they passed each other both pulled round into a turning circle which tightened rapidly. After the second circle the Government pilot broke away and dived – the classic error. Larios followed it down (albeit a dangerous thing to do), set the Chato on fire and watched it spin into the ground. That afternoon Larios, in another air battle, shot down two more Chatos. The first was guilty of not keeping a sharp look-out above, the second one failed to watch behind while trying to shoot down another Fiat.

In time, however, the Spanish pilots had learned most of the pitfalls of air fighting. Certainly a good number of Spanish pilots on both sides achieved a large score of their opponents' aircraft shot down. On the Nationalist side twenty pilots became 'aces'.

Bombers too had developed. They were no longer predominantly biplanes, for all-metal fast monoplanes had begun to appear. The German Heinkel 111 and Dornier 17s both achieved a measure of success, and another new bomber type had seen action in the war. This was the Ju87 dive-bomber – the notorious 'Stuka' that was destined to be met in WW2 by the RAF, French and Russians in large numbers.

The Germans for their part had gained immeasurable experience in real air warfare. No maneuvers or training schools, however realistic their exercises, could compare with the real thing. Both bombers and fighters had progressed swiftly and by 1939 the reports sent back to Germany had enabled aircraft designers to accelerate their development programmes because of the refinements needed in combat conditions. Thus by the opening of the Second World War, Germany was well ahead in aircraft design and know-how. Experienced pilots who had flown in Spain became the young air leaders who would take the Luftwaffe into two years of victorious air battles at the start of WW2.

FIRST CLASHES IN A WORLD WAR
By the time the Spanish Civil War came to an end, the shadows of this wider conflict were stretching over Europe. Neither the politicians nor the public harbored any illusions about the role of air power in a future war, although the experience in Spain had been used to draw exaggerated conclusions about the effect of mass bombing raids on the

civilian populations of big cities. Nevertheless, it was in an atmosphere of almost eerie calm, tinged with uncertainty, that Londoners filed into their air raid shelters on the morning of September 3 when the sirens sounded only minutes after Prime Minister Neville Chamberlain's 11am radio announcement that Britain was at war with Germany.

Poland was first in the firing line. Early in the morning of September 1 a force of about 120 Heinkel He111s and Dornier Do17s, escorted by Messerschmitt Bf110 fighters, were reported by Polish ground observation posts to be heading for Warsaw. The Luftwaffe had made giant strides since the first German pilots went into action with the Condor Legion in 1936. It now possessed 3652 first-line aircraft comprising 1180 medium twin-engined bombers (mostly He111s and Do17s), 366 Stuka dive bombers, 1179 Me109 and Me110 fighters, 887 reconnaissance aircraft and 40 obsolescent ground-attack Hs123s. Transport was provided by 552 Ju52s, and there were 240 naval aircraft of various types. For the Polish campaign the Luftwaffe deployed 1581 of these aircraft.

German intelligence had estimated the front-line strength of the Polish air force at some 900 aircraft. In fact on 1 September the figure was nearer 300, made up of 36 P37 'Los' twin-engined medium bombers, 118 single-engined 'Karas' P23 light reconnaissance bombers and 159 fighters of the PZL P11c and P7 types. Light gull-winged monoplanes, with open cockpits and fixed undercarriages, they had been an advanced design in the early 1930s but were now hopelessly outclassed by the Luftwaffe's modern aircraft. Neither the PZL P11c nor the P7 could get high

enough to intercept the high-flying Do17 reconnaissance aircraft.

On the opening day of hostilities, however, the German attack came in at low level, aiming to knock out the Polish air force on the ground. The Luftwaffe failed to achieve its objective as during the last days of peace the Polish air force had dispersed its aircraft to a number of secret airfields. On the morning of September 1 not one Polish squadron remained at its pre-war base. As a result only 28 obsolete or unserviceable machines were destroyed at Rakowice air base.

The first air combat of WW2 took place during this action when Captain M Medwecki, commanding officer of 111/2 Fighter 'Dyon' was shot down by a Ju87 soon after he took off. Another pilot, Lieutenant W Gnys attacked the Ju87 and later shot down two low-flying Dornier 17s – the first Polish kills (see pages 72-73). Warsaw too was attacked by Luftwaffe bombers and the first to be shot down, a low-flying HE111, was destroyed by Lieutenant A Gabszewicz.

A more spectacular victory occurred later that day during a running air battle above Warsaw. Second Lieutenant Leopold Pamula shot down a He111 and a Ju87 but ran out of ammunition when the fighter escort came down on the P11s. Pamula rammed one Me109 before parachuting to safety. In the same battle Aleksander Gabszewicz had his P11 set on fire and had to bale out. On his way to the ground he was shot at by a fighter, an event experienced by other parachuting Polish pilots as the battles continued.

Despite the inferiority of the Polish fighters, they achieved at least a dozen victories on the first day of WW2, although they lost 10 fighters with another 24 damaged. This gave the Polish pilots some confidence. Even with their outmoded aircraft they seemed able to cope with the Germans. Their pilots found that one good method of attack was to dive head-on where a tail-chase was more or less out of the question. This collision-course tactic unnerved the German bomber pilots and was most effective in breaking up formations and inflicting damage on the Heinkels and Dorniers. The Polish fighter pilots unexpectedly found the twin-engined Me110s more dangerous than the single-engined Me109s. The first German kill of WW2 was in fact scored by a 110 pilot, Hauptmann Schlief, who shot down a P11 on September 1.

By mid-September German pincers from north and south had closed around Warsaw. Then on September 17 the Red Army intervened from the east, destroying the last Polish hopes. Warsaw surrendered on September 27 and the last

Poland's main front-line fighter in September 1939 was the PZL P11c. Obsolete in comparison with the German Me109s, it nevertheless gave a good account of itself before Poland fell. Here a P11 of 152 Squadron stands on Szpondowo landing strip, camouflaged with grass and straw against low-flying German aircraft.

STANISLAW SKALSKI

WHEN GERMANY INVADED Poland in 1939, Stanislaw F Skalski was in his early 20s, and a regular Polish Air Force officer, flying PZL fighters with 142 Squadron. On the second day of the war, he destroyed two Dornier 17s, and by the end of the brief Polish campaign was the top-scoring fighter pilot with 6¼ victories. He escaped to England, and joined 501 Squadron RAF in the Battle of Britain, scoring four victories. In June 1941 he was made a flight commander in 306 Polish Squadron and shot down five more German aircraft. He received the British DFC, having already won the Polish Silver Cross and Cross of Valor. He then had a spell as an instructor before commanding 317 Squadron in April 1942, winning a bar to his DFC.

In 1943 he led a group of experienced Polish fighter pilots into the Middle East, flying Spitfire IXs attached to 145 RAF Squadron. This 'Fighting Team' or 'Skalski's Flying Circus' as it was also called, operated during the final stages of the Tunisian campaign, Skalski adding three more personal kills. He was then given command of 601 Squadron – the first Pole to command an RAF fighter squadron. He received a second bar to his DFC as well as the Polish Gold Cross before returning to England.

As a Wing Commander in April 1944 he commanded 133 (Polish No 2) Fighter Wing, flying Mustangs, raising his score to 19 victories when he forced two FW190s to collide on June 24. He ended the war as a gunnery instructor, decorated additionally with the British DSO. Returning to Poland after the war he was imprisoned by the Russians; and, following his release, drove a taxi in Warsaw.

organized resistance collapsed in the first week of October. Despite the obsolescent equipment of the Polish air force, and its inferiority in numbers, it had inflicted heavy damage on the Luftwaffe, which had lost 285 aircraft with almost the same number so badly damaged as to be virtually non-effective. Polish fighter pilots were officially credited with 126 victories, which indicates modest claiming by them, for Polish anti-aircraft fire claimed less than 90, leaving an unclaimed deficit of some 70 aircraft. The last German aircraft shot down by a Pole in this campaign was claimed on September 17 by Second Lieutenant Tadeusz Koc. The highest-scoring Polish pilot was Second Lieutenant Stanislaw Skalski, with 6½ kills. The highest-scoring German, and Germany's first 'ace' of WW2, was Hauptmann Hannes Gentzen, who scored seven victories in a Me109D.

A total of 327 aircraft were lost by the Polish Air Force. Of these 260 were due to either direct or indirect enemy action with around 70 in air-to-air fighting; 234 aircrew were either killed or reported missing in action. One of the chief lessons learned by the German bomber force operating over Poland (and as the RAF bombers were soon to discover) was that they were susceptible to fighter attack. The immediate requirement, therefore, was for the bombers to have heavier defensive armament and additional armor protection for their crews.

FINLAND VERSUS RUSSIA

No sooner had Poland fallen than another conflict broke out, this time between Finland and Russia. This, called 'The Winter War', began on November 30. The Finnish Air Force had a variety of aircraft. Its fighters were 31 combat-ready Dutch built Fokker D.XXIs, a low-wing monoplane with fixed spatted undercarriage. It was armed with four 7.9-mm Browning machine-guns. Experienced pilots could handle the Fokkers fairly well although novice pilots needed to take care, especially when landing. Further fighter types were Gloster Gladiators from England and even Bristol Bulldogs, front-line RAF aircraft back in the early 1930s. Their bombers were British Bristol Blenheims.

On the Russian side were many of the types that had flown with the Republicans in Spain: Ratas, Chatos and SB-2 bombers. The Chatos, however, were soon replaced by the I-153 'Gull', another stable biplane type – extremely maneuverable and superior to the Finnish aircraft in dogfights. Like many bombers at this time, the Russian SB-2s were faster than most fighters, so

the Finnish pilots needed to use a rapid dive from height to catch them. (The 'SB' stood for 'Skorostnoi Bombardirovshchik' – Fast Bomber.)

Yet it was a 'Fast Bomber' that became the first victim of a Finnish fighter pilot on December 1, 1939. So excited was the Finnish pilot, Lieutenant Eino Luukkanen, flying a Fokker D.XXI, that he later admitted to not even thinking about tactics or firing angles – his reactions had been merely automatic.

He and his wingman dived after two SB-2s, Luukkanen placing himself behind one, exchanging fire with the Russian rear-gunner. He used no tactics, unlike the Russian pilot, who lowered his wheels as the Fokker closed in, causing Luukkanen to pull up to avoid a collision. The Finn was not deceived twice, throttling right back on his next attack. His fire knocked out one engine and the SB-2 crash-landed in a field.

On other occasions SB-2s were able to keep ahead of pursuing Fokkers and in a tail chase it took a patient and determined pilot to overhaul the Fast Bombers – especially after they were free of their heavy load.

Another problem in this area during the particularly cold winter of 1939–40 arose when trying to close with high-flying Russian bombers. At height these would leave vapour trails that could be seen from afar, but so too could those of the intercepting fighters; the bombers could thus either retreat or climb further.

On December 23 Luukkanen destroyed a Russian light observation plane, then, when leading his flight against some SB-2s, saw ten I-16s diving on them. Luukkanen turned to meet the danger, and opened fire head-on at the first I-16 he met. He claimed a probable as the fighter began a sporadic air battle before both sides broke off the action.

The Finns used the two-man flying unit, having already abandoned the close vic formations. In this they copied the Germans, with whom they became allied when the 'Continuation War' began in the early summer of 1941. The Winter War had ended on March 13, 1940, but the uneasy peace lasted only a little over a year. In the second war with the Russians Eino Luukkanen raised his score to 54 by August 1944.

Meanwhile, the war in Europe had begun, although slowly. Following the attack on Poland, the British and French declared war on Germany on September 3, 1939, then waited for their war to begin in earnest. The period from September 1939 to the early part of May 1940 became known as 'The Phoney War', as each side warily eyed the other, and waited.

POLAND EASTERN FRONT SEPTEMBER 1, 1939

P11c VERSUS
THE LUFTWAFFE

During the summer of 1939 the Polish air force found itself dealing with repeated violations of its airspace by photo-reconnaissance Do17s of the Luftwaffe, and the experience of the P11c, the principal Polish fighter, was not encouraging. Unable to reach either the speeds or the altitudes of the German intruders, the P11c was clearly obsolescent by this time, and the intruders were able to evade the Polish fighters' attempted interceptions virtually at will.

In preparation for the conflict which by this stage was widely anticipated, the Polish Air Force had been reorganized in the spring, with around a third of the available fighters concentrated around Warsaw and the remainder allocated to the various armies. By the end of August most of the operational aircraft had been dispersed to concealed airfields in preparation for the assault, which duly began before dawn on September 1.

Because of heavy fog on the opening day of the war, German plans were changed, with the intended mass attack on Warsaw postponed in preference to raids against airfields and other tactical targets. Flying low to locate the airfields, the bombers of Luftflotte 4, allocated to the advance against Kracow in the south, gave the defending fighters a chance at interception.

TIMETABLE

1 As dawn breaks, the P11cs of 121 Fighter Squadron, Dyon III/2, are scambled from their campaign base at Balice, 5 miles west of Kracow; led by Capt Mieczyslaw Medwecki, they are responding to raids on the airfields in the region by He111s of I and III/KG 4.

2 Still climbing, the Polish fighters are attacked by Ju87s of I/StG 2: given no time to react, Medwecki is hit and crashes in flames.

3 Lt Wladislaw Gnys turns on one of the attackers and fires; he stalls away before seeing the result of his action.

4 Regaining height, Gnys sees a pair of Do17Zs about 600 ft below him: the Dorniers, of KG 77, are flying at some 3000 ft on their way back from bombing Kracow.

5 Gnys dives on the tail of the rear bomber, opens fire with his four 7.7 mm machine-guns, then turns to engage the second enemy aircraft.

6 Again Gnys attacks from above and behind the Dornier, and again he turns away before seeing either aircraft's fate.

7 Both Do17s have been hit, and both crash near Zurada.

8 Returning to his base, Gnys sees a lone He111 and makes a quick firing pass, but finds he is out of ammunition.

9 Gnys returns to his base having scored the first aerial combat victory of World War 2.

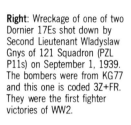

Right: Wreckage of one of two Dornier 17Es shot down by Second Lieutenant Wladyslaw Gnys of 121 Squadron (PZL P11s) on September 1, 1939. The bombers were from KG77 and this one is coded 3Z+FR. They were the first fighter victories of WW2.

CHAPTER SIX

DUELS OF DESPERATION

AT THE END OF THE FIRST World War the RAF was the largest air force in the world, with 2 7 333 officers (over half of whom were trained pilots) and 263 837 non-commissioned men. It had 22 171 aeroplanes in service and in store and the delivery of new aeroplanes was averaging 2668 a month.

With the arrival of peace came demobilization and the wholesale dismantling of Britain's air arm. By the beginning of 1920 27 087 officers, 21 259 cadets and 227 229 non-commissioned ranks had left the service. The wartime force of 188 squadrons had shrunk to a mere 33, of which eight were still in the process of formation. When the first postwar permanent commissions list was published in the summer of 1919, it contained the names of 1065 officers, one third of whom were of senior rank.

For the next 15 years the RAF was maintained at a very low level. Its principal operational activity – for most of the period almost its *raison d'être* – was the highly effective exercise of 'air control' in the Middle East and on India's Northwest Frontier. The biplane era was extended into the mid-1930s. On July 6, 1935 King George V attended an inspection of the air service at Mildenhall and then a fly past at Duxford. All 37 of the squadrons which took part in the day's activities were equipped with biplanes, and on special display was the Gloster F7/30, the prototype for the Gloster Gladiator.

It was only in the face of the massive German aircraft development and manufacturing programme that Britain in turn launched her own rearmament drive. The expenditure devoted to air defense rose from £39 million in 1936 to £88.5 million in 1937 and £111.5 million in 1938. By April 1937 the RAF had a paper strength of 100 squadrons in the United Kingdom and 26 based overseas. In addition there were another 26 squadrons in the Fleet Air Arm, which was shortly to come under Admiralty control.

Although the government had been jolted into increasing expenditure on air defense, it placed its faith in numbers rather than quality of aircraft. It was left to a few farsighted engineers and designers to provide the RAF with aircraft which were equal to the test which lay ahead of them. The Hawker Hurricane, designed by Sydney Camm, flew for the first time on November 6, 1935 and entered service with the RAF a year later. The Supermarine Spitfire, designed by Reginald J Mitchell, flew for the first time on March 5, 1936 and entered service with the RAF in August 1938, a month before the Munich crisis.

Left: The Hawker Hurricane saw the brunt of the early air fighting of WW2 over France, before flying alongside the Spitfire over Dunkirk and during the Battle of Britain. This picture is of two Mark 1 Hurricanes that served with 71 'Eagle' Squadron, 1940-41.

Right: Me109E – the personal mount of Major Helmut Wick when Kommodore of I/JG2, on October 6, 1940. On its tail are marked 42 of his eventual 56 victories. He was killed in action on November 28, 1940.

If nothing else, the much-maligned Munich Agreement bought the RAF vital breathing space. In September 1938 Fighter Command (which had been formed in July 1936) consisted of 573 obsolete biplanes and a mere 93 modern monoplane aircraft. Delivery of the Spitfire I had only just begun and the Hurricane lacked the gun heating to allow it to operate above 15 000 ft. By September 1939 the situation had improved. Of Fighter Command's 37 squadrons (still 16 fewer than its commander Air Chief Marshal Sir Hugh Dowding's minimum requirement of 53) 27 were equipped with Spitfires and Hurricanes. When war was declared in September 1939, the RAF flew machines to France as it had done in 1914, but unlike 1914 it did not send its total strength. The day before war was declared it sent ten Battle squadrons of No. 1 Group to form the Advanced Air Striking Force (AASF) – about 160 aircraft, followed by two Blenheim squadrons at the end of the month. It also sent four Hurricane squadrons, the latter forming the Air Component. The squadrons were Nos 1, 73, 85 and 87. None of these squadrons were immediately swamped by hordes of enemy aircraft, as was half-expected; instead, they and their French counterparts just waited. They had to wait until the early spring of 1940, meanwhile experiencing one of the worst winters of recent times.

The Luftwaffe, however, were not asleep and nor were Bomber Command in England. Both made exploratory raids upon each side's naval forces, neither wishing to risk bombing towns or civilians. The RAF dropped leaflets on cities and bombs on naval installations or ships around Kiel and Wilhelmshaven.

OPENING SHOTS

The first attack on Britain was by a force of Ju88 bombers of 1/KG30 on October 16, 1939, against shipping anchored near the Forth Bridge, Scotland. Flight Lieutenant G Pinkerton, flying a Spitfire of 603 Squadron, shot down the leading Ju88, the RAF's first kill over Britain since WW1; 602 Squadron, also in the air, sent another into the sea. There were other encounters over the winter months of 1939-40, mostly in the north of England or over Scotland. One victory, on February 22, 1940, involved Squadron Leader A D Farquhar DFC, Commanding Officer of 602 Squadron. He attacked and crippled a He111p near St Abbs Head, Berwickshire. With him was Flying Officer G V Proudman, flying one of the first Spitfires fitted with experimental 20 mm cannon (No L1007). As the crippled Heinkel began to go down, Farquhar ordered Proudman to try out his cannons, then watched as Proudman proceeded to knock large pieces off the German bomber – an impressive effect unobtainable with 0.303 shells. The bomber made a crash-landing on the Scottish coast and in true WW1 tradition Farquhar landed near by in order to stop the Germans setting fire to

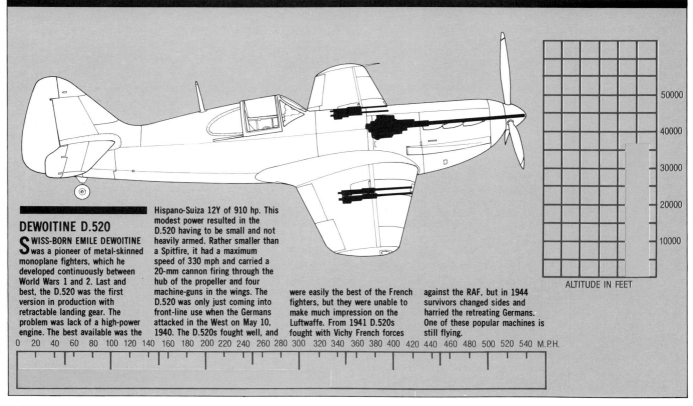

DEWOITINE D.520

SWISS-BORN EMILE DEWOITINE was a pioneer of metal-skinned monoplane fighters, which he developed continuously between World Wars 1 and 2. Last and best, the D.520 was the first version in production with retractable landing gear. The problem was lack of a high-power engine. The best available was the Hispano-Suiza 12Y of 910 hp. This modest power resulted in the D.520 having to be small and not heavily armed. Rather smaller than a Spitfire, it had a maximum speed of 330 mph and carried a 20-mm cannon firing through the hub of the propeller and four machine-guns in the wings. The D.520 was only just coming into front-line use when the Germans attacked in the West on May 10, 1940. The D.520s fought well, and were easily the best of the French fighters, but they were unable to make much impression on the Luftwaffe. From 1941 D.520s fought with Vichy French forces against the RAF, but in 1944 survivors changed sides and harried the retreating Germans. One of these popular machines is still flying.

ALTITUDE IN FEET

0   20   40   60   80   100 120 140 160 180 200 220 240 260 280 300 320 340 360 380 400 420 440 460 480 500 520 540 M.P.H.

50000
40000
30000
20000
10000

their aircraft. Unfortunately he ran onto soft ground and turned over, having to be rescued by the German crew – but ironically not before they had set fire to their Heinkel.

The Germans made their first claim of WW2 in the West on September 4 when Blenheims and Wellingtons raided Wilhelmshaven. Five Blenheims and two Wellingtons were lost, one Wellington falling to Feldwebel Alfred Held as the Luftwaffe's first victory over the RAF. On October 31 came the first victory for Hurricanes based in France. Pilot Officer P W O Mould attacked and shot down a Dornier 17, the first German aircraft shot down by the RAF over France since 1918. On November 2 Flight Lieutenant R Voase-Jeff of 87 Squadron shot down a He111, the first victory for 87 Squadron in WW2 and the first Heinkel to be brought down in France.

The RAF's approach to the conduct of the air war was colored by the assumption that in 1939 – as in 1914 – fighting between Germany and the Allies, when it came, would be in Belgium. The Maginot Line, the fortress system which ran along the Franco-German border, provided France with a seemingly impregnable defensive breakwater. It was less clearly grasped that this purely defensive posture also provided Germany with greater security. The Maginot breakwater would channel the flow of the German attack through Belgium, along whose frontier were stationed the 10 divisions of the British Expeditionary Force. If there was another stalemate, as there had been in 1915, each side's air forces would undoubtedly attack the other, the Luftwaffe flying bomber sorties from Germany, the RAF sending their bombers out from eastern England. With the distances involved, it followed that escort fighters would not be present, therefore opposing fighters would be used almost exclusively for aerial defense.

In this contest the RAF's Bomber Command was convinced that its fast modern bombers, 'bristling' with power-operated turrets would be able to fight their way to and from any target. The concept of the self-defending bombing force flying in tight formation – Douhet in action – was about to be put to the test.

On December 3 a force of 23 Wellingtons had been despatched on a shipping strike off Heligoland and sank a minesweeper. Although 12 of the Wellingtons returned with their bombs still on board, there were no losses. On December 14, a second operation was mounted against the

Schilling Roads, off Wilhelmshaven. The results were less encouraging. Five out of 12 Wellingtons from No. 99 Group, based at Mildenhall, were shot down and a sixth was blown up by its own bombs. Four days later another formation of 24 Wellingtons flew to the same target on an 'armed reconnaissance' mission. Two turned back with engine trouble and the rest pressed on. Although the Germans were at this time not as advanced in their radio location (later called radar) as the British, their Freya radar installations in the Heligoland area were operational. These detected the bomber force and pinpointed their progress as they turned in two groups to fly on a westerly course to the north of the Frisian Islands.

Luftwaffe Me110s and Me109s from bases in northern Germany intercepted the RAF aircraft over the sea. During a running fight 11 Wellingtons were shot down, a 12th later ditching during its return across the North Sea. Six more were so badly shot-up that they either crashed or crash-landed upon reaching England. The other five had all been damaged. The Germans lost three Me109s with three more and two Me110s damaged (another seven fighters had very slight damage). The Germans had originally claimed 38 Wellingtons shot down, later revised to 26 or 27 (still too high). For their part, the RAF gunners claimed 12 German fighters.

THE BOMBERS' FAILURE
Despite exaggerated claims on both sides – a feature that would continue throughout the war, the unescorted Wellingtons had been beaten. The bomber had not got through. Lacking armor plating and self-sealing fuel tanks, the Wellingtons were fatally vulnerable to beam attacks from the cannon-armed fighters. When the fuel tank in the port wing was hit the Wellington immediately caught fire. Those that did not burn lost huge quantities of fuel which poured through the holes punched by cannon fire in the tanks. A priority programme was immediately put in hand to fit extra armor to the fuel tanks of all Bomber Command aircraft; and all further daylight operations by Hampdens, Whitleys and Wellingtons were suspended.

The RAF now began to consider the effect of German air attacks in force against England. Their training and tactics evolved during the late 1930s and, revised only slightly to allow for the higher speeds and greater fire-power of their new monoplane fighters, were in the text books; and superb *theories* they were too. For instance, the thinking was that now the era of the comparatively slow biplane was fast receding, the dogfight was a thing of the past. In the RAF training manual dated 1938, the chapter on 'Air Fighting Tactics' quoted: 'MANEUVER AT *high speeds in air fighting is not now practicable, because the effect of gravity on the human body during rapid changes of direction at high speed causes a temporary loss of consciousness.'*

While this last fact was not in doubt, it had in reality very little effect on the pilots themselves. Pilots did 'black out' for a few moments as blood drained from the brain in a high-speed turn, but it lasted only momentarily and the subconscious continued to control the aircraft in those seconds. But this theorizing led the fighter tactics doctrine along certain defined lines. The manual continued: 'SINGLE-SEATER FIGHTER *attacks at high speed must be confined to a variety of attacks from the general direction of astern.'*

It was obvious to those who prepared for Britain's defense in the years of peace that the only likely threat would come from bombers flying from Europe (Germany) across the North Sea. Unlike the airships and long-range German bombers of WW1, these would be liable to interception by both RAF fighters based in eastern England and by Allied fighters in France or Belgium. Because of the distances involved they would be unable to have escorting fighters to protect them, just as RAF Bomber Command would be flying far beyond the range of British fighters. The only chance of escort came from possible two-engined fighters that could carry more fuel to extend their flying radius. The difficulty was that with two engines and the weight of this extra fuel they would be no match for defending short-range single-seaters and therefore far more vulnerable than the bombers they were trying to protect.

RAF DEFENSIVE TACTICS
On this basis, RAF Fighter Command developed its defensive tactics.

FIGHTER COMMAND ATTACK NUMBER ONE
With the basic fighter section being a vic of three aircraft, the leader, upon sighting an enemy bomber, would order his two wingmen into line astern behind him. Diving to the attack the three fighters would drop just below the height of the bomber to avoid return fire from the enemy rear-gunner. The fighters would close and in turn open

fire from about 400 yards and then one by one would break away outwards and then down. They would then turn and regain height behind the enemy aircraft in order to reposition themselves for a possible further attack.

Fortunately for RAF fighters during the war, German bombers never did position a rear-gunner in the extreme tail as RAF bombers did. The Germans relied on a dorsal gunner positioned roughly in line with the trailing edge of the bomber's wings. When it became apparent that opposing fighters would make their attacks in a shallow upward curve from below and then break out and down, the Germans added a ventral gun position immediately below the dorsal gun. All guns were virtually on free-standing mounts and not in power-operated turrets as in RAF bombers. The exception in the RAF was its twin-engined Handley Page Hampden, but the others – the Whitley, Wellington and later the Stirling, Manchester, Halifax and Lancaster – all had two or three such turrets. But they lacked any form of ventral gun – which was perhaps unfortunate.

FIGHTER COMMAND ATTACK NUMBER TWO

In this tactic, two three-plane sections spot an enemy bomber formation and the leader of the six fighters orders his pilots into line astern. Positioning themselves behind the target bombers and slightly below, the leading section attacks the right flank bomber with the second section going for the left flank bomber. As the attack goes in, the sections, which should ideally be separated fore and aft by about 200 yards, form rear echelon. The leading three go into a starboard echelon, the second three into port echelon. After the attack, the leading section breaks to the right and down, the second section to the left and down. They all then pull up and round for subsequent attacks.

FIGHTER COMMAND ATTACK NUMBER THREE

This tactic was very similar to Number Two, except that it was designed to attack a larger number of bombers with perhaps a squadron strength of four vics of three fighters. It was more complicated and as the fight began the section would endeavour to attack simultaneously from the rear, beam and rear quarter.

All three attacks were only really effective if the German pilot obligingly kept on a straight and level course without taking too much evasive action. Only in this way could a text-book attack be made to look like a text-book example! On early Fighter Affiliation exercises, when Bomber Command would put up a target bomber for Fighter Command to practice their attack techniques, the bomber would just cruise along smoothly. The three or six Spitfires or Hurricanes came curving down, slipped below the target then closed in before winging over and down. It looked splendid but was almost totally useless.

AIR WAR IN FRANCE

Fighter Command's conviction that its pilots needed to be equipped to oppose only German bombers seemed to be confirmed in France in the first eight months of the war. Over the winter of 1939-40 the Hurricanes of the Air Component and those attached to the AASF, met, for the most part, lone German aircraft flying reconnaissance missions over the Maginot Line, or along the Belgian border. Like the French fighters, the British did meet German fighters too, but usually these were flying fighter patrols and were not a direct escort to their bombers.

Both Allied and German air leaders had by this time begun to take a little more seriously the possible disadvantage of their fighters' limited range of action. Both sides had twin-engined fighters, the most advanced being Germany's Me110. It had already proved itself in action over Poland and against British Wellingtons in December 1939. The Luftwaffe, and especially its commander, Hermann Göring, had high hopes of its potential. The French had the Potez 631, but the RAF had only the fighter version of the Bristol Blenheim which was no real challenge in an air battle. As the war progressed, improved twin-engined types began to appear while single-engined machines later carried long-range fuel-tanks to extend their combat radius. Early 1940 knew none of this.

Paul Richey was in France with No. 1 Squadron at this time as a young pilot officer. He was later to write a world-famous book *Fighter Pilot* on his experiences in the Battle of France. He told me: '*B*EFORE THE WAR WE HAD THIS *rather rigid air drill, with rigid attacks laid down, Number One Attack, Number Two Attack, and so on. However, when we got to France we learnt a lot from the French. They used to fly in much looser formations than we did. We flew in threes, the French flew in fives. We had a flight of six in two sections of three, all flying more or less straight and level in open formation, 50 to 100 yards apart. The French used to fly a flight of five, three aircraft 50-100 yards apart, flying straight* *and level, and two weavers astern and above of them. We picked this up from the French and used it in France and as a result we were not bounced once.'*

Paul Richey shot down the squadron's first Me109 on March 29, 1940. While on patrol near Metz, in company with two other Hurricanes he saw bursting anti-aircraft fire and flew to investigate. Then two Me109s appeared above, and as they climbed towards them three more suddenly dived in their direction. Richey continued in a left-hand turn, watching his tail as a 109 closed in and began to fire at long range. He twisted his Hurricane round and under the 109. Then the 109 roared over his cockpit, having lost sight of the Hurricane in the maneuver. The 109 pilot pulled up in front of Richey, stall-turned to the left and dived, with Richey on his tail. The Messerschmitt was much faster than the Hurricane and Richey could not get within range, but after a descent of some 10 000 feet the 109 throttled back as it climbed again. This allowed Richey to gain on it and when he was in range he opened fire. The 109 streamed smoke then went into a vertical spiral, to fall inside German territory. Not till years later did he discover the identity of the German pilot who was with 111/JG53, led by Werner Mölders.

On the same day another member of 1 Squadron, Flight Lieutenant Johnny Walker claimed the first Me110 shot down by an Allied fighter pilot. Walker and his two wingmen fought nine 110s north of Metz, Walker staying behind one despite some violent maneuvers before it fell to the ground.

The Phoney War came to an end on May 10, 1940 with the German invasion of Holland and Belgium and it is possible to pinpoint the precise moment when the Battle of France was lost – at 3pm on May 15 when the first German troops crossed the Meuse. The British evacuation from Dunkirk began 11 days later on May 26.

In that short period the four RAF Hurricane squadrons, supported and reinforced by other Hurricane and even Gladiator squadrons from England, fought themselves to a standstill. The damage which they and the French Air Force inflicted upon the Luftwaffe was enormous, but eventually numbers overwhelmed them and their bases were gradually overrun by the speed of the German assault.

Whatever the tactics employed by the fighter pilot, the paramount necessity was to be able to shoot straight. Strangely enough, this was lacking in a number of pilots in the early war years. They discovered that like the pilots of WW1 they had to get in close. Peacetime thinking that the firing-range should commence at 400 yards was very rapidly altered in the event of active combat. Dennis David, who was a pilot in 87 Squadron in France in 1940, told me on one occasion that he soon realized that he was not a particularly good shot. He was, however, a good pilot, so quickly realized that he would have to use his flying skill to get into such a close firing position that he could not miss. Using these tactics he shot down a dozen German aircraft over France, raising this total to 19 by the end of the Battle of Britain.

By the time the evacuation of the British Army at Dunkirk had begun on (officially) May 26, the

The Supermarine Spitfire, along with the Hurricane, helped defeat the Luftwaffe in the Battle of Britain. Its various Marks remained in front-line service throughout the war and saw action on all major fronts. This picture shows Spitfire Is of 610 Squadron on patrol during the Battle of Britain.

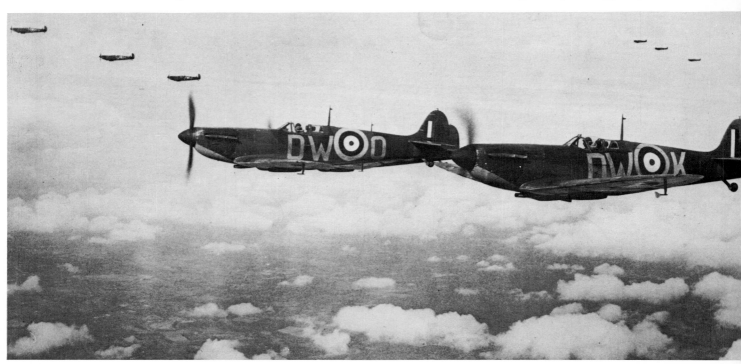

HAWKER HURRICANE I versus MESSERSCHMITT Me110C-4

SIR SYDNEY CAMM DESIGNED the Hurricane in 1935. He made things simple and tough. Structurally the Hurricane was old-fashioned, with fabric covering and a fixed-pitch wooden propeller; on the other hand it had a monoplane wing into which the landing gear retracted. From the start it handled well, and thanks to the nerve of the Hawker management in laying down a production line of 1000 before they had a single order, the RAF had plenty at the start of World War 2. Scores were lost in France, but in the Battle of Britain Hurricanes shot down more enemy aircraft than all other aircraft and anti-aircraft guns combined. It was easy to fly, easy to aim at an enemy and easy to repair. Many of its victims were Me110C series escort fighters. Much more modern than the Hurricane in most ways, they were planned to spearhead the Luftwaffe's onslaughts. In the Battle of Britain they proved unwieldy, and needed escorts themselves! Most ended up as night-fighters defending the Reich.

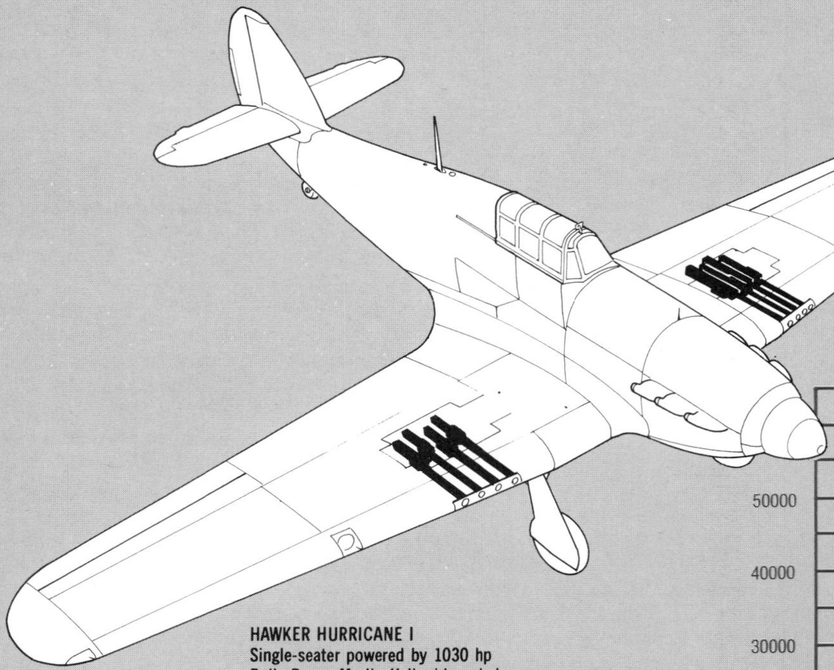

HAWKER HURRICANE I
Single-seater powered by 1030 hp Rolls-Royce Merlin II liquid-cooled V-12 engine, giving speed of about 310 mph, ceiling of 34 000 ft and range of 460 miles. The revolutionary armament comprised eight 0.303 in Browning guns in the wings. Altogether 14 533 Hurricanes were built.

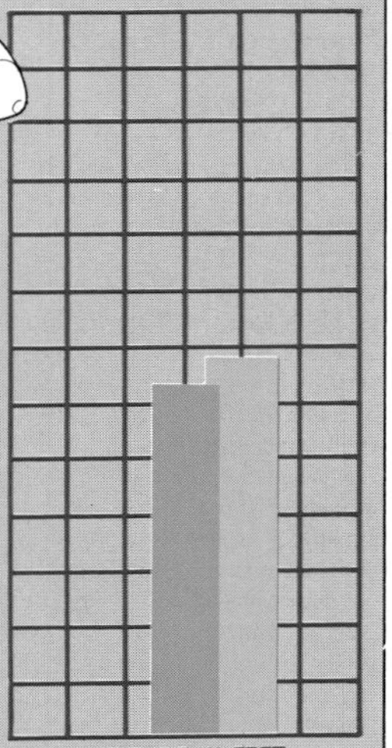

50000
40000
30000
20000
10000

ALTITUDE IN FEET

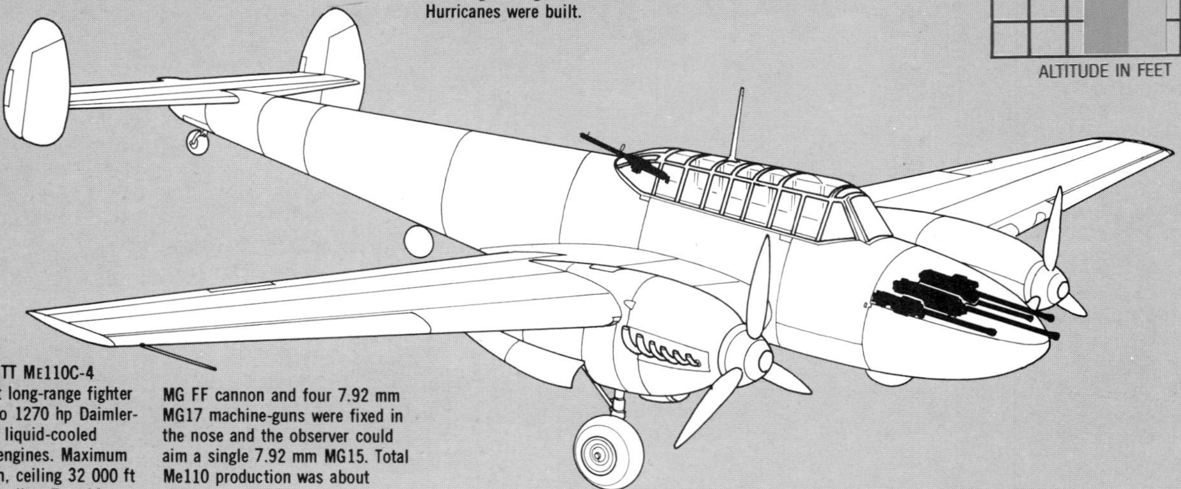

MESSERSCHMITT Me110C-4
Two/three-seat long-range fighter powered by two 1270 hp Daimler-Benz DB 601N liquid-cooled inverted V-12 engines. Maximum speed 349 mph, ceiling 32 000 ft and range 680 miles. Two 20 mm MG FF cannon and four 7.92 mm MG17 machine-guns were fixed in the nose and the observer could aim a single 7.92 mm MG15. Total Me110 production was about 6050.

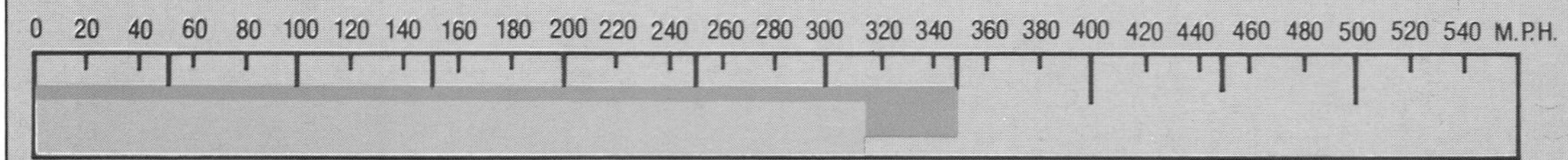

0 20 40 60 80 100 120 140 160 180 200 220 240 260 280 300 320 340 360 380 400 420 440 460 480 500 520 540 M.P.H.

EDGAR KAIN

THE FIRST 'ACE' OF THE ROYAL Air Force in WW2 was a New Zealander, Flying Officer E J 'Cobber' Kain, born on June 27, 1918. He learned to fly before coming to England to join the RAF, which he did on his second attempt in 1937, having failed his medical the previous year. When war began, 73 Squadron went immediately to France and Kain opened the squadron's account on November 8 when his Hurricane shot down a high-flying Dornier 17, and claimed another Dornier on November 23.

The severe winter of 1939-40 restricted much of the air activity during this 'Phoney War' period, but in March 1940 both sides began to fly more sorties. On March 2, Kain and his wingman chased a He111 towards Germany when they were in turn attacked by some Me109 fighters. In the resulting dogfight, the New Zealand pilot shot down one 109 in flames. Another 109 shot up his engine, yet he managed to glide down to a safe landing. He was awarded the DFC. A few days later he brought his score to five, becoming the first RAF 'ace' of WW2. When the German attack in the West commenced on the morning of May 10, 1940, the RAF Hurricane squadrons in France bore the brunt of the air assault. Kain shot down a Dornier 215 on the first day, another on May 11, and also damaged a 109. On May 12 he claimed an Hs126 observation aircraft, and his 10th victory, a 109, went down on May 13.

By May 27 'Cobber' Kain had shot down 17 German aircraft. He was one of the few survivors of the original pilots who had flown to France the previous September. He was awarded a bar to his DFC and on June 6 was ordered back to England. As he took off, he gave spectators a show of aerobatics, crashed and died instantly.

whole of 11 Group of Fighter Command, covering south-east England, had been alerted. This group had not only to protect the men awaiting rescue from the port and later the beaches of Dunkirk but also to cover and escort the ships that plied between France and England, taking the rescued soldiers home.

THE RAF'S HARD LESSON

The German *blitzkrieg* had been bad enough for the pilots of Fighter Command and indeed the light and medium bombers of Bomber Command in France. Fairey Battles and Bristol Blenheims had been shot out of the sky by a buoyant Luftwaffe as they tried vainly to stem the German onslaught. Suddenly, above Dunkirk, all their tactical thinking and all their peacetime training were found wanting.

True, over Dunkirk Fighter Command pilots were fighting a battle in a way and in conditions that were very different from what they had prepared for, but their problems were many. For one thing they were flying across the English Channel, having to cover perhaps 60 miles or more to get to their patrol areas. This was very different from a defensive sortie above London or the east coast of England.

British radar, while more advanced than Germany's, was still in its infancy and, over France, RAF fighters were almost outside its modest range and were also beyond the control of ground radio communication. Fighters damaged in combat, or pilots having to bale out, had to come down over a hostile country or a battle zone.

Height has always been significant in air combat, but the anomaly over Dunkirk was that to be able to engage German dive-bombers and strafing fighters, the Spitfires and Hurricanes had to be at low level and thus were vulnerable from above. As this problem unfolded, the RAF fighters began to patrol higher; this left the beaches vulnerable and led to the belief among soldiers and sailors that the RAF were not protecting them sufficiently.

Yet another major factor was numerical strength. The Germans were able to put large numbers of aircraft into the Battle of Dunkirk. Fighter Command was small in comparison and 11 Group, bearing the brunt of the battle, had an average of only 16 squadrons available on any one day. Indeed, only 31 squadrons passed through Keith Park's 11 Group during the period of the battle. With this small force he had to cover Dunkirk through the hours of daylight and with a force reduced by battle damage.

Because the British fighters were constantly outnumbered, Park was forced after the first few days to group squadrons together in wings for some form of self-protection, but this in itself caused problems. Firstly it created gaps in air cover because his 16 available squadrons, flying in two or three squadron wings, could give less overall coverage than the same number flying one or two squadrons at a time in rotation. Secondly, as Fighter Command tactics did not provide for large formations flying together, they were not prepared or trained for it. Therefore, more often than not the leader of the 'wing' formation merely led the squadrons to the French coast, where they split up and acted on their own, and were rarely co-ordinated in any offensive or defensive battle plan.

Without exception all squadron and flight commanders were peacetime airmen who had been promoted to these positions through length of service and leadership potential. None, of course, had seen action. They were quite happy, therefore, to fly out in their peacetime formations of tight vics of three aircraft, which the Germans had discarded more than two years earlier in Spain. The practise of flying in sections of three had part of its basis in the need for a leader to be able to take his squadron up through cloud that often prevailed over Britain. With four section-leaders each having two wingmen tucked in close beside him, 12 fighters had far more chance of breaking cloud without everyone having been scattered about as the pilots spread out to avoid colliding with an unseen colleague. Tight vics of three also aided discipline in the air; the leader could look back and see at a glance anyone who was straggling and not keeping a neat formation. There was another factor: a number of pilots who flew during that period have said to me that they believed the three-plane vics were retained for so long because in the air 'they looked nice'.

They were, in fact, a death-trap. The wingman (two of them in each three-man vic) was so busy keeping station and ensuring that he did not run into his leader that his opportunity to search the sky for hostile aircraft was vastly reduced. The leader, too, while his job was also to search the sky, often relied on his wingmen to protect the rear, so that in fact almost nobody was regularly looking behind – from where the danger would strike. The leader too could make no sudden movements without giving his men a warning in case one or other of them should collide with him, so valuable seconds were lost in starting a sudden maneuver.

Because of this rigid and inflexible vic formation, German Me109 pilots were able to

'SAILOR' MALAN

BORN IN SOUTH AFRICA IN 1910, Adolph Gysbert Malan served in the Merchant Navy in his youth, and did not join the RAF in England until 1935. By the time WW2 began he was a flight commander with 74 Squadron, flying Spitfires, and saw action for the first time above the beaches of Dunkirk, in May 1940. Within a few days he had shot down five enemy aircraft and won the DFC.

In early June 1940 he shot down two He111 bombers which brough him a bar to his DFC and instant fame. During the Battle of Britain, he brought his score to 14 and, after the winter fighting with Me109s, raised this to 18. In 1941 'Sailor' Malan commenced a phenomenal rate of scoring, flying at the head of the Biggin Hill Fighter Wing of three squadrons – 74, 92 and 609. Between March and July 1941, Malan destroyed 14 Me109s, and damaged a further ten, for which he received the DSO and bar. His final score was 35 destroyed or shared destroyed, seven probables and 14 damaged, making him the highest-scoring pilot of the RAF in Europe, until 1944 when Johnny Johnson topped this score.

Malan was an innovative tactician, and his 'Ten Rules of Air Fighting', published in 1942, were distributed to all fighter units in the RAF. He later commanded RAF Station Biggin Hill, and held commands at the time of D-Day. After the war he returned to South Africa, and died in 1963.

inflict losses on RAF squadrons, who simply had no idea that they were there until the German pilots opened fire. The number of squadron, flight and section leaders lost, not to mention ordinary squadron pilots, during the second half of May was a crippling blow to an already outnumbered Fighter Command.

Roland Beaumont, a pilot with 87 Squadron stationed at Lille Marque, recalled an incident during the Battle of France: '*My third combat was a classic example of the weakness of inflexibility. We were now operating full-time from the grass field at Lille Marque and had been ordered off at three-squadron strength to patrol the ground battle area at Valenciennes at 10 000 feet. We made a fine sight as 36 Hurricanes formed up in the late afternoon sun in three squadron boxes, line-astern, four sections of vic-threes to a squadron. I was flying No. 2 in the right-hand section of 87 Squadron, leading the Wing, and it made one feel quite brave looking back at so many friendly fighters. And then without fuss or drama about 10 Messerschmitt 109s appeared above the left rear flank of our formation out of some high cloud. The Wing leader turned in towards them as fast as a big formation could be wheeled, but the 109s abandoned close drill and, pulling their turn tight, dived one after the other on to the tail sections of the Wing. Their guns streamed smoke and one by one four Hurricanes fell away. None of us fired a shot – some never even saw it happen – and the enemy disengaged, while we continued to give a massive impression of combat strength over the battle area with four less Hurricanes than when we started. We had more than three times the strength of the enemy on this occasion and had been soundly beaten tactically by a much smaller unit, led with flexibility and resolution.*'

SPITFIRE MEETS 109

The first Spitfire versus Me109 clash came on May 23, 1940. It came during a dramatic rescue of the commanding officer of 74 Squadron, who had been forced to land on an airfield in France when his engine was damaged. Fifty-four Squadron, which shared RAF Hornchurch with 74 Squadron, flew a two-seat Miles Master aircraft to France escorted by two of its Spitfires. These were flown by Pilot Officer Alan Deere and Pilot Officer Johnny Allen.

Over the airfield, which was all but abandoned by this stage, the Master went down to land while Deere circled above and Allen climbed to keep guard above some cloud. No

sooner had the two-seater landed than Allen reported Me109s and that he was engaging. As he battled with the 109s above, Deere lost height above the airfield but then a 109 dived out of the low cloud, making towards the taxiing two-seater. It flew right across Deere's nose and Deere opened fire. The 109 pilot pulled away rapidly but Deere turned his Spitfire after it, fired again and sent it crashing into the edge of the sea.

Climbing to help Allen, Deere ran into two 109s, knocked pieces off one then fought the second until his ammunition ran out. Then he decided to see if he could take on the 109! For several minutes he dived, turned and chased it before commonsense urged his getaway. However, he had convinced himself that the Spitfire was a match for the Messerschmitt, and except for certain parameters, was even superior to it. This stood him in good stead in later battles and Al Deere ended the war with 22 victories, and as a proven Wing Leader and Air Commander.

The Me109 pilots fought in pairs over Dunkirk while the RAF flew in threes. Oddly enough, there are any number of personal combat reports of this period where the RAF pilots record that the Germans too were flying in vics of three. This was pure auto-suggestion: the RAF flew in threes, so when sighting German fighters in groups they believed they saw 109s in similar formations. No one knows who first saw or realized that the Germans' basic unit was a pair and their basic section two pairs.

Nevertheless, the RAF did have some tactical, progressive thinkers within its ranks. A number of the up-and-coming leaders and air fighters, even the innovators, discovered for themselves the inflexibility of their vic formations and the need for a more open formation.

Flight Lieutenant A G 'Sailor' Malan of 74 Squadron discovered over Dunkirk the need for change and began altering the way the squadron flew during that period. RAF squadrons flew in sections, each given a color for quick radio identification. The leading section was usually known as Red Section (eg Red 1, Red 2, 3, 4). Others would be Yellow, Green, Blue, etc. If still flying in vics of three they would be Red 1, Red 2 and Red 3. Each squadron would also have a radio call sign in order to identify the squadron to a ground controller, ie: a call name might be 'Brutus'. Thus the leader would be called and in turn identify himself as 'Brutus Red One.'

Malan had the sections break into pairs when they encountered German fighters. On May 27 he led 74 Squadron on a patrol between Calais and Dunkirk, spread out between 2000 and 15 000 ft.

Near Dunkirk several high-flying Me109s were seen, so Malan ordered his men into pairs and they began to climb. He attacked a 109 while still on the climb, the German pilot rolling into a dive. Malan followed with his wingman and his fire set the 109 smoking.

The Spitfires had become separated in this fight but Malan joined up with his Red 4 and despite their fuel running low they attacked two sections of Dornier bombers, going for the leader of the rear vic of three. To spread the bombers' return fire, Malan attacked the Dornier from the right flank, the other Spitfire pilot from the left. Malan aimed at the Dornier's port engine which he set on fire. As he broke away and came round for another pass, he saw that Red 4 was streaming glycol, having been hit by return fire.

A WW2 fighter with a liquid-cooled in-line engine could not last long with a ruptured coolant tank. It took only a minute or two before the engine overheated and stopped, with the added risk of fire if petrol lines had also been damaged. It was a problem with fighters particularly, as the glycol tank was always at the front of the aircraft, cooled by the air intake which also needed to be at the front. It required only one bullet to pierce or smash the coolant unit, and let out the glycol (the equivalent of a car's anti-freeze water) for the fighter to be out of the battle. It was, therefore, very vulnerable to fire from a rear-gunner in a German bomber.

On this occasion Malan's Red 4 crash-landed on the beach at Dunkirk and returned by ship. The Dornier had to be left only damaged. Later that afternoon Malan led his men into several Dorniers off Dunkirk and with no Me109s around he took his section into a Number One Attack in true text-book style, except that he had two pairs rather than a vic of three. He and his Red Three – Pilot Officer Hugh Dowding, son of Sir Hugh Dowding, Commander in Chief of Fighter Command – selected one. They made sweeping passes firing from 250 to 50 yards, while the Dornier pilot headed down to ground level to prevent the Spitfire getting beneath him. Despite the bomber's burning engine and smoke coming from the fuselage, they eventually had to let it go after they had chased it some distance inland over France.

THE NOT-SO DEFIANT

Another fighter with RAF Fighter Command was the Boulton Paul Defiant, a two-seat single-engined monoplane. The Defiant had been designed to Air Ministry Specification F.9/35, which called for a two-seater fighter in which the entire armament was concentrated in a power-operated centrally mounted turret permitting a 360 degree radius of fire in the hemisphere above the aircraft. The theory was that the Defiant would fly in formation with enemy bombers and destroy from below, where they were unable to bring their guns to bear. No forward-firing guns were fitted on the Defiant, which prevented the pilot from engaging in a private war of his own. Nor, it seems, was any thought given to the Defiant's own vulnerability to fire from below.

It first saw action with 264 Squadron over Dunkirk and, as it resembled a Hurricane, its four rearward guns gave a nasty shock to a number of Me109 pilots, attacking what they thought was a normal fighter formation. Indeed, what the Germans thought was a perfect target was really a Defiant formation waiting for the attackers to

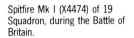

Spitfire Mk I (X4474) of 19 Squadron, during the Battle of Britain.

get within range of their guns. Once the German fighter pilots became aware of the danger, they no longer attacked them from the rear. The heavy Defiant was no match for the nimble 109 and was very soon withdrawn from front-line use, and relegated to night-fighting. Nevertheless the Defiant, during its period over Dunkirk, had of necessity got its tactics down to a fine art, based on keen co-operation between pilot and gunner as the pilot needed to put the aircraft into the best firing position for his guns to be effective.

Against unescorted bombers they would swoop down and under the bombers, in vics if possible, and as the bombers came in sight above them, the gunners would open up on them. It was a nasty experience for the German pilot and crew suddenly to have a devastating burst from four 0.303 guns smashing up through the floor of the cockpit or slamming into their engines and wing tanks. Another Defiant tactic was to fly ahead and below the bombers and let the bombers overtake them. This was fine if the bombers did that, but there was a certain naiveté in it. If the bombers saw them to be Defiants they would not fly over them and if they thought they were Hurricanes would they likewise ignore the danger and just fly on? Another Defiant tactic was to fly parallel to the bomber and fire sideways – a success only if the bomber kept straight!

The difficulty encountered by Fighter Command having to operate over the French coast and some distance from their home bases is a fact taken for granted today. Yet, as explained earlier, this was a position almost undreamed of by the theorists in the peacetime expansion of the late 1930s. After Dunkirk and the subsequent loss of all France to the invading Germans, Britain now faced an airborne threat not only from distant Germany, but from just across the English Channel. With Norway also occupied, the Luftwaffe could also raid northern Britain from bases on the Norwegian coast.

This possibility had not occurred to the leaders of Fighter Command in late 1939. Now, it was a fact. Germany had the use of captured airfields along the whole coastline from Norway to Cherbourg in France. This meant not only that the Luftwaffe would be able to strike Britain from any point, or from a number of points simultaneously, along that coastline, but also that the RAF would be thinly stretched to protect Britain, from Scotland in the north, to London in the south, and Wales in the west. It also meant that the Luftwaffe, certainly that portion based in France, would be able to use short-range fighters – Me109s – as both an escort to its bombers or to fly

fighter sweeps over vast areas of southern England. With France lost, the tactical and strategic planning of Fighter Command needed complete revision.

NEW GERMAN STRATEGY

The Luftwaffe too had to replan its strategy. Essentially the Luftwaffe was a support weapon for its ground forces. The German *blitzkrieg* method was to blast a way through enemy troops, armor and fortifications with its dive-bombers in order for the ground troops to advance and mop up. With attention now turned towards Britain, its aircraft would need to obtain air superiority so that an invasion by sea could take place without catastrophic casualties.

In several respects, Fighter Command was in a better position to defend the British Isles than the Luftwaffe was to attack. As was to be proved conclusively throughout the summer of 1940, Britain's radar was to be a deciding factor. The Germans were altogether unable to understand how the Spitfires and Hurricanes regularly succeeded in intercepting their aircraft.

Development of radar (initially known as Radio Direction Finding or RDF and Radio Location) had made great strides in the late 1930s. By 1937 results of tests from early RDF installations were making contact pick-ups at ranges of 100 miles and trained operators could identify mock formation raids. By the beginning of 1940 nearly 30 RDF stations had been set up along Britain's coast line from Land's End to Newcastle. Each site consisted of a number of 350-foot transmitter aerial masts and 250-foot receiver masts, a transmitter and a receiver office where the radar screens were situated.

From these CH (Chain Home) stations, radio signals were transmitted in all directions from the aerials and, should an aircraft be in the range of the transmitter, a signal would be reflected back. Picked up by the receiver aerials a plot would show on a cathode ray tube in the receiver office. By measuring, by calibration on the tube, the elapsed time between transmission and the returned signal, the range of the aircraft could be determined. Using similar methods height and location were established. This information, quickly fed to the fighter sector stations by way of a filter room, gave the fighter controllers a fairly accurate picture of all aircraft in the air covered by the RDF network.

Germany too had its own radar equipment but it was not as advanced as Britain's. Yet the Germans felt certain that Britain was well behind them in radar development.

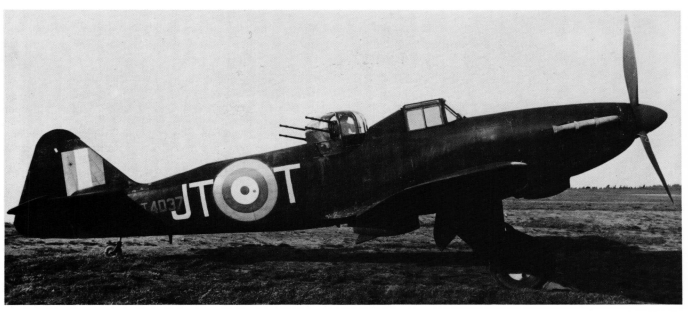

Relegated as a day fighter, the Defiant was later used as a night fighter. One serious drawback was that the pilot did not have a single forward-firing gun, so he had always to maneuver his aircraft in order for his gunner to fire at the enemy.

The RAF was also fighting over its own territory so that a bale-out or crash-landing meant only the loss of an aircraft, not a pilot. Its chief disadvantage was in being constantly outnumbered. The German bombers were numerous, and their defensive fire was a constant threat. The Me109s were deadly, escorting above and behind the bombers, always in a position to pounce from a shimmering blue sky and a blazing summer sun. The Germans too still had a certain amount of faith in their Me110 long-range fighter. With the scale of operations undertaken during what later became known as the Battle of Britain, the disadvantages of the short-range Me109 became evident. As a fighter it was, like all fighters, basically designed as a free-flying weapon, a hunter. Restricted to escorting slow, lumbering bombers, its full potential was hampered.

The RAF fighters, for their part, were doing the exact job for which they had been designed – high-speed fighting and interception. The only difference was that they had to deal with enemy fighters rather than be free to attack a more substantial bomber.

BATTLE FOR BRITAIN

The Battle of Britain was fought between July and October 1940 and the tactics used by both sides are of great interest because they formed the basis of those employed in Europe for the following four years.

When it became clear to Hitler that Britain would reject all his peace overtures, he began to consider plans for an invasion, Operation Sealion, the date for which was set to be September 15. Control of the air over the Channel and south-eastern England was essential to the success of Sealion – the same type of 'air superiority' which had first been contested over the trenches of the Western Front during the 'Fokker Scourge' of the winter of 1915–16.

Hermann Göring, head of the Luftwaffe, believed that it would take four days to eliminate the RAF south of a line from Chelmsford to Gloucester, an indication of the combination of over-optimism and faulty intelligence which was to characterize the German conduct of the battle. At his disposal were three air fleets with a total of about 3500 aircraft. Ranged against the Luftwaffe were 1100 fighter aircraft of Air Chief Marshal Dowding's Fighter Command, of which 704 were immediately available for operations.

The battle passed through a series of stages, marked by the Luftwaffe switching its targets as it went along. Hindsight has given these stages a sharper definition than was apparent at the time. Initially both sides were groping in the dark, neither of them in full control of their forces or of the course the battle was taking. Every day they were breaking new ground, absorbing tactical lessons which were to be put to use throughout the rest of the war.

In the first phase of the battle the Luftwaffe

launched attacks on coastal targets and convoys, seeking to entice Fighter Command squadrons over the Channel to be engaged and cut up by superior numbers. Frequently they flew fighter sweeps in the vicinity of the raiding force. The RAF learned to ignore the sweeps, provided they could be identified in time. During this period, July 10 to August 10, the Luftwaffe lost 227 aircraft against the RAF's 97.

After the initial sparring the attrition began in earnest. On July 30, Hitler ordered Göring to prepare 'immediately and with the greatest haste ... the great battle of the German air force against England'. On August 2, Göring issued final orders for *Adlertag* (Eagle Day), on which the destruction of Fighter Command was to be accomplished.

IMPORTANCE OF RADAR
Bad weather delayed the beginning of the operation until August 12. On that day German attacks were concentrated on No. 11 Group's forward coastal airfields at Hawkinge, Lympne and Manston and five radar stations in Kent and Hampshire. The station at Ventnor in the Isle of Wight was put out of action until August 23, but the rest were all operating again the next day. The radar stations, whose tower masts offered the most conspicuous of targets, were crucial to Britain's air defense. Reports from the radar stations, along with those from coastal and inland observation posts, were transmitted to Fighter

Command HQ at Bentley Priory. Here they were cross-checked and then the 'filtered' information was transmitted simultaneously to the relevant Group and sector stations. Allowance had to be made for the six-minute time-lag between the radar observation and the plot of the enemy formation on the map. Interceptor squadrons were allocated by the Group Controller and scrambled by the Sector Controller, who directed them to meet the incoming aircraft.

At this stage radar was capable of extremely accurate bearings but was less reliable when it came to estimating the height and numbers of the attacking force. Nevertheless, its value can be gauged from the subsequent assessment of Adolf Galland, then commander of II/JG26: '*I*N *battle we had to rely on our own human eyes. The British fighter pilots could depend on the radar eye, which was far more reliable and had a longer range. When we made contact with the enemy our briefings were already three hours old, the British only as many seconds old – the time it took to assess the latest position by means of radar to the transmission of attacking orders from Fighter Control to the already airborne force'.*

Fatally, the Luftwaffe did not press home its attack on the radar stations. On August 15 Göring, presiding over a meeting of his three air fleet commanders, concluded, 'It is doubtful whether there is any point in continuing the

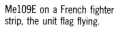
Me109E on a French fighter strip, the unit flag flying.

attacks on radar sites, in view of the fact that not one of those attacked has so far been put out of operation'. On such musings was German **strategy based**.

The blunder was compounded by failures of intelligence. Throughout August the attack continued on Britain's fighter stations but repeatedly effort was wasted on airfields not in use by Fighter Command. On the day Göring met his three air fleet commanders, the Luftwaffe entered the most intensive phase in its campaign. For the first, and last, time all three fleets combined to throw five successive waves (some 1790 aircraft in all, although only one-third of them were bombers) against targets as far apart as Portland in the south-west and the Tyne in the north-east. Among Luftflotte 2's targets in the south-east were such key fighter bases as Biggin Hill and Kenley, but the formations which fought their way through attacked Croydon, West Malling and other less vital stations. Losses were heavy. Luftflotte 5, operating from Norway and Denmark and attacking targets in the north-east, was particularly severely handled. Just after midday the first of its formations - comprising some 100 He111s escorted by about 70 Me110s - was picked up by radar while still one hundred miles out to sea. As it crossed the coast Spitfires of No 72 Squadron split the formation into two sections, one of which was then savagely mauled by fighters of No 79 Squadron. The Me110 escort, running short of fuel and harassed by Spitfires and Hurricanes, turned for home, leaving the He111s to unload their bombs relatively harmlessly on a suburb of Sheffield. Not one military objective was hit. A second formation of 50 Ju88s managed to blow up an ammunition dump at Bridlington and damage the airfield at Driffield, but this was Luftflotte 5's only success on a day during which it lost one-eighth of its bombers and one-fifth of its long-range fighters. It was never again committed to daylight operations against England.

On the night of August 15, the BBC announced German losses of 182 aircraft and another 53 'probables'. This was one of the classic instances of overclaiming in the heat of battle - actual German losses were 76 against the RAF's 34. On a wider scale the numbers game was reaching a critical point. By August 18 the RAF had downed a total of 367 aircraft against its own losses of 183 in combat and 30 on the ground. However, Spitfire and Hurricane production was running at only a little over 100 a week and the reserves were down to 230 aircraft. The training organization had supplied only 63 pilots to replace the 154

killed, missing or severely wounded. Another worrying factor was the success of the night raid on the Castle Bromwich Spitfire factory by Kampfgruppe 100, whose He111s were equipped with the 'Knickebein' radio navigation aid.

With the prize still eluding its grasp, the Luftwaffe now narrowed its aim to the destruction of No 11 Group's seven key sector stations - Biggin Hill, Debden, Hornchurch, Kenley, Northolt, North Weald and Tangmere - the nerve centers of the air defense system, each of which controlled three squadrons. Kenley was badly hit on August 18, then bad weather caused a lull until the 26th when North Weald was heavily attacked. Between August 30 and September 1 Biggin Hill was hit six times. Most of its buildings were wrecked and its vital equipment had to be operated out in the open. On September 4 the sector stations enjoyed a respite, but so many other raids were being plotted at Bentley Priory that the operations table was temporarily saturated. As a result no air raid warning was received at the Vickers aircraft factory at Weybridge - producing two-thirds of the RAF's Wellingtons - which was hit by 20 Me110s with considerable loss of life. Two days later it was the turn of the Hawker plant at Weybridge, which was producing more than half the total supply of Hurricanes.

OPPOSING STRATEGIES
The cumulative effect of this slogging match was beginning to take its toll. The Luftwaffe continued to suffer heavy losses and of the 1000 German aircraft crossing the Channel every day only about 25 per cent were bombers. But the RAF's reserves of Hurricanes and Spitfires were down to 125, and the attacks on the Vickers and Hawker plants suggested that aircraft factories might follow the sector stations as priority targets. The two weeks during which the Luftwaffe had driven home its attacks on the inner ring of airfields on which the Sector Stations were deployed had cost 378 German aircraft against the RAF's losses of 277. This was five British machines for every seven lost by the enemy - the best loss ratio achieved by the Luftwaffe during the Battle of Britain. As Churchill wrote later, 'The scales had tilted against Fighter Command ... There was much anxiety'.

At this point German strategy took one more turn. Late in the afternoon of September 7 the Luftwaffe began its first concentrated daylight raid on London. Ordered by Hitler partly at least in retaliation for the RAF raid on Berlin on August 24-25, it gave Fighter Command - reeling on the

JEAN ACCART

IN MAY 1940 CAPITAINE JEAN Accart, the commander of French fighter squadron 1/5, flying Curtiss 75A Hawks, led his men into a head-on attack on a formation of German Me110s, and followed up by shooting down two Dorniers, in one of which Accart himself claimed a share. Later that same day, May 10, Accart again took off from his base at Suippes and shot down three Dorniers. On May 11 he claimed a He111 and on May 12 a Dornier 215, despite being wounded in the head and face by the enemy rear gunner's fire.

Accart's unit was mentioned in despatches for achieving 33 air victories without loss in the first three days of the battle for France. By the end of May Accart's personal score was over a dozen. On June 1, leading three Hawks in company with a patrol of Dewoitine 520 fighters, he attacked a formation of He111 bombers. Making his attack, he was again hit by gunfire as the enemy airplane slowed down leaving a trail of smoke. Half-conscious, he baled out, landing alive but gravely injured.

Accart's official score during the Battle of France was 12 destroyed and three probables. In 1942 he escaped from occupied France to Spain, but was interned until early 1944. After release, he helped to form 345 Squadron of Free French pilots in the RAF, leading this unit during the final stages of the war under the pseudonym of 'Major Bernard'. Air fighting was rare by this time, and his squadron flew mostly ground-attack missions. After the war he served as a Colonel in the French Air Force.

KENT ENGLAND SEPTEMBER 20, 1940

SPITFIRE VERSUS ME109

During the Battle of Britain there was a marked contrast in the tactics used by the opposing RAF and Luftwaffe pilots. The German Me109s operated in formations evolved during the Spanish Civil War — the Rotte, or pair, and the four-plane Schwarm: the leader and wingman in a Rotte would fly some 200 yards apart, the wingman normally slightly below and to the rear, so that they could cover each other effectively; two pairs together would form a Schwarm, graphically described as 'finger four' by the RAF.

During the early stages of the battle, when they were operating free-ranging sweeps against RAF fighters, the tactical flexibility afforded by these loose formations enabled the Messerschmitt pilots to exploit their superior performance and inflict heavy losses on the more rigid formations of British fighters, and although the advantage disappeared when they were committed to close escort of bombers, the loose pair would become the universal standard fighter formation.

Right: Flying ground-controlled interceptions, RAF fighters were committed to rigid formations of three aircraft ('V's): all but the formation leader had to devote too much attention to maintaining their positions, and standardized attack patterns were a further handicap.

TIMETABLE
1 Ten Spitfires of No. 92 Sqn are scrambled from Biggin Hill: circling at 5000 ft over Gravesend, on the Thames estuary, they expect to link up with No. 41 Sqn.
2 Having failed to achieve the rendezvous, the squadron is ordered to climb to 20 000 ft by the Fighter Controller to intercept a high-altitude raid detected by radar.
3 The Spitfires are then vectored south and instructed to continue climbing to a height of 27 000 ft.

4 At 1130 hours, over Dungeness on the English Channel coast, and still climbing in formation, the Spitfires are attacked by the Me109Es of JG 51.
5 Led by the Spanish Civil War ace and Germany's leading fighter pilot, Werner Mölders, the Messerschmitts dive out of the sun on the struggling Spitfires.
6 The Spitfire formation breaks up under the German attack.

7 Covered by his wingman, Mölders is able to pick his targets: he succeeds in shooting down two of the Spitfires to register his 39th and 40th victories.
8 Pilot Officer H P Hill crashes at West Hougham, near Folkestone.
9 Sergeant P R Eyles goes down in the sea: like Hill, he is killed.

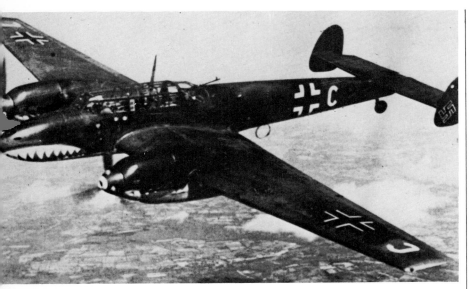

Me110C of the Destroyer Group, ZG76, in 1940. Most of the major air forces tried to develop a twin-engined, long-range fighter for bomber escort, but all failed. The weight of guns, armor, two engines and extra fuel ruined any chance of a maneuverable fighter that could defend itself. The Me110 was no different and was quickly relegated to night fighting, in which it excelled.

ropes – a vital breathing space. The battle over London reached its height between September 7-15. By the end of the month, the battle was won. Daylight raids ceased on October 5 and Operation Sealion was postponed on October 12. More than 1700 German planes had been shot down.

The Germans found, just as the RAF and later the USAAF found, that to provide escort to bombers needed a good deal of tactical fore-thought, and the Luftwaffe did not have the time in 1940 to learn all the lessons and to acquire the ability to introduce changes that would help them then.

Fighter Command fought gallantly with what it had and tried desperately to adapt to the changing air war. By necessity during the battle it fought in squadron strength – 12 aircraft pitted against any number of German machines. Occasionally two or more squadrons would intercept together but this was not a set plan or pattern. If some were able to rendezvous, the Spitfires often took on the escorting fighters while the Hurricanes attacked the bombers, but it was not always so well defined.

In an attempt to overcome the problem of small numbers of RAF fighters engaging numerically superior German formations, 12 Group of Fighter Command put squadrons into a Wing Formation. Developed by Squadron Leader Douglas Bader, the famous legless pilot commanding 242 Canadian Squadron, and supported by 12 Group's AOC, Trafford Leigh-Mallory, the idea was to scramble three or four squadrons and not to engage hostile formations

until these units had formed into their 'Big Wing', well north of London.

Arguments continue to this day on the merits of this formation tactic. The 'Wing' supporters defend the method because they felt that with more attacking fighters, more damage could be inflicted and more mutual support be obtained. Those against it argue that, as it took time to assemble and form up the Wing, the hostile raid was often on its way home by the time any engagement took place, the target having been bombed. Meanwhile, individual squadrons from, say 11 Group, (which bore the brunt of the Battle) had usually inflicted some casualties on the raiders, but perhaps more importantly, had succeeded in breaking up the raid, forcing some bombers to jettison their bombs, and upsetting German cohesion.

The German Me110 fighters proved vulnerable to both the Spitfires and the Hurricanes and on several occasions had themselves to be rescued by the single-seat 109s. The 110 pilots fell back on a tactic used in WW1, that of the defensive circle, each plane and rear-gunner covering the plane ahead and behind. A number of RAF pilots tried various ways to combat the 110 circle, one being Flying Officer Count Manfred Czernin of 17 Squadron – an Englishman despite his Austrian/English background and family lineage.

Czernin had seen action in France and flew right through the Battle of Britain, winning the DFC. On August 25, 17 Squadron were 'scrambled' to intercept a reported 100-plus enemy aircraft heading for Weymouth. The Hurricanes were climbing, trying to gain the height needed to do battle, when ahead of them the pilots saw the vast armada of German aircraft. The German fighters saw them too and about 15 to 20 Me110s, taking advantage of their own height, began to dive towards the British fighters.

As the two formations met, the leading 110 burst into flames but so too did the leader of the British squadron. Czernin was also in the head-on clash and, after the first pass, the 110s began to form their circle. Pilot Officer H A C Bird-Wilson (later Air Vice-Marshal, DSO DFC AFC) was with 17 Squadron in 1940 and said of Czernin's subsequent tactics against the 110s: *T*o

most pilots it was extremely hard to penetrate this German tactic once the 110s had formed up. It was Czernin's firm conviction that the only way to attack them was to carry out a head-on attack and go round in a circle in the opposite direction to the Germans! This may have not been a very

ADOLF GALLAND

PERHAPS THE BEST-KNOWN OF the Luftwaffe's successful fighter pilots, Galland saw action in the Spanish Civil War, but it was not until the Battle of France in 1940 that he claimed his first combat victory. This was as Kommandeur of the III Gruppe of JG26, and by August 1940, he had become Kommodore of JG26 and been awarded the Knight's Cross following his 17th victory in the skies over England. Six weeks later his score had risen to 40 and he was the third pilot to be awarded the Oak Leaves to his Knight's Cross.

After the Battle of Britain, Galland continued to lead JG26 in France against the RAF which had started to take the air war to the Luftwaffe. By June 1941 he had scored 70 victories and became the first pilot to win the Swords to his Knight's Cross. After Mölders' death in November 1941, Galland became General der Jagdflieger, promoted to Generalmajor – at 30, the youngest General in the German armed forces.

By this time his score had climbed to over 90, and in January 1942 he became the second pilot to win the Diamonds to his Knight's Cross. As the head of the Luftwaffe's fighter arm, Galland did much to develop fighter tactics and strategy, but it was an uphill struggle not only against an ever-growing powerful Allied air assault on Germany, but also in the face of internal politics and opposition from his superiors. Galland was relieved of his strategic duties at the beginning of 1945, but continued the fight as leader of JV44, equipped with Me262 jet fighter aircraft. He brought his score to 104 before being wounded.

successful manoeuvre to shoot down 110s but it usually meant that the formation broke up and thus became easier kills for fellow RAF pilots.'

On this occasion, however, Czernin shot down three Me110s. The head-on attack was another tactic some RAF squadrons managed to initiate although it was not easy to set up, or to perform. When used it often had the effect of splitting up the enemy formation and as the German bombers had only one light machine-gun in the front cockpit area, it made for a less dangerous attack. However, the closing speeds made aiming difficult and the attacking pilot had to choose quickly whether to fly over or under the fast approaching target. If the RAF pilots attacked in line abreast there was no chance of breaking off to the left or right before reaching the bombers.

Whatever happened to the bombers, attacking Spitfire or Hurricane pilots invariably became embroiled with Me109s at some stage. In 1940 the Spitfire, as Al Deere had discovered over Dunkirk, was superior to the 109 except in the initial climb and dive. The Hurricane was also more maneuverable but was slower and was no match for the 109's rate of climb. In the turning battle, both RAF fighters could turn inside the Messerschmitt. More often than not the Me109 pilots avoided close action with RAF fighters by adopting 'dive and zoom' tactics, yet another maneuver from WW1 days. Another problem with the early Spitfires and Hurricanes was their inability to follow a 109 in the classic fighter maneuver of a half-roll and dive. The 109's fuel-injection system enabled it to turn onto its back and pull down into a dive, whereas the RAF fighters performing the same maneuver, or just pushing the stick forward, drained their carburettors and the engine began to cut out. In later versions of the Merlin engines this problem was solved so the RAF pilots were able to follow German fighters and also use the same tactic to get out of trouble.

Adolf Galland flew with JG26 during the Battle and recorded in his famous book *The First and the Last*: '**T**HE "DESTROYER" (ME110) aircraft was born from an accurately recognized shortcoming of the Me109 – its restricted range. The modern Vickers Supermarine Spitfires were slower than our planes by about 10 to 15 mph but could perform steeper and tighter turns. The older Hawker Hurricane ... compared badly with our Me109 as regards speed, and rate of climb. Our armament and ammunition were also undoubtedly better. Another advantage was that

our engines had injection pumps instead of carburetors used by the British, and therefore did not conk out through lack of acceleration in critical moments during combat.

'The short range of the Me109 became more and more of a disadvantage. During a single sortie my group lost 12 fighter planes, not by enemy action but simply because after two hours flying time, the bombers we were escorting had not yet reached the mainland on their return journey.'

One drawback in the system as far as the RAF were concerned was the apparent failure to disseminate information that would be useful to others. Although Fighter Command were engaged in an unequal and deadly struggle, no one seemed to think it important to pass on valuable ideas.

As we have already seen, some fighting leaders, like 'Sailor' Malan, had already begun to use the pair system rather than the vic. Other squadrons were using two 'weavers', who flew behind the squadron, weaving back and forth to protect the main force. While this was an improvement, the 'weavers' usually ran short of fuel before the others. They might also be the most junior or inexperienced pilots liable to be picked off and unaware of what had hit them. In any event, the fact was that nobody told the other squadrons that this new idea, or that tactic, was worth using. In consequence, some squadrons were using the vic formations, for instance, up to the end of 1940 and into 1941. Additionally there was almost no circulation of information about German tactics or German aircraft. Even lessons learned and knowledge gleaned from the men who had fought over France reached no one except fellow squadron pilots. This shortcoming has to be laid clearly at the door of the Air Commanders, who obviously lacked a total understanding of the basic operational needs of their front-line pilots.

KNOW YOUR ENEMY

It was not until March 1941 that the following tactical information, prepared and circulated by the Deputy Directorate of Air Tactics at the Air Ministry, concerning German aircraft types, was released:

1. Me109

In this type the pilot is very vulnerable to deflection attacks owing to the position of the armor, which is some 50 inches astern of his seat. The glycol, radiator and oil coolers are also very vulnerable to attack from below, and many aircraft have been brought down by having their cooling systems shot through. Me109s frequently adopt dive and zoom tactics, which are not always easy to follow and for Hurricane Is the best counter-measures seem to be to attempt to make surprise attacks. If the Me109s form defensive circles, it is best to attack them by flying round inside the circle in the opposite direction. When Me109s are escorting bomber formations and form defensive circles, it is best for the fighters to make feint attacks to try and occupy the attention of the fighters while allowing the bombers to proceed unescorted. Small numbers of fighters have successfully achieved this, allowing the greater concentration of our fighters to attack the enemy bombers. Me109s seem to prefer avoiding combats where numbers are more or less equal, but sometimes go away to gain height and then return in an attempt to surprise our fighters.

2. Me110
The Me110 is usually treated in a similar manner to the Me109, but head-on attacks on the former are not recommended. Beam or quarter attacks with bursts aimed just behind the pilot usually have the effect of setting the aircraft on fire. At close range of 100 yards or under, the Me110 shows a tendency to disintegrate owing to its light construction. It is well to avoid getting in front of this aircraft on account of the heavy forward armament, which can hit at long range. Its rear gun fire has usually been found to be ineffective. The pilot is well armored against head-on attack, but usually no other armor has been found in the aircraft brought down in this country.

3. Do17
Beam, head-on, and port bow attacks have been found the most effective against this type, which is heavily armored against attacks from astern. It is usually found that fire from the top rear gun is effective owing to the twin rudders and it has been found that it is best to attack from slightly below when coming in from astern, as there is usually only one lower rear gun. Prisoners of war state that the Do17 can be got home on the port engine alone, but it will not maintain height if only the starboard engine is running.

4. He111
Head-on and beam attacks have been found best, otherwise attacks should be made from dead astern and slightly above. The engines of the He111 have hitherto proved very vulnerable. The enemy's tactics with this type have usually been to fly in close formation with well organized mutual supporting fire.

5. Ju87
It has not proved possible for monoplane fighters to attack the Ju87 when it is dive bombing, as owing to the steep angle of dive and the slow speed attainable with the diving brakes, our fighters over-shoot. It is therefore recommended that fighters should try to attack the Ju87 before it commences to dive, or, failing this, when it has pulled out of its dive. The Ju87 has been found to be well armored behind and below the rear gunner so that attacks from directly astern and below are less effective. Formations of Ju87s are usually preceded, or accompanied, by large fighter escorts which endeavor to distract the attention of our fighters.

6. Ju88
Beam and head-on attacks are recommended as being the best against this type, and it is interesting to note that the gunner cannot change from one top beam gun to the other without first stowing the original gun. It is therefore best to make a feint attack on one beam, followed by the real attack on the opposite beam. In general, astern attacks from below seem to produce the least opposition. The engines have been found to be very vulnerable. Enemy tactics usually take the form of steep, high speed, dives to ground level.'

The year 1940 ended with the Luftwaffe using only fighters over southern England. Me109s flew with a bomb under the fuselage which caused little damage but created a nuisance. It did provoke Fighter Command sufficiently to fly interception sorties against them, in a cloudy grey sky, where other Me109s flying 'Frei Jagd' missions at height were ready to pounce on the climbing Spitfires and Hurricanes, many of whom were still flying in vics of three.

By the end of the Battle of Britain, the German fighter pilots had reluctantly to face the bitter truth that despite their own strenuous efforts, they had failed to knock out the RAF and gain the necessary air superiority over southern England. They felt too that the fight had been lost not because of any shortcomings on their part but by the Luftwaffe High Command, headed by Göring. He had plainly under-estimated the strength and determination of the RAF to defend its island fortress. Worse still, he refused to acknowledge his mistakes and merely blamed his fighter pilots for letting him down. In continuing tactics that were clearly not helping to win the struggle, he sacrificed many valuable aircrew to death or capture, aircrew who could never be replaced and

The deadly Ju87 Stuka dive bomber struck terror into the hearts of Allied soldiers and sailors in WW2. Flying over England, however, in 1940, it proved vulnerable to defending Spitfires and Hurricanes, and had to be withdrawn in August. This was because RAF fighters that followed Stukas in their dive had a sitting target as they pulled out and lost their forward speed.

who were sorely missed in the battles that were to follow. The fighter pilots of both sides came to appreciate each other as hard fighters.

One of the outstanding German fighter pilots of 1940 was Major Helmut Wick of JG2. Towards the beginning of November 1940 his victory score was nearing 50. On November 6, Wick led a sweep over the Southampton area of southern England.

'WE THEN MET A CROWD OF HURRI- canes flying lower than ourselves. Just as I was about to start the attack, I saw something above me and immediately called on the intercom: "Attention; Spitfires ahead." The Spitfires were sufficiently far off that I could still launch the attack on the lower-flying Hurricanes. Just then the Hurricanes made a turn which proved to be their ruin. We shot down four of this group almost at once, one of which fell to me. The remaining Hurricanes turned away but began to climb again and during the climb I caught one of them flying on the right-hand side of the formation. The Hurricanes then dived steeply. I cannot fully explain my next experience, perhaps I was not quite fit or my nerves were frayed, but after my second Englishman went down, I only wanted to fly home. I still had fuel for a few more minutes of action, but the desire towards France, I spotted in front of me three Spitfires coming in from the sea. I saw them first and reached them quickly and the first one fell immediately. Now, I said to myself, we must get them all. If we let them get away today they will probably kill some of my comrades tomorrow, now away with them! I set my teeth and started the next attack. The second Spitfire fell after a few bursts leaving only one whom I was determined would not return home to report his defeat. I fired at him with my machine- guns and soon white smoke poured from him. The pilot appeared to be hit because the aircraft went down out of control, but suddenly it recovered and I was forced to attack it again. The Spitfire slowly turned over and crashed to the ground. Now it really was time to fly home. When I arrived back over my airfield, I did not perform the usual stunts to indicate my victories as my fuel was almost exhausted. When I jumped out of the plane I hugged the first person who came across to me, who by chance turned out to be an old friend from my training days. I have now scored 53 victories and need only the one more to draw level with my old instructor Werner Mölders.'

Helmut Wick scored his 54th kill the next day when again he led his Staffel over Southampton

and the Isle of Wight. Here they fought with 145 Squadron, claiming six of the Hurricanes shot down. Their tactics were to box in the eleven RAF fighters, with their estimated 50 Me109s spread out in three groups: one ahead, one astern and one to the side. The Hurricanes were unable to attack any one of the three groups without exposing themselves to the other two, and if they turned inland, the 109s would be right behind them. The Hurricanes began a climb but then the 109s began to attack in pairs, picking off the RAF fighters as they tried desperately to fly above the German fighters. Five Hurricanes went down, two pilots being killed, three injured. One of those killed was Nigel Weir DFC, who had fought over Dunkirk and throughout the Battle of Britain, gaining six victories. Wick himself was killed before the end of the month, falling in action over the Channel on November 28 having scored 56 victories.

As the winter of 1940–41 gave way to spring, there was every reason to believe that the Luftwaffe would return to continue its air war against Britain. The RAF, however, had its own plans for action as the weather improved. Having survived the battles of the previous summer, flying and fighting on the defensive, the air leaders were keen to start taking the war to the enemy. The switch to offensive would need a new set of tactics.

CHAPTER SEVEN

FLEXIBLE FORMATIONS

THE SPRING AND SUMMER OF 1941 saw the beginning of the Allied offensive air effort against Germany. Initially it was undertaken by the British RAF, with later years seeing the build-up of the American air force when the United States came into the war. The task was daunting. The RAF, especially its Fighter Command, had hardly begun to recover from its battles in France, over Dunkirk and during the Battle of Britain. Bomber Command, now almost totally committed to raiding Germany by night, had its light bomber force available only for daylight operations. Where to attack was the problem. Germany occupied almost all northwest Europe, Italy was now a major ally; and in the Middle East, Germany and Italy were threatening North Africa, Greece and the Mediterranean.

The RAF in 1941 was in many ways like the RFC in WW1 where the Channel was 'no-man's-land' and their operations over Northern France, Belgium and Holland were like the offensive patrols and bomb raids of WW1. A major factor in the air war for the RAF fighter pilots was that their operations were now almost totally offensive. This meant that, as with the Luftwaffe over England in 1940, a lost aircraft would mean a lost pilot or perhaps a lost crew. Like the scouts in WW1, they would also have to fight their way back to England, with exhausted fuel supplies and perhaps a damaged machine. The Germans, like their counterparts of WW1, could choose when to attack, waiting for the RAF to appear.

For their part the RAF, in deciding to take the offensive, had to get the Germans up to fight and to design tactics to cope with a still very superior Luftwaffe. These they refined over the year of 1941 – the 'shooting season', as the RAF fighter pilots called it. The operations they mounted had colorful names:-

Circus
A small force of bombers, usually twin-engined Blenheims – later even four-engined Stirlings – perhaps six in number. They were usually enough to entice the German fighters into the air but needed heavy protection. This might be provided in the form of ten fighter squadrons.

Rodeo
A fighter sweep over enemy territory without bombers. These might be opposed, but if there were no bombers the Luftwaffe fighters might well ignore it, for it posed no threat in itself.

Ramrod
A similar operation to the Circus but in which the

Left: Pilots and a Spitfire of 609 Squadron, 1941, when the RAF began to take to the offensive over France. As the RAF began to form Fighter Wings, 609 Squadron became part of Sailor Malan's Biggin Hill Wing. Left to right standing: Sgt Ken Laing, P/O Joe Atkinson, Sgt Bob Boyd, F/O Bauduoin de Hemptine, P/O Peter MacKenzie (in cockpit), Flight Lieutenant Paul Richey DFC, F/O Jean Offenberg, P/O Jimmy Baraldi. Seated: P/O Vicki Ortmans, F/Sgt Tommy Rigler, F/O Keith Ogilvie, Flight Lieutenant John Bisdee DFC, P/O Bob Wilmet. Sailor Malan's dog 'Spit' is far right.

prime objective was the destruction, by bombers, of a specific target. These too would be heavily escorted. The Germans had no idea, of course, that there was any difference between the Circus operation and the Ramrod, but if there were bombers about they usually tried to attack them.

Sweep

A general term for fighters mounting an offensive mission over enemy territory. It differed specifically from the Rodeo in being flown in support of a Circus or Ramrod, but not perhaps in close proximity. It would be designed to cover the area which the bombers would be attacking shortly. This was intended to 'sweep' the sky of any hostile aircraft. Support sweeps might also be flown after a raid.

By the spring of 1941, Fighter Command in the south of England had begun to form its squadrons into specific wings. Among the first wing leaders were men of proven leadership and air combat qualities: Douglas Bader, who had led a 12 Group Wing in the latter part of the Battle of Britain; 'Sailor' Malan, leader and later commanding officer of 74 Squadron; Bob Tuck, who had seen action over Dunkirk and the Battle of Britain with 92 Squadron and in command of 257 Squadron. These were the first, many others followed their example throughout the war. These were the men who could lead two, three or even four fighter squadrons in the air and whose anticipated task was to inflict the greatest damage on the enemy with the minimum loss.

On Circus and Ramrod operations there were generally four protective elements: Close Escort fighters surrounded and stayed with the bombers, Escort Cover gave protection to the Close Escort fighters, High Cover covered both Close Escort and Escort Cover squadrons and prevented enemy fighters from positioning themselves above them, Top Cover flew high above the bombers' route but had a roving commission to seek out enemy fighters in proximity to the bombers' route.

In addition there was a Target Support Wing which was routed independently to the general target area, and then maintained cover over it. Withdrawal Cover Wing flew out to support the returning fighters whose aircraft would be running low on fuel and, if they had been in a fight, ammunition. There might also be flown Fighter Diversion sweeps, especially when a Ramrod was being flown. It was very complex yet well planned, but, as the Germans had found over England the previous year, the Close Escorts had difficulty with the fighters' freedom of action.

By now the RAF had finally abandoned the three-plane vic. 'Sailor' Malan had helped to devise a scheme whereby a squadron formation flew three sections of four, each in line astern. This would be improved upon in other units, but it survived for some time in the RAF. One of the squadrons in Malan's Biggin Hill Wing was 609; the other two were 74 and 92 Squadrons. Paul Richey DFC, by now recovered from the wound received in France in May 1940, was one of 609's flight commanders. He recalled: '*W*HEN *I eventually got back to air fighting in 1941, I found that although we'd gone over to pairs and fours, we were still flying a very rigid formation, in 609 Squadron for instance. I had several rows with Michael Robinson, who was both my Commanding Officer and my brother-in-law, about this. We used to take off in three fours, climb up to the French coast, each section in line astern, four in front, four on the right and four on the left – but all in line astern.*

'*Michael Robinson wanted these fours to stay very close to him and stay very close to each other. The result was, they were so busy with their formation flying they couldn't see what was going on. This was fairly general throughout Fighter Command at that time.*

'*Having already seen this in France I knew we must loosen up this sort of formation. Not only couldn't you see what was going on but it was a frightfully easy target, flying straight and level. Anyway, Michael went on leave for a fortnight and I introduced my own theories. What we then did was that we had the leader's four in longish line astern at the bottom gently weaving, then above him we had the second four, snaking from side to side across him and above that was the third four, also snaking, in order to keep the two fours below always in sight. So, as the bottom four weaved to the right, for instance, the second four would turn left and then right so they could look down on the leading four, while the top four would be doing the same in sequence. Then the whole squadron would snake along, very fluidly. In this fashion we were never bounced over France in 1941.*

'*Later, Michael said to me at the end of that shooting season, "You were absolutely right, although I didn't say it at the time." Even when he came back from that fortnight's leave he didn't say anything.*

'*But the "Snake" as we called it, didn't catch on generally in Fighter Command. The Tangmere Wing had quite a different thing; they had the finger-four formation under Douglas Bader and*

"Cocky" Dundas etc. We had, of course, learnt the pairs from the Germans.'

Tangmere Wing was led by Douglas Bader and, as one would expect, he had his own ideas on tactics, which he formulated with his pilots. The result was the 'Finger-Four'.

THE 'FINGER FOUR'

This tactic involved a section of four aircraft spread like four fingers. Each pilot could easily cover the whole area of sky, the four men were in a flexible and open formation and if attacked the pilots would subdivide into two pairs. Initially it was agreed that when attacked the pairs would break in opposite directions, and turn tightly so that both would be able to curve in behind the attackers. Bader was keen to try it in action, so one morning he grabbed Hugh 'Cocky' Dundas and two other pilots and flew out to see if they could get some 109s to attack them.

They flew down the Channel at 25 000 ft between Dover and Calais in line abreast. Dundas was out to the left, Badar 50 yards to his right, the No 3 100 yards to Bader's right with No 3's wingman 50 yards the other side. It worked. Five Me109s were spotted turning above and behind them. As the Messerschmitts came in, Bader kept his four Spitfires on an even course, keeping a running commentary as the 109s approached. Then he ordered them all to break! Bader and Dundas hauled round to the left, the other pair to the right. So steep and tight were the Spitfires' turns that the four of them had actually turned inside the two rearmost 109s and both Dundas and the other wingman were hit as the 109s opened fire. Bader saw smoke pouring from one of the leading 109s but then had to cover Dundas as he broke towards England, badly shot-up. He got down safely and the other No 2 had to force-land in a field.

Analyzing what had gone wrong, Bader decided they should all have turned the same way to stay together and keep the enemy in sight. Bader tried it again, this time using other Spitfires to perform the attack; within a few days they had perfected the 'Finger Four' tactic and used it from then on. Other wings soon copied it and it was used by RAF fighter pilots for the rest of the war, and indeed is still in use today.

The Canadians in 401 Squadron - which had been No 1 RCAF Squadron during the Battle of Britain - had devised, and by 1941 had perfected, another variation in battle formation. The Spitfires would fly in a wide, loose-V formation in sections of twos which would stay together

whatever happened. When they reached enemy territory the leader would order one pair to fly 'figure-of-eights' behind the two arms of the 'V' as look-outs. As these would use more fuel, they would be relieved by other pairs from time to time. During formation turns the leader of the section composing the 'V' would slide underneath him and take up the same position on the other side.

The air war over France was becoming a team effort. The wing leader was the team captain. People like Harry Broadhurst, leader of the Hornchurch Wing, left his pilots in no doubt that they would have to act and fight as a team. There would be no room for individual heroics, the issue was too serious now. In taking the war to the enemy they would have to fight to win.

For many, the air battles over France in 1941 - and again in 1942 - were a campaign on their own. The Sweeps and Circuses mounted by Fighter Command and Bomber Command, to 'take the war to the enemy', were, however, a disastrous phase. One might even suggest that, just as the German fighter pilots felt aggrieved at their leaders for the way they directed the Battle of Britain in 1940, so too could the British fighter pilots record the same feelings for the 1941-42 period. In many respects, the figures must speak for themselves.

After the German invasion of Russia on June 22 1941, only two Luftwaffe fighter Gruppen, JG2 and JG26, were left in France with part of another in Holland. On July 26 1941 German fighter strength on the Western Front was just 238.

At the end of 1941 the RAF admitted the loss of 849 fighters in addition to a number of light bombers of 2 Group while involved in Circus operations. German fighter pilots claimed about 950 kills, so the figures seem fairly accurate. On the other hand, Fighter Command claimed 909 victories while actual German losses were 183 from all causes! The comparable figures for 1942 were around 900 RAF fighter losses while Luftwaffe claims were 972 - including bombers. The RAF claimed some 500 victories, while actual Luftwaffe losses from all causes were just 272.

Thus in two years, Luftwaffe day fighter pilots on the Western Front shot down a possible 1900 RAF fighters, of more than 5000 losses. (1) Their own losses amounted to around 450 from all causes. It can be seen therefore that, although the RAF continually took the war to the Germans, the offensives proved costly, the RAF losing four fighters for each Luftwaffe fighter destroyed. This had to be, in mathematical terms, a victory for the Luftwaffe. As, however, the RAF claimed

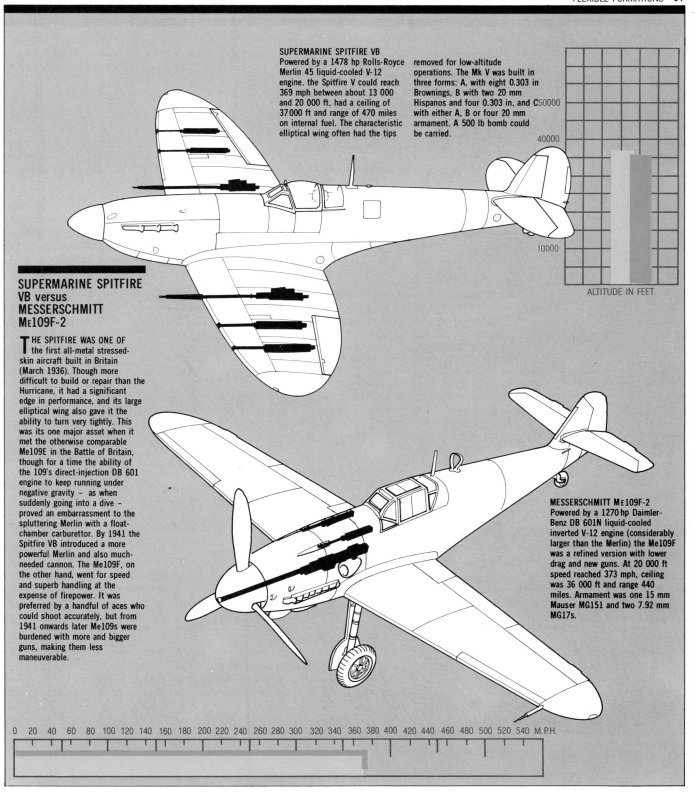

SUPERMARINE SPITFIRE VB
Powered by a 1478 hp Rolls-Royce Merlin 45 liquid-cooled V-12 engine, the Spitfire V could reach 369 mph between about 13 000 and 20 000 ft, had a ceiling of 37 000 ft and range of 470 miles on internal fuel. The characteristic elliptical wing often had the tips removed for low-altitude operations. The Mk V was built in three forms: A, with eight 0.303 in Brownings, B with two 20 mm Hispanos and four 0.303 in, and C with either A, B or four 20 mm armament. A 500 lb bomb could be carried.

50000

40000

10000

ALTITUDE IN FEET

SUPERMARINE SPITFIRE VB versus MESSERSCHMITT Me109F-2

THE SPITFIRE WAS ONE OF the first all-metal stressed-skin aircraft built in Britain (March 1936). Though more difficult to build or repair than the Hurricane, it had a significant edge in performance, and its large elliptical wing also gave it the ability to turn very tightly. This was its one major asset when it met the otherwise comparable Me109E in the Battle of Britain, though for a time the ability of the 109's direct-injection DB 601 engine to keep running under negative gravity – as when suddenly going into a dive – proved an embarrassment to the spluttering Merlin with a float-chamber carburettor. By 1941 the Spitfire VB introduced a more powerful Merlin and also much-needed cannon. The Me109F, on the other hand, went for speed and superb handling at the expense of firepower. It was preferred by a handful of aces who could shoot accurately, but from 1941 onwards later Me109s were burdened with more and bigger guns, making them less maneuverable.

MESSERSCHMITT Me109F-2
Powered by a 1270 hp Daimler-Benz DB 601N liquid-cooled inverted V-12 engine (considerably larger than the Merlin) the Me109F was a refined version with lower drag and new guns. At 20 000 ft speed reached 373 mph, ceiling was 36 000 ft and range 440 miles. Armament was one 15 mm Mauser MG151 and two 7.92 mm MG17s.

0   20   40   60   80   100 120 140 160 180 200 220 240 260 280 300 320 340 360 380 400 420 440 460 480 500 520 540 M.P.H.

GEORGE BEURLING

B'UZZ' OR 'SCREWBALL' TO HIS friends, the Canadian George Frederick Beurling was a natural fighter pilot. A rebel and a loner, who kicked against authority and discipline, he ran up a score of over 30 victories, mostly in the blue skies over the island of Malta in 1942. In many ways he resembled the 'lone-wolf' fighter aces of the early days of WW1.

Initially he flew from England with Canadian and RAF Squadrons, before being posted to Malta, with a modest score of just two kills. There he flew with 249 Squadron. He was awarded the DFM after bringing his score to 11, but within days this had risen to 17, including four kills in one day, July 27. By August 1942 he had 19 victories and he was persuaded, not without some difficulty, to become an officer. By October his victories totaled 28 but on October 14 he was shot down and wounded. By that time he had scored twice as many victories as any other pilot during Malta's blitz. He returned to England with a DSO and DFC, and even survived a crash at Gibraltar when the airplane in which he was a passenger went down into the sea.

Back in England, he joined 403 RCAF Squadron, following a hero's reception and tour in his native Canada. Still the rebel, he came into conflict with his CO, but he added three more victories over FW190s above France, bringing his score to 31 ¼. He became a gunnery officer, and at the end of the war left the RCAF and for a while was a civil pilot. In 1948 he was recruited to fly for the Israeli Air Force but in May of that year he was killed in a crash in Rome when ferrying an aircraft to the Middle East.

over 1400 victories, they thought they were, at the very least, inflicting heavy casualties on their opponents.

Among Fighter Command's armory in 1941 were a number of Commonwealth and European manned squadrons. Canada, New Zealand and Australia all had fighter and bomber squadrons and there was a sprinkling of South Africans too. The Poles, Czechs, French, Dutch and Norwegians also had squadrons of nationals, who had escaped from advancing Germans or made their way to England after their countries had been occupied. And, as in WW1, there were American volunteers who had come to England, some via the Royal Canadian Air Force, to fight against the Nazi régime.

The Americans had been grouped together within No 71 Squadron RAF, but just as in WW1 the American volunteers were collectively known as the Lafayette Squadron rather than No N124 Escadrille, so the WW2 flyers were known as the Eagle Squadron. Led by British RAF squadron commanders, it became operational in April 1941, initially flying Hurricanes, then Spitfires. Shortly afterwards two other American squadrons were formed, 121 in May (operational in July), and 133 in August (operational by the end of the year).

The most successful Eagle pilot was Gus Daymond, who won the DFC and bar for shooting down eight German aircraft, while with 71 Squadron. During one air battle above a German base in France, Daymond and Johnny Flynn became separated. Flynn was chased out to sea by two Me109s, one of which he then shot down. Daymond was engaged by four others. He later recorded: '*T*HOSE KRAUTS COULD REALLY fly their airplanes and they could shoot mighty straight. Every time I looked round one of them was firing at me. It seemed as if fire was just streaking out of their planes in my direction. And they hit me plenty: they pretty much shot the hell out of my plane alright.*

'At the time they were all above me, but I didn't know when two of them might go down and attack from underneath, so I stopped that possibility myself by diving down to the deck. Once there, I went all out but they had me sort of headed off from home and I knew I had to do

*(1) Total RAF losses for 1941 and 1942

	Fighters	Bombers	Coastal
1941	849	1328*	339
1942	900	1616*	352

*including night losses.

something and do it fast because they had already hit me, and I didn't know when something was going to blow up or catch fire.'

When America later came into the war, all three squadrons were transferred into the embryo US 8th Air Force in England. Seventy-one Squadron's Eagles had by that time claimed 45 German aircraft shot down and produced the first four American 'aces' of WW2.

While the Battle of Britain raged and while the RAF in England began encroaching upon Europe in 1941, there were other areas where air fighting was growing in intensity. One of the most important was the Middle East. Here, the Italians were advancing towards Egypt in North Africa, invading Greece and trying to bomb the island of Malta into submission.

DEFENDING MALTA
Malta's strategic position in the Mediterranean was a constant thorn in the side of the Italian and German forces. Under siege conditions its defense was a handful of fighters – at first a few Gloster Gladiator biplanes, later Hurricanes and then Spitfires. The fighter pilots were always outnumbered but rarely outfought and were eventually victorious.

The Gladiators were slow, and when they first met Italian SM79 bombers over the island, the bomber pilots just pushed the throttle forward and flew away. With Sicily just 60-odd miles away, warning of the approach of Italian bombers gave little time for the Gladiators, when scrambled, to reach their height and the bombers were usually on their way home by the time the Gladiators had climbed to them. And once the Gladiators' presence was known, the Italians sent escorting fighters – in this case Fiat CR42, the updated version of the CR32 that fought in Spain. In fact, Malta's first kill was a fighter which the nimble Gladiator was able to out-turn in a scrap. Nevertheless, Gladiators often managed to break up Italian bombers and forced several to jettison their load into the sea.

The Italian bomber pilots tried their own tactic to try to shoot down the Gladiators. One of a group of five SM79s under attack – they usually flew in vics of five – would begin to straggle. This was an inviting target and, as the biplane closed in, the bomber would accelerate, bringing the Gladiator into the range of the bombers' lower ventral guns. Fortunately the Gladiator pilot, though his aircraft was shot up, landed safely and alerted his brother pilots to this trap.

The Italians then began to send over their

TOP-SCORING FIGHTER PILOTS IN THE MIDDLE EAST DURING WW2

RAF

	Total	Location	Final Score		Nationality
S/Ldr M T StJ Pattle	40+	Desert/Greece	(40+)	Killed in action	South African
F/Lt G F Beurling	26	Malta	(31)		Canadian
S/Ldr N F Duke	26	Desert/Italy	(28)		British
W/Cdr L C Wade	25	Desert/Italy	(25)	Killed, accident	United States
S/Ldr V C Woodward	22	Desert/Greece	(22)		Canadian
F/Off W Vale	22	Greece	(22)		British
S/Ldr C R Caldwell	20½	Desert	(28½)		Australian
Capt John J Voll	21	Desert	(21)		United States

LUFTWAFFE

	Total		Final Score	
Hpt Hans-Joachim Marseille	151		(158)	Killed in action
Hpt Werner Schroer	86		(102)	
Hpt Heinz Bar	65		(220)	
Oblt Ernst-Wilhelm Reinert	63		(174)	
Oblt Hans-Arnold Stahlschmitt	59		(59)	Killed in action
Hpt Gustav Rodel	57		(98)	
Oblt Franz Schiess	52		(52)	Killed in action

ITALIAN

	Total	Location		
Major Adriano Visconti	26	Desert /Italy		Killed in action
Sgt Teresio Martinoli	23	Malta/Desert/Italy		Killed, accident
Capt Franco Lucchini	21	Malta/Desert/Sicily		Killed in action
2/Lt Leonardo Ferrulli	21	Malta/Desert/Sicily		Killed in action
Capt Mario Visentini	20	East Africa		Killed, accident

Macchi 200 fighters – fast, sleek monoplane fighters, but not as agile as the Gladiators, which continued to survive. The Gladiator pilots found that they could out-fly most of the Italian fighters, who would overshoot in attacks, fail to follow a sudden turn and would often put their aircraft into a spin to evade, appearing not to understand that once in a spin they became an easy target for the attacker. The Fiat or Macchi would be slow in a spin, allowing the Gladiator to circle it and take pot shots at it. The Gladiators' second confirmed kill was, at last, a SM79, hit and set on fire by a diving attack from height. It went into the sea and two Italians parachuted onto the island. Later, in July 1940, the first Hurricanes arrived – from North Africa.

There were few Hurricanes available in the Middle East at this time. In England the Battle of Britain was about to start and the war in North Africa was escalating. In fact, throughout the rest of 1940 no more than six Hurricanes at a time were available for the island's defense. Then, in September, the Luftwaffe came on the scene: Ju87 dive-bombers at first, later Me109s. The defenders nonetheless had their successes. During the first five months of hostilities over Malta, Gladiators and Hurricanes intercepted 72 raids and shot down 37 Italian and German aircraft. When the 109s appeared, the Hurricane tactic, after the initial clash, was to form a defensive circle and keep turning till the 109s ran short of fuel and flew back to Sicily.

In April 1941 the first Hurricane IIAs arrived. These were a slightly better match for the 109s, but only a maximum of 11 were available. One was flown by Flight Lieutenant Donald Stones DFC, who arrived in Malta in July 1941, and remained there until the spring of 1942, having previously flown Hurricanes on night intruder sorties over enemy airfields in Sicily. He recalled:

'O N MALTA, WITH THE GERMANS AND Italians only 63 miles away, but depending on what the radar plot was, and what height they were (and the radar wasn't bad on Malta), we'd climb south to gain height before coming back over the island. If they were at a medium height we'd climb straight towards them. We were flying in finger-fours by then, pretty wide out so everybody could look around.

'You had to change your mind very quickly in combat. I remember Ju88s over Malta, escorted by Me109s. On this occasion they were going for the flying-boat base at Kalafrana Bay when we first picked them up visually, and it was difficult to see which way they were heading. We were going full out, full revs, full throttle – through the gate, then we suddenly realised they were more frontal than flank. I had to yell "Line astern!" and go in to do almost a beam attack on them. Not the most accurate way to take a squadron in, but it did split them up.

'When I left Malta, we had only 13 Hurricanes and four Spitfires serviceable. Some of the more witty boys would say, "Oh, there go the Hurricanes with the fighter escort!"'

Ron Noble arrived on Malta in November 1941, staying till March 1942. He had flown Spitfires in England and found conditions on Malta very different: 'W E OPERATED IN "THREES" ON occasion despite having flown "fours" in the Coltishall Wing. Being a young Pilot Officer though, I really thought little of it.

'Usually we flew south when scrambled to gain height before coming back at height. We thought nothing about the odds – three or four aircraft going in to attack 40–50 enemy aircraft. Quite often it was a case of diving down, make a pass, then get the hell out. We opened fire 800 yards to 600 yards, coming back with great claims but probably did very little damage at that range especially with just 0.303 guns. Later, with confidence, we would get in closer which was the secret of success.

'Eventually, however, we had to land back on the island. Me109s would fly sweeps designed to catch the RAF fighters landing or refuelling. Casualties were high, but more aircraft were destroyed on the ground than in the air combats.'

AIR WAR IN NORTH AFRICA

While fighting developed over Malta, the air war over North Africa had also begun. Again the Italians were the aggressors. They had their Fiat CR42s with which to patrol or to escort their SM79, SM81 or Cant Z1007 bombers. In the early days they retained some CR32s of Spanish Civil War fame which they used, with Breda 65s, for ground attack.

Italy had come into the war in June 1940 when the RAF in Egypt had only three fighter squadrons, each equipped with Gloster Gladiator Is. There was just one Hawker Hurricane in the whole of North Africa! The first clash came on June 14 when Gladiators of 33 Squadron shot down a Caproni 310 and a CR32, with another probably destroyed.

By August the air battles became more frequent and all three Gladiator squadrons were in action. Eighty Squadron moved one flight from its base near Alexandria to Sidi Barrani at the end of July, as the British Army took the offensive into Libya. This squadron saw a good deal of action over the next two months and developed its own set of combat tactics.

In these first clashes the RAF pilots found that the CR42 biplanes used a dive-and-zoom method of attack. In an initial attack where they hoped to surprise the British fighters, they would attack individually from all directions. They would then make simultaneous attacks from the beam and quarter, using speed in a dive to regain lost altitude after each firing pass.

After a fight on August 4 in which a four-man escort mission to a Lysander were all shot up (three forced down and one landed at base wounded), retaliation was planned. It was decided to fly a squadron show of 14 Gladiators in an Italian patrol area where large formations of CR42s has been observed.

The RAF pilots were concerned that if the Italians saw such a 'large' formation of Gladiators they might not wish to engage, but the RAF had been ordered to employ at least a dozen Gladiators for self-protection. The squadron, however, did not take this as specifying 14 in one formation. Accordingly they flew in four sub-sections. The 'bait' would be three Gladiators flying at 8000 ft, with three more at 10 000, four at 12 000 and a top section of three at 14 000 ft. They flew in the broad vic formation which was the standard search pattern during the early days of the desert war.

The high vic leader controlling the battle formation spotted 27 (actually there were only 16) CR42s and some RO37 reconnaissance aircraft at 6000 ft. He led the Gladiators into the sun, then ordered the low sub-section to attack. The Fiats too were in vics and as the first three Gladiators made contact so the other sections were ordered down. Several Fiats were shot down before they realized that they were under attack. It was a complete surprise. Nine CR42s were shot down for the loss of two (the Italians claimed five), although one pilot walked back.

The Gladiator pilots over Libya, like those in Malta, found great difficulty in matching the speed of the faster Italian bombers. In a tail chase they would invariably be left behind. One pilot in 80 Squadron, Pilot Officer V A J Stuckey, caught

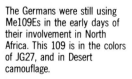

The Germans were still using Me109Es in the early days of their involvement in North Africa. This 109 is in the colors of JG27, and in Desert camouflage.

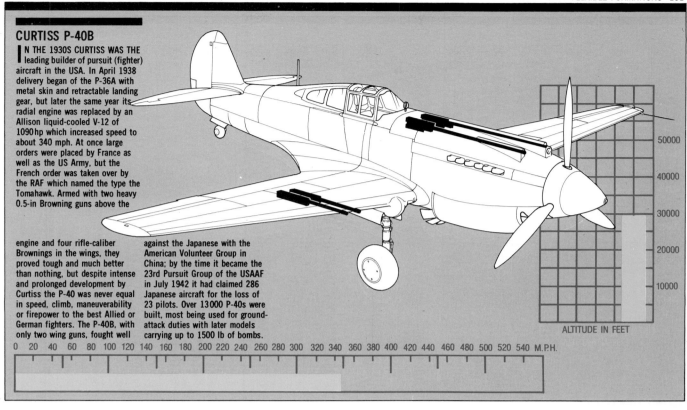

CURTISS P-40B

IN THE 1930S CURTISS WAS THE leading builder of pursuit (fighter) aircraft in the USA. In April 1938 delivery began of the P-36A with metal skin and retractable landing gear, but later the same year its radial engine was replaced by an Allison liquid-cooled V-12 of 1090 hp which increased speed to about 340 mph. At once large orders were placed by France as well as the US Army, but the French order was taken over by the RAF which named the type the Tomahawk. Armed with two heavy 0.5-in Browning guns above the

engine and four rifle-caliber Brownings in the wings, they proved tough and much better than nothing, but despite intense and prolonged development by Curtiss the P-40 was never equal in speed, climb, maneuverability or firepower to the best Allied or German fighters. The P-40B, with only two wing guns, fought well against the Japanese with the American Volunteer Group in China; by the time it became the 23rd Pursuit Group of the USAAF in July 1942 it had claimed 286 Japanese aircraft for the loss of 23 pilots. Over 13 000 P-40s were built, most being used for ground-attack duties with later models carrying up to 1500 lb of bombs.

50000
40000
30000
20000
10000

ALTITUDE IN FEET

0 20 40 60 80 100 120 140 160 180 200 220 240 260 280 300 320 340 360 380 400 420 440 460 480 500 520 540 M.P.H.

an SM79 on one occasion above Mersa Matruh. He managed to creep up on the Italian without being seen and in his first attack silenced the rear-gunner in his dorsal position as well as knocking out one of the aircraft's three engines. In this damaged state the bomber was unable to outpace the Gladiator and the British pilot fired until all his ammunition was gone. However, the bomber continued to fly and the frustrated Stuckey closed in, slid back his canopy and fired a Very flare at the enemy cockpit. This so upset the Italian crew that they baled out and the bomber, set alight by the flare, fell in flames.

THE 'SCIENCE OF AIR FIGHTING'

Acknowledged as most probably the highest-scoring RAF fighter pilot in WW2, Flight Lieutenant T M St John 'Pat' Pattle DFC also flew Gladiators with 80 Squadron at this time. Pattle was another thinking pilot, a tactical innovator and a superb marksman, qualities which made him a formidable opponent. He kept notes about what he called the 'science of air fighting', jotting down details of the enemy aircraft's weaknesses and strong-points. Thus he was able to tell his men how best to attack the various aircraft they encountered.

Among these notes was his plan for attacking the SM79s. The best method, he believed, was not to try to close in unseen from behind, but rather to use a head-on attack. In doing this, he would aim for an engine and if he was successful the bomber, with the loss of a third of its power, would be easier to pursue. The next task was to silence the rear gunner, and then he would aim at the fuel-tank in the starboard wing root. If this could be damaged to allow fuel to stream out, tracer shells fired into the vaporizing fuel would ignite it – and that would be that.

When Italy invaded Greece on October 28, 1940, the Gladiators of 80 Squadron, resting while being re-equipped with Mark IIs, were sent to Greece. Despite being outnumbered, they outfought and outflew the Italians – and Pat Pattle claimed almost all of his 40-odd victories between November 1940 and March 1941, using tactics he had devised in the desert.

On December 21 the Squadron, still flying in threes, in the absence of any suggestion that they should use other than peacetime formations, attacked Italian bombers. As the bombers were split up in a diving attack, escorting CR42s began to engage the British aircraft. They too still flew in threes, but there were an estimated 50 Fiats.

NEVILLE DUKE

BORN IN KENT, ENGLAND IN January 1922, Neville Duke found himself in 1941 flying Spitfires, often as Number Two to the redoubtable 'Sailor' Malan on sweeps over France. In these early battles, Duke shot down two Me109s before leaving 92 Squadron for the Middle East.

Joining 112 Squadron, he traded his Spitfire for a P40 Tomahawk and shot down his third 109 a few days later. Both German and Italian aircraft were now his adversaries, but very quickly, following his apprenticeship in England under leaders like Malan, Duke began scoring regularly. By the end of 1941 his score had risen to 7½. The squadron then re-equipped with Kittyhawks and had a new CO, Clive Caldwell DFC. By March 1942 Duke also had received the DFC and completed his first tour of ops. After a period as an instructor, he rejoined 92 Squadron now part of the Desert Air Force. Duke scored again on January 8, 1943 over a Macchi 202, then three days later, celebrated his 21st birthday with two more, (piloted, as he discovered later, by an Italian Wing Leader and a Squadron Commander respectively). Two days later he scored another double, both Ju87s, and afterwards gained a bar to his DFC and promotion to Flight Lieutenant. In March 1943 he added seven kills to his total (now 20), his reward being an immediate DSO, and when he increased this to 22, he was again rested, taking another instructor post. In 1944 he commanded 145 Squadron in Italy, winning a second bar to his DFC with four victories in three missions. Two Me109s on September 3, 1944 brought his score to 28 in 496 missions, and with a further six probables and ten damaged, Duke became the highest-scoring fighter pilot in Middle East Command. After the war he became chief test pilot for Hawker.

However, Pattle was astounded that the Fiats, diving down in threes, all fired at long range and made no attempt to close with the Gladiators before zooming back to height. Seeing this and as usual quickly sizing up the situation, he decided to take the initiative. As the next three CR42s dropped to swing away before continuing down in a curve to about 1000 feet below the Gladiators, Pattle prepared to pounce. He followed them with his two wingmen as the Fiats curved down, watching out for a further three Fiats who would be beginning their next pass. Before the three lower Fiats could begin their climb back to the others, Pattle had dived and closed in behind one CR42 and fired at point-blank range. It reared up, shedding shot-off fragments before diving earthwards in flames.

ACES OF THE AMERICAN VOLUNTEER GROUP IN CHINA

Name	Total	
Robert H Neale	16	Scored 17¼ victories in WW2
David Hill	12¼	Scored 18¼ victories in WW2
Edward F Rector	12	
William N Reed	11	Scored 16½ victories. Killed Dec 19 1943
George T Burgard	10¾	
William D McGarry	10½	Interned in Indo-China, March 24 1942
Kenneth A Jernstedt	10½	
John Van Kuren Newkirk	10½	Killed by ground fire, March 24 1942
Robert L Little	10½	Killed by ground fire, June 22 1942
Charles H Older	10¼	Scored 18¼ victories in WW2
Charles R Bond	9	
Robert T Smith	9	First US ace in one combat
Frank Lawler	8½	
Charles W Sawyer	8	
Percy R Bartelt	7	
William E Bartling	7	
Robert Moss	7	
Frank Schiel Jr	7	
James H Howard	6½	Scored 9½ victories WW2, won CMH
John Bright	6	
Robert P Hedman	6	
Gregory Boyington	6	Scored 28 victories in WW2, won CMH
Robert J Raines	6	
John R Rossi	6	
Lewis S Bishop	5½	Interned in Indo-China, May 28 1942
Thomas Haywood	5½	
Parker Dupouy	5	
C H Laughlin	5	
Joseph C Rosbert	5	
Edward Overend	5	Scored 9 victories in WW2
John Petach	5	Killed by ground fire, July 10 1942
Louis Hoffman	5	Killed in air combat, January 26 1942
Robert J Sandell	5	Killed in flying accident, February 7 1942
Robert H Smith	5	Scored 8 victories in WW2
George McMillan	5	Scored 8¼ victories in WW2
R W Prescott	5	
Noel R Bacon	5	
Fritz E Wolf	5	

During the Greek campaign, 80 Squadron finally received the long-awaited Hurricane fighters. Pattle was just as deadly with these, although the Italians were now using the better G.50 monoplane fighter. In a Hurricane, a British pilot could fight on equal terms with the radial-engined G.50, although as some 80 Squadron pilots found, the G.50 pilots fought shy of Hurricanes!

There were two pilots in 80 Squadron who epitomized the two main types of successful air fighter. Pattle, as we have already seen, was the tactician, the thinker, a superb pilot who used his skill and foresight to take on an opponent and win. Fellow-pilot Flying Officer R N 'Ape' Cullen was the exact opposite. A pre-war racing motor-cyclist, he had his own method – which was just to see the enemy and go for him. He used no tactics; he just relied on bold courage and a killer instinct that served him worthily. Both pilots were later to die in Greece, but not before each in his own way had achieved a measure of success. Pat Pattle was later assessed to have shot down between 40 and 50 enemy aircraft, thus becoming the RAF's 'unofficial' top-scoring fighter pilot in WW2. Ape Cullen DFC was credited with 16½ victories before his death on March 4 1941. He had been taught to fly fighters by Pattle after managing to transfer to 80 Squadron from a transport unit in 1940.

In April 1941 the Germans came to the assistance of a flagging Italian drive into Greece. The Luftwaffe came too. It was like the Malta campaign repeated. Malta held out because it was an island and inexplicably had no invasion force sent against it. Greece fell. Yet again the RAF was outnumbered, but not outfought.

1941 – AMERICA AT WAR

On Sunday, December 7, 1941 the Japanese made a devastating air strike from a force of aircraft carriers upon the American naval base at Pearl Harbor in Hawaii. It was prepared and carried out by the Japanese Navy under the direction of one of the world's greatest war planners and strategists, Admiral Isoroku Yamamoto. The parameters of the conflict now spread to the Far East and Pacific – from as far south as the shores of Northern Australia to the borders of India in the west – and introduced two new and powerful air forces.

The Japanese had been fighting in China since 1937, and her pilots, like the Germans who flew with the Condor Legion in Spain, had acquired combat experience before their war with the Allies began. A number of their aircraft would see extensive action in WW2, but none more so than

Curtiss P40 Tomahawk in the markings of the American Volunteer Group (AVG). The AVG, under General Claire Chennault, flew in defense of China against the Japanese and later from airfields in Burma. The P40 proved a superb performer against the early Japanese fighters and bombers but like all the Allied aircraft, found difficulty in dogfighting the Zero.

the Mitsubishi A6M1 – Type O fighter – the famed Zero (later code-named 'Zeke' by the Americans).

During the early hostilities in China the Japanese main fighter type was Mitsubishi Type 96 'Claude', a stubby low-wing open-cockpit, radial-engined machine with a fixed spatted undercarriage. It was revolutionary as a fighter in a Japan that, like other air forces, was loath to give up the biplane. As in all successful fighters it was exceptionally maneuverable and, despite its short range and slow speed, was outstandingly success-ful.

The Chinese Air Force operated with a variety of European and American fighters, among them Gloster Gladiators, Curtiss Hawks, and Russian I-15 Chatos and I-16 Ratas, but these aircraft were often outnumbered by the Claudes and it was this factor as much as any which was responsible for the latter's success.

However, it had only a short range. Because of the distances involved, bombers often flew unescorted and suffered accordingly. On August 14, 1937 Japanese bombers from Formosa carried out their first heavy air attack on Shanghai, a distance of 1250 miles. A day later they struck again, followed by carrier-based bombers and fighters on August 16.

But during a raid on Nanking, the Chinese fighters, guided by an American, Claire Chen-nault, waited until the Japanese bombers turned for home, seemingly victorious, before striking. Relaxed and probably over-confident, the Japanese suddenly found a mass of Chinese fighters plummetting down upon them in curving dives from a brilliant summer sky. Eight of the 18 bombers were shot down. Chennault had flown with the US Army Air Corps and had at one time been an instructor with the Air Corps Tactical School. In 1935 he had written a book entitled *The*

Role of Defensive Pursuit. He retired in 1937 and was later invited by the Chinese to command their Air Force in the fight against the Japanese.

Chennault had formulated his own ideas when in the American Air Corps and soon introduced a 'combat element' of pairs. He told the Chinese pilots that if in action they became separated they were to join the nearest friendly two-man element and, in doing so, act as a sort of tail cover for them. Within days of Chennault's tactics being implemented, 54 Japanese aircraft had been shot down. This put a speedy end to unescorted bombing raids until a fighter could be found capable of escorting bombers to any target in China.

The answer was supplied by the Mitsubishi Zero.

This machine, destined to be Japan's front-line fighter for most of the period 1938–43, and still carrying out this function in 1945, was a superb fighter despite a number of drawbacks. It was heavily armed with two 20-mm cannon and two 7.7-mm machine-guns. At 300 mph the Zero could cope with all opposition in the air, and its agility and rate of climb ensured its safety in combat. As it was a naval fighter, used on Imperial Japanese aircraft carriers, range was important – and the Zero's was good. In 1940 it set world records for combat range over China – 1000 miles on one round trip. Some marks of the type in WW2 could operate at up to 1500 miles.

One tactic demonstrated by the Zero pilots on September 13, 1940, was particularly effective. Thirteen Zeros escorted bombers on a raid against Hankow. After the raid the Zero pilots, led by Lieutenant Saburo Shindo and Sub-Lieutenant Ayae Shirane, flew off with the bombers. They wanted to lure the Chinese aircraft into the air and, as expected, as they left the target the

BALIKPAPAN, BORNEO JANUARY 25, 1942
ZERO VERSUS B17

In the opening stages of the Pacific war the B17 Flying Fortress was one of the few USAAF aircraft available with the range for offensive operations against the Japanese, and even for the skilled Zero pilots of the Japanese Navy the big bomber posed novel problems. Operating at altitudes above 20 000 ft, where the Mitsubishi fighter grew more sluggish, and at speeds that forced the Zero pilots to use full throttle to catch it, in early encounters its very size tended to make them misjudge their firing distances, while its speed caused their rangefinders to misread.

With no tail turret, the B17D was vulnerable to close-range stern attack, but even then it was capable of absorbing a considerable weight of fire: the Zeros' machine-guns were ineffective and their cannon shells exploded on the outer skin until new fuzing arrangements were made. By the spring of 1942, when the first B17Es with tail turrets were in the Pacific theater, the Zero pilots had already tired of stern attacks that frequently had no apparent effect, and had turned to head-on attacks, aiming for the pilot or engines. These in turn were negated by evasive maneuvers allowing the bombers to bring their heavy machine-guns to bear, and ultimately it was found that the most effective tactic was a rolling dive from above, repeated as necessary.

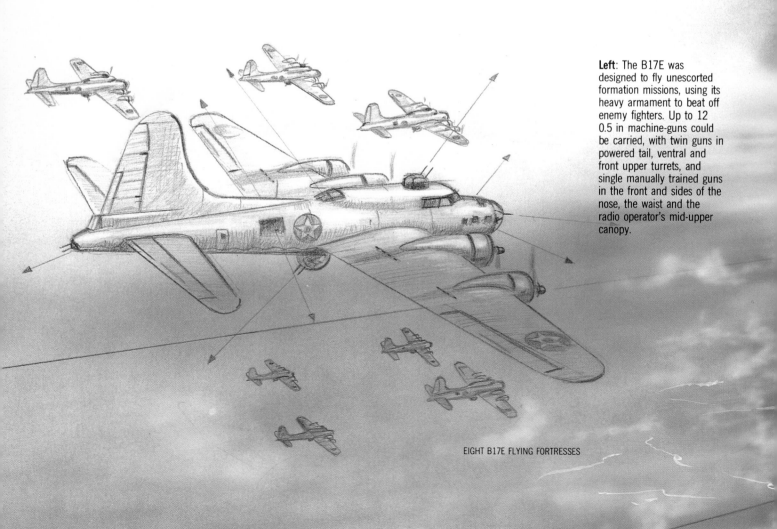

Left: The B17E was designed to fly unescorted formation missions, using its heavy armament to beat off enemy fighters. Up to 12 0.5 in machine-guns could be carried, with twin guns in powered tail, ventral and front upper turrets, and single manually trained guns in the front and sides of the nose, the waist and the radio operator's mid-upper canopy.

EIGHT B17E FLYING FORTRESSES

TWO A6M2 ZEROS

NAVAL PILOT
SABURO SAKAI

NAVAL PILOT
2/C SADAO UEHARA

TIMETABLE

1 Patrolling over the invasion fleet at Balikpapan, Borneo, at 22 000 ft, Sakai and Uehara see aircraft approaching from the direction of Java.

2 It is soon clear that the aircraft are B17s: two flights of four at around 20 000 ft, the rear flight slightly above the leading group. Sighting the Zeros, the rear group closes up to form a defensive box.

3 During their first attack the Zeros pass out of range, but the bombers miss the ships of the convoy and Sakai and Uehara climb for a second attempt: this time one of the B17s is hit.

4 Sakai sees lumps of metal fly off in the slipstream, and the dorsal and waist guns cease firing, but the bomber continues in formation, apparently unaffected.

5 The two Zero pilots continue to press home their attack, climbing and diving again and again, scoring repeated hits with cannon and machine-guns but without visible effect.

6 After the sixth attack the B17s split into two flights: one of the bombers is seen to have oil streaming from one of its port engines and is steadily dropping behind. Sakai chases and catches the damaged bomber, emptying his guns into it from a range of 150 ft; finally, emitting a cloud of black smoke, the bomber noses down into the cloud below. Despite coming under fire from the massed guns of eight B17s, Sakai returns to his base with only three bullet holes near his wingtips.

Chinese fighters – I-15s and I-16s – arrived on the scene, while, high overhead, a Japanese reconnaissance plane remained to report their arrival. With this information, the Zeros turned, gained height and reappeared over Hankow, taking the 27 Chinese Chato and Rata fighters completely by surprise. Half an hour later the Zeros had swept them from the sky, claiming to have shot them all down. The Japanese had four Zeros damaged. Flight Warrant Officer Koshiro Yamashita accounted for no less than five Chinese fighters.

By this time, the Japanese tended to adopt a fairly open formation – more like ragged line-astern sections, all but the leader gently weaving back and forth, one hundred yards separating the individual aircraft. This was not dissimilar to 609 Squadron's tactics in 1941 as described by Paul Richey, except that the whole formation was tighter.

By the outbreak of WW2, the Zero had had 16 months of active combat over China. And only two Zeros had been lost to the Chinese – to anti-aircraft fire, not to their fighters. Its impact on the war in China was simply overwhelming, for by the end of that conflict it had shot down 99 Chinese aircraft.

No sooner had Pearl Harbor been attacked than the Japanese launched an offensive against the Philippines. The established range of the Zero fighter actually enabled it to escort bombers from Formosa to Clark Field, in the Philippine Islands – a round trip of some 900 miles. Over the target the force was intercepted by five American Curtiss P40 fighters. Seeing the Zeros, four of the P40s

half-rolled and scattered; the other spiralled to the left and was pounced on by a pilot, Saburo Sakai, who later became the highest-scoring Japanese pilot to survive the war. His fire brought the American down – the first to be shot down over the Philippines, and his third victory, the others having been achieved over China. He was to register a total of 64 victories by the war's end.

Japanese forces quickly overran the Philippines, invading New Guinea to the south and Malaya to the west. Sakai's unit – the Tainan Wing – took part in the move towards New Guinea. Before that, however, the Tainan pilots had met the American B17s – Flying Fortresses.

ZEROS TAKE ON B17s
The Boeing B17 first flew in 1935 and by 1941 over 100 were in service in America, Hawaii, in the Philippines and other bases in the Pacific. It was one of the largest four-engined aircraft in service, with a 10-man crew, and bristling with defensive armament. B17s were formidable opponents for Japanese pilots, as they would also prove later for German pilots over Europe. The Tainan pilots first met them on December 10, 1941 when flying a patrol over Japanese naval vessels.

Part of the B17's defense was the height it could attain. On this occasion it was bombing from 22 000 ft, and the Zero did not excel at height. The Japanese pilots also found it difficult to judge their firing distance because of the bomber's size. The return fire from 14 guns posed another problem for the attackers. One vulnerable area in early B17 models was the tail, where the absence of a turret enabled an attacking pilot to stay right behind the bomber, sheltered by the Fortress's huge tail-fin.

Once the Japanese began encountering the B17s, both over the Philippines, and over their own ships and convoys, they began to devise better ways of using their Zeros to bring them down. In the spring of 1942 the E-Model B17 began to reach American squadrons; it had a tail-gun position which greatly helped the defense of the bomber. Until it arrived the Zero pilots' tactic was to dive behind the Boeing in a sweeping, firing pass, hoping to rake the bomber from tail to nose. They found however, that it had little effect on the heavily armored aircraft and this fact and the introduction of the new tail-turret caused the Zero pilots once more to revise their tactics.

The Americans found the Japanese Zero fighters almost impossible to cope with. Before the war they had spoken disparagingly against reports that Japan could ever produce a fighter that might be superior to anything America could

Nakajima Ki27 (later codenamed Nate) was a standard Japanese Army fighter from 1937 until 1942. Important as the first Japanese fighter with an enclosed cockpit, it saw extensive service in Manchuria, China and then in the Philippines and the south-west Pacific. It was the forerunner of the Nakajima Ki43 Oscar. Before the Zero came onto the scene, the Ki27 was the most maneuverable, fast-climbing and speedy fighter in the east, surpassing every other fighter it met.

Along with the P40, the P39 Airacobra saw much action in the opening stages of the Pacific war in the Philippines and over New Guinea. It was, however, totally outclassed by the Japanese fighters, especially the Zero. Nevertheless, with its strong armor and self-sealing fuel tanks it could withstand a fair amount of punishment. Poor speed and a low ceiling were major drawbacks, but its pilots liked the 37-mm cannon, firing through the propeller spinner, mounted in the forward fuselage. The P39 was rejected by the RAF but was used extensively by the Russian Air Force.

produce. Admittedly the Americans were at a disadvantage in the early months of the Far East war, and they soon discovered that their fighters were simply no match for the Zero. American equipment was inferior, too. They still had P36 Mohawks, early P40B Tomahawks, Brewster Buffaloes, even ancient P26s – very much a plane of the 30s – and Seversky P35s that were both slow and underarmed. Nor were the P40E Kittyhawks and P39 Airacobra a match for the Zero.

The Zero was light in construction, carried no armor or self-sealing tanks, and no radio, while its pilots rarely flew with parachutes. It was able to turn almost in its own length, and flick-roll out of danger. The Japanese fighter was faster, could outdive any American aircraft, and often had a better ceiling. The Zero's controls became progressively sluggish above 26 000 ft and it took well over an hour to reach 30 000 ft – but nonetheless in a straightforward contest the Zeros had the advantage.

JAPANESE AIR TACTICS

Despite all this, the factors which made the Zero so nimble were also its undoing. Because it had no armor to protect the pilot and engine, and no self-sealing tanks, the Zero could catch fire or explode, or the pilot could be knocked out if an American pilot did manage a burst of fire on target. Without radios, contact between the pilots themselves or with any ground control was non-existent. The Japanese communicated by hand signals or wing-wobbling, which was very limiting and next to impossible once a battle had started. A parachute was not considered essential. The pilots were issued with them but few used them, for they felt that the extra straps and harness restricted movement in an already cramped cockpit. Also, as combat in the early part of the Far East war was usually over enemy territory, for the Japanese to fly with life-saving apparatus bespoke a willingness to surrender which was completely at variance with their Bushido code as warriors of their Emperor. To be taken prisoner was unthinkable.

It is as difficult for a European or an American to understand this code of conduct as it was later almost impossible to comprehend how a Japanese pilot could, as a kamikaze, dive headlong to certain death into a British or American ship. Nevertheless, their code of conduct demanded it, and there really was no honorable alternative.

Indeed, as the American, British and Commonwealth flyers in the Pacific found, the Japanese airmen were well trained, skillful,

disciplined and far superior to the crude stereotypes so disparaged by the popular press and cartoonists. And in a Zero they were highly dangerous.

They continued to fly in three-plane vic formations – a leader with two wingmen – but in a slightly more open formation than the RAF in England had used. However, the Japanese suffered, surprisingly, from a lack of teamwork in combat. They rarely worked as a closely knit team.

The formation commander would lead his men into a battle area but once they met hostile aircraft the Japanese pilots more often than not split up and it was every man for himself. This was where aircraft radios would have helped the leader to co-ordinate and direct his men. In a way they fought like WW1 pilots. After an initial clash combat became an individual matter. This was relatively successful in the early months of the war when the Zeros were overwhelmed by the opposition, which was to a certain degree disorganized and outclassed. But once the Allied pilots began to predominate, they were less inclined to start dogfights with the Japanese – it was silly to do so, especially against aircraft that could cut inside them every time.

The Japanese tactics were based on the Zero's ability to turn inside the turning-circle of its opponents. Maneuverability was essential to their thinking and their strategy of air combat. Once the Allied pilots understood this, they were able to cope with the Zero and later types of Japanese fighters.

CHAPTER EIGHT

EMPHASIS ON THE OFFENSIVE

WHEN, IN JUNE, 1941 THE Germans invaded Russia, all but two German fighter Gruppen left Northern France to support the invasion. For the young fighter pilots Soviet air space was to provide a new arena for their Messerschmitts as Hitler's march to the east contributed to the temporary cessation of the Battle of Britain.

The Luftwaffe were far from ready for the attack having scarcely recovered from the air battles against England. However, the Russians in the air were so hopelessly inferior in aircraft, weaponry, tactics and training that the German fighter pilots had no difficulty in finding targets. In the first months following the invasion the Germans claimed nearly 500 Russian aircraft shot down, with a further 1200 destroyed on the ground in the northern sector alone. Adding those from the central and southern sectors, it is estimated that the Russians lost nearly 4000 aircraft in this period.

From the very beginning the main Russian strategy was to saturate the air with aircraft in an attempt to swamp the opposition. The result of this was to provide more targets for the German guns. For the Germans, with their experience of combat, their tried and tested fighter formation and tactics, it was all too easy. The German 'aces' – the *Experten* – ran up enormous scores. For men of the calibre of Werner Mölders, it was little more than target practice. Flying on the Eastern Front, he was the first German pilot to achieve 100 victories, and with 101 he was forbidden by Göring to fly further operations. He was made, at just 28 years of age, General of the Luftwaffe's Fighter Arm.

The Germans were now flying the Me109F while the Russians had the I-151 and I-153, being replaced by the MIG-3. The MIG flew faster than the 109F and had a greater range, but the Russian Air Force tacticians were strait-jacketed with pre-war thinking, as the RAF had been. The Soviet doctrine was to teach her pilots to fly and to fight in horizontal maneuvers which was extremely limiting. Before long, and impelled by the urgency of the situation, some far-sighted Russian pilots realised the need for a change of tactics.

THE SOVIET STAR

One of these was Alexander Pokryshkin. He was 28 when the Germans attacked his country and had been an aircraft mechanic before becoming a pilot. His hero was René Fonck and he adopted many ideas from the French pilot's book *Mes*

Left: Grumman F4F-4 Wildcat on Henderson Field, Guadalcanal, February 1943. The Wildcat was the standard US Navy fighter at the beginning of the war with Japan and saw action at Coral Sea and Midway in 1942. Marine units also flew the Wildcat, especially in the fighting for Guadalcanal in the summer and autumn of 1942. Once the American pilots had learned not to dogfight with the Zero, they found they could more than hold their own in combat with this deadly enemy.
Above: Lavochkin LaGG-3 Russian fighter which was extremely rugged but a little underpowered and not as maneuverable as its German opponents. However, many pilots thought it better than its running mate, the MIG-3 and it remained in front-line service until superceded by the La-5 in 1943.

Combats. Pokryshkin kept a diary in which he noted all the innovations he made when flying in mock combat with his brother pilots. In these exercises and later in action he found the climbing spiral to be best for evasion. He also developed the snap-roll to reduce speed and make an attacking German pilot overshoot and get ahead of him. He converted his fellow pilots to flying and fighting according to his ideas which achieved results and prolonged survival. He also studied the enemy, their aircraft and tactics, and noted their weaknesses. He instilled in his pilots the doctrine of 'Altitude, Speed, Maneuver and Fire'. Relying on good marksmanship and seeing the need to close the range before firing, Pokryshkin later flew with an élite Guards Regiment – comprising units of the best pilots grouped together, and posing a formidable threat to the Luftwaffe.

His first victory, shortly after the invasion, came when he shot down a Me109. He watched it fall in flames but, like so many other pilots, became so engrossed in watching his first kill go down that he nearly fell victim to the attack of a second Messerschmitt. Lucky to escape, he put his MIG into a screaming dive to ground level, levelled out and zig-zagged home. By the end of the war this able tactician who gave so freely of the fruits of his ideas and experience, had shot down 59 German aircraft. It has been said that Alexander Ivanovich Pokryshkin was to the Russian Air Force what Werner Mölders was to the Luftwaffe.

With his help the Russians revolutionized the hitherto accepted tactics of aerial combat. He had himself learned and mastered the tactic of the sudden, swift, violent attack maneuver. The object of this tactic was to win the psychological battle, to unnerve the enemy pilot, who would then be an easier target. In practice it was obviously more difficult, but on occasions it was successful, and it broke up the German formations.

The Russians had a number of technical and geographical advantages over the Germans; these included greater endurance in the air of their fighters and having their bases located well behind the front line. The Luftwaffe was based very near the front line and (like the RFC against the Germans in WW1) its pilots constantly took the air war to the Soviets, who tended to remain on the defensive. The Soviets used their fighters to protect their ground attack and reconnaissance aircraft, two well known types of these being the Petliakov PE-2 and Ilyushin Il-2.

The PE-2 was a very fast reconnaissance aircraft. If a PE-2 pilot was not surprised he could outdive and outfly a Me109 but his aircraft was known to be lightly built and therefore vulnerable to enemy fire. This was illustrated when Günther Rall, who scored 275 victories, fired at one at the limit of the range of his guns; he noted strikes on the PE-2's wingroot and the wing then sheared off.

Flying a Focke Wulf 190 A-4, a mark that began to reach front line Luftwaffe squadrons towards the end of 1942, was Leutnant Günther Schack of III/JG 51. His first sortie with an A-4 came on December 17, 1942 during which he met PE-2s. '*WE HAD TO FLY ESCORT FOR JU88 bombers. When we came near to the target we were immediately attacked by Soviet fighters. But when we came among them with our new birds they disappeared very quickly. During the action I suddenly saw five "Cementers" [Ilyushin Il-2 bombers] fly off in an easterly direction. We hastened to catch them but in spite of my two cannons and two heavy guns, I could not make a kill, only causing some damage to them.*

'*On the return flight, at an altitude of 6500 feet, we met unexpectedly four Petliakov Pe-2s close to our own airfield. I called to the pilot of my nearest aircraft, "Max, you take the right, I'll take the left one." I closed slowly on the Pe-2s. When I was at a distance of about 500 feet, I was travelling almost exactly at their speed and their tail gunners opened fire on me. I took careful aim, and had hardly pushed the firing button, when flames burst out of my target. Max hurried near like mad, and fired, but did not register a single hit, then slipped away over the Soviets. I got a quick shot* at the next one and, to my surprise, this aircraft also went down in flames.

'Now the other two began to bank and turn away to the east. I followed, firing at them alternately, wondering all the time how long my ammunition would last. Suddenly both burst into flames at the same time. Max was only able to witness my kills. One of the Pe-2s kept its altitude for a long time, trailing a long black smoke-cloud behind. Two of the crew baled out and soon after the plane crashed some miles away from the other.

'Meanwhile, we had crossed the Russian lines and on the way home we met three more Pe-2s. Max hurried at them again like mad, and this time he got one. My ammunition was almost gone, only one MG still firing, so I turned away. Hardly had we set course for home when we spotted three more Pe-2s ahead. Max now had to attack alone, but he was so nervous that he didn't get a single hit.

'As we were well in the German area I was not willing to let them go unpunished. I stalked near with my single MG, aimed between fuselage and engine where the tank was situated, and fired. I shouted with excitement when flames came out. I did not waste a moment, and fired at the next one. Smoke began to pour from it too, but now all my ammunition had gone. The Russian aircraft, which was burning, glided down and made a belly landing, continuing to burn on the ground.'

Günther Schack scored a total of 174 victories and was awarded the Knight's Cross with Oak Leaves.

The Il-2 'Stormovik' fighter-bomber was a major target for Luftwaffe fighters and ground flak gunners. It was a heavily armored airplane and a number of Luftwaffe pilots reported seeing their cannon and machine-gun strikes bouncing off. Most Luftwaffe pilots agreed that it was the most difficult aircraft to bring down as it could take an enormous amount of punishment and the Il-2 pilots were also capable of inflicting considerable damage.

Erich Hartmann, who later became top-scoring pilot of all time with 352 kills, developed his own tactics for dealing with the Stormovik. He would try to swoop below and behind the fighter-bomber to fire into its belly or try to hit its oil-cooler. If, however, the Il-2 was flying too low for fire to reach its underside, Hartmann would aim for its wingroot.

The Il-2 pilots' tactic was usually to fly to the front-line target area at around 4500 ft, going at full speed in one all-out attack to avoid Luftwaffe fighters and penetrate German ground fire. They would often fly in large groups of anything up to 60 aircraft.

As they neared the lines the Il-2s dived to low level and headed straight in. Hartmann's tactic on these occasions would be to fly at 15 000 ft from where he could detect the incoming Stormoviks. He would then begin a shallow dive and easily overhaul the relatively slow fighter-bombers.

Hartmann and his pilots would level out several thousand feet above the Il-2s, flying over and past them. The Russians would watch the Me109s going over and assume that they had not been spotted. Then, however, Hartmann would

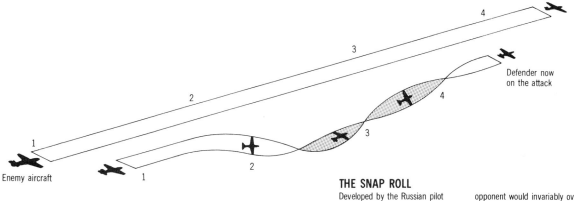

Enemy aircraft

Defender now on the attack

THE SNAP ROLL

Developed by the Russian pilot Aleksandr Pokryshkin – the 'father' of Russian fighter tactics – the snap roll was used by him when attacked from behind by a fast-approaching enemy. By using this tactic, the opponent would invariably overshoot and end up ahead of the Russian, thus himself becoming the target. Pokryshkin scored most of his kills flying the American P39 Airacobra.

roll over and pull down, and followed by his men would assail the Russians. This worked on several occasions, until the Russians learned how to deal with the German tactic.

TACKLING THE ZERO

In the Far East the biggest problem for the Americans was how to combat the Zero. At the end of 1941 and for the first half of 1942 the Zero was all-conquering. In March 1942 the Japanese Tainan Wing left Formosa and moved to Bali Island in the East Indies, then to Rabaul in New Britain. In early April they moved to Lae on the east coast of New Guinea. From here they flew operations over Port Moresby, where they encountered American P40 and P39 fighters and Australian P40s. Still flying in vics of three, the Japanese Zeros would cross the 15 000-ft high Owen Stanley Mountains and on to Moresby, with the Coral Sea in the distance.

Once over the mountains the P40s and P39s would climb to challenge the Japanese. Quite often the Zeros would be amongst them before the Americans knew it; they would have height and speed and the experience to take advantage of cloud or sun before pouncing. But the Japanese still lacked the essential teamwork. Consequently, Saburo Sakai tried to instill some discipline into his Lae Wing companions in April 1942.

This was provoked by an incident when seven B26 Marauder bombers had attacked Lae to be met by nine Zeros. With no radio control the Japanese as usual rushed pell-mell and simultaneously at the bombers only to get in each others' way and as a result claimed only one B26 shot down. The bombers had at that time no fighter cover, being outside escort range.

Sakai lectured his pilots at some length on what they should do and how only their working together as a team would bring success. It seemed to work and co-ordinated attacks followed. The culmination came on May 24. Six B25 Mitchells of the 3rd Bomb Group USAAF attacked Lae. They flew through a pass in the Owen Stanley Mountains, then swept east for their target. They were met on their bomb-run by 11 Zeros coming in head-on.

Hiroyoshi Nishazawa pumped a short burst of cannon fire into one B25, which exploded and fell into the sea. Toshio Ota got a second, Sakai destroyed a third, while Junichi Sasai exploded a fourth. Sakai then got his second, to make it five. The Zeros tore into the last Mitchell but it survived although ripped to pieces. The pilot crash-landed his machine at Moresby. These Japanese pilots were among the best. Four of them gained high victory scores: Nishazawa 87, Sakai 64, Ota 34, Sasai 27. Nishazawa shot down 20 American aircraft in a month and by November 1942 his score reached 30.

These pilots of the Imperial Japanese Navy flew from land bases, but those who took off from aircraft-carriers also had their successes – as well as their failures. Their opponent, the US Navy, had as its main fighter the Grumman F4F 'Wildcat', equipping seven of its eight squadrons. Three of the US Marine Corps' four squadrons also flew Wildcats.

Wake Island, far out in the Pacific, had a small garrison, including Wildcats. Japanese bombers raided the island on December 8, 1941, but four Wildcats had been scrambled and had reached 12 000 ft to the north of the island. However, the bombers were hidden by a rain squall and came in low. They destroyed seven Wildcats on the ground and killed 20 men, including three pilots, reducing Wake's fighter defense to five Wildcats and eight pilots. In another raid, one bomber was shot down by a Wildcat. Two more were shot down in a raid two days later (December 10). The pace continued throughout the month, the defenders even thwarting a landing attempt. By December 22 the Japanese had reduced the American force to just two Wildcats. These met a force of 39 aircraft from two Japanese carriers. One pilot went down in a fight with six Zeros, while his companion, contending with the bombers, shot down two. He was then wounded, and returned to Wake where he crash-landed. Wake Island fell to invasion shortly afterwards. The defending Wildcats had destroyed nine Japanese aircraft against odds.

THE PACIFIC WAR

Because of the vast distances involved, the fight in the Pacific theater became one of carrier warfare and 'island-hopping'. Aircraft carriers, however, were not plentiful and took a long time to build, but in order to have air cover for naval vessels, convoys and assault ships, they were essential. Equally essential was the need to protect them. Each carrier had fighter planes to defend the ships and carriers from air attack from both land-based aircraft and enemy carriers.

The US aircraft carriers' first raid was against the Japanese-held Marshall and Gilbert Islands on February 1, 1942. The carriers (*Yorktown* and *Enterprise*) sent bombing aircraft to attack the Japanese naval air base while escorting Wildcats made strafing attacks. Eleven Claude fighters attacked them and Lieutenant (jg) W E Rawie, as he pulled out from his second strafing pass, saw

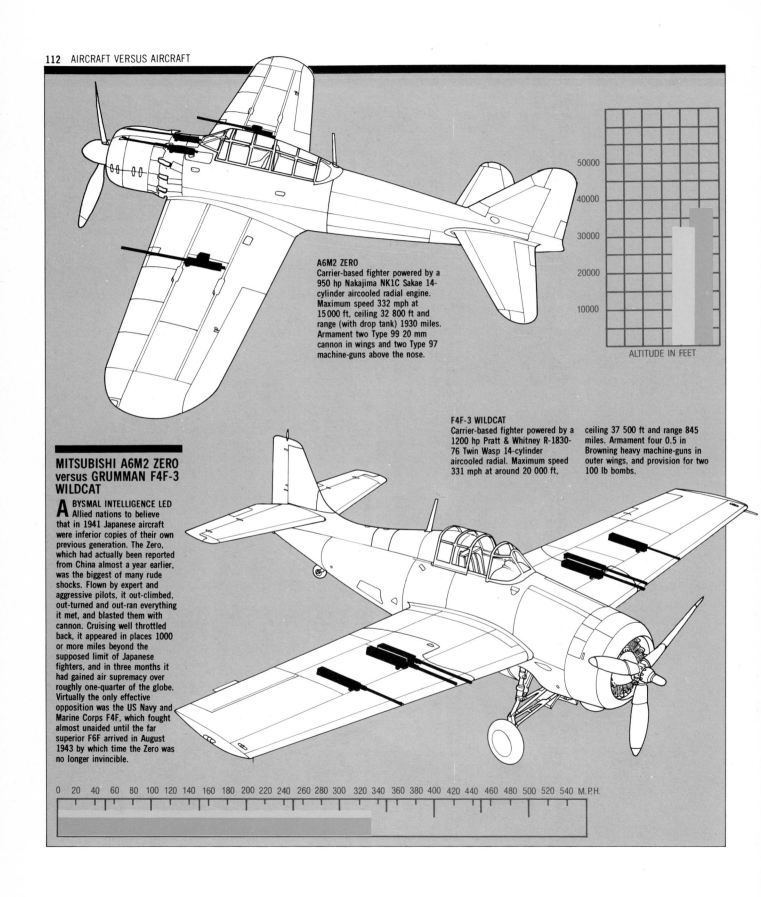

A6M2 ZERO
Carrier-based fighter powered by a 950 hp Nakajima NK1C Sakae 14-cylinder aircooled radial engine. Maximum speed 332 mph at 15 000 ft, ceiling 32 800 ft and range (with drop tank) 1930 miles. Armament two Type 99 20 mm cannon in wings and two Type 97 machine-guns above the nose.

ALTITUDE IN FEET

F4F-3 WILDCAT
Carrier-based fighter powered by a 1200 hp Pratt & Whitney R-1830-76 Twin Wasp 14-cylinder aircooled radial. Maximum speed 331 mph at around 20 000 ft, ceiling 37 500 ft and range 845 miles. Armament four 0.5 in Browning heavy machine-guns in outer wings, and provision for two 100 lb bombs.

MITSUBISHI A6M2 ZERO versus GRUMMAN F4F-3 WILDCAT

ABYSMAL INTELLIGENCE LED Allied nations to believe that in 1941 Japanese aircraft were inferior copies of their own previous generation. The Zero, which had actually been reported from China almost a year earlier, was the biggest of many rude shocks. Flown by expert and aggressive pilots, it out-climbed, out-turned and out-ran everything it met, and blasted them with cannon. Cruising well throttled back, it appeared in places 1000 or more miles beyond the supposed limit of Japanese fighters, and in three months it had gained air supremacy over roughly one-quarter of the globe. Virtually the only effective opposition was the US Navy and Marine Corps F4F, which fought almost unaided until the far superior F6F arrived in August 1943 by which time the Zero was no longer invincible.

0 20 40 60 80 100 120 140 160 180 200 220 240 260 280 300 320 340 360 380 400 420 440 460 480 500 520 540 M.P.H.

two Claudes coming at him head-on. Rawie kept his course, narrowly avoided collision, and fired a quick burst at one of them. The Claude went down – the first victory to a carrier-based Wildcat in WW2. Lieutenant Jim Gray claimed two more, but had his Wildcat shot to pieces and landed back aboard his carrier as his fuel gave out.

On February 20 the carrier *Lexington* prepared to attack the Japanese base at Rabaul, New Britain. Instead the 'Lex' became the first US carrier to be the target of a land-based air attack. She was well defended by the Wildcats of squadron VF-3. This outfit was commanded by a man whose name became famous in the early months of the Pacific war – Lieutenant Commander John S Thach.

'Jimmy' Thach graduated from naval academy in 1927 and by early 1942 was an experienced pilot with about 3500 flying hours and definite ideas on fighter tactics. These he put into action and proved in combat during battles in the first half of 1942.

One of his pilots was Lieutenant Edward 'Butch' O'Hare, aged 27. Both these men had been part of the squadron gunnery team in 1940 that won the fleet trophy. Under their tuition, the pilots of VF-3 became superb shots and eager for action. The legend of Jimmy Thach was about to be written.

The American Navy pilots had quickly assessed their Wildcats in relation to the Zero fighters. They had discovered the folly of dogfighting the Zeros but were also aware of other liabilities. The Wildcat was heavier than the Zero and so the latter could out-turn it. However in a straight fight the Wildcat's pilots considered its speed adequate. Maneuverability, rate of climb and range were, however, no match for the opposition.

During the Battle of the Coral Sea in May 1942 – which was the first carrier-versus-carrier battle in history – the US Navy pilots learned more lessons.

In this ferocious battle the Americans lost the carrier *Lexington*, and the *Yorktown* was damaged. The air squadrons lost 27 planes. The Japanese lost the *Shoko*, with two other carriers damaged, and were forced to abandon their move against New Guinea. In the air the Japanese Navy squadrons lost 32 aircraft in combat plus a number of damaged machines that were pushed over the side to make room for the lost carrier's planes.

This first carrier battle made the Americans realize the need for earlier interception tactics rather than more ship defense. From now on the carrier-based fighters began to fly Combat Air Patrols (CAP) some distance from the Task Force vessels. Controlled by radar, these fighter patrols were able to engage incoming aircraft earlier and could intercept reconnaissance or shadowing aircraft. Cooperation between the fighters and the fighter controllers improved too. Until the Coral Sea battle the CAPs flew only 10–12 miles from the Task Force; this was extended in mid-1942 and better radio and improved ship's radar gave the controllers – the Fighter Direction Officers (FDOs) – greater help in locating the enemy. The FDO could pre-position the Wildcats above incoming planes, although he needed to take care in case low-flying torpedo aircraft were coming in.

The Zero was still better in combat but the American pilots were learning that success could be achieved if they kept together, stayed at altitude and maintained a high speed. Their chance to even the score was just weeks away.

BATTLE OF MIDWAY

At the beginning of June 1942 the Japanese attacked Midway Island, 1300 miles north-west of Pearl Harbor and a potential base within striking distance of Hawaii. Four carriers escorted the invasion force with 254 aircraft. Against them the Americans disposed three carriers with 232 aircraft, plus 82 Navy, Marine and Army planes from Midway itself, mostly Brewster Buffaloes but including seven F4F-3 Wildcats.

The Japanese made an air strike against Midway on June 4. Twenty-six defending aircraft intercepted the attackers but lost 16 of their number. The American plan was for 12 aircraft to meet the raid – which was 107 aircraft strong – while the others orbited ten miles from Midway. As the 71 attack planes headed in, the 36 Zero fighters shot the defenders to pieces. The Zeros were initially behind and below their bombers, expecting to catch the Americans as they were still climbing, but the latter had made a good climb and at 30 miles out were 2000 feet above the Japanese. They attacked and did some damage before the Zeros got in amongst them and began to destroy the Buffaloes.

One Wildcat pilot, Captain Marion Carl, who was to end the war with 18½ victories – mostly on Wildcats – was being attacked by a Zero when he found himself suddenly alone. The Marine pilots had heard about the Zero's speed, maneuverability and better climb but knew it was inferior in a dive. Carl had height, so he pushed everything forward and dived for the sea. Heading into a cloud, he crossed his controls, to put the Wildcat into a skid. The Zero overshot but when Carl attacked his four guns jammed under negative 'G' and the Zero escaped.

Coming back over the island, Carl could see the air base smoking and on fire. He also saw three Zeros well spread out. Deciding to get at least one, the Marine rolled over and got behind one Zero and, having cleared his guns, shot it into the sea. This was Marion Carl's first victory and his Zero was one of only two lost on the first strike against Midway. Of the 19 Buffaloes only six reached base. All but two of the Wildcats got back. Most were shot up with only two airworthy.

The Brewster Buffalo was very similar to the Wildcat to fly although the Buffalo was 'more fun' – because it was more docile – yet harder to land. The Wildcat was more stable and therefore a better gun platform. Carl had often flown a Buffalo and had only just converted to the Wildcat. The conversion undoubtedly saved his life. The Buffalo pilots found, as did other American pilots, that it was suicide to try to dogfight the Zero – one just played into the enemy's hands. For the loss of 13 Buffaloes and two F4Fs, the Japanese lost 10 aircraft; yet they claimed more than 40 defending fighters shot down plus a number of 'probables'!

Meanwhile the two carrier groups were searching for each other. Leading one escort group of six Wildcats was Jimmy Thach.

In the Battle of Midway, the Navy flyers had flown the new version of the Wildcat, the F4F-4, which, unlike the F4F-3, had folding wings to help in storing the planes below decks, and six as against four 0.50 machine-guns. The Wildcat squadron also had its complement of aircraft

raised from 18 to 27. However, the extra guns and added armor affected the Wildcat's performance, making it sluggish, something the Wildcat pilots did not care for when it was still inferior to the Zero.

The increase to six guns in fact gave the pilot less firing time. Added fire-power reduced the total duration of firing because the overall amount of ammunition carried remained the same. The firing time lost was five seconds, which could be the difference between life and death in an air battle. Each gun now carried 240 rounds instead of 360. The total was the same, 1440 rounds, but six guns fired them off faster. The view of some pilots, notably Jimmy Thach, was that increased fire-power was no substitute for marksmanship.

Every factor had to be weighed relative to other requirements. The F4F-4 was unpopular with pilots owing to its reduced climb, range and firing time, but aircraft carriers could carry greater numbers of the stubby fighters, with their folding wings, which was a consideration when carrier groups were out in mid-Pacific, far from replacements. The F4F-4 was blooded at Midway and in combat with defensive and escorting Zeros it produced a profit rather than a deficit in the Coral Sea. The Wildcat had now taken the brunt of the Pacific war for the first six months and new battles were about to begin, on land as well as sea.

GUADALCANAL
In August 1942 the Americans took their first offensive step against the Japanese since Pearl Harbor, the first of dozens of islands to be invaded and retaken being Guadalcanal in the Solomon Islands chain. The US Marines stormed ashore on

Mitsubishi A6M3 Zero (Zeke). The most famous of all the Japanese fighters of WW2, the Zero in all its forms and models dominated the air war over China and later in the Pacific. The A6M3 was initially called the Hamp until it was recognized as the Model 32 (Zeke 32). It began to arrive in front-line squadrons in 1942. The earlier production Model 21 was in service at the time of Pearl Harbor.

SABURO SAKAI

HIGHEST-SCORING PILOT OF THE Imperial Japanese Navy to survive the war, Sakai saw action during the war in China in the late 1930s where he scored his first two aerial victories. When WW2 began he was based on Formosa as part of the Tainan Wing, flying Zero fighters. On the morning of the first day of the Pacific war, Sakai was escorting bombers to attack bases in the Philippines, and over Clark Field he shot down a P40- the first aircraft shot down over the Philippines in the war.

Two days later he shot down his first Boeing B17 bomber, the first B17 lost in combat. At the end of December 1941 the Tainan Wing moved to Sulu Island, encountering more B17s and then began flying operations over Borneo, engaging Dutch and American fighters – P36s, P39s and P40s. By February 1942, Sakai had 13 official victories. In March the pilots moved to Lae, New Guinea, and began flying against the Americans and the Australians around Port Moresby, again encountering P39 and P40 fighters as well as twin-engined B25 and B26 bombers. On April 11, Sakai scored his first double victory – two P39 Airacobras.

These sorties over Port Moresby continued through 1942, and Sakai's victory score rose to 59. In August 1942, the Lae pilots were sent to the Japanese base at Rabaul. Flying over Guadalcanal on August 8, Sakai damaged a Wildcat so badly that the pilot baled out, and went on to attack two Avengers which were seen to go down on fire, before he was seriously wounded. Nevertheless, he flew again, on one occasion over Iwo Jima fighting 15 Hellcats and surviving, and in action over Japan scored two more victories. He ended the war with 64 scores to his name.

August 7 and captured a nearly complete fighter strip on the island's northern plain. This was a vital foothold if the Americans were to succeed in fighting their way up the Solomons. The island would be a static yet unsinkable aircraft-carrier. The obstacle to be overcome would be the defense of the island by its Japanese garrison and air support from Rabaul, some 600 miles to the north-west, from which Japanese bombers could easily reach Guadalcanal with, of course, fighter escort. There began a mammoth struggle which lasted for many months.

On the first day the Japanese reacted by sending 27 Betty bombers and 17 Zeros to attack the invading forces. They also sent nine Val dive-bombers on a one-way trip, as they had not the range to reach Guadalcanal and return home. At the end of this day, the Japanese had lost 16 aircraft – five Bettys, two Zeros and the nine Vals (five shot down, four ditching out of fuel).

At first carrier-based Wildcats gave air cover to the Marines, but on August 20 Marine Air Group 23 with one fighter and one dive-bomber squadron arrived on the island airstrip. The Wildcats were commanded by Major John L Smith, one of his pilots being Marion Carl of Midway fame.

The air battles over Guadalcanal were similar to those over Malta – plenty of attacking enemy aircraft, limited food, supplies, spares and fuel. Yet, unlike Malta, half of the island was still occupied by the Japanese, who daily seemed able to overrun the Marine position only to be pushed back again. After some minor skirmishes, when Carl's advice to the others about out-diving the Zeros saved one or two of them, came the first big clash, on August 24.

Japanese carrier planes and Rabaul-based bombers and fighters attacked in strength. In the fight that followed, Marion Carl led his division (section of four) over a group of Bettys, peeled off and in an overhead pass shot one down into the sea. He went on to claim two more, and a Zero, to make him the first US Marine Corps 'ace'. The Marines claimed 20 shot down, but the Japanese lost, perhaps, only a dozen all told. After the Marines were reinforced on August 30 by another fighter and bomber squadron, the battles continued.

When the Marines attacked Guadalcanal, the Japanese pilots at Lae were recalled to Rabaul, including Saburo Sakai, whose victory tally was nearing 60. He and his brother pilots were immediately ordered to escort bombers against the island, and over Guadalcanal had a battle with Wildcats from the US carriers *Saratoga* and

Enterprise. Sakai shot down one Wildcat after quite a struggle, but was puzzled by the American tactics. Each time they attacked and the Zeros turned to meet them they would scatter and dive. Other Wildcats would then attack in sections from out of the sun, fire, roll over and disappear below without giving the Japanese pilots the chance to use their maneuverability to close with them. The Japanese could comprehend the American tactics but noticed too that their gunnery was sadly inferior; only one Zero went down.

Sakai's commander, Tadashi Nakajima, was attacked by two Wildcats. He pulled round onto the tail of one but before he could fire the second Wildcat pilot was on him as the two Americans 'scissored'. This was the first time that the former Lae Wing pilots had met the Navy Wildcats and they were now meeting the Thach Weave, also for the first time. Nakajima was forced to break away and make off. Shortly afterwards Sakai shot down his 60th victim, but was seriously wounded when he attacked two Avengers, losing the sight of his right eye and sustaining severe head wounds. He managed to fly back to Rabaul, but was out of the fighting for 20 months.

The fighting above Guadalcanal continued with bombers and Zeros flying down 'the Slot' from Rabaul to be met by the Marine fighters, scrambled after sighting reports radioed in by island coastwatchers along the Japanese route. With the island strengthened by more fighters, the bombers were often badly mauled. In late September the Japanese suddenly changed their tactics and sent smaller formations of bombers escorted by larger numbers of Zeros. It was like the RAF 'rodeos' over Northern France, and the Japanese intentions were similar. They sought to lure the Marine pilots into a fighter action and wear them down in battles of attrition. Sometimes they succeeded.

On one occasion coastwatchers failed to detect the Japanese sweep and Guadalcanal radar did not identify the raiders in time. Thirty-three Wildcats, struggling to gain height after take-off, were attacked and six aircraft were lost; the others accounted for four Zeros.

These battles went on almost daily, each side gaining and then losing the advantage. In October while some of the surviving aces were being rested on the American side, a fresh batch of Marines arrived. One of these was 27-year-old Joe Foss.

During the next weeks Foss opened his score against the Japanese as he welded his flight into a real 'hot-shot' team. Seventy-two enemy aircraft

MIDWAY, PACIFIC OCEAN JUNE 4, 1942

THE THACH WEAVE

Pilots being trained for the US Navy during 1941 were taught to fly in the same three-plane 'V' formation used by the RAF. Lt Cdr John S 'Jimmy' Thach, CO of fighter squadron VF-3 in San Diego, was unhappy with the rigidity of this formation and during training at San Diego he began to develop a German-style fighter tactic, using two-plane elements in a more fluid squadron formation.

His idea was that a properly spaced two-plane unit attacked by an enemy fighter had only to turn toward the nearest friendly unit to evade the threat and pull the opponent across the front of another fighter. Thach himself named this tactic the Beam Defense Maneuver, but inevitably it was more often called the Thach Weave. Like the RAF, the US Navy did not change its tactical thinking overnight: some of Thach's fellow squadron commanders saw the sense of the idea and adopted it themselves, but others were reluctant to abandon the three-plane section until combat experience forced them to acknowledge the need for change.

By February 1942 VF-3, equipped with F4F Wildcats, was aboard the carrier *Lexington*: on 20 February the squadron was due to mount a raid on the Japanese base at Rabaul, but preparations were interrupted by the approach of a Japanese reconnaissance aircraft. Six Wildcats were scrambled and the intruder was shot down, but not before it had confirmed the American presence, and at 1630 hours the carrier's radar screens showed more aircraft approaching.

During the ensuing attack by a total of 17 G4M 'Betty' land-based bombers in two waves, VF-3's Wildcats earned more honors, with 15 'Bettys' either being shot down or ditching during the return journey. Lt Edward 'Butch' O'Hare, one of a number of exceptional fliers who were to gain fame flying with the squadron, personally claimed five victims in his first combat, a feat which earned him the Congressional Medal of Honor.

Four months later, during the Battle of Midway, VF-3 was based aboard the carrier *Yorktown* and was involved in the action depicted here.

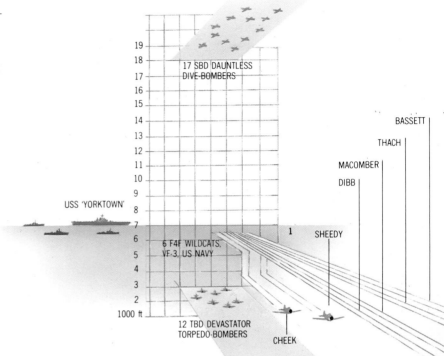

Theory of Beam Defense
Elements of two aircraft 3-400 yards apart: each pilot can watch his partner's tail, and a unit under attack breaks toward the next unit, which simultaneously breaks toward the threatened pair. The attackers, following the first unit, meet the second pair almost head-on.

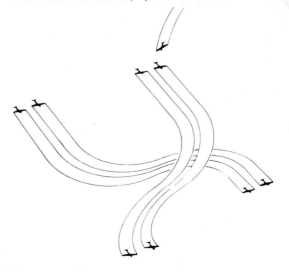

15 A6M2 ZEROS,
IMPERIAL JAPANESE NAVY

TIMETABLE

1 Six of VF-3's Wildcats, led by Jimmy Thach, set off to escort a strike force of torpedo- and dive-bombers in an attack on the Japanese carriers accompanying the invasion fleet toward Midway.
2 After a long search the Japanese carriers are located: the dive-bombers make an unopposed attack, but the defending Zeros shoot down ten of the 12 low-flying torpedo-bombers; the remaining pair subsequently ditch.
3 At the same time, the top two pairs of Wildcats are attacked by 15 Zeros: one Wildcat is shot down immediately.
4 Thach turns hard, meeting a Zero head-on and flaming it with his first burst.

5 The formation continues to apply the defensive weave.
6 Another Zero follows a Wildcat through the scissors, bringing it in front of Thach.
7 Thach opens fire to claim his second Zero.
8 The Wildcats maintain the defensive weave pattern as the battle develops. Thach goes on to claim a third Zero, while another pilot registers one probable kill. Meanwhile, the other two Wildcats fight it out with more Zeros, claiming two kills and one probable. Of the original six Wildcats, five make it back to 'Yorktown' with one pilot wounded; despite VF-3's efforts, 'Yorktown' is torpedoed and has to be abandoned.

JOE FOSS

BORN IN SIOUX FALLS, SOUTH Dakota, in April 1915, Joseph Jacob Foss became the second-highest-scoring US Marine pilot in WW2 with 26 kills, second only to Gregory Boyington with 28. However, Foss was the highest-scoring Marine pilot in the Pacific air battles and was awarded the Congressional Medal of Honor and the DFC. Foss arrived in the Pacific in the summer of 1942, being sent to Guadalcanal in September as a Marine Captain and flight commander in VMF 121, leading the famed 'Flying Circus' flight, that accounted for 72 Japanese aircraft.

The US pilots were usually outnumbered in the air, and shelled by Japanese ships and army artillery when on the ground. Yet between October 9 and November 19, Foss shot down no fewer than 23 Japanese aircraft in his Grumman F4F Wildcat, including five in a single day on October 25, 1942. On November 7 he shot down two 'Pete' floatplanes and a 'Rufe', a Zero floatplane. On this occasion he lost his way home and had to ditch north of the 'Canal', but scrambled ashore on the island of Malaita, being picked up next day by a rescue plane. His score reached 20 five days later, making him the first American pilot of WW2 to reach this figure, and by January 15 he had raised it to 26.

On January 25, 1943, Foss led eight Wildcats and four P38s of the Army to stop a large force of Japanese raiders from carrying out their mission, at first by ordering his men not to engage but to circle to and fro between Savo Island and Cape Esperance. Unable to draw Foss into a fight, the Japanese simply turned round and flew home.

fell to his eight men, six of whom became 'aces', Foss himself claiming 26 shot down. On October 25 Foss, in two missions, knocked out five Japanese airplanes – the first Marine pilot to do so in one day. This brought his own score to 16. Foss, like Jimmy Thach, had grown up hunting game-birds on the wing. Interestingly, fighter pilots who had this background found little difficulty in hitting enemy aircraft in combat. He also liked the Wildcat's six guns, and had his sighted two each at 250, 300 and 350 yds. As there was a period when guns jammed through defective ammunition, Foss considered six guns ample to be sure of hitting a target.

On November 12, Joe Foss became the first American in WW2 to score 20 victories. And he survived. He and pilots like him understood their enemy. Foss once remarked that a saying on Guadalcanal was: 'If you're alone and you meet a lone Zero, run like hell – you're outnumbered!'

By this time Guadalcanal was more or less secure. From then on began the American build-up which gradually enabled them to overrun and regain all the islands in the South and Central Pacific areas, then move on towards the Philippines and, eventually, Japan.

The Battle of Midway and the prolonged struggle for Guadalcanal had been a slogging match between the Zero and the Wildcat. Like the RAF in 1940, the American pilots had to evolve their fighter tactics in the light of their day-to-day experience and use their aircraft to the best of its ability. What these same pilots were able to do was to produce enough feed-back to help with the design of the new Navy fighter that would shortly arrive in the Pacific – the new and exciting Grumman F6F Hellcat.

AUSTRALIAN OPERATIONS

In the South-West Pacific area at the beginning of 1943, the Japanese, still fighting for New Guinea, were also threatening Northern Australia. In New Guinea itself there were nine American and two Australian fighter squadrons. The latter flew P40 Kittyhawks, as did the Americans, the P39 by now being obsolete.

The Americans were in fact gradually replacing their Kittyhawks with P38 twin-engined, twin-boomed Lightnings. The Kitty-hawk had not fared well against the Zero mainly due to its slower rate of climb and its failure to operate successfully at high levels. Above 18 000 ft the P40 became sluggish while the Zero just continued upwards and out of sight, or, more dangerously, reached a tactically advantageous position. The P40 pilots had to be satisfied with

hit-and-run tactics, hoping to hit the light Zero with their .5 machine-guns before being seen.

To the south, on the Australian mainland around and to the south of Darwin, the RAAF had six squadrons: two equipped with Spitfires, one with long-range Beaufighters, two with Hudson bombers and one with Vengeance dive-bombers. There were also an RAF Spitfire squadron, an American B24 Liberator outfit and a Dutch Mitchell squadron. The three Spitfire squadrons were merged to form No. 1 Australian Fighter Wing, comprising 452 and 457 Squadrons RAAF and 54 Squadron RAF.

Japanese aircraft based in Celebes were ordered to make monthly forays over Darwin and the surrounding area. They made two attacks in March, inflicting heavy damage on some fuel-storage depots, but lost seven of their number to Spitfires.

There followed a lull in Japanese activity which the Allies assumed to be a reluctance on the enemy's part to engage the redoubtable Spitfire. Of the 95 Spitfire pilots in the wing, six had gained vast experience in fighting the Germans and Italians over occupied France or in the Middle East. A further 37 had some combat experience, so they felt confident that they could oppose the Japanese with some expectation of victory. A few American pilots (one being Joe Foss), while on leave, warned the Spitfire pilots to take care when faced with Japanese fighters. Understandably, however, this was something that the Australian Wing pilots would have to find out for themselves.

The leader of No. 1 Wing was Wing Commander Clive 'Killer' Caldwell DFC, an Australian who had scored 20 victories in North Africa. In his Spitfire VC he had already shot down a Japanese torpedo-bomber on March 2, 1943 as well as a Zero.

On May 2, radar plots identified Japanese planes heading for Darwin and the Spitfires were scrambled. Ordering rendezvous at 10 000 ft over Hughes Airfield, the fighter controller told Caldwell to expect 20-plus hostile aircraft (actually 18 bombers and 27 Zeros) at 25 000 ft. Caldwell ordered the wing into a right-hand climb into the sun, heading up to 30 000 ft. When he saw them, at 27 000 ft crossing Darwin harbor, his 33 Spitfires had reached only 26 000 ft. Caldwell continued to lead his men higher but no sooner had he reached the height of the bombers, than he saw the Zeros at least 4000 ft above them.

Caldwell was in no position to attack the bombers, as this would expose his pilots to the Zeros, so he went on climbing with the sun behind him. Eventually gaining height and position, the Australian ordered 54 Squadron to take on the Zeros while 457 Squadron came out of the sun at the bombers. As the attacking pass ended, 457 was to regain height and if needed the leader could call on 452 Squadron to protect them from any Zeros that came down to attack.

By this time the Japanese had bombed, turned and were heading out to sea, and the Spitfires were at 32 000 ft, the Zeros at 22 000 and the bombers at 10 000. Caldwell signalled 54 to begin the attack, the Squadron diving almost vertically onto the Zeros. The CO, Squadron Leader E M Gibbes, sent one very surprised Zero pilot down with smoke streaming from his machine as the battle began. Meanwhile 457 Squadron attacked the bombers from a vertical position but the Zeros turned towards the Spitfires head-on and prevented all but one from reaching the bombers.

Caldwell then led 452 Squadron down to assist, aiming at a Zero, but only one of his cannons fired, which slewed his Spitfire to one side. Two Zeros attacked but he turned under them as a third came up beneath him. Pilot Officer K J Fox turned his Spitfire after this Zero and managed to put a few bullets into it, but then the quick-turning plane was round and behind him. Moments later Fox was struggling free of his shattered Spitfire to parachute into the sea.

The battle ended with claims of six Japanese planes down, four probably destroyed and eight damaged. Five Spitfires were lost but three pilots were rescued from the sea. Five more Spitfires force-landed short of fuel, one being written off, while three more suffered engine-failure and had to land, one being destroyed. In all, two pilots were killed, seven aircraft were destroyed and three damaged. The Japanese pilots claimed 21 victories and reported six bombers damaged.

Following this action, which received adverse publicity in the newspapers, it was concluded that the Spitfires should carry more fuel, that interception should be made earlier, and the pilots (as the Americans had warned them) should be strictly enjoined not to dogfight the Zeros.

SPITFIRE VERSUS ZERO
The Spitfire, as a fighter, was superior to the Zero, though less maneuverable at low speeds. In straight and level flight, as well as in a dive, the Spitfire was faster, but the Zero had the better climb. Tactics in future should be restricted to

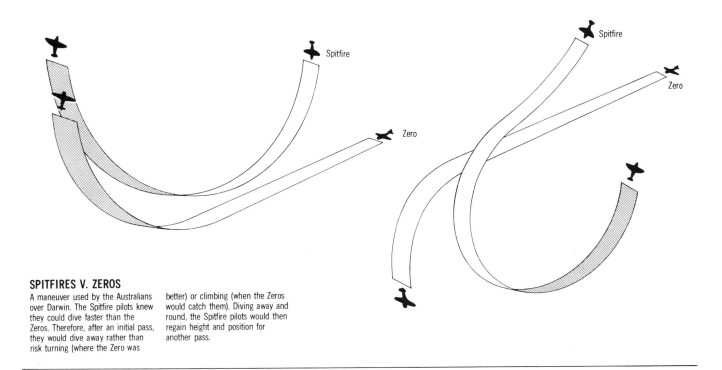

SPITFIRES V. ZEROS
A maneuver used by the Australians over Darwin. The Spitfire pilots knew they could dive faster than the Zeros. Therefore, after an initial pass, they would dive away rather than risk turning (where the Zero was better) or climbing (when the Zeros would catch them). Diving away and round, the Spitfire pilots would then regain height and position for another pass.

fast attacks, then a dive away to regain speed to climb for another attack.

On June 20 the Japanese returned to Darwin. The wing put up 46 Spitfires, but Caldwell's radio failed. Squadron Leader Gibbes, who was to take over, had engine failure, so the three squadrons decided to engage independently. The first to see the enemy, at 27 000 ft, were 54 Squadron, who dropped their external tanks and attacked as the Japanese crossed the Australian coast. They shot down four bombers and a Zero; 452 also engaged and shot down three more bombers and an escorting Zero.

After bombing an army camp, the Japanese headed north. Caldwell, despite his broken radio, together with Group Captain A L Walters, continued the attack and they shot down one Zero each.

A new tactic by the Japanese on this occasion was that, while the Spitfires were engaged higher up, ten bombers slipped in at low level to attack the airfield at Darwin and an army camp. But they were seen by some of 54 Squadron, who shot down one of them. In all, nine Japanese bombers and five fighters were claimed for the loss of two pilots, which restored some of the Spitfire pilots' confidence.

The usual hint of another impending attack came in early July when the Japanese sent a reconnaissance aircraft over the Darwin area. On July 6 an approaching Japanese force was intercepted by 33 Spitfires, while another two stayed low in case a raider slipped in beneath them. A third Spitfire flew out to make visual contact with the raiding force to report its direction of approach to base controller.

Caldwell made rendezvous at 6000 ft; the controller then directed him towards the Japanese, who were at 20 000 ft and coming in over the Timor Sea from the north-west heading for Fenton, south of Darwin. The radar plot showed a slow approach, indicating that they were climbing, whereupon the Spitfires continued their climb and when they reached 32 000 ft they saw the Japanese three thousand feet below. They could make out 26 bombers flying in three wide V-formations. The large Vees were subdivided into three smaller vics of three aircraft. Escorting them were 21 Zeros.

The Spitfires were between them and Fenton. Caldwell had planned that 452 Squadron would engage the escort while 54 went down head-on at the bombers, 457 being kept in reserve at 7000 ft above the bombers to observe the battle as it developed.

At 11.35 am the Japanese aircraft crossed the Australian coast, and Caldwell ordered 452 onto the fighters, who began to form a defensive circle. Two Zeros were shot down and the others were unable to defend the bombers, but three Spitfires were lost, two to engine failure and one to enemy action.

Then 54 Squadron went for the 27 bombers, although several Spitfires were having engine problems, so that only seven were able to attack. They shot down four but lost two more Spitfires. Caldwell then ordered two four-man sections of 457 down onto the bombers. They were engaged by the Zeros who shot down three of the Australians, but two more bombers were destroyed. Another bomber went down over Fenton, then the raiders headed for the coast. Caldwell positioned himself ahead of them, made a lone head-on pass on a bomber, and was engaged by a Zero, and then by two more, but he evaded, half-rolled and dived away.

This was the last major Japanese raid over Darwin. The Spitfires had had some success but had sustained losses in aircraft and pilots. A significant number of Spitfires had been lost by engine failure. Nevertheless, the Japanese did not relish further combat with the Spitfires and in fact their next effort in August was at night, when only reconnaissance aircraft came over. Three were over Darwin on August 20, the Spitfires shooting them all down. Caldwell shared a fourth with his wingman later that afternoon after a 300-mph chase out to sea.

These losses forced the Japanese to change their tactics. They began to escort their reconnaissance aircraft. On September 7 they sent a heavily escorted reconnaissance plane towards Darwin. No 457 Squadron were scrambled and positioned themselves over likely spots where the reconnaissance plane might turn for base. At first the radar plot seemed to show just one machine. As it closed, the plot revealed the fighters as well. The rest of the wing was scrambled, only to be caught while climbing by the escort Zeros. Three were shot down, including the commanding officer of 452, but he and a second pilot baled out. Then the pilots of 457, having already gained height, dived on to the Zeros and for no loss shot down four and damaged others. The Japanese reverted to night raids. In October, Flight Lieutenant J H Smithson, patrolling over Darwin Harbor, found a vic of three bombers in the searchlight, attacked from dead astern and shot down two.

The threat from the Japanese air effort over Darwin was ended, except for a few more scrambles against elusive reconnaissance aircraft.

Designed to replace the Hurricane as a day fighter, the Typhoon did not come up to expectation and by 1943 was developed as a ground-attack fighter-bomber. However, excelling at low level, it proved its worth in combating low-level hit and run raiders over the English Channel in 1942-43. This picture is a Mark 1B (EK183) of 56 Squadron, the first squadron to receive the Typhoon, in September 1941.

The Spitfires won the battle despite their bad engines. They had opposed the Zeros, learned the best way of fighting them, inflicted damage on the bombers, and caused the enemy to change their tactics several times – and they had won.

NEW AIRCRAFT IN EUROPE

On the Western Front, known to the Luftwaffe airmen as the Channel Front, the war in Europe had continued much as it had done in 1941, with the RAF Fighter Command still trying to pin the German Air Force down by flying Sweeps, Rodeos, Ramrods and Circuses over Belgium and Northern France.

Fighter Command's main equipment was the Spitfire, the Mark II of early 1941 having been replaced with the Mark V with two 20-mm cannon and four 0.303 machine-guns. The Hurricane had been relegated to night fighting and night intruding, with four 20-mm cannon and long-range fuel-tanks to allow them longer periods over the Continent waiting for night raiders to return to their bases from missions against England.

Some new fighter types had been flown and tested in combat, but most failed the high standards needed to survive. The RAF had tried the P39 Airacobra and P40 Tomahawk, but the former found little favor, and the Tomahawks were relegated to a few tactical reconnaissance operations or sent to North Africa where the Italians were easier opposition because of their substandard aircraft – until the Germans began to dominate the desert skies.

A replacement for the Hurricane from the

Hawker stable was the Typhoon. It began to enter squadron service in September 1941, but not enough testing time had been given which would have avoided the faults which were subsequently encountered. It was a big, heavy airplane of seven tons, but its engine was to suffer teething troubles, a number of Typhoons lost their tailplanes and, surprisingly, one early fault was the lack of rearward view. Early pilots were staggered to discover that they could not see behind them because of the armor-plating that not only covered the pilot's head and back but extended sideways to the edge of the fuselage. When this was put to the designer, Sydney Camm, who had also designed the Hurricane, he said somewhat angrily, 'My bloody aeroplane's so fast you don't have to see behind you!' He was wrong, of course, and soon the rear view was cleared and later models in 1944 had a 'tear-drop' canopy which gave the excellent all-round view so essential in any warplane, especially a fighter.

Nevertheless, the Typhoon, as a pure fighter, was disappointing and it was eventually assigned to ground-attack duties. This was due, in the main, to its excellent low-level capabilities, but an experienced pilot could still hold his own in fighter-versus-fighter combat when necessary.

In late 1941 some Spitfire pilots over France began to report seeing a radial-engined Me109 (some even thought the Germans were using captured Curtiss Hawks) during fighter sweeps. This was identified as Germany's new Focke-Wulf 190 fighter, which became the dominant Luftwaffe fighter for the remainder of the war. As with most WW2 fighters the design went through a number of variants and most of the FW190 ones were good. The FW190A-3 for instance was armed with two 20-mm cannon in the wingroots and two 7.9-mm machine-guns atop the fuselage in front of the cockpit, plus two 20-mm cannon in the wings. The two machine-guns carried 1000 rounds each, the inboard cannon had 200 RPG (Rounds per Gun) while the wing guns had 55 RPG. It had a speed of 312 mph at 20 000 ft, 418 mph at 21 000 ft. It could climb to 26 000 ft in 12 minutes, had a service ceiling of 35 000 ft and a range of 497 miles.

It became painfully apparent to the RAF that here was a new fighter that was able to outperform their Spitfire Vs on almost every count. It could outrun them, outdive them, outclimb them and outgun them. The only advantage was that the Spitfire had a tighter turn. For the next seven or eight months the RAF were on defensive/offensive missions. It was an echo of WW1 when the German Fokkers dominated with the Germans choosing the moment to engage, and the RAF fighting their way out by constantly turning into the Focke-Wulf's attacks. Not until the Spitfire IXs came on the scene in 1942 could the RAF operate on nearly equal terms with the 190. Initially they held an advantage in that the early Mark IXs were almost impossible to distinguish from the Mark V, which was most disconcerting for the 190 pilots.

The FW190's fire-power at first was not as good as the Spitfire's, the wing-root guns' rate of fire being restricted by the synchronization required for the shells to pass through the propeller arc. The FW190A-2 carried more shells for its cannon than the Spitfire Vs. The A-2 could fire for 17 seconds, the RAF's 20-mm Hispano 404 Mk II for just 10 seconds.

By the spring of 1942 the RAF pilots in their Spitfire Vs were well matched against Me109Fs, but were wary when tackling the 190s. In March 1942 Fighter Command lost 32 Spitfires, 103 in April and 61 in May. Little wonder that they welcomed the arrival of the Mk IX that summer.

However, the transition period continued to be traumatic for the RAF. Al Deere, who had shot down one of the first Me109s over Dunkirk in 1940, was, by the early summer of 1942, in command of 403 Canadian Squadron in the North Weald Wing. On June 2 they were part of a fighter sweep – an operation which some pilots felt to be a waste of time. Usually the Luftwaffe ignored a fighter sweep that could do no damage, and only a Circus or Ramrod with bombers stirred them into action. But today it was a different story.

On that June morning the Hornchurch and North Weald Wings joined forces to sweep over

the St Omer area, while 403 Squadron flew as top cover in the North Weald Wing at 27 000 ft. Soon after the Spitfires crossed the enemy coast, the controller warned of German reaction, followed by other warnings, but nothing was seen until the Spitfires were on their way out, when about 12 FW190s were seen behind, at 403's height, and closing fast. Fortunately, 403 had rehearsed just such a tactic. On Deere's order, one four-man section was to break upwards while the other two would turn into the approaching 190s. Deere had already approved of this tactic when he saw it being used by Me109s during the Battle of Britain.

When the FWs were almost upon them, Deere gave the order to break left. To his right, Yellow Section broke upwards while Red and Blue Sections turned hard towards the 190s. As they turned, Deere looked for Yellow Section and was dismayed to see a second group of FW190s coming through a thin cloud layer some 2000 ft above and right on their beam. The first group of 190s were now almost head-on to Deere's Red Section and there was only time for a quick burst of fire before the 190s pulled up over the Spitfires. More 190s came down from the right. Deere immediately turned to meet this new threat and then the air was full of twisting, turning 190s and Spitfires. The 190s, unlike the Me109s Deere had often met before, were keen to stay and give battle whereas 109 pilots usually made a quick pass and vanished before the Spitfires could out-turn them. These 190s seemed to be spoiling for a fight. Deere and his Squadron fought their way out but lost seven Spitfires and four pilots to this very determined group of Focke-Wulf pilots.

FIGHTERS OVER DIEPPE

The summer of 1942 saw the Dieppe Operation, code-named 'Jubilee'. This was a Combined Operations raid on August 19 on the French port, planned to keep up the pressure on the Germans in France, test the feasibility of an eventual landing on the Continent, entice the Luftwaffe to battle, and boost Russian confidence in Britain's potential.

At the commencement of the Dieppe raid, the RAF had made available 70 squadrons, 48 with Spitfires, including three USAAF squadrons (the 307th, 308th and 309th Fighter Squadrons), as well as the Eagle Squadrons [71, 121 and 133], soon to become the nucleus of the 4th US Fighter Group.

The Luftwaffe had 190 serviceable FW190s and 16 Me109 fighters of JG2 and JG26, while KG2 had 45 Dornier 217 bombers. The day after the battle, KG2's strength had been more than

The Focke Wulf 190 fighter gave the RAF a shock when it was first encountered over France in the later summer of 1941. It outclassed their Spitfire Vs and it was not until the Spitfire IXs arrived that Fighter Command was able to hold its own with the deadly 190. The Focke Wulf was also used by the Luftwaffe as a fighter-bomber.

halved, while JG2 and JG26 had been reduced to just 70 available fighters.

One of the pilots with 71 Eagle Squadron was Pilot Officer Harold Strickland. The Eagle Squadron flew in this formation.

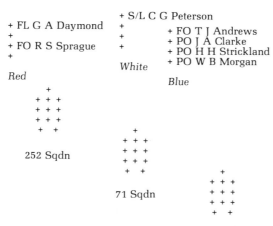

In his diary Strickland recorded: '*S*QUADRON *took off before dawn. In the darkness navigation lights were burned. My No. 2 did not retract his wheels and could not keep up, causing me to hold back. Andy (Blue One) turned off his lights before reaching Beachy Head. I lost him but contacted him before heading out to sea, then lost him again in the darkness.*

'*I set course for Dieppe and five minutes before my ETA, began to climb to 5000 feet. Blue Section was to guard the west flank of the assault forces over the beach. I saw flashes of heavy gunfire to my left, which was towards the sun, which was still below the horizon. In all other directions it was dark.*

'*As I proceeded towards the convoy I could see the outline of four aircraft patrolling east to west, line astern. I closed towards them from out of the darkness and identified them as four FW109s. I attacked the No. 4 with cannon and machine guns with about 45 degrees deflection and saw my explosive shells strike the fuselage. He dived. The other three turned into me. I turned right, pulled into a steep climbing turn and entered the cloud. Was counter-attacked three times upon leaving the cloud cover. Landed at Gravesend shortly after dawn.*

'*Second Sortie: we arrived at Dieppe with many air combats in progress. Blue Section attacked and chased away Me109s, believed to be*

carrying bombs. Dornier 217s and Ju88s were chased away after jettisoning their bombs. Enemy reaction was reaching its peak. We encountered terrific flak and on two occasions flew through our own flak maneuvering for position.

'*Red and White Sections damaged two FW 190s.*

'*Third Sortie (which I missed): Squadron arrived at Dieppe during a dive-bombing attack by some 20 Ju88s protected by screens of 190s and 109s. With another squadron they attacked and damaged or destroyed all the dive-bombers. Unfortunately Pete was struck by rear gunner of a Ju88, caught fire and baled out. McPharlin was hit by a 109F and his instruments shattered. He baled out.*

'*Fourth Sortie: We arrived off Dieppe to find all our assault boats and transports away from the beaches and on course for England. We covered the convoy at prescribed altitude. A large force of 190s appeared. Wing Commander Duke-Wooley ordered the Debden Wing to prepare for attack.*

'*We maneuvered into the sun and climbed. The 190s were above. When we turned towards them from below, they retreated, heading towards Le Touquet.*'

Harold Strickland was 39 years of age during these events, and two years later went back to France with the US IX Tactical Air Force Command HQ, on D-Day +10. He was well aware that the sacrifices made at Dieppe in 1942 gave the Normandy invasion planners much experience and good intelligence.

Fighter Command put up an almost complete air umbrella above the French port and the Channel to cover the returning convoy at the end of the day. Unlike the Dunkirk situation two years earlier, Fighter Command had 48 Spitfire squadrons in action, and three Typhoon squadrons, in addition to eight Hurricane squadrons used for ground attack.

The tactics employed had to cover and protect the attacking Canadian and British Commando forces, the ships that carried them there and back, and the Hurricanes, Bostons, Blenheims and reconnaissance Mustangs that flew in support.

In some ways the Spitfire squadrons were faced with similar tactical problems – other than numbers – to those of the RAF over Dunkirk. Air fighting in a three-dimensional battle arena always demands that patrols must be flown at all levels, especially in operations such as Dieppe – high (approximately 27 000 ft) in order to be above the battle and if possible above the enemy;

Above and **Right**: Me109G fighter being attacked by a Typhoon pilot low over Northern France. The Messerschmitt had just taken off from its base when attacked. The Typhoon pilot opened fire from 175 yards, closing in to 75 yards. Hit, the 109 went down with engine and port wing burning to crash on the airfield's perimeter track. In pictures 2 and 3 cannon shells can be seen exploding on the fuselage and port wing.

lower to deal with low-flying fighters and bombers who would need to fly at under 2000 ft to be effective against ground and naval forces. The RAF therefore also needed to be available between the very high and the very low to support both levels. This meant, at Dieppe, that some squadrons were heavily engaged while others saw no action whatever. Most Spitfire squadrons flew three or four patrols over Dieppe or the Channel in the 16 hours of daylight and those patrolling at low or medium heights were in constant danger of being attacked from above. The high squadrons often kept station, and while at times they could engage Me109s or FW190s at medium levels, many squadrons saw nothing.

At the end of the day the RAF claimed 96 Luftwaffe aircraft destroyed. Actually, only 23 fighters and 25 Dorniers were lost, with a further 24 damaged. The RAF's great effort cost them, in fact, 100 aircraft lost and 66 more damaged, 62 pilots and aircrew killed in action, plus two more in accidents, 17 taken prisoner and another 30 injured or wounded. The RAF did, however, succeed in its aim of protecting the light bombers and the returning convoy.

The Luftwaffe too achieved some success, although it was well below strength considering its overall numbers in France. The Dorniers arriving to bomb the ships off Dieppe were escorted by FW190s, and came in under the main German fighter force that was engaging the RAF cover patrols. Fortunately British radar detected their approach and alerted squadrons to engage them. It was obvious too that German radar was supporting the Luftwaffe's effort in sending their aircraft in when the RAF cover seemed to be either a little thin or heavily engaged already.

Four of the Spitfire squadrons at Dieppe were new Mark IXs that were gradually coming into service. The Spitfire IX had been flown in test trials against a captured FW190 and the Spitfire V. The RAF were forced to admit that the 190 was about the best all-round fighter in the air at that time. The 190 was faster at every level than the Spitfire V and faster than the Mk IX at 2000 ft, 5000 ft and between 18 000 and 21 000 ft. The Mk IX was faster at 8000 ft, 15 000 ft and above 25 000 ft. The 190 and the Mk IX were equal in a climb, the 190 faster in a dive and more maneuverable, except in a turn. The 190's superior rate of roll enabled it to avoid the IX if attacked in a turn, as it could flick over into a diving turn in the opposite direction, which was almost impossible for any Spitfire to follow.

It was found that the Mk IX's best form of defense was to attain a good speed, then if its pilot saw the 190 before the German got into firing range, it could outfly the attack. But if it was flying at low speed its slow acceleration gave the 190 a good chance of closing in. If the Mk IX could hold the initiative the pilot was considered to have a fair chance of outwitting the 190.

HIT-AND-RUN BANDITS

In the late summer and fall of 1942, and again in the first half of 1943, the Germans, as part of the offensive in the West, flew 'hit-and-run' raids against England's south coast. By now they were unable to operate large formations as in 1940 and night raids were becoming more costly as RAF techniques improved. Consequently, small or medium formations of bomb-carrying Me109s or FW190s would cross the Channel, bomb coastal towns or ports and get away as quickly as possible.

They were extremely difficult to catch. The Luftwaffe tactics for these raids were of two kinds. The pilots would either fly across at low level, below the British radar, or, having gained a good height, cross the Channel in a prolonged diving swoop, drop their bombs and make off at top speed.

It was useless to scramble fighters as by the time the Spitfires were up, the enemy would be back across the Channel. The only real counter to these raiders was to have standing patrols in the air, out to sea, hoping to be in the right place when the hit-and-run fighters came over. Even then they were almost impossible to stop. Coming in under the radar meant that unless the defenders and attackers actually collided, the flyers on standing patrol could not be advised of their presence until they had bombed. And only then – too late – could they be directed to intercept.

The Typhoon with its low-level capability became much more successful against these raiders than the Spitfires. Several of the new Typhoon squadrons were detailed for these operations, although the RAF, by having to fly standing patrols, were almost reverting to WW1 tactics.

The New Zealand-manned 486 Squadron was one unit engaged on these operations. Vaughan Fittall from Auckland told me: '*W̶E WERE rostered to have two Typhoons in the air during all daylight hours with a further two at readiness on the airfield. Our patrol lines were between Dover and Dungeness or Dungeness to Eastbourne, or Bognor to Beachy Head, or Selsey Bill to St Catherine's Point.*

'*When the weather was completely against us, we would fake operational conversations in the*

hope that we could bluff the Germans into thinking we had our patrols up. When flying these operations at low level with our, then, unreliable Sabre engines, it was quite nerve-racking for we had no height for escape if we had an engine failure.'

Fellow pilot Allan Smith, also from Auckland, shot down a Me109 on one of these missions on April 29, 1943: '*O*UR *PATROL LINES ranged between North Foreland and Beachy Head and it was difficult to make an interception unless you were right above the target area where the German aircraft made their attack. Initially we flew at 500 feet, which gave us a chance to speed up an interception by increasing our speed in a shallow dive.*

'I was scrambled on April 29 with Frank Murphy and headed straight out to sea keeping low on the water. The Controller plotted bandits approaching from the south and we were positioned between the bandits and the French coast. Later, after other vectors, I saw two aircraft low on the water. At about the same time the bandits either saw us or received a message from their base that they were being intercepted, and turned for France. This gave us a chance to close the gap and I identified them as Me109s. We tucked in behind them and it must have been very difficult for them to know just where we were because they were not flying far enough apart to cover each other's tail effectively.

'We were flying about 10 feet above the water and as we got into range I told Frank to attack the second 109 while I kept an eye on the leader. Frank was having trouble with his reflector sight and was having to use the splashes of his cannon shells on the water to direct his guns. There were a number of strikes on its wings and fuselage and the 109 moved to the left. As it came into my sights I gave it a couple of short bursts and shortly afterwards it crashed into the sea.

'I then closed in on the leader and fired. Pieces started to come off and it burst into flames. I moved to the left to avoid the debris and as the 109 lost speed I ended up in close formation to it. The German pilot turned and looked at me but shortly afterwards he hit the sea.'

Later, Typhoons began flying sorties over France, Belgium and Holland. Squadrons based at Manston often flew operations over the Dutch Islands, which was a happy hunting ground for the 'Tiffie' pilots. This was before the 'Tiffie' began carrying rockets, yet with four 20-mm

cannons they were able to inflict a good deal of damage on trains, road transport and especially shipping off the Dutch coast or on the inland rivers and canals. They were also intercepted by Messerschmitts and Focke-Wulfs but at low level they had some advantage over the Luftwaffe fighters. They had occasional success when meeting formations of Do217 bombers. They also tried to entice the German fighters up by simulating slow-flying Hurricanes on German radar, as Vaughan Fittall recalled. He was, by late 1943, a flight commander with 198 Squadron:

'*W*E WERE OFTEN DISAPPOINTED *the Luftwaffe seldom had a go at us, so sometimes we used to cross the sea with our flaps down and our engines throttled back in the hope that we would appear on the German radar as slow-flying Hurricanes and tempt the 190s to have a go at us.*

'On 7th October, 1943 we saw some 190s and then it was a matter of full throttle and after them as we expected them to head for the clouds. However, two 190s chose to hug the ground and gradually Mike Bryan (C.O. of 198) and I drew ahead of the squadron and once in range fired alternate bursts until one went down. It was 198's first confirmed kill.'

On November 30, 198 Squadron flew a sweep over Holland in support of American B17s that were raiding Germany. The Typhoons were to fly near German fighter bases to engage any fighters going to or returning from the battle areas. Instead they suddenly came across four Dornier 217s. Seeing no hostile fighters about, they thought it was a trap. However, the attack began. Fittall circled with his section to cover the other as it went in, then flew in himself. All four bombers were shot down. Some miles away the Typhoons of 609 Squadron also found a formation of Dorniers and shot down seven of them.

Another memorable encounter for a Typhoon pilot took place on January 24, 1944. Flying Officer W G Eagle of 198 Squadron, who had seen considerable action in the Western Desert in 1941, was flying alone at sea level over the North Sea. He had become separated from the squadron and ran into 12 Me109s fitted with long-range tanks.

Being well placed to attack, Bill Eagle climbed up under the leading 109 – they were at 300 feet – and fired. The 109's tank blazed and exploded, enveloping the 109 in burning fuel. Eagle fired into a second 109, which trailed smoke, lurched to one side and crashed into a third 109. All three went into the sea as the others rammed home their throttles and sped for base.

CHAPTER NINE

DAY AND NIGHT FIGHTING

FROM THE VERY BEGINNING OF the war neither the Luftwaffe nor especially the RAF were prepared for night fighting. However, when their attempts to dominate with daylight bomber operations failed, both sides resorted to night raids.

The RAF strengthened their night-bombing groups from early 1940, the Germans switching to night raids towards the end of that year when their daylight losses over England became disastrously high. If they were both ill-prepared for a night war they were equally so for defense against night bombers. The RAF quickly pressed Blenheim fighters into night service while the Luftwaffe used twin-engined Me110s for night defense.

Over the next few years each side made strenuous efforts to combat the other's night bombers. Airborne radar changed blind stalking above a blacked-out England or Germany into more of a science and its skilled use enabled ground controllers and the airborne radar operator to put the pilot into an attacking position.

The RAF's first successful night-fighter was the twin-engined Bristol Beaufighter. Armed with four 20-mm cannon in the nose and six 0.303 machine-guns in the wings it had formidable fire-power. It also had speed, range and endurance.

Airborne radar – AI (Airborne Interception) – sent out a series of radio waves. If there was an aircraft within range an echo bounced back and showed on two small radar screens. One screen gave elevation, the other the azimuth. Once in contact, the radar operator/navigator could guide his pilot close enough for a visual sighting. It was a skill that in some night-fighter crews was highly developed. John Cunningham and his radar operator Jimmy Rawnsley flying with 604 Squadron had considerable success. It was very much a team effort and it is axiomatic that every successful night-fighting crew had had long and hard experience together – in many cases, years. However skilled or whatever a pilot's marksmanship, his shooting ability was nothing without a capable and unflappable partner guiding him onto a target.

LUFTWAFFE NIGHT-FIGHTERS

The Germans too had their airborne radar, the Lichtenstein (FUSG 202). Installed in Me110s and later in Ju88s and Dornier 217 night-fighters, it would relay ground instructions to guide pilots onto the RAF bombers. The use of such aircraft as the Ju88 and Do217 was encouraged when it was

Left: The most deadly American day fighter of WW2 – the P51D Mustang. This example, with long-range fuel tanks under the wings for maximum range, was flown by Colonel John D Landers, CO of the 78th US Fighter Group. He had already shot down six Japanese aircraft over New Guinea flying P40s with the 49th Fighter Group. Then in England with the 8th Air Force he added 8½ air-to-air kills, plus another 14 destroyed on the ground, with a number of probables.

Right: Night-fighter, night intruder and bomber support fighter, the Bristol Beaufighter was the RAF's mainstay in night operations in the mid-war years. This Mark 1F is equipped with Mark IV AI radar.

realized that a night-fighter did not need maneuverability but staying and hitting power. They could carry a large fuel supply, heavy armament and the necessary radar and electrical equipment. Their ground controller received radar information from Giant Würzburg scanners which had a range of 40 miles. Once guided to the proximity of a target, the airborne Lichtenstein operator – his set having a range of some 2½ miles – also guided his pilot to the night raider.

Armament in the Me110 was two 20-mm cannon and two 7.9-mm machine-guns in the nose. The rear gunner also had a machine-gun. A further gunnery development was the introduction into Me110s of two upward-firing 20-mm cannon, mounted in the fuselage at an angle of 10 to 20 degrees, which was known as 'Schrage Musik'. Using non-tracer ammunition to conceal both his position and the new guns, the German pilot, when put in visual touch with a bomber, needed only to fly beneath it and fire upwards – not into the fuselage/bomb bay, but into wings, engines and fuel tanks. Few bomber crews attacked from such a position had any idea of what or who were responsible.

The Germans' general tactic was for a night-fighter, once airborne, to fly to a radio beacon where it would circle until the ground controller located a target aircraft. He would then be guided to a position where his radar operator could pick it up. It was not difficult to locate the RAF bombers as they generally formed stream, easily identified on ground radar. Only the ultimate target would be unknown.

Hauptman Wilhelm Johnen shot down 34 Allied aircraft while flying night-fighting Me110s with NJGs 1, 5 and 6. On the evening of April 28, 1944, when Johnen, now with 3/NJG 6, was based at Hagenau, it looked as if the RAF would not be flying over Germany because of the weather. However, soon after midnight, orders came to take off and fly to the Nancy sector – RAF bombers were making for Southern Germany. Oberfeldwebel Mahle was his gunner, Brinos his wireless operator. '*I*T WAS 1.10 HOURS *precisely by the time we reached our combat height of 15 000 feet. Brinos tuned in on the ground station wave and learned that the head of the British bomber stream was flying west of Nancy on a course south-south-east. In a few moments we should get the first contact in our radar. I circled west of the city and explored the night sky with my SN2. Brinos reported calmly, "Achtung. The first enemy zig-zags have appeared. Turn slightly to port."*

'*The gyro compass showed 160 degrees and changed on a slight left-hand turn to 130 degrees. Brinos now reported, "Target about two and a half miles ahead. Give her full gas."*

'*My C9+ES was very fast. Within a few minutes the distance was reduced to 1,000 yards. At any moment the enemy bomber must appear. I closed in until I could see the black shadow of the bomber. The British machine was flying peacefully, weaving slightly to avoid attack. I recognised the type by its wings – a four-engined Lancaster. Brinos switched off his SN2 and concentrated on each phase of the ensuing air combat. Slowly we stalked the bomber with the moon behind us. Distance 200 yards. The British pilot must have spotted us for he suddenly did a*

Top: The Me110, relegated to the night-fighter role, flew defense sorties over the Reich from 1941-1945. This 110 of 6/NJG6 carries the 'Lichtenstein' radar aerials.
Above: The demand for long endurance rather than maneuverability in night-fighters, was answered by using Dornier 217 and Ju88 heavy fighters in the battles over Germany. This Ju88G-6 carries FuG 220d and FuG 350 radar aerials. Note too the position of the two 20 mm oblique guns (Schräge Musik) halfway down the fuselage.

vertical turn to starboard to give his rear gunner a better chance to fire. I stuck on his tail. The perspex of the gunner's turret glittered in the moonlight. Just as I got it in the centre of my sights he opened fire with all his guns. The glow-worms shaved my machine, but with a slight pressure on the rudder I slipped out of the danger zone. Now I was flying below him and approaching at "elevator" speed. In this way the rear gunner could not fire at me, although the mid-upper gunner was still a danger. This time I would shoot first; of that I was certain. Slowly the long narrow wings rose in the air. As soon as I could see the glowing exhaust pipes, I fired between the two engines.

'The enemy must have opened fire at the same moment for his tracers hit my wings. I immediately took avoiding action. "The Tommy's on fire," screamed Brinos into the R/T, nearly deafening me. He was right. Flames were pouring from the trailing edge of the wing, but the crate continued to fly calmly on its way.

'"Shall I give him another burst?" I wondered, drawing closer. But the enemy was badly hit and the greedy flames were glowing eerily in the darkness, lighting up the red, white and blue circles. One of the crew baled out. For the fraction of a second his body gleamed in the light of the flames before he fell into the yawning depths. One after another followed suit and eight men in all baled out. It was high time, for a moment later the port petrol tank exploded and the machine hurtled to the ground, leaving behind it a long fiery tail.'

Twenty minutes later Johnen shot down another bomber that fell in flames into Lake Constance. He chased another across the border into Switzerland although it was forbidden to fly over neutral territory. As the two aircraft exchanged gunfire, Johnen's Me110 was hit in the port engine which caught fire. He was forced to land on a Swiss airfield where both crewmen were interned. Within a month they were back in Germany, exchanged for three British officers who had escaped from a prison camp in Germany, and were thus allowed to return to England while Johnen and his crew took a train back to the Fatherland.

Naturally each side was anxious to try to outdo and out-think the other. Throughout the war they were constantly trying to jam one another's night radar or devising other counter-measures which would stop the bombers being intercepted.

During one period of serious jamming the Luftwaffe began sending single-engined Me109s and FW190s into the German night skies. They went up on nights that had some moon and operated over the RAF target city which was, when they reached it, well lit with flames, exploding bombs and defensive searchlights. These fighters, termed 'Wild Boar', gained some measure of success, although they were limited to 'light' nights, favorable weather and not a little luck.

The RAF too used single-engined fighters in the early days simply because the raiders outnumbered the Beaufighters and Blenheims. The Hurricane was used mostly; but so too was the Defiant. Both the German Me110 and the RAF's Defiant were failed daylight fighters but both fared better at night. Hurricanes or Defiants were guided to the area of the German raid, then it was just good fortune if they got close enough to see the glow of the German bombers' exhaust stubs. They usually flew at half or quarter moon, and, of course, if a raider was caught in searchlight, the fighter without radar was able to fly into the attack.

These two fighter types were also used with some success in intruder missions over France. Granted that it was often difficult to locate bombers in the darkness over England, it was obvious that they had eventually to return to base. Hurricanes, and sometimes Defiants, would be sent over France and try to pick off the returning Heinkels or Dorniers as they landed, the enemy airfield betraying its presence by having to switch on landing-lights which were visible from some distance.

Gerry Gray flew Defiants with 264 Squadron.

He reported: '*INTRUDING IN DEFIANTS was incredible. Once we'd located the enemy airfield and saw bombers landing I'd dive and we'd go right up underneath the bomber, pull up and my gunner would fire a squirt right in the chap's faces as they came in to land. On May 7, 1941 we attacked Merville like this, got a Heinkel and a couple more probables. From the German's point of view it was ghastly, for they would have very little control with their wheels and flaps down, then suddenly we'd pop right up in front of them, all guns blazing.'*

THE RADAR WAR

By late 1942 the German night-fighter force had evolved new tactics to combat the RAF bomber streams. They began to infiltrate the stream on both its outward and return journey. Individual crews, once in the stream, were then able to pick up their own radar contacts and conduct their own pursuit, rather than be vectored onto individual bombers by ground control.

Successes were many, not least, for instance, on the night of March 4-5, 1944 when the Luftwaffe night-flyers shot down 75 heavy RAF bombers and on March 30-31 when the RAF lost 94 with 13 more written-off through combat damage. Bomber Command could not for long have sustained such losses, but fortunately RAF technicians and radar experts were gradually winning the airborne radar war and had by the fall of that year virtually neutralized the German system.

German night-fighters built up high scores during the night war over Germany. Their top scorer was Major Heinz-Wolfgang Schnaufer, with 121 victories, all achieved in 164 sorties. He scored many multiple kills: on May 25, 1944 he shot down five Lancasters in 14 minutes, on February 21, 1945 he destroyed two in the early morning, followed by a further seven that evening, making nine in one day.

Helmut Lent was the first night-fighter to score 100 victories, before being killed in a crash in late 1944. His total of 102 made him night 'ace' No 2. The third highest was Prince Heinrich of Sayn-Wittgenstein, with 83, who also flew at night on the Russian front; but his greatest success was over Germany. On one July night in 1943 he shot down seven bombers and on January 1, 1944 scored six. Then on May 21, 1944, he had just accounted for his fifth of the night when he was shot down.

German night-fighters were undoubtedly causing severe losses to Bomber Command, who, never without offensive initiative, had to find a way to beat the threat. The question was how to locate an enemy night-fighter flying near the bomber stream over Germany with AI operating. The British crew would not know how to distinguish, say, an Me110 from a British bomber until the pilot was close enough to see it. This could be a long and tedious process; actually finding a German fighter would be more by luck than judgement.

However, a German Ju88 night-fighter fell into Allied hands and the 'boffins' were able to get their hands on the Lichtenstein airborne radar set. The RAF were soon provided with a small receiver called Serrate that could pick up signals from the Lichtenstein set. Suddenly the RAF night-fighters were able to tell a German night-fighter from an RAF bomber – although the contact might prove to be an Me109 or FW190 (that did not carry radar) flying 'Wild Boar' sorties.

The Beaufighters of 141 Squadron RAF, commanded by Wing Commander Bob Braham, began operating near RAF bomber streams or in the vicinity of target areas to combat German night-fighters. These began in June 1943, Braham and his men being the pioneers of this type of operation. Bob Braham was a prewar airman who had been involved in night operations since 1939. As the war progressed he became one of the RAF's outstanding night-fighter pilots. Teaming up with AI operators such as Sergeant 'Sticks' Gregory and Flight Lieutenant 'Jacko' Jackson, he ended the war with 29 victories, mostly at night, although he was shot down and taken prisoner in June 1944 on a day Ranger operation over Denmark.

Michael Allen was one of Braham's men, and flew with Flying Officer Harry White. Trained as a radar operator, Mike Allen had crewed with his pilot, Harry White, in 1941 and flown extensively on night defense duties. By the summer of 1943 they had the experience and confidence to use the new Serrate over enemy territory with success. Mike Allen recalls: '*WE NORMALLY operated around 17–18 000 feet – the height of the bomber stream. Our objective was to find and destroy German night-fighter aircraft, and indirectly to cause confusion to the German ground controllers and night-fighter crews. To do this we used our aircraft as individual freelance high level patrols, using them in the following ways:*
1. Patrol between German night-fighter airfields and the path of the bomber stream.

2. When German night-fighters were vectored to a radio beacon, and would orbit there waiting for their Group Controller to send them onto a bomber. As months went by so our intelligence gave us the known locations of some of these beacons. We ourselves could not pick up their signals but knowing the locations we could fly into the vicinity and hope to find a night-fighter orbiting there.

(Element of surprise in early days when [Enemy] night-fighters didn't know RAF night-fighters were operating over Germany etc.)

3. Knowing where the bomber stream was headed one could sometimes reckon that at a given time the night-fighters would have been vectored into the stream and we could then fly a freelance patrol on the edge of the stream hoping to pick something up either entering or leaving the stream. With our Serrate we knew we might pick up very long range signals – 20–25 miles away – that gave us the indication there were night-fighters in that area.

4. On Berlin trips, or other large target areas, go into the area as the last of the bombers were going through. If, for instance, the bombing times were midnight to 0025, we would aim to be in the target area at around 0025, knowing that the night-fighters already up in that area, particularly the single-seaters, [would be] flying around by the light of the fires and searchlights and not necessarily know the bombing was finished. We then had a reasonable chance of picking up one of these boys. Our [radar] tubes would be clearing and the Germans would be hanging around and there [they] would be. We would spend 15–20 minutes in the target area between 18–20 000 ft. It was dangerous so perhaps we would prefer just to stand off the area.

5. As the bomber stream came out of the target area, say Berlin, and turned and began to head back home across the northern plain we could patrol near it. In the early days we would use our own initiative of where we would like to patrol, and hope to pick up any night-fighters flying either side of it.

6. Another variation was that if the Main Force was going out across the North Sea and 100 Group laid on a spoof raid further south to divert night-fighters, then some RAF fighter activity would be needed to back up the spoof raid. In this way we would be able to intercept any night-fighters diverted south away from the main stream.

'The range of our Mark IV AI was governed by our height above the ground – about four miles at 20 000 feet. Once we got a contact I would throw a switch on the side of the viewing unit and the pictures on the radar tubes would change. If our contact was indeed a night-fighter we would receive 'herring-bone' pictures from the emanations of the German's radar equipment. We would pick up Serrate contacts at considerably longer ranges than the normal AI set, so we would also search by constantly switching from AI to Serrate, and then guide my pilot towards the Serrate contact until I picked it up on the AI.

'I would then concentrate on the Mark IV and hope to be able to complete the interception and bring Harry to a visual – about 1 000 to 600 feet – and ideally the target would be a little bit above so we would come in below it.

'One of the frightening things was to see the number of Lancasters and Halifaxes who we would "intercept" and they would never know we were there. We would often pursue to get a visual and in many cases the RAF rear-gunners or mid-uppers never saw us at all. We could see any number being shot down like flies and we could do little about it.

'The Beaufighters lacked endurance and nearly all our trips we did were 4 to 4½ hours, especially if we'd had a chase and a combat. Later, on Mosquitoes we could go 5 or even 6 hours. Our longest was to Chemnitz which was 6 hours, 40 minutes. By that time we were using two 100-gallon drop tanks to extend our range. With the Beau we were also hampered by lack of speed.

'On July 15, 1943 we shot down a Me110 but in actual fact he must have got us on his forward-looking radar because we did have, as far as one can at night, something of a dogfight with him. Eventually we arrived up behind him – he, unlike us, had no rearward radar – and shot him down.

'On this occasion Harry opened fire with one two-second burst from 750 to 600 feet, using 60 rounds of 20 mm and 168 rounds of .303, from dead astern and from slightly below.

'Twice we shot down "Wild Boar" Me109s and on another occasion a He177 that was dropping flares to illuminate the target area for "Wild Boar" fighters. Later we used the Mark X AI. The difference between IV and the X was that where the range of the Mk IV was governed by our height, with the Mk X centimeter AI we did not have that restriction and our range was up to 5–10 miles. However, with the Mk X there was no rearward-looking area so we needed "Monica". (This was a rearward-looking radar set, providing a warning of the approach of a German fighter coming in from behind.)

'What Bob Braham had started in June 1943 by

The Ta 152C, a refined development of the much-feared FW190 and which saw service on the Eastern Front against Soviet tanks.

two years later had resulted in something like 200 German night-fighters having been destroyed by 141 Squadron and later the squadrons within 100 Group, Bomber Command. We also achieved much confusion among the Germans who knew we were around and were concerned that while they might be going for a Lancaster, one of us might be behind them.'

US DAY BOMBING

In 1942 the US 8th Army Air Force began arriving in Britain to begin nearly three years of bombing French and German targets by day. With the RAF attacking at night, the Allies opened round-the-clock bombing to rain death and destruction on Hitler's Third Reich. It began a mammoth struggle for the American day bombers which saw some of the bloodiest and yet most courageous air battles of WW2.

The Americans, still learning the lessons in the Pacific where their B17 Flying Fortresses were meeting strong opposition from the Japanese Zero fighters, continued to sustain the pre-war belief that their bombers could fight their way to and from enemy targets in Europe. But they wisely flew with escort fighters, reinforced and assisted by RAF Spitfires. Initially their targets were in France and well within escort range but, as the war continued and the strength of the 8th Air Force grew, Germany itself became a tempting target.

Their first raid on Germany was mounted on January 27, 1943, sending 64 B17s and B24 Liberators to Wilhelmshaven. The Luftwaffe retaliated, and lost seven of their fighters for just three bombers shot down.

From August 1942 American heavy bombers flew in combat boxes of 18 aircraft, with succeeding boxes 1½ miles behind. This was changed soon after attacks on Germany began, for the more distant targets would have to be beyond the range of their escort fighters. To improve their defensive formation they started to send out their bombers in wing formations, each of three 18-plane groups. Instead of flying behind each other, the groups positioned themselves at high, medium and low level. The medium level, or lead squadron, would fly slightly ahead of the other two, the high squadron above and to the right, the low squadron beneath but to the left. Thus the 54 four-engined bombers occupied a huge stretch of sky, 600 yards long, a mile or so wide and half a mile deep. Other wings would fly identical formations at intervals of about six miles.

It was these large armadas that fought their way into Germany in the first half of 1943, pitting themselves against a Luftwaffe fighter force of from 600 to 800 single-engined fighters, which, once scrambled, would wait for the fighter escort to turn for home as their fuel gave out; they would then be able to attack the bombers to and from the target before relieving escorts could reach them.

Attacking a B17 bomber wing was a considerable undertaking, for the defensive fire was considerable. The B17F which equipped the 8th Air Force at this stage had 12 0.50 defensive guns. Therefore a wing of 54 bombers could put up a veritable hail of fire from 648 guns. In 1943 the average B17 carried about 9000 rounds of ammunition. A simple calculation shows that a combat wing had over 486 000 rounds to blaze at the attackers from 648 guns. Not surprisingly, devising tactics for attacking these groups tested the ingenuity of the Luftwaffe pilots. The 0.5 guns could fire 14 rounds a second and had an effective range of 600 yards. And that was not all. The two-ounce bullet was lethal up to four miles on a human body.

As the Japanese had found in the Pacific, the B17s and B24s were difficult targets from the conventional astern position. The mass of return fire directed at them was tremendous, and to break away was never easy. To go under meant running the gauntlet of fire from the ball-turret gunners hunched up right below the bomber's fuselage, as well as fire from left or right waist-gunners. To pull up and over brought fire from the waist-gunners, top-turret gunner and a gun from the B17's radio room. If attacking the American low or medium groups, climbing meant meeting fire from the group(s) above, so often it was the low box that was hit the hardest and then the German pilots just risked the fire from the ball gunners as they dived down and under.

The Luftwaffe fighters then began to attack from head-on. Unlike the more scattered B17s in the Pacific, the European B17s in massed formations were not free to maneuver or swing about to thwart a head-on pass and bring other guns to bear. For both sides it was a nerve-racking experience. If the German pilots found the B17s when they were ahead of them, and decided to make head-on attacks, they would go into a shallow dive, bringing them level when within gun range. If they were behind the bombers they would fly over to reach a point ahead, then half-roll and come curving down and back to put them at the same level approach height.

The combined closing speed of the two aircraft formations gave neither side enough time to fire. Apart from the bomber's top turret gunner and the navigator and bomb-aimer firing single 0.50 guns from the nose area, the other gunners could not fire. At first they could not see the approaching fighters, and when they could, there was the danger that they would hit other B17s in their formation as the fighters flashed past beneath or over them.

The attacking fighter too had little time to fire. Coming in at perhaps 500 mph, he would close with the B17s at 200 yards per second and at 500 yards might get in only a brief half-second burst before taking avoiding action. It was a test of nerves for both sides.

The two pilots in the bomber's cockpit were of course very vulnerable to frontal attack and if they were put out of action it was almost certainly the end for the aircraft. This threat was countered by the introduction in late 1943 of the B17G with two 0.50 calibre guns in a chin turret beneath the bomb-aimer's window and bombing panel.

A FW190 pilot might have a variety of ammunition in his guns – tracer, high-explosive, armor-piercing – and with all guns functioning about 70 rounds per second would strike the B17. The Germans estimated that about 20 hits from 20-mm ammunition were enough to shoot down a Boeing.

HITTING THE BOMBERS

As the dangers to attacking fighters increased, so the Luftwaffe conceived other methods of stemming the huge armadas of four-engined bombers. At one stage they even dropped pre-set bombs on them, which were timed to explode when they were at the same height as the bombers. However, the airborne rocket was more successful.

Initially twin-engined Me110 or Me410 aircraft were employed to carry two rockets under each wing. They were 210-mm rocket mortars, adapted from the weapon used by the German infantry. They were launched from tubes slung beneath the fighter's wings, each projectile weighing 248 pounds, 80 pounds of which comprised the warhead. They could have a pre-set range set to explode, usually between 600 and 1 200 yds. Impact with a four-engined bomber would also detonate the rocket.

However, its disadvantage was that while it increased the Luftwaffe's hitting power, it reduced the performance of the carrying aircraft because of the weaponry attached to the wings. Me110s and 410s, already easy targets for American escort fighters, were even more vulnerable when hampered by rocket tubes. So too were Me109s and FW190s when they were adapted to carry one under each wing. If, however, there was no escort, or the attacking aircraft closed in unhindered, they could keep out of the lethal range of the bomber's 0.50 guns and from this vantage-point send rockets into the closely-packed bomber formations. To inflict damage the rocket need only explode within 50 ft of a target. If hit, an exploding B17 had been known to cause enough damage to neighbouring aircraft to bring down one, perhaps two, of them.

If he reacted quickly enough, a crewman could warn his pilot that rockets had been fired so that he could take avoiding action. B17 crews would often fan out momentarily and see rockets streaking past where they had just been.

As a result, most German pilots considered the rockets only good for breaking up American formations so that other fighters could go to work during the confusion.

Crews of Me410s especially, if caught, were extremely vulnerable to US fighters. Their top speed was only about 15 mph more than a B17's and flying at the B17s' height they became sluggish and lost any hope of turning sharply enough to avoid a US Thunderbolt escort fighter. The added drag of tubes and rockets was considerable.

Another method used by attacking fighters against the four-engined Americans was similar to that also used by the Japanese in 1942, the dive from above. To achieve any success a pilot had to position himself at least 1500–2000 ft above the B17 and to be some 800 ft ahead. Diving at speed gave the pilot a perfect planview target, and perhaps only the top gunner would be able to fire up at him. The disadvantage was the time it took to set up this tactic and if Thunderbolts were near the Germans would quickly be engaged while waiting to get into position.

The Luftwaffe also introduced the 30-mm heavy cannon – the Mk108 – firing an 11-oz high-explosive shell at a high rate. It was estimated to

In order to combat head-on attacks by German fighters, B17 crews had to ensure forward defensive fire. On this B17F there are four 0.5in guns, two in an improvized mounting. Later the B17G had a chin turret with two 0.5 in guns to help thwart head-on attacks.

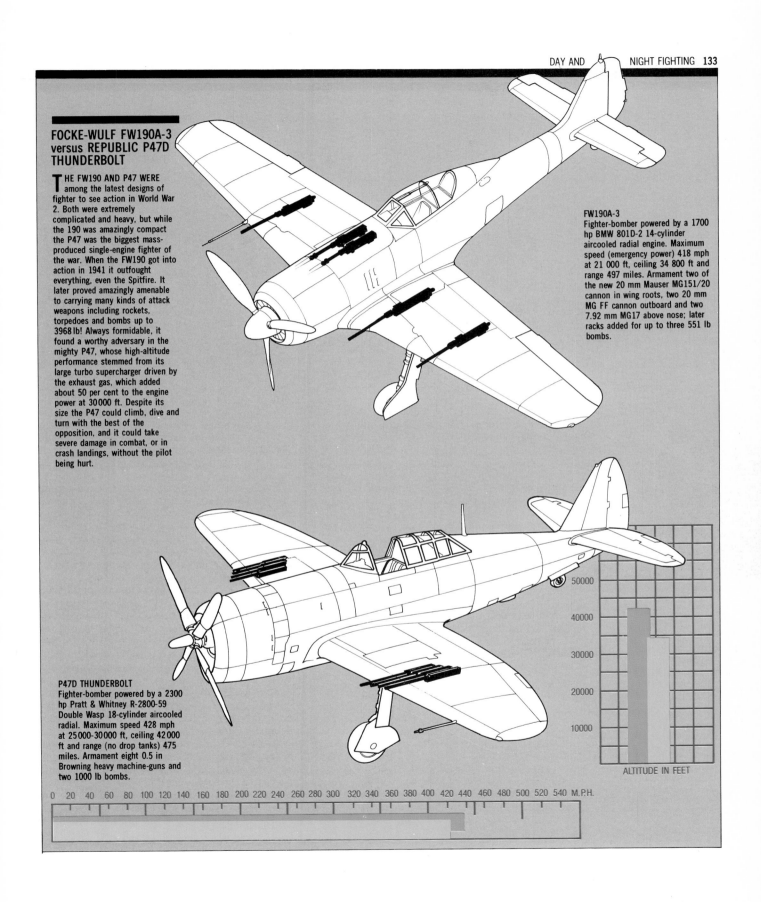

FOCKE-WULF FW190A-3 versus REPUBLIC P47D THUNDERBOLT

THE FW190 AND P47 WERE among the latest designs of fighter to see action in World War 2. Both were extremely complicated and heavy, but while the 190 was amazingly compact the P47 was the biggest mass-produced single-engine fighter of the war. When the FW190 got into action in 1941 it outfought everything, even the Spitfire. It later proved amazingly amenable to carrying many kinds of attack weapons including rockets, torpedoes and bombs up to 3968 lb! Always formidable, it found a worthy adversary in the mighty P47, whose high-altitude performance stemmed from its large turbo supercharger driven by the exhaust gas, which added about 50 per cent to the engine power at 30000 ft. Despite its size the P47 could climb, dive and turn with the best of the opposition, and it could take severe damage in combat, or in crash landings, without the pilot being hurt.

FW190A-3
Fighter-bomber powered by a 1700 hp BMW 801D-2 14-cylinder aircooled radial engine. Maximum speed (emergency power) 418 mph at 21 000 ft, ceiling 34 800 ft and range 497 miles. Armament two of the new 20 mm Mauser MG151/20 cannon in wing roots, two 20 mm MG FF cannon outboard and two 7.92 mm MG17 above nose; later racks added for up to three 551 lb bombs.

P47D THUNDERBOLT
Fighter-bomber powered by a 2300 hp Pratt & Whitney R-2800-59 Double Wasp 18-cylinder aircooled radial. Maximum speed 428 mph at 25000-30000 ft, ceiling 42 000 ft and range (no drop tanks) 475 miles. Armament eight 0.5 in Browning heavy machine-guns and two 1000 lb bombs.

ALTITUDE IN FEET

50000 40000 30000 20000 10000

0 20 40 60 80 100 120 140 160 180 200 220 240 260 280 300 320 340 360 380 400 420 440 460 480 500 520 540 M.P.H.

require just three good hits with this gun to score a victory. These guns were generally attached externally – to the undersides of a Me110, for instance. The problem with all these heavier type guns, whatever machine carried them, was that they increased drag and thereby impeded maneuverability which was so essential when ranged against Spitfires, Thunderbolts and later P51 Mustangs. For their part, the Allies had little reason to increase the caliber of their guns for everyday use as they rarely had to meet opposition heavier than Me110s or Ju88s, and certainly had no call to engage anything so formidable or resilient as a B17.

FLYING ESCORTS

The defense of the B17 and B24 formations could only be improved if escorting fighters could be given the ability to reach any target area in Germany. The Americans had been made to realize that unescorted bombers could not fight their way to and from Germany without suffering unacceptable losses. In the fall of 1943, for instance, the 8th Air Force lost 27 Fortresses, three Liberators and three Thunderbolts on October 8 bombing Bremen and Vegesack, 25

more Fortresses a day later against Marienburg, 30 B17s on October 10 attacking Münster, and 60 Fortresses on October 14 when bombing Schweinfurt, with a further 17 written off in crashes or because of battle damage. (The 8th had lost 60 bombers on the first Schweinfurt raid on August 17, 1943, the previous highest having been 26 lost on June 13 against Kiel.)

The P47 Thunderbolt's range was extended by the fitting of 200-gal drop-tanks made from resinated paper. These proved unsatisfactory as atmospheric pressure above 23 000 ft interfered with the flow of fuel. Designers overcame the problems of pressurization and control valves but production and delivery were slow, so the original tanks were used for initial climb and flight to enemy-held territory which extended ranges by about 70–80 miles.

By the late summer the new 108-gal metal drop-tanks began to arrive, which further improved the P47's range and staying power. However, the Luftwaffe's counter-move was merely to try to draw the American fighters, who would then jettison their drop-tanks ready for combat, whereupon the Luftwaffe turned away, having succeeded in reducing the P47s' range. The Germans need only wait around until shortage of fuel forced the fighters to leave the bombers unguarded.

Thunderbolts could fly escort up to 340–375 miles before having to turn back. This took them into Germany, but not as far as every target area that needed to be visited. Staying close to the bombers, however, reduced this range owing to their having to weave to stay with their slower charges. Only by sending other fighter squadrons directly to a target or pick-up area could the P47s get the full range from their tanks, so various Fighter Groups would fly cover while others flew target support or withdrawal support missions. Additionally, the Americans made sure they engaged any German fighters trying to make them drop their tanks early, and forced them to use up valuable fuel and ammunition, so they would have to land, to refuel and re-arm.

In the hope of extending escort cover the twin-engined P38 Lightning was eagerly awaited. In North Africa in combat with Me109s and FW190s at low and medium altitudes where most of the air fighting took place, the P38F had given a good account of itself. It had been able to turn with the single-seaters, could usually outclimb them, and was faster. It had also done well against the Japanese in the Pacific. The Lightning had a longer range than the Thunderbolt, and began to fly target leg escort and support missions on deep

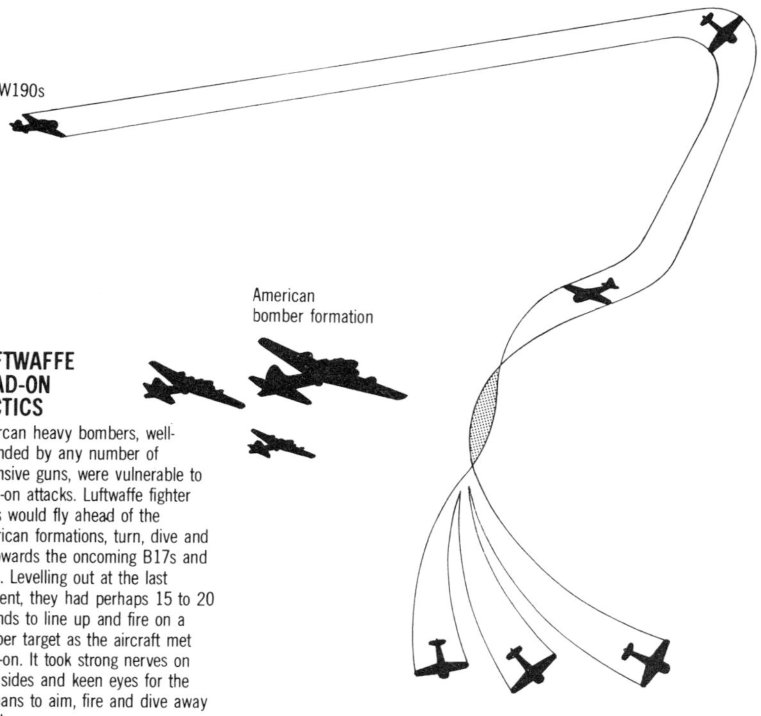

FW190s

American
bomber formation

LUFTWAFFE HEAD-ON TACTICS

American heavy bombers, well-defended by any number of defensive guns, were vulnerable to head-on attacks. Luftwaffe fighter pilots would fly ahead of the American formations, turn, dive and fly towards the oncoming B17s and B24s. Levelling out at the last moment, they had perhaps 15 to 20 seconds to line up and fire on a bomber target as the aircraft met head-on. It took strong nerves on both sides and keen eyes for the Germans to aim, fire and dive away – fast.

The American P38 Lightning fighter saw extensive service in Europe, North Africa, Italy and the south-west Pacific. America's top aces, Dick Bong and Tommy McGuire scored 40 and 38 victories respectively in P38s with the 5th Air Force over the Philippines. It was also used as a fighter-bomber, carrying 500lb or 1000lb bombs.

bomber penetrations. However, although the P38 was excellent below 20 000 ft, it was inferior above this altitude and, of course, most of the fighting over Germany was well above that height. The P38s also experienced engine problems. They had a good record against Luftwaffe fighters, but by mid-1944 they were being replaced by the P51 or assigned to ground-attack sorties.

THE FAR-RANGING MUSTANG

Meanwhile P51Bs had arrived in England and were soon operating with the 8th Air Force on long-range sorties carrying 75-gal drop-tanks. Their first long-range missions took place in December 1943, flying as far as Emden, Kiel and Bremen, round trips of 800 to 1000 miles, taking four to five hours.

The Mustang had only four 0.50 machine guns against eight in the Thunderbolt. Gun-jamming was a problem, usually occurring during tight turns when centrifugal forces affecting the ammunition belts caused the gun breech to block.

By the spring of 1944 the Mustangs had increased their range to 1200 miles, much to the alarm of Luftwaffe pilots now faced with an even more versatile fighter almost on their doorstep. Slower Me110s and Me410s [which were beginning to cause the heavy bombers concern with their 30-mm guns and their rockets] became

particularly vulnerable when attacking bomber formations beyond the gunners' effective range. But it was not all one-sided. On March 4, 1944 one new Mustang group was set about en route to Berlin while lost in cloud near Hamburg. I/JG1 stalked the Mustangs and surprised them with the help of their ground control. Eleven of this unit's P51s failed to return.

In May the bubble-canopied P51D reached England, the first examples going to squadron and flight commanders because of the enhanced view from the cockpit. The D models had reinforced wings allowing greater fuel loads and an increase to six 0.50 guns. The P51Ds could climb and dive faster than the latest Me109Gs; the two were fairly well matched in level maneuvering flight. The P51D carrying two external drop-tanks could escort the B17s all the way to any target, and even on shuttle missions which flew on to land in Russia. They could remain aloft for over nine hours. The guns were more dependable in the D model, and the total of rounds carried was increased from 1260 in the P51B to 1880 in the D. The inboard guns usually carried 400 each, the two outer guns having 270 each. Each gun was loaded to fire five incendiary rounds before the final 25 to warn the pilot that his ammunition was nearly exhausted.

THE MIGHTY THUNDERBOLT

For the remainder of the war over Europe the Thunderbolts and increasingly the Mustangs defended their 'big brothers', the Fortresses and Liberators. The Thunderbolt was a large machine, weighing about seven tons. At first the pilots felt that in such a huge beast with its slow acceleration they could never hope to dogfight the 109s and 190s. But the P47 had hidden strengths.

At top speed the P47 could reach 400 mph if first put into a gentle dive. Once reached, this speed could be maintained. When the American pilots discovered how good their P47s were they delighted in the fact that above 22 000 ft they were faster than either the 109 or 190. The P47 could out-dive both of them, it had a superior rate of roll and turning radius above 22 000 ft, and a good rate of roll at almost any altitude provided the pilot maintained airspeed. With such good diving ability, the zoom to regain lost height was equally impressive. Another advantage was the P47's capacity to absorb damage and still get safely home. Its main disadvantage against the Luftwaffe fighters was that the 109 and 190 had a tighter turn. However, by this stage in the war the tactic was, in these circumstances, not to be drawn into this sort of encounter but to use, in the case of the Thunderbolt, its superior dive, zoom and roll.

There were many successful P47 and P51 pilots, among them some outstanding air leaders. Perhaps two of the latter should be mentioned as exceptional, Don Blakeslee and Hub Zemke. Although not among the very high scoring USAAF pilots, Blakeslee was valued for his capabilities as a leader and tactician. He had flown in the Eagle Squadron in the RAF before joining the 4th Fighter Group, which he later commanded, flying P51s.

Hub Zemke, too, was not one of the most prolific scorers but, at the head of the 56th Fighter Group – mainly flying P47s – his brilliance also lay in his ability to command in the air and achieve successful interceptions and equally successful defensive actions while escorting the 'heavier'. He later recalled:'

A FIGHTER PILOT must possess an inner urge to do combat. The will at all times to be offensive will develop into his own tactics. If your enemy is above, never let your speed drop and don't climb, because you'll lose too much speed. If you're attacked on the same level, just remember you can outclimb him. Beware of thin cirrus clouds – the enemy can look down through them but you can't look up through them. Don't go weaving through valleys of cumulus clouds, either with a squadron or by yourself. The enemy can be on your tail before you know it.

'When popping down out of a cloud, or up, always do a quick turn and look back. You may have jumped out directly in front of a gun barrel. When attacked by large numbers of enemy aircraft meet them head-on. In most cases half of them will break and go down. Handle all those remaining in an all-out fight until you're down to one – then take him on.

'If there are twenty aircraft down below, go screaming down with full force to pick out the most logical target at the point of firing. Then pull up to a good altitude and develop an attack on one of those remaining enemy pilots who had been shaken out of his helmet by your sudden onslaught.

'I stay with the enemy until he is destroyed, I'm out of ammunition, he evades into the clouds, or I'm too low on gas and ammo to continue. When you have your squadron with you and the enemy has so much altitude you never would get up to him, stay below and to the rear of him – he'll be down.

'Learn to break at the proper time to make a head-on attack – the enemy doesn't like it. Don't run. That's just what he wants you to do. When caught by the enemy in large force, the best policy is to fight like hell until you can decide what to do...'

Among the pure fighter pilots were Francis Gabreski, who not only destroyed 30 German aircraft but added 6½ victories in the Korean war; John Meyer, who destroyed 24 in the air and 13 on the ground, and added two victories in Korea as well; and Dave Schilling, whose tally was 22½ in the air and 10½ on the ground in 132 combat missions. The 'terrible twins' of the 4th Fighter Group were Don Gentile and John Godfrey who, often working together, destroyed between them about 60 enemy aircraft in the air and on the ground. They first teamed up when the 4th was flying P47s and they used the tactic, adopted by others, that whichever pilot of the two first spotted an enemy aircraft and was in the better position in relation to it, would attack. If this was the wingman then the No 1, or leader, would simply change position and cover his No 2 when he attacked. The pair would then make co-ordinated attacks. For this tactic to work successfully each man had to have implicit faith in the other, each had to be good, and know almost

P47 Thunderbolts were used by the Americans in Europe and the Far East Pacific areas, as well as by the RAF in India and Burma. With long-range tanks it could penetrate deep into Germany or into Burma to seek out air and ground targets. Many of the top American aces gained high scores on the Thunderbolt, a superb aircraft with a good speed and rate of roll. It could take a tremendous amount of damage and still bring its pilot home.

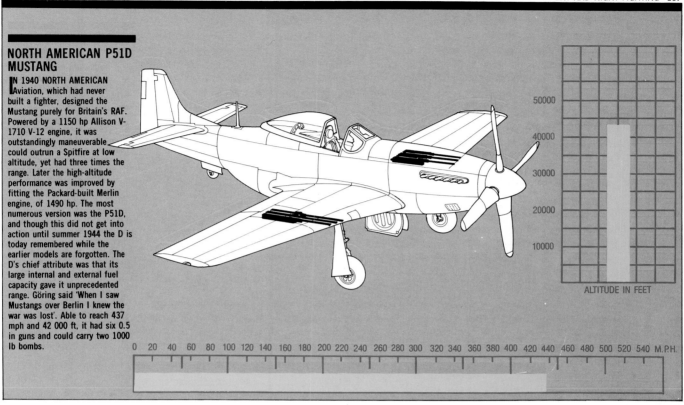

NORTH AMERICAN P51D MUSTANG

IN 1940 NORTH AMERICAN Aviation, which had never built a fighter, designed the Mustang purely for Britain's RAF. Powered by a 1150 hp Allison V-1710 V-12 engine, it was outstandingly maneuverable, could outrun a Spitfire at low altitude, yet had three times the range. Later the high-altitude performance was improved by fitting the Packard-built Merlin engine, of 1490 hp. The most numerous version was the P51D, and though this did not get into action until summer 1944 the D is today remembered while the earlier models are forgotten. The D's chief attribute was that its large internal and external fuel capacity gave it unprecedented range. Göring said 'When I saw Mustangs over Berlin I knew the war was lost'. Able to reach 437 mph and 42 000 ft, it had six 0.5 in guns and could carry two 1000 lb bombs.

instinctively how the other was going to react in any given situation. In an actual battle, the leadership of the pair might change several times but this was irrelevant if the enemy was shot down.

Another top 'ace' was Bob Johnson, flying Thunderbolts with the 56th Fighter Group. He shot down 28 German fighters in only 91 combat missions in less than twelve months. He was also an intelligent pilot who during these months had endured many experiences which taught him how to overcome his German opponents – experiences such as the one on May 19, 1943 when he was present on a Circus mission in his Thunderbolt.

The Circus was intended as a feint to draw off German interceptors. As the main striking force flew to the primary target, a smaller group of bombers with fighter escort attacked a diversionary target.

The heavy bombers roared unescorted to Kiel and Flensburg, while the fighters shepherded the Circus force of 40 Flying Fortresses to The Hague. The escort route took them, with fighters from the 4th and 78th Groups, on a sweep from Ijmuiden to south of The Hague, and return. The decoy bomber force suddenly changed course, and Johnson never rendezvoused with them. Instead, he made a wide, high-altitude fighter sweep, the

kind of a mission in which he was free to look for trouble. He later recalled: '*E*VERYTHING went fine until we had turned and were nearly over the Dutch coast on our way home. Again I was Tailend Charlie and the last fighter over the mainland. Barron, the second man in my flight, broke radio silence. "Two bandits, six o'clock, in the sun." I looked around and saw the two German fighters, far above and a long distance behind our formation. Too far, I estimated, ever to catch us. For the next several minutes I held formation, turning my head only occasionally to check the two reported fighters.*

'They were decoys, and I was too green to recognize the fact. Once I had spotted the two planes, still high and far behind, I concentrated on flying my formation slot. My head should have been on a swivel, and it wasn't. I never saw the four black shapes hurtling from high altitude. I knew something was in the air when white flashes appeared magically all around my fighter, uncomfortably close. I was so green that I thought the flashes to be light flak, never considering that light anti-aircraft guns don't throw shells to 30,000 feet.

'To evade what I still thought were anti-

aircraft shells, I skidded the Thunderbolt sharply to the left and right and changed altitude in a broken line of flight to keep any shrapnel from falling onto me after the shells had exploded. No one had said a word since Barron's warning. I decided to have a look, and cocked the Thunderbolt on its side, to the right of the flight, and glanced back.

'"Blue Flight – break!" I yelled, and then almost exploded into action. My heart jammed into my throat, and in a blur of arms and legs my left hand slammed the throttle all the way forward, my right hand jerked the stick hard to the right, my right foot jammed down on the rudder pedal. The Thunderbolt whipped over on her back as I threw the fighter into the start of a split-S. The moment I was inverted I glanced down and saw the enemy coast. "Oh, no, Johnson!" I told myself. "That's Jerry's hunting grounds. Let's go home!"

'I held the straining fighter upside down, streaking earthward in a 45-degree dive, and ran

for it. The inverted Thunderbolt raced for the sea while I kicked the rudder pedals, slamming the fighter from side to side to present a poor target for any pursuers. My finger poised over the Mayday button, for at the first sign that my fighter might be hit, and that I would have to bail out into the drink, I wanted to be certain that Air-Sea Rescue would be on its way to fish me out of the Channel.

'I didn't realize then that my decision to race for home probably saved my life. The moment the lead German pilot saw my wing go up and over, he immediately started to roll his own fighter, snapping around and down into his own split-S maneuver, nicely co-ordinated to bring him out of the diving half-loop smack on my tail – with a perfect setup shot. I never identified the enemy planes; seeing the black wings alive with the sparkling flame from their cannon was enough for me!

'The Jerries were masters at the art of cutting up enemy fighters. When the lead plane rolled and arced over in the split-S, his wingman continued straight ahead, snapping out bursts of cannon shells as he closed the distance between our two planes. High above the pursuit one of our squadron leaders, "Pappy" Craig, burst into laughter as he watched my Thunderbolt fairly leap ahead. We were permitted to race our engines to a reading of 52 inches manifold pressure and my instrument read 57 inches, with me pounding at the throttle in an attempt to squeeze even more speed out of the plunging fighter. By the time I reached 25 000 feet, the Thunderbolt was running wild and had streaked away from the pursuing German. I don't know how fast I was going. I was so scared that I don't even remember remaining upside down and kicking rudder back and forth at that terrific speed. At 15 000 feet I rolled the P-47 right side up, leveled out and took a careful look behind me. Not an airplane in the sky. Whew – what relief! Now for home!'

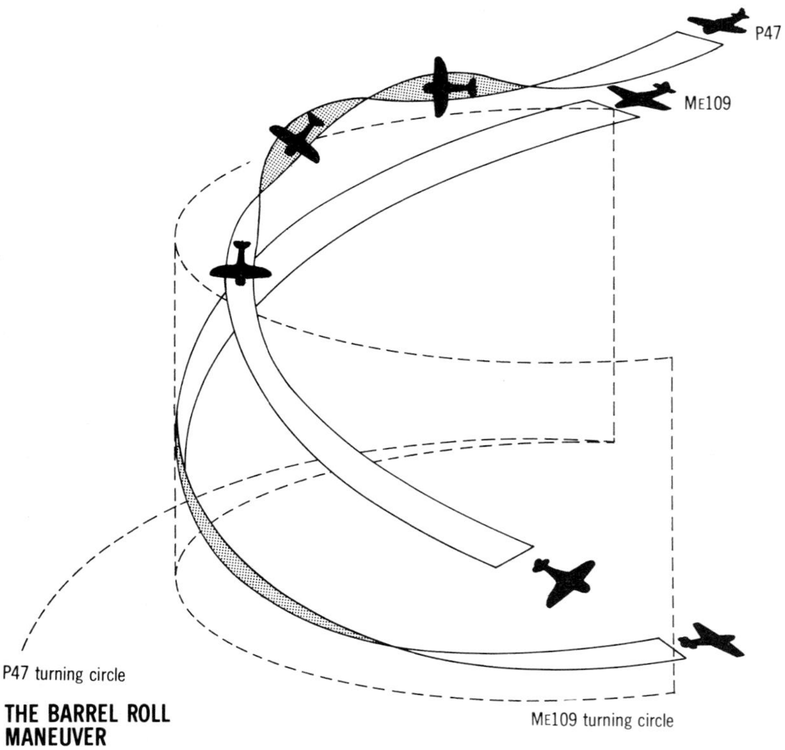

Little by little he learned, as was shown by an incident on March 6, 1944 during a raid on Berlin. Johnson saw two Me109s that had just shot down a Fortress. The 109s were above him, but Johnson climbed, seeing black exhaust smoke pouring from their engines showing that they were on full power. The German pilots saw the approaching P47 and raced for safety, but Johnson went for the leader as he dived. Then the smoke stopped, a sure sign to the American that the 109 pilot had closed his throttle. Johnson quickly cut his own power and skidded his Thunderbolt to the right to prevent over-shooting, then half-rolled to the left.

P47 turning circle

ME109 turning circle

THE BARREL ROLL MANEUVER

The German Me109 could turn better than the P47 Thunderbolt. If attacked, the Luftwaffe pilot might throttle back and pull into a hard turn. The American would be unable to follow, but by rolling in the opposite direction to the 109's turn, then pulling round, he ended up on the tail of the 109 in an attacking position.

ROBERT S JOHNSON

BORN IN OKLAHOMA IN 1920, Bob Johnson was a member of the 56th Fighter Group flying from England in mid-1943 as part of the 8th American Air Force. In his first combat missions he had an unfortunate tendency to leave formation and chase any enemy aircraft he saw. This happened on June 13, when he peeled off after some FW190s which his formation had failed to attack. He managed to shoot down one of the German fighters, but he was reprimanded when he returned to base. Nevertheless, he disagreed with the strategy and felt that if a pilot saw the enemy, he should attack. Eventually Thunderbolt pilots flying escort to bombers were allowed greater freedom to attack and Bob Johnson began building his score of victories, beginning on his 30th mission on August 24 when he shot down a 190 near Paris. In October he claimed two more 190s and a Me110, his sixth on November 3 and by the end of 1943 two 190 kills on his 54th mission brought his score to 10. Adding two more successes in early January 1944, Johnson went on to multiple victories: two over Brunswick on January 30, two over Hanover on February 20, two on March 8; March 15 saw three kills – two 190s and a Me109. Another double on April 13, then a damaged 109 on May 4, later upgraded to a confirmed, made 26 victories. On his 91st mission, on May 8, he shot down a 190 and a 109 – giving him 28 victories. Soon afterwards he ended his tour and returned to America as the top-scoring 'ace' from the air fighting over France and Germany, his victories achieved in just 11 months of combat. In air-to-air kills, Johnson shared top place with Colonel Francis Gabreski, also of the 56th FG.

The 109 turned sharply to the left and Johnson rolled over after it. The German pilot, convinced he could out-turn the P47, suddenly found Johnson right behind him as he pulled round. Johnson had not turned inside him, but the superb rolling capability of the Thunderbolt had allowed it to roll in the opposite direction to the 109 to defeat the better turning ability enjoyed by the German pilot. The 109 was burning on the ground just moments later.

Colonel Jesse Thompson flew with the 55th Fighter Group of the 8th Air Force, equipped with P51D Mustangs. He recorded: '*I* HAD, AND have, an enormous respect for the P51D as a combat machine. There is no doubt in my mind that, on the whole, it was the best single-seater to see action in the European theatre.

'The P51D's best climbing angle was far less than that of the Spitfire and while the '51 could not equal the Spit in level turns, you could shake one by pulling into a fast diving turn. The Me109G and the P51D were fairly evenly matched in level maneuvering flight but the '51 could climb and dive faster although the 109 had an advantage in initial acceleration in a dive – which often was sufficient to allow the 109 to get away. In long full power dives, the P51D could run into compressibility with disconcerting results. Pulling out of these dives could be thrilling also . . . popped rivets (it happened to me) was the least one could expect and one pilot I knew strained his wings so much that the gear would not come down when he got home.

'Another less endearing characteristic of the P51D was the difficulty of baling out. Once the canopy was jettisoned the air circulation around the cockpit was such that it tended to trap the pilot behind the armor plate against the radio. How this came about I have never fully understood but it did happen. I'm sure level flight bale-outs were accomplished, although I never knew of one, but so far as I was concerned the only certain method was from inverted flight.

'Nevertheless, despite its peculiarities the P51D was an extremely good airplane, its pilots had complete confidence in its ability to perform any reasonable mission and its most serious detractors cannot but admit that it fulfilled its role in a superior fashion.'

Lieutenant Colonel Richard Turner scored 12 air-to-air victories with the P51 with the US 9th Air Force, flying from England. He also destroyed nine more on the ground, all scored while with the 356th Fighter Squadron, of the 354th Fighter Group – flying Mustangs. On June 30 1944, south of Vire-Caen, over the Invasion Front in France: '*T* HE WEATHER WAS GOOD WITH ONLY A suggestion of cirrus clouds at high altitude. Climbing out from the forward strip towards Vire with my two flights, I saw what appeared to be bogies at 12 o'clock high and approximately 30 000 feet. Going to maximum climb and flipping on gun and sight switches, I informed the flight of the bogies' location, and gave chase. We seemed to be closing well from the rear. We were making a perfect blind approach. After ten or fifteen minutes of climbing we reached their altitude about a thousand yards behind them, and we recognised them as a flight of Me109s flying to the south. Hoping that they wouldn't see us creeping up on them, I kept pressing on to get within good range, telling my flights to keep closed in tight until we were in range.

'As I closed in, I sighted on the 109 to the left of the formation, leaving the others for my flights to pick up. I put the pip right on his tail and fired off a burst. The range was deceptive at this high altitude, and the tracers dropped away under the aircraft without scoring a strike. Naturally, the other 109s saw the fire, and broke to the right with my Mustangs hot on their tails. For some inexplicable reason my target kept right on course without breaking, so I raised the pip to just over his rudder top, and fired another long burst. This time multiple strikes blossomed all over the plane causing it to stream volumes of black smoke. I couldn't see any visible flame, and the pilot didn't bale out, so I pressed in for another attack as he began a slow descent. I scored another cluster of strikes and the smoke increased as he wobbled into a turn to the left, still losing altitude. Now I realised why there had been no flame. We were at an altitude of 25 000 feet, and there wasn't enough oxygen at this height to support a freely burning fire. On the chance the plane might still be flyable, I fired again, hitting the whole length of his wingspan and fuselage. The 109 yawed wildly from the impact, and cartwheeled over into a vertical plunge. As he hit lower altitudes, the black smoke turned into a cloud of bright yellow flames which soon enveloped the entire craft.

'Suddenly I saw tracers flash past me on the right, closely followed by two Me109s travelling at great speed, who were obviously about to overrun me. Dropping downward in a following trajectory, I fired a burst at the leader's flight path missing him, but managing to hit his wingman as he followed the leader through my line of fire. The

Mustang fighters with Invasion markings, summer 1944, of the 375th Fighter Squadron, 361st Fighter Group, US 8th Air Force in England. The nearest P51, coded 44-13410 E2-C and named LOU IV was the mount of the Group Commander, Colonel Thomas Christian. He was killed in action on August 12, 1944. Note the long-range fuel tanks.

leader continued his dive for the deck, but his wingman straightened out ahead of me, evidently somewhat damaged by my chance hits. I let the leader go, and followed the wingman. I closed to close range to finish him off. Intent on completing this job, I held fire until I was sure I was in range, and then poured fire from all six guns. He blew apart instantly. I turned in search of my patrol mates wondering fleetingly if I wasn't getting a little bit flak-happy. I joined the flight, and we proceeded with the patrol for a while before returning to base.'

One of the 8th Air Force's top fighter aces was Major George E Preddy Jr, who shot down 28 German aircraft between December 1 1943 and December 25 1944, the date of his own death in combat. He flew both the P47 and the P51 first with the 487th Fighter Squadron, then as CO of the 328th Fighter Squadron of the 352nd Fighter Group. He had previously flown against the Japanese from Northern Australia, damaging two Japanese aircraft in his 13 months in that war zone, during 1941–42. In March 1944, Preddy was asked to write down his knowledge of air fighting to pass onto other pilots. Among his advice was the following: '*IN FLIGHT THE NO. 2 MAN flies on the leader's left wing with Nos 3 and 4 on the right. In the squadron the flights fly line astern stacked down. The whole outfit is in very close, and if each man flies a steady position it is possible to take 16 or 20 ships through an overcast.*

'*On the climb out, the flights and individual ships fly close formation as this reduces throttle-jockeying and saves gas. When we approach the enemy coast, everybody moves out into battle formation, ie: line abreast and five or six ships' length apart for individual ships and line abreast for each two flights. This is an easy formation to fly when flying a straight course and offers excellent cross-over.*

'*When escorting several large boxes of bombers it is impossible to keep the groups together, so squadrons and sections of squadrons are assigned a particular section of the task force. We usually fly two flights of four planes each. The flights fly line abreast to offer cross-over, but if the lead ship is turning a lot, it is necessary to fall in string. Normally the flight leaders and element leaders look for bounces with the wingmen on the defensive. This doesn't mean that leaders never look back or wingmen never look down. It is impossible to see everything, but each pilot must keep his head moving and look to find.*

'*When the leader is preparing to make a bounce he should inform his squadron of his intentions. If* a wingman sees an enemy plane which would get away if he didn't act immediately, he goes down on the bounce calling in as he does so. In this case the leader becomes the wingman.

'If a pilot sees an enemy aircraft behind him in firing range he must take evasive action immediately. He slips and skids the ship as much as possible giving the Hun maximum deflection. It is a good idea to turn in the direction of friendly planes, so they can shoot or scare Jerry off your tail.

'As a conclusion, in escorting bombers it is a good idea to range out to the sides, front and rear and hit enemy fighters before they can get to the bombers unprotected.'

On May 30 1944, flying a Mustang, George Preddy shot down two German fighters and shared another while on bomber escort. His wingman was Lieutenant William T 'Whis' Whisner – a future ace in his own right, ending the war with 15½ air-to-air and three ground kills. Later in Korea Whisner claimed 5½ Migs. Preddy's combat report states: 'AS THE BOMBERS were approaching the vicinity of Magdeburg, I was leading a section of seven ships giving close escort to the rear box which was quite a distance behind the main formation. I noticed 20 to 30 single-engine fighters attacking the front boxes so we dropped our tanks and headed towards them. We came up behind three Me109s in rather tight formation. I opened fire on one from 300 yards and closed to 150 yards. The 109 burst into flames and went down.

'I then slipped behind the second 109 and fired while closing from 200 to 100 yards. He started burning and disintegrating immediately. He went down spinning.

'The third enemy aircraft saw us and broke down. I followed him in a steep turn, diving and zooming. I got in many deflection shots getting hits on the wing and tail section. I ran out of ammunition, so my element leader, Lt. Whisner, continued the attack getting in several good hits. At about 7000 feet the pilot baled out.'

In 1944 Robert 'Bazi' Weiss was the commander of the Luftwaffe III Gruppe of JG54, operating from Villacoublay airfield in France. Soon after the Allied landings in Normandy, Weiss led a mission of FW190s against American bombers. His Gruppe records describe how: 'WEISS LED the 40 FW190s to attack a large formation of Fortresses, above which Spitfires prepared themselves for the attack, whilst about 30 Mustangs came from the far side of the formation to place themselves between the Forts and the enemy.

'The FW190s, in close formation, climbed rapidly and then, just as suddenly, launching their attack from above and at the rear of the formation, dived down through the mass of the bombers, whose close formation was torn apart, passed through them, turned on their wingtips and attacked again from directly in front. Startled by this fierce attack, many of the B17s droppd their bombs, although still well clear of their target. Weiss shouted – "Forward, then right turn into the sun," and again the pilots drove through the fiery hell of the bombers' defensive fire, pulled hard back on their control columns and climbed steeply towards the sun. The American gunners, completely dazzled by the sun, were unable to continue their fire.

'Hardly had they gained comparative safety when a voice shouted: "Defensive circle, quickly. Indians right above!" In a headlong dive about 35 Thunderbolts sought to catch the FW190s unaware. Whilst all other planes of the Group formed a circle, Hauptman Lang's Staffel continued to climb and within seconds engaged the enemy fighters, Lang himself, and Weiss, acting as guards over the circling and banking FW190s. The action, which started at 19 000 feet, was now down to 6000 feet, and still the deadly combat went on. But whilst the defending force was steadily growing smaller, the Allied fleet was growing larger, as reinforcements kept coming in from all sides, so the FW190s that were still able to escape quickly made their way to the area of Paris, where they were protected by a strong girdle of anti-aircraft fire. When the remnants of the force landed at Villacoublay, the airfield was still undamaged, but there were only 15 FW190s still available for the next action. At this time, the ratio of strength between the German fighter forces and the Allied air forces must have been in the order of about 200 to 12 000! The German 'Jager' (hunter-fighter) had become the 'Gejagter' (hunted one).'

GERMAN INGENUITY

German fighter pilots too had the odd trick up their sleeves which, while not strictly a tactic, was a good enough ploy to get them out of trouble. Adolf Galland, perhaps the best known of the Luftwaffe pilots in the West, still flew the occasional mission despite his high rank and position (General of the Fighter Arm). On one occasion, after trying to attack a Fortress, he was set on by four Mustangs. Galland was wise enough not to attempt a dogfight in his FW190, so he dived to try to escape. However, the Mustangs stayed with him, tracer shells zipping up round his machine. Finally, Galland did something that had saved him before – he fired his guns. The resulting streams of smoke that wafted back towards the American pilots perhaps gave the illusion of backward-firing guns or even perhaps bullets passing over their own aircraft from the rear. They also were showered with spent cartridges and links which added to the illusion of hits being scored on their machines. In the event it succeeded, and the four P51 pilots broke into a right-hand climbing turn, allowing Galland to escape.

In desperation to inflict losses on the seemingly unending and undiminishing number of American daylight raids, the Germans took more desperate measures against the 'heavies'.

Galland himself introduced a new tactic, using more heavily amored attack fighters to go into the maelstrom of return fire from the Fortresses and Liberators, while lighter fighters took on the American escort fighters. These 'Sturmgruppen' were equipped with the FW190A-8/R8, carrying extra armor plating of 5-mm to 12-mm thick steel plates around the pilot and engine cowling, and 50-mm thick bullet-resistant glass in the windscreen. It also carried two 30-mm cannon in addition to two 20-mm cannon. Consequently, the Sturm 190s could weigh up to five tons!

In view of the size of the American bombing formations, this Gruppe and its escort could normally attack only a single bomber group, approaching it in a special battle formation called 'Gefechtverband'. Its one Sturmgruppe and two light fighter Gruppen totalled about 100 aircraft.

The Sturmgruppe would attack in three waves each in a large 'V' with one close escort Gruppe and the second Gruppe as top cover. The Sturm fighters would then begin close infighting with the bombers protected by the other fighters. The Sturm pilots were also expected, in the event of their failure to shoot it down, to ram a bomber. Failure to do so could lead to a court martial.

The 30-mm cannon had a relatively low muzzle-velocity, so that its accuracy diminished very quickly as the range increased. As it also carried a total of only 55 rounds per gun, pilots could not afford to waste them, and the total firing time was only five seconds. It really meant the pilot getting so close that he could not miss. At such a range the 30-mm gun was devastating, and often the pilot fired at 100 yds or less with the shortest of bursts. Only if a pilot found his guns

jammed was it considered necessary to ram. In this position a pilot needed only to pull up slightly then dive, aiming perhaps to slice off the B17's huge tailfin with a wing, or to smash one of the B24's two large tailplane rudders. Rammings were not very frequent, and of those which occurred about 50% of the pilots survived unhurt. By late 1944 the lack of trained pilots removed the obligation to ram.

The whole operation was at risk if American fighters reached the battle formation while it was forming up or actually attacking. Generally the German escorts were able to keep the P47s and P51s occupied, but if any did break through to the Sturmgruppe, the escorts' general tactic was to continue to approach the bombers and risk being shot down, hoping by that time to have got at least one bomber. Very occasionally a Staffel of the Sturmgruppe might be ordered to turn to engage approaching fighters, but as they were so heavy and therefore vulnerable to attack it was often better to continue against the 'heavies' and hope for the best.

SPITFIRES GO EAST

The war in Burma was, like the Pacific, equally dominated by the Zero and another exceptional Japanese fighter, the Nakajima Ki43 – code-named 'Oscar'. By late 1943, they totally outclassed the RAF Hurricanes, and generally the RAF or Indian pilots would dive for the trees and keep in tight circle at low level until the Japanese pilot flew off.

To combat these fighters a new type of Spitfire, the Mark VIII began to arrive in India in December 1943. This was designed to take the Merlin 61 engine with its four-bladed propeller. It was found to be equal to the Japanese fighters in many respects and superior in others. Only in the turn were the Zero and Oscar still better.

The Spitfire VIII first saw action over the Arakan and during raids on Chittagong and Calcutta. On December 31, 136 Squadron destroyed a large number of attacking Japanese bombers and fighters. During the siege of Imphal between March and June 1944, the defense of the Imphal Valley was almost exclusively undertaken by a handful of Spitfire VIII squadrons. One pilot involved was Alan Peart, a New Zealand pilot with 81 Squadron who, with this squadron, had seen considerable action in North Africa and Sicily: '*T*HE MARK VIII WAS A beautiful machine with retractable tail-wheel, clean lines and pointed tail. The Stromburg carburettor permitted negative "G" without the* engine cutting out and it had (like the Mark IX) a two-stage supercharger which provided considerable additional power above 18000 feet. Our armament was two 20-mm cannon and four 0.303 machine-guns, all of which were effective against the Japanese.

'Our first sight of the Japanese was during a raid on Calcutta and then in the Arakan where we had quite a number of engagements against Japanese Oscars (plus the odd Zeke) and where we had the opportunity of developing our fighter tactics against opponents with characteristics entirely different from those of the Germans.

'In the Arakan the Mark VIIIs met the enemy in force in February 1944. Within a period of 14 days the Japanese suffered severe fighter losses and lost a lot of their aggressiveness. Until then they appeared to roam at will over Allied territory.

'I recall that after an encounter with a large force of Oscars over the Arakan, 81 Squadron had few claims of aircraft destroyed but claimed many damaged. Some time after, we received reports that up to 30 enemy aircraft were seen to crash. Not all 81s but it indicated that, under the rules, our claims could be very much an underestimation.

'The Mark VIII had a considerable advantage over the Oscars and Zekes, being armoured, more highly powered, faster and better armed. The Japanese on the other hand were extremely manoeuvrable, had great endurance in the air and generally outnumbered the intercepting Spitfires.

'Our tactics were to position ourselves above the Oscars, attack at speed using the sun, surprise if possible and power to climb away out of range. Thus we could mount continuous attacks with relative impunity. This was similar to the German fighter tactics. The Japanese defence was to fly in circles, each fighter covering the one in front and taking snapshots at the Spitfires as they passed.

'They were not heavily armoured and our .303s could put a lot of destructive metal into them. The cannons caused obvious and serious damage. This was not the case with Me109s, where I have hit one with machine-guns from behind only to see the bullets ricocheting off. In such cases we could only claim a damaged. Similarly with the Japanese aircraft, unless it was badly on fire or seen to crash, or the pilot baled out, it could not be claimed as destroyed. I never did see a Japanese pilot bale out!'

North of Burma, in China, was the American 14th Air Force, now commanded by the former leader of the American Volunteer Group, Claire Chennault. He still had his very singular methods of fighter tactics. By this stage of the war his pilots had late-model P40s and the twin-boom P38 Lightnings. Because Chennault's methods were so different, the tactics of the 14th, and particularly those of the 23rd Fighter Group, had no parallel anywhere else during the war. As was the now accepted custom, the 14th flew flight fomations of four aircraft which could break down into pairs. However the fours flew in four distinct echelons back from the center of the whole formation.

The leading flight, called the Assault Flight, led the way with the aircraft in echelon starboard. From 100 to 200 yards behind them flew two flights, one each in echelon port and starboard, both known as Support Flights. The final four, also in echelon starboard, flew 100 yards further to the rear.

The two Support Flights flew from 200 to 400 yards outward of the Assault Flight leader, and between 1000 and 2000 feet higher. The Reserve Flight which usually contained the squadron leader, flew another 1000 feet above the rest. Although this arrangement was less flexible than the normal finger-four formations, it was designed for quick 'in-and-out' fighter strikes, and the leader in the rear flight could oversee, order attacks, and give support with his Reserve flight as necessary. The only shortcoming was that his rear four might easily be the first to be bounced in a high attack by Japanese fighters, and his leadership lost. With the other three flights ahead and below, they would be unable to support him.

The Spitfire Mark VIII used by the RAF in India and Burma from early 1944 until the end of the war. This machine was one of 607 Squadron's aircraft used during the defense of Imphal in mid-1944, and helped to defeat the Japanese Oscar pilots in that battle.

IMPHAL PLAIN, BURMA, MAY 11, 1944

DEALING WITH DIFFICULT TERRAIN

In the spring of 1944 the Japanese were preparing to invade India. On the central Burma front the natural features of the Chin and Naga Hills were an obstacle, but a good road through the mountains to the railhead at Dimapur made this route the most attractive. Defending the Imphal Valley astride the road, along with the British 14th Army, were RAF Spitfires and Hurricane fighter-bombers based at seven airstrips — themselves vital staging posts for the aircraft supporting the invasion.

By March 1944 the Imphal Plain and the garrison town of Kohima to the north were surrounded, and only air supply by RAF Dakotas was sustaining the defenders. The severe fuel rationing essential in the circumstances prohibited the use of standing patrols, and the defending fighters' problems were further compounded by the mountainous terrain limiting radar range. Japanese fighters were able to approach low across the Burma plain and through the valleys with a good chance of surprising the transports. The Spitfires could only scramble quickly to intercept the intruders, which then tried to use their superior maneuverability to nullify the Spitfires' performance advantage.

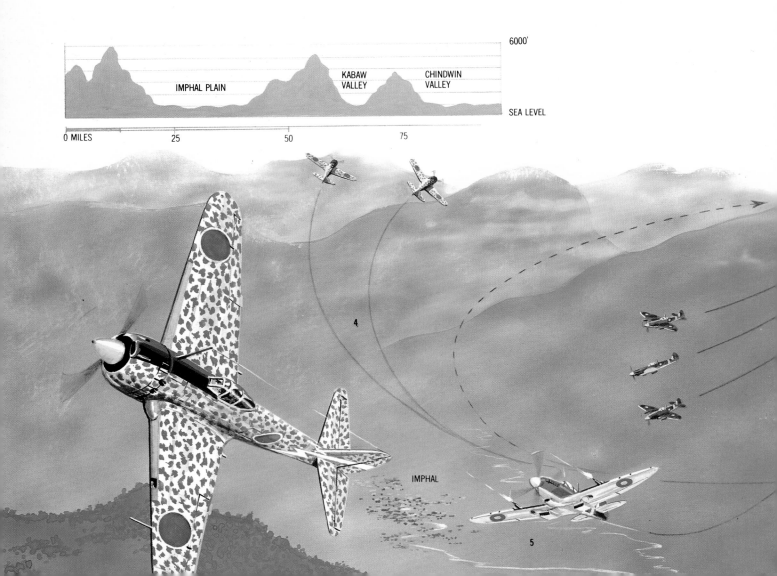

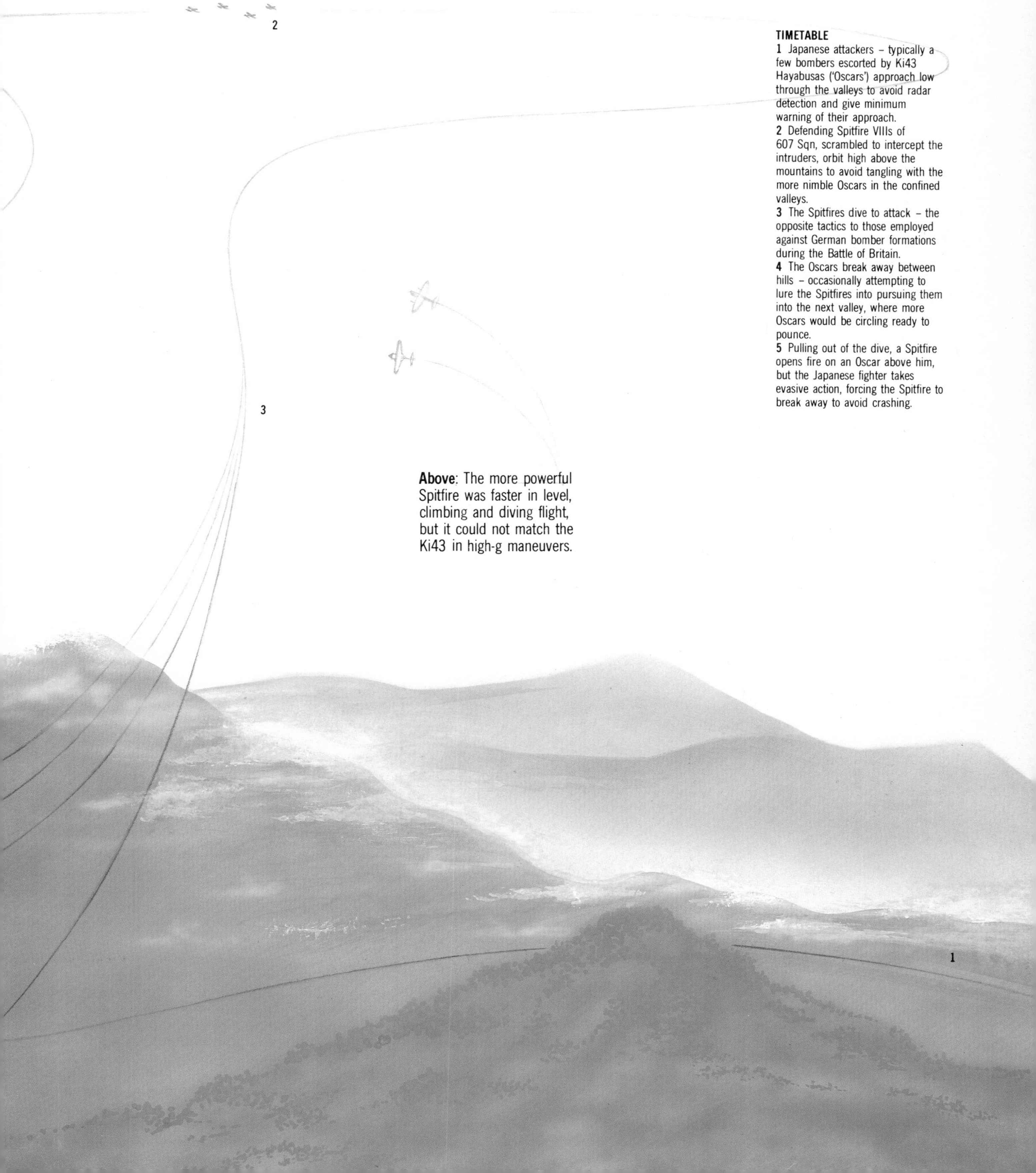

2

3

Above: The more powerful
Spitfire was faster in level,
climbing and diving flight,
but it could not match the
Ki43 in high-g maneuvers.

TIMETABLE

1 Japanese attackers – typically a
few bombers escorted by Ki43
Hayabusas ('Oscars') approach low
through the valleys to avoid radar
detection and give minimum
warning of their approach.
2 Defending Spitfire VIIIs of
607 Sqn, scrambled to intercept the
intruders, orbit high above the
mountains to avoid tangling with the
more nimble Oscars in the confined
valleys.
3 The Spitfires dive to attack – the
opposite tactics to those employed
against German bomber formations
during the Battle of Britain.
4 The Oscars break away between
hills – occasionally attempting to
lure the Spitfires into pursuing them
into the next valley, where more
Oscars would be circling ready to
pounce.
5 Pulling out of the dive, a Spitfire
opens fire on an Oscar above him,
but the Japanese fighter takes
evasive action, forcing the Spitfire to
break away to avoid crashing.

1

CHAPTER TEN

ZENITH OF THE FIGHTER PILOT

IN THE PACIFIC THE AMERICAN Grumman F4F Wildcat had been replaced by its big younger brother, the F6F Hellcat, a machine designed to defeat the Zero fighters of the Japanese Imperial Navy. Following the early shock of meeting the Zero in combat, and especially after the Coral Sea and Midway battles, the US Navy pilots had begun demanding more speed and better climb.

The Hellcat equipped the first US Navy squadron at the beginning of 1943, as the might of the American production effort began to make a decided difference. Two and a half years later – by the end of the war – it dominated the Pacific skies and had helped to defeat Japanese air units at sea and over land – even over Japan. It was some time, however, before the F6F saw combat.

The American Navy's new fighter proved faster in level flight than the Zero at all altitudes and above 10 000 ft it could match or slightly exceed its climb. The Hellcat had nearly twice the all-up weight of the Zero so, like the big P47 in Europe, it could easily outdive an opponent. The Japanese Zero maintained its advantage in the turning circle and below 230 mph it could outmaneuver the Hellcat even though the latter's airframe permitted more 'G'. At higher speeds, however, the Zero's control surfaces induced stiffer responses, enabling the Hellcat to match it in the turn.

Armament in the Hellcat was six 0.50 machine guns, each carrying 400 rounds – an increase from 1440 of the Wildcat to 2400. The American pilots welcomed this. The first Japanese plane to feel the Hellcat's increased fire-power was a large 'Emily' flying-boat (Kawanishi H8K) which Lieutenant Richard L Loesch and his wingman shot down on September 1, 1943.

Another first came on October 5 when the Americans raided enemy-held Wake Island, and 47 Hellcats flew a strike mission from carriers, only to be intercepted by 27 defending Zeros. Before dawn the fighters clashed and three Zeros went down, two to Robert W Duncan. His fire smashed the Zero's cockpit as the fighter burst into flames. Duncan then followed another Zero up into a loop, and his fire sent it blazing into the sea. Shortly afterwards a fourth Zero went down to the guns of Lieutenant M C 'Boogie' Hoffman, who knew the Zero well as he had test-flown a captured specimen some months before.

WEAVING HELLCATS
Over the preceding two years the Navy formations had slowly improved so that by 1944 their expertise had been honed to a sharp edge.

They were now flying in sections of four instead of three and flew the 'stepped-down' rather than the 'stepped-up' formation, which gave their pilots better upward visibility. The 'Thach Weave' was used almost exclusively by the four-man sections, which quickly subdivided into pairs when under attack. Once patrolling over hostile territory the sections would weave in and out in a continuous series of turns so that no opening would be offered for Japanese pilots to make an unopposed attack.

Nevertheless, the Japanese pilots did try to master the 'weave tactic'. If they outnumbered the Americans and had the skill, the Japanese would try to hit the Hellcats as they made a swing on the outside of a turn. If the Hellcat pilots were pulling a lot of 'G', their guns tended to jam with centrifugal force, which immediately put them at a disadvantage.

Identification was and is an essential adjunct to successful air combat, coupled with good eyesight. He who sees the enemy first has big advantages. To see and then to identify your enemy are very important – sometimes crucial – criteria. Robert A Winston, Commanding Officer of the US Navy Squadron VF-31, learned all about identification during operations in support of the American attack on the Paulau Islands off the Philippines at the end of March 1944.

VF-31 were flying an evening Combat Air Patrol (CAP) when his division was vectored 75 miles out from the task force to investigate a radar plot of a suspected 'bogey'. The four Hellcats found what Winston thought in the darkening sky was a formation of nine Zeros in three vees.

Coming down with the evening sun behind them Winston led the attack, going for the leading vic. That three had begun to pull round to the left. Suspecting a trap from more Zeros above, Winston quickly fired a burst in the turn and set one ablaze before zooming up to check his tail. He saw his wingmen just beginning high-side runs on the rest of the enemy aircraft, but could see no more Japanese above. Below he saw the two remaining planes of the lead vic in a high-speed glide, making no attempt to turn and fight. Ignoring this, Winston dived and shot down both planes. Only then, when one of his pilots called to say the enemy were not Zeros but 'Judy' (Yokosuka D4Y) dive bombers, did Winston realize why they were not as aggressive as he had expected. Winston and his division shot down all nine dive bombers as the sun set.

THE 'TURKEY SHOOT'

The record for enemy aircraft shot down in one air battle by an American pilot went to Commander David McCampbell of the US Navy, flying Hellcats aboard the carrier *Essex* in 1944. Already an experienced F6F pilot, he commanded Air Group 15, shooting down his first Japanese plane in June off Saipan in the Marianas. This was just before what was perhaps the most famous day in the annals of air combat, June 19, 1944.

On that day – known later as the day that saw the Great Marianas 'Turkey Shoot' – US Navy pilots shot down about 300 Japanese aircraft for the loss of 16 Hellcats and 13 pilots. McCampbell, in two sorties, shot down seven, but his greatest success was four months later, on October 24,

Left: The F6F Hellcat, introduced by the US Navy to combat Japanese power in the Pacific.
Below: Kawasaki Ki61 'Hien' – (Flying Swallow) codenamed 'Tony'. American fighter pilots who began to meet this in-line engined fighter that equipped Japanese Army squadrons in late 1942, thought at first that it was a licence-built version of Germany's Me109. Despite the use of German Mauser cannon and a Japanese version of the German DB601 engine, captured versions soon disproved the theory of it being a 109. It was in production until 1945 and 2735 were built.

DAVID McCAMPBELL

BORN BESSEMER, ALABAMA IN January 1910, David S McCampbell joined the American Naval aviation in 1934, so he was an experienced flyer by the time the USA joined the war in 1941. Even so it took him till mid-1943 to get into combat at which time he was 33 years old. Commanding Air Group 15 aboard the USS carrier Essex flying F6F Hellcats, he first saw action over the Marianas, claiming his first Japanese aircraft – a Mitsubishi A6M 'Zeke' (Zero) on June 11 1944. On June 19 he shot down five 'Judy' dive-bombers in one morning sortie, then added two Zekes during another mission that same evening.

Over the Philippines in September he shot down a further seven Japanese aircraft in two days. On October 24, Commander McCampbell, with one other pilot, engaged an estimated 60 enemy fighters, and in a running battle they shot down no less that 15, McCampbell scoring nine – a record for an American pilot. This won for him America's highest reward, the Congressional Medal of Honor, which he added to the Navy Cross, Silver Star, Legion of Merit, the Distinguished Flying Cross with two Gold Stars and the Air Medal.

Continuing the fighting over Leyte Gulf in the Philippines, McCampbell downed a 'Zeke' and a 'Val' dive-bomber on November 5, followed by an 'Oscar' four days later bringing his score to 34. Air Group 15's tour of operations then ended. Dave McCampbell's 34 was the highest score by an American pilot during just one tour. His Air Group, the 'Fabled Fifteen' shot down a record 318 enemy aircraft during its tour, plus 348 on the ground.

1944, off the Philippines during the landing of US forces on Leyte, with the US Fleet including the *Essex* covering the assault.

Knowing the Japanese reaction to the landings, the US Navy pilots were flying sorties in support. Aboard the *Essex*, her pilots were delayed flying an air strike as enemy aircraft were reported, heading for the Task Force. McCampbell, who had by this time scored 21 kills, was ordered not to fly on air defense missions, but only as leader of air group strike operations. On this day, however, he was ordered up and was quickly heading out to engage inbound enemy planes. Owing to a mix-up on take-off, McCampbell found he had fewer Hellcats than he should have had and, when sending one division into an attack, he found himself alone with his wingman, Lieutenant Roy Rushing, to cope with any aircraft they found at high level.

Then they found themselves in the middle of a group of bomb-carrying Japanese fighters which immediately pulled into a defensive circle. The two Americans tried unsuccessfully to find an opening, so they gained some height and cruised around above the 40-odd Zeros and Oscars. Time was on their side. They were only about 30–40 miles out from the task force; the Japanese were a good distance from their bases around Manila, with dwindling fuel supplies.

The two Navy pilots had not long to wait before the Japanese pilots, unnerved and concerned about their draining tanks, began to turn towards home base. McCampbell had been calling for additional men to help out, but only one other F6F joined them. There followed a running fight for over an hour and a half, during which the

three F6F pilots harassed the enemy fighters. The third F6F pilot finally ran out of ammunition, but not before he had shot down at least four fighters. McCampbell and Rushing continued the action, keeping above the Japanese, from where they continually swooped down like a pair of wolves after a herd of sheep. Scissoring all the time, the two F6Fs kept at it; although the Japanese were flying similar tactics, they were hit and fell away one by one. Occasionally a Japanese fighter would pull out, turn and try to attack them, but each time the Americans would pounce from their vantage point and shoot him down.

At the end of the action, McCampbell had shot down no less than nine – seven Zeros and two Oscars – plus two probables. Rushing scored over five Zeros and an Oscar, damaging three others. This was achieved in 18 to 20 passes – the Japanese keeping their bombs under their wings. When McCampbell landed on the *Essex* his engine sucked the last drop of petrol from his tanks, and he found just two rounds of 0.50 ammunition left in his guns. For this action, David McCampbell received the Congressional Medal of Honor – America's highest bravery award, not bad for an 'old guy' of 34, who went on to gain a total of 34 victories.

FAR EAST SLOGGING MATCH

By this stage in the Pacific war the American Navy and Marine fighter pilots had the measure of the Japanese aircraft and had suitable machines in which to fight them – the F6F Hellcat and the F4U Corsair. From then on it was effectively a slogging match until the Japanese finally surrendered in August 1945.

Above: The distinctive features of its gull-wings made identification of the Chance Vought Corsair easy in the air or on the ground. The F4U Corsair was considered by many Japanese pilots to be the best American combat aircraft at any altitude, and it was used both as a fighter and fighter-bomber in the Pacific. These Corsairs are of the British Fleet Air Arm in September 1944 during operations against Sumatra.

pilots to get in a good shot at them. The American pilots tried to keep a minimum 250 mph airspeed in their P38s, avoiding steep climbs or tight turns which would reduce this speed. Having all the Lightning's guns in the nose section – generally one 20-mm cannon and four 0.50 machine-guns – gave a more concentrated fire-power and they were less affected than guns in the wings of other types, by wing movement or centrifugal force.

A number of pilots made names for themselves in P38s. Dick Bong in fact became the top-scoring US pilot of the war with 40 victories. He wrote down his tactics for a 5th Air Force survey to help fighter pilots.

In Dick Bong's own words: '*F*ROM THE experience I have gained in individual combat in this theater against a number of different types of Japanese fighters and bombers, these facts stand out.

'Defense against Jap fighters is resolved around the superior speed of our fighters. If you are jumped from above, dive to pick up an indicated speed of at least 350 mph, then level out and start a shallow climb at high airspeed. Generally speaking, a Jap fighter will not follow you in a high-speed dive, but occasionally one does and if such happens, a turn to the right for 90 degrees will throw the Jap behind. The controls stiffen up to excess in high-speed dives, and he cannot follow a sharp-diving turn. A turn into the Jap is always effective because they have a healthy respect for the firepower of our planes. An indicated airspeed never less than 250 mph in combat is good life insurance.*

'Offensive measures go according to the

The US Army Air Force too slogged it out with the Japanese in the last year of the war, mostly in the P38 Lightning. Flying and fighting through New Guinea and over the Philippines, the P38 pilots took on the best that the Japanese could send against them – and won.

Many of the pilots flying P38s had been through the mill of flying P39s or P40s. Like many others, they had learned the danger of dogfighting with the Zeros and Oscars. They concentrated on dive-and-zoom tactics, developing a sort of 'yo-yo' maneuver which made it difficult for the Japanese

HIGH-SIDE ATTACK

A favourite of the US Navy, this tactic involved a Hellcat attacking a Japanese enemy aircraft. Beginning at a higher altitude, the Hellcat sights his enemy and starts a smooth nose-high turn. The pilot drops the Hellcat's nose to keep the enemy in sight, and then begins to bank in the opposite direction to reverse the turn, making sure to fire ahead of his target.

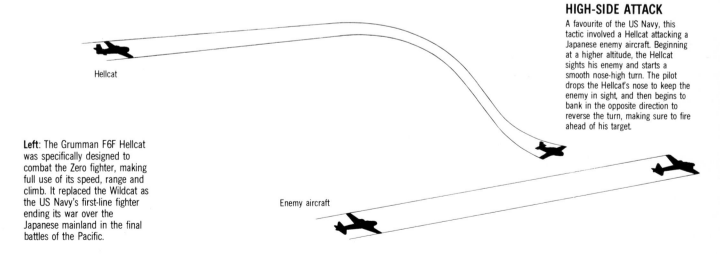

Hellcat

Enemy aircraft

Left: The Grumman F6F Hellcat was specifically designed to combat the Zero fighter, making full use of its speed, range and climb. It replaced the Wildcat as the US Navy's first-line fighter ending its war over the Japanese mainland in the final battles of the Pacific.

PIERRE CLOSTERMAN

REACHING ENGLAND FROM Brazil in 1942, Closterman joined 341 'Alsace' Squadron of the Free French Air Force in the summer of 1943. With this unit he destroyed two German FW190s on July 27 and a third one month later. Commissioned, he joined 602 Squadron RAF in October and between then and July 1944 claimed five more kills and was awarded the DFC.

After some test flying, he returned to operations in March 1945 as a flight commander with 274 Squadron, flying Hawker Tempests in France and Holland. Three days after his arrival he shot down a Me109 and got another on March 14. Then he went to 56 Squadron where he added three more victories, plus a number of German aircraft destroyed or damaged on the ground. In the last month of the war he joined 3 Squadron, still flying Tempests, and in the last few days of the war, shot down three FW190s, two Dornier 24s and a Ju252, to bring his score to 19 in air-to-air combat. In his various ground attack sorties he destroyed at least four German aircraft and damaged several others, as well as claiming 72 trains, and 225 trucks and lorries plus two R-Boats. He received a bar to his DFC as well as the French Legion of Honor and Croix de Guerre. He had flown 293 missions, and in addition to his confirmed successes had claimed five probables and eight damaged.

Closterman left the RAF in August 1945, and later became a Member of the French House of Representatives. He was called-up during the Algerian crisis and served in the Armée de l'Air throughout that conflict. He is the author of 'Le Grand Cirque' (The Big Show).

number of the enemy, but they are always hit-and-run because the Jap can out-maneuver us about two to one. Any number of Nips can be safely attacked from above. Dive on the group, pick a definite plane as your target, and concentrate on him. Pull up in a shallow high-speed climb and come back for another pass. Single enemy planes or small groups can be surprised from the rear and slightly below a large percentage of the time. He seems to be blind, or he does not look directly behind him enough to spot you, and your first pass should knock him down. Against bombers, it is quite safe to drive right up on the tail of any of them with two exceptions – the Betty and the Helen. These two planes have 20-mm cannon which cover a 30-degree arc to the rear, and a beam attack broken off before you reach this one is the best attack.'

Tommy McGuire scored 38 kills. He too put down his observations on tactics in the survey. He agreed with Bong that the shallow high-speed dive or climb was the best defense against a rear attack. Keeping a high speed in combat was a must and staying in pairs at all times was essential. Never chase single enemy planes from a group, as the Japanese often used this trick to isolate American planes from the rest, when they would be attacked by others away from the cover of the main P38 formation. His attack maxim was: 'Go in close, and then when you think you are too close, go on in closer.'

Bong and McGuire were each awarded the Congressional Medal of Honor. Both had considerable success over the Philippines in late 1944, but McGuire was killed in action on January 7, 1945, over Los Negros Island while trying to defend a fellow-pilot from attack. Ironically, he died breaking his three cardinal rules of air combat.

On that day, Tommy McGuire set course for a new Japanese air strip on Los Negros, planning to come in at 2000 ft to surprise any fighters climbing up. Flying in below broken cloud, a single Zero came down from the clouds in the classic fashion and in total surprise. The Japanese pilot was Shoichi Sugita, whose score was to reach 80 before his own death in combat.

At the last moment McGuire saw the Zero and pulled his P38 into a vertical bank and a steep turn. His three pilots circled, boxing in the Zero. Sugita broke to the left to get away but McGuire's four planes continued round in the circle, all five aircraft dropping down to about 200 ft. This had broken No 1 rule – never attempt combat at low altitude.

Above: A Messerschmitt 262 sits abandoned on a German air strip at the end of WW2. Messerschmitt 262s – either 'Sturmvogel' (Stormbird) bombers, or 'Schwalbe' (Swallow) fighters – could have caused devastation against Allied aircraft had development not been delayed by Hitler. In the event the jet came to the front too late to turn the tide in favor of the Luftwaffe.

Left: The Hawker Tempest V, developed from the Typhoon, which reached RAF squadrons in the spring of 1944. Because of their high speed, they were retained on defensive operations over England against the German V1 flying-bombs and destroyed 638 between June and September. Once employed on the Continent in the last months of the war, they matched their speed against the German jets. This Tempest is of 274 Squadron – note the long-range fuel tanks.

The P38s now scattered, but it was a fatal mistake for the Americans. Sugita, able to turn quickly in his nimble Zero, got behind a P38 and stayed there. The American called for help. McGuire responded, reduced speed, and pulled round. This broke rule No 2 – never fly under 300 mph in combat. Also he still had on his drop-tanks, violating rule No 3 to drop them in a fight. The Zero now had the advantage over both P38s. McGuire pulled round in a tight turn but with his tanks still on and at an already dangerously low speed, his P38 stalled and plunged into the jungle where it exploded.

Gerald R Johnson had 22 victories flying P38s and was Commanding Officer of the 49th Fighter Group. He knew, as did the other American pilots, that by and large the quality of Japanese fighter pilots was diminishing as the war progressed. Their ranks had been thinned by the Allies and training of replacements was below the earlier high standard.

Johnson studied the opposition and had found that generally the enemy pilots were what he called 'stick-and-rudder' men. In this they were excellent, but their maneuvers were too evenly coordinated and could be anticipated. They seldom used skids, side-slips or sudden, violent uncoordinated maneuvers to avoid trouble. They also seemed less alert and, as Dick Bong discovered, they could often be surprised from below and behind.

Johnson always attacked first in squadron strength, before breaking into pairs, but he taught his pilots to stay in the general area for mutual support and not go chasing a retreating enemy plane. If one lost a leader or wingman, the remaining pilot had to join up immediately with another pair. To be alone was fatal. Hit-and-run he knew was the best tactic. Most kills came in the initial clash, so his maxim was 'attack, do the most damage, then re-form'.

There were other Army aircraft in the Pacific at this time, besides the P38s. The P47 equipped some groups. One pilot who recorded his tactics was William D Dunham, of the 460th Fighter Squadron, who scored 15 victories. He felt the best individual defensive tactic to be a hard and fast offensive action – the old saying that 'the best form of defense is attack'. Dunham, like other Thunderbolt pilots in the Pacific, used his machine as did his contemporaries in Europe, taking full advantage of its superior speed and diving ability. It enabled them to make an attacking pass at enemy aircraft, followed by a fast dive, with little danger of being shot down. If the P47 pilot was attacked from above, his best defensive tactic was a sharp aileron roll to the right and down, diving out 180 degrees from the direction of the attack. For the best results it should be executed just before the attacker was within range, for the slow aileron action of the Japanese fighter at high speed made it almost

HAWKER TEMPEST V versus MESSERSCHMITT Me262A-1a

IN 1939 CAMM DESIGNED THE Typhoon as a much more powerful successor to the Hurricane, with stressed-skin construction. Despite prolonged engine troubles it became a famed ground attack aircraft. The Typhoon's wing was thick. Given a thinner wing (of elliptical shape, like the Spitfire), the resulting Tempest proved an outstanding fighter at low levels, and the most successful of all in destroying flying bombs (V-1 cruise missiles). They even shot down 20 Me262s in air combat, even though the German twin-jet was over 100 mph faster. The 262 was the most modern fighter of the war, a delight to fly and with devastating firepower. Its drawback was the tricky and unreliable nature of its immature engines, to the extent that its victories were outnumbered by its severe losses.

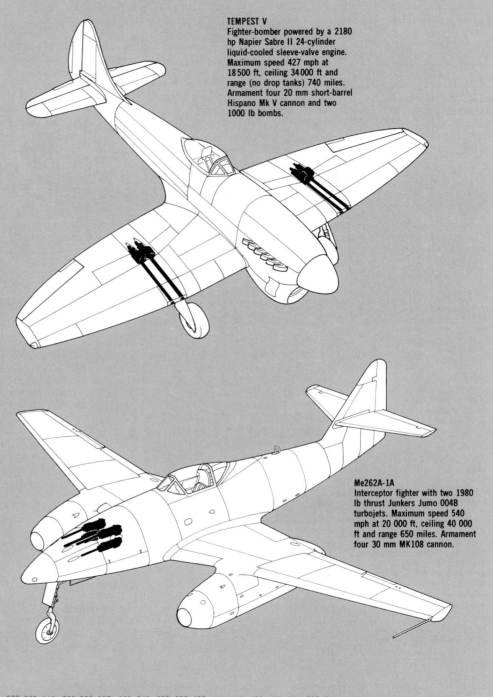

TEMPEST V
Fighter-bomber powered by a 2180 hp Napier Sabre II 24-cylinder liquid-cooled sleeve-valve engine. Maximum speed 427 mph at 18 500 ft, ceiling 34 000 ft and range (no drop tanks) 740 miles. Armament four 20 mm short-barrel Hispano Mk V cannon and two 1000 lb bombs.

Me262A-1A
Interceptor fighter with two 1980 lb thrust Junkers Jumo 004B turbojets. Maximum speed 540 mph at 20 000 ft, ceiling 40 000 ft and range 650 miles. Armament four 30 mm MK108 cannon.

50000

40000

30000

20000

10000

ALTITUDE IN FEET

0 20 40 60 80 100 120 140 160 180 200 220 240 260 280 300 320 340 360 380 400 420 440 460 480 500 520 540 M.P.H.

Right: The fast RAF Mosquito which was opposed by the new German Me262 jet.

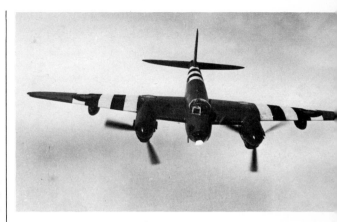

JOHANNES STEINHOF

BORN IN 1913, 'MACKY' Steinhof joined the German Navy in 1934 but transferred to the Luftwaffe in 1936. By 1939, aged 26, he commanded the 10th Staffel of JG 26, and in February 1940 he took command of 4/JG52. His first two victories were Wellington bombers, shot down on December 18, 1939 (although one was later disallowed) in the battle of Heligoland Bight. By August 1941 he had shot down 35 Allied aircraft and was awarded the Knight's Cross.

Steinhof flew in Russia, and later over Sicily, having been made Kommandeur of II Gruppe of JG52 in February 1942. In September of that year he received the Oak Leaves to his Knight's Cross, having scored 100 kills by August 31. On February 2, 1943 this total had increased to 150. In March 1943 he was given command of JG77. In July 1944 he was awarded the Swords to his Knight's Cross, having now scored 167 victories and in December he was made Kommodore of JG7.

In the last weeks of the war, Steinhof joined Adolf Galland's élite JV44 squadron, flying Me262 jet fighters. With this unit he raised his score to 176, shooting down Russian aircraft near Berlin in March and April 1945. His six kills on the 262 made him one of the first aces of the new jet age. On April 18, 1945, when taking off for a mission, his jet crashed and exploded. Steinhof survived, badly injured and terribly burned. Yet he fought back from the brink of death to fly again. He later went to America to fly jets and rose to high rank within the new West German Air Force, becoming a Major General in 1962.

impossible for him to pull through and change direction. By the time he had done this, the P47 pilot would have enough speed to outdistance him.

The Japanese were rarely able to combat successfully the American weave or scissoring tactic. They considered the Corsair to be the top American combat fighter at any altitude, the P38 Lightning best at high level and the later version of the P40 – the Warhawk – the best fighter at low level.

THE JET ENTERS COMBAT

Over Europe in the last months of WW2 the Luftwaffe operated the first jet fighter to see combat – the Messerschmitt 262. It was perhaps fortunate for the Allies that Hitler at first insisted that this aircraft be used as a bomber, but his senior pilots later had their way and diverted enough onto fighter operations to cause the Allies considerable concern.

Test-flown by such pilots as Adolf Galland as early as 1943, the Me262 was a powerful weapon in their hands. It was faster than anything else in the air and, used correctly, it could seriously interfere with American daylight raids, to the extent of making them too costly to continue. Fortunately Hitler's decision to postpone full production at first and then use it as a bomber not only saved countless American lives, but could be said to have prevented the war from extending beyond May 1945. In Hitler's defense, he did see in the Me262 something that most war leaders had been looking for – a bomber that could outfly all opposition, bomb a target successfully and, equally important, return home. Unfortunately (for him) the idea was sound but his timing was out.

While the arguments raged, Galland used the Me262 jet to combat the RAF's fast photo-reconnaissance Mosquito aircraft. Few conventional fighters could catch these light wooden aircraft, but the 262s were able to climb and intercept them and thus proved how successful the Messerschmitt could be.

Despite Hitler, Galland was able to form a jet fighter wing – JG/7 – especially when the Arado 234 jet bomber became available. JG/7 was given to Walter Nowotny who, by the summer of 1943, had a score of 150 on the Eastern front and by October of that same year had become the Luftwaffe's top ace with 250 victories – in only 442 missions.

The fighter version of the Me262 could fly at 540 mph – it could far outstrip the Mustangs, and it could reach 30 000 ft in seven minutes. It could

fly for only an hour, which was a drawback, but its 30-mm guns could pack an awful punch. Later it added the new R4M rockets to its armament, being able to carry 24 of these high-velocity air-to-air rockets which were ripple-fired to form a dense pattern. Fired at a B17 formation, a single rocket was usually more than enough to cause lethal damage.

The tactic used by Me262 pilots when attacking US bombers was generally to place themselves about three miles behind the bomber 'box' and about 6000 ft above. From this position they began a dive to reach a speed of over 540 mph with which to penetrate any fighter screen. Continuing down to 1000 to 1500 ft below the 'box' the German pilot would then pull up, throttle back in order to lose some of this forward speed, then level out some 1000 yards behind the target at about 100 mph, firing rockets (if carried) at 650 yards, then following up with his 30-mm from closer range. The pilot would accelerate away and over to avoid flying debris, as his target bomber disintegrated.

Me262 jets were involved during the Luftwaffe's attack on Allied airfields in Holland on the first day of January 1945. Mostly they flew as lead aircraft, a task shared with Ju88s, guiding the FW190s and Me109s to the various airfields selected for attack. The mass attack had its own tactics, the Germans coming in low and fast to achieve surprise. The Ardennes battle had been raging for some time, although bad weather had kept both sides grounded. January 1 happened to be the first morning in several days that weather permitted the attack. Because by this stage in the war the Luftwaffe, like the Japanese, were being forced to use inexperienced and poorly trained pilots, the Germans could not take the risk of flying a low-level attack at dawn, for they would

HEINZ BAR

LIKE A NUMBER OF HIGH-scoring Luftwaffe fighter pilots, "Pritzl" Bär was in action when WW2 began and was still flying operationally when it ended. Born near Leipzig in March 1913, his early ambition was to become an airline pilot and to this end he obtained his private pilot's license in the 1930s. In 1937 he joined the Luftwaffe, and became an NCO fighter-pilot. Once war began, he flew in action on the Western Front, scoring his first kill on September 25, 1939, a French Curtiss P36. During the Battles of France and Britain he flew with JG51 under Werner Molders, was commissioned and ended 1940 with 17 victories. Several times he was badly shot up in combat with RAF fighters, and on September 2 he had to bale out over the Channel.

When Germany invaded Russia, Bär and JG51 were assigned to the invasion force, and within two months, he had scored his 60th victory and won the Knight's Cross and Oak Leaves. He scored no less that six kills on August 30, 1941, but the next day baled out over enemy territory but managed to walk back to the lines, although injured. He was out of action till 1942 but soon ran his score up to 90 to receive the Swords to his Knight's Cross.

In 1942 he took command of JG77, flying over Malta and North Africa, adding 45 kills to his tally, and although shot down several times, always survived. In April 1944 his score reached 200, over 20 of which were four-engined American bombers. With 204 victories by early 1945, he flew Me262s with JV44, scoring a record 16 kills by the war's end, the highest number for a 262 pilot in the war. With 220 confirmed victories during over 1000 missions, he was second only to the German ace Marseille in downing the most British and American aircraft. Bär died in an air crash in April 1957.

have needed to take off and fly into Holland while it was still dark. So they took off at first light. In consequence, although they surprised a number of bases and destroyed a fair number of aircraft on the ground, they would, had they hit the airfields half an hour earlier, have caught and destroyed many others that were themselves taking off at dawn to support the American battle front.

THE WAR IS WON

In many ways this attack became the death throe of the Luftwaffe's fighter arm. That morning they not only lost some 300 aircraft to ground fire and air-to-air combat, but more significantly over 200 fighter pilots were killed, missing, taken prisoner or wounded. The enemy never recovered from this reversal of their effort designed to knock out the RAF's Second Tactical Air Force.

The last German airplane shot down over Europe by the RAF was a Siebel 204, destroyed by Flight Lieutenant Gibbons and Warrant Officer Seymour of 130 Squadron. This occurred early on May 5, 1945, over Hamburg, the British pilots flying Spitfires XIVs. The next day Germany surrendered.

By the last months of the war in the Pacific, the American and British carrier task forces were sending their aircraft over the Japanese mainland. From China and from captured islands (initially the Marianas), American land-based aircraft were now within striking distance too, and with

GERMAN JET ACES OF WW2		
Name	Jet Score	Total
Oberst Heinz Bar	16	(220)
Hpt Franz Schall	14	(137)
Fwbl Hermann Buchner	12	(58)
Maj Georg-Peter Eder	12	(78)
Maj Erich Rudorfer	12	(222)
Ltn Karl Schnorrer	11	(46)
Fwbl Buttner	8	
Heinz Lennartz	8	
Oblt Rudolf Rademacher	8	(126)
Oblt Walter Schuck	8	(206)
Guenther Wegmann	8	
Maj Theodor Weissenberger	8	(208)
Lt-Gen Adolf Galland	7	(103)
Fritz Mueller	6	
Oberst Johannes Steinhoff	6	(176)
Fwbl Baudach	5	
Maj Heinrich Ehrler	5	(209)
Oblt Hans Grunberg	5	(82)
CWO Heim	5	
Maj Klaus Neumann	5	(37)
Ltn Schreiber	5	
Hpt Wolfgang Spaete	5	(99)

escorting P51 Mustangs.

The USAAF now had the B29 Superfortress, a new bomber which had flown its first raid against Japan itself in June 1944. Defending Japanese Army and Navy fighters found the B29s difficult targets, as they were well defended with heavy caliber machine-guns in remote-controlled turrets and a 20-mm cannon in the tail. They also flew at even greater heights than the earlier B17s the Japanese had fought in the first year or so of the war. It was not until August 20 that enemy fighters made their first successful interception when they shot down one of 60 raiding B29s. As it was an evening raid, night-fighters were also sent up. It was in fact a twin-engined Nakajima J1N1 (Irving) flown by Lieutenant Endo that scored. Unusually, he carried upward-firing 20-mm cannon, like the Germans' 'Schrage Musik', and it was the use of the German tactic of flying beneath the B29 that proved successful. The success prevented further B29 raids until October.

The battles with the bomber giants continued into 1945, the Kawasaki Ki45 'Toryu' night-fighter (Nick) helping the defense of the homeland. Most models of the Nick carried a 37-mm cannon and two 20-mm guns. A single-seat version – the Ki46 – was evolved from this design and had a number of successes against the B29s but it was no match for the American fighters. The Zero (Zeke) still bore the brunt of the air battles although new fighters continued to reach front-line squadrons, two being the Kawanishi 'Shidon' (George) and Mitsubishi 'Raiden' (Jack). The George was designed to combat the Hellcat. It possessed good speed, four 20-mm cannon and armor plating. Despite its heaviness in flight it proved maneuverable, though lacking range. Another drawback was that inexperienced pilots found it difficult to handle and several died while trying. The Jack was meant to combat B29s – Japanese pilots equating it with the FW190 – and it was able to fly above 400 mph. It was excellent for its job as a bomber-killer with armor plate and a heavy fire-power but it lacked maneuverability in battle with Mustangs or Hellcats.

When Saipan Island was captured the B29s began operating from it and the first bombers appeared over Tokyo in November. On November 21 Lieutenant Mikihiko Sakamoto took a leaf out of the German Sturmgruppe tactic book and crashed his fighter into a B29. He was not the first nor the last.

The Japanese tactic with either the Irving or Nick was a dive from behind to build speed to catch the B29 which could fly at 370 mph – faster than these two Japanese fighters. They would

LEADING BRITISH EMPIRE ACES OF WW2

Name	Total	Nationality
S/Ldr M T StJ Pattle	40+	South African
W/Cdr J E Johnson	38	British
G/Cpt A G Malan	35	South African
W/Cdr B Finucane	32	Irish
F/Lt G F Beurling	31	Canadian
W/Cdr J R D Braham	29	British
W/Cdr R R S Tuck	29	British
S/Ldr N F Duke	28	British
W/Cdr C R Caldwell	28½	Australian
W/Cdr F R Carey	28	British
S/Ldr J H Lacey	28	British
W/Cdr C F Gray	27½	New Zealand
F/Lt E S Lock	26	British
W/Cdr L C Wade	25	American

AMERICAN ACES OF WW2

USAAF

Name	Total	Unit
Maj Richard I Bong	40	Far East Air Force
Maj Thomas B McGuire Jr	38	Far East Air Force
Col Francis S Gabreski	31	8th Air Force
Capt Robert S Johnson	28	8th Air Force
Col Charles H MacDonald	27	Far East Air Force
Col John C Meyer	26	8th Air Force
Maj George E Preddy	26	8th Air Force

US NAVY

Name	Total
Capt David S McCampbell	34
Ltd Cdr Cecil E Harris	24
Cdr Eugene A Valancia	23

US MARINE CORPS

Name	Total
Col Gregory Boyington	28
Brig Gen Joseph J Foss	26
Lt Robert M Hanson	25
Maj Kenneth A Walsh	21
Capt Donald N Aldrich	20

LEADING FRENCH ACES OF WW2

Name	Total	War Zone
Capt Marcel Albert	23	France/Russia
W/Cdr Jean Demozay	21	RAF
S/Ldr Pierre Clostermann	19	RAF
Lt Pierre Le Gloen	18	France/Syria
Capt Roland de la Poype	17	RAF/Russia
2/Lt Jacques Andre	16	France/Desert/Russia
Cdt Louis Delfino	16	France/Desert/Russia
Cdt Edmund Marin la Meslee	16	France
2/Lt Roger Sauvage	16	France/Russia
Lt Georges Valentin	15	France/Desert/Corsica

LEADING GERMAN ACES OF WW2

Name	Total
Maj Erich Hartmann	352
Maj Gerhard Barkhorn	301
Maj Guenther Rall	275
Oblt Otto Kittel	267
Maj Walter Nowotny	258
Maj Wilhelm Batz	237
Maj Erich Rudorfer	222
Oberst Heinz Bar	220
Oberst Hermann Graf	212
Maj Heinrich Ehrler	209
Maj Theodor Weissenberger	208
Oberst Hans Philipp	206
Oblt Walter Schuck	206
Oblt Anton Hafner	204
Hpt Helmut Lipfert	203

LEADING JAPANESE ACES OF WW2

Name	Total	Service
Lt Tetsuzo Iwamoto	94	Navy
Lt Hiroyoshi Nishazawa	87	Navy
Ens Shoichi Sugita	70	Navy
Lt Saburo Sakai	64	Navy
WO Hiromichi Shinohara	58	Army
WO Takeo Okumura	54	Navy
Sgt Satoshi Anabuki	51	Army

then dip below the Superfortresses in order to fire their upward-mounted 20-mm cannons – aiming for the two pilots rather than the self-sealing and protected fuel tanks.

The single-seat fighters attacked from the rear also but, as the Germans found, it was a slow approach, with the air full of defensive fire. The pilots then resorted, like their German counterparts, to coming in head-on. They would position themselves ahead and above, then curve down to a rapid head-on pass, aiming for cockpit or engines, then half-roll, dive beneath the huge aircraft and away. Some Jack fighters also carried a single 20-mm cannon mounted behind and to the left of the pilot's seat in order to attack from below and behind, firing upwards into the belly, wings or cockpit area.

By the time Mustangs from the captured island of Iwo Jima and carrier-based Hellcats could roam freely over Japan it was obvious that the end of the war was near, although experienced pilots, even flying Zeros at this late stage, could outfight the Americans. Flight Warrant Officer Kinsuke Muto while test-flying a George was attacked by 12 Hellcats over the Atsugi Navy airbase. He shot down four of them. On February 17, 1945 near Tokyo, Lieutenant Sadanori Akamatsu in a Zeke shot down two Hellcats in one fight, then two more later in the day. Sadly for the Japanese, most of their experienced pilots had long since fallen – another parallel with the Luftwaffe's fate in Europe.

The end finally came in August 1945, when two B29 raids dropped atomic bombs on the cities of Hiroshima and Nagasaki. WW2 ended less than a week later.

WESTERN FRONT SEPTEMBER 26, 1944

P51 VERSUS Me262

The pilots of RAF and USAAF piston-engined aircraft had to use new tactics to combat the German jets they began to encounter during the last months of World War 2. The jets were so fast that a tail chase was totally out of the question — even the Mosquito pilots, whose speed had made them immune from interception, found themselves overhauled with ease by Me262s — and Allied pilots were able to get within firing range only if they spotted the jet well below and were able to close with it during a high-speed dive. Even then inaccurate fire would warn the jet pilot that he was under attack, to simply push his throttles forward and speed away from his assailant.

An edge could be gained if the attacker's fire damaged one of the engines of an Me262,

Below: As seen through the P51's gunsight, the Me262 maintains a deflection angle great enough to avoid being hit, turning too fast to allow the Mustang's guns to be brought to bear.

reducing its power enough to enable the piston fighter to stay with it. Alternatively, excessive maneuvering on the part of the German pilot might enable his pursuer to stay with him. Otherwise, the jets were really vulnerable only when taking off or landing.

Wing Commander John Wray, DFC, saw combat with German jets while leading 122 Wing, RAF, in 1944-45, flying Tempest Vs. He recalls: '*So far as the German jets*

were concerned you'd got to be above them, by at least 3000 ft, because all we could do was open everything up and dive. But as soon as they knew you were there they were off like shit off a shovel, so we just had that moment when you could catch the chap, when he couldn't see you, when you came down, going like the clappers hoping to get close enough to get in a burst before he saw you. He just had to open his throttle and he was gone! And that really was the name of the game'.

TIMETABLE

1 Flying at 20 000 ft escorting a bombing raid on Hamm, Drew sees an Me262 10 000 ft below him. Leading his flight down he begins to chase the jet, dropping his tanks to gain maximum speed.
2 Despite his airspeed hovering around 500 mph, Drew fails to reduce the range on the jet, which is easily outpacing the Mustangs in a 30° dive.

3 Just as Drew is about to give up, the 262 begins a shallow turn to port.
4 The Mustangs attempt to cut inside.
5 The 262 responds by tightening his turn.
6 As the two aircraft pass each other the deflection angle of 90° is too great for Drew's fire to be effective.

7 The Mustangs pull round to resume the chase.
8 The four P51s find themselves over a German airfield: probably warned by the German pilot, the airfield's guns put up a massive flak barrage, hitting one of Drew's men and forcing him to bale out.
9 Drew then finds himself over a marshalling yard in the middle of more flak. Despite registering a level speed of 410 mph on the deck, Drew fails to gain on the jet.

10 Another 262 appears out of cloud, but Drew's wingman sees it and turns sharply before it can make a pass: both jets pull away with ease and the Mustangs are finally forced to abandon the chase; Drew has fired 1376 rounds and hit nothing.

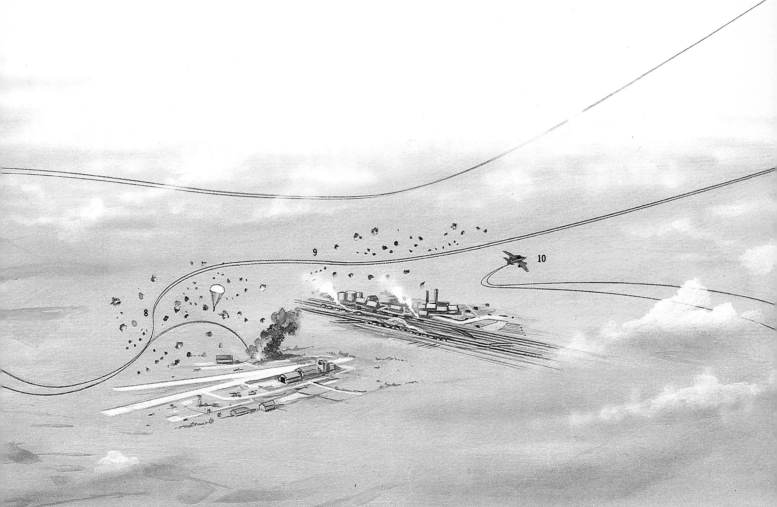

CHAPTER ELEVEN

PISTONS TO JETS

THE WORLD'S FIRST JET-VERSUS-jet combats took place over Korea from 1950 to 1953. With the jet came a new breed of fighter pilot. Gone to some extent were the 'seat-of-the-pants' flyers of WW1 and WW2, since the jet aircraft needed a new touch. With faster speeds and more sophisticated instrumentation requiring feather-light flying, accuracy and precision were essential. A far more professional approach was necessary.

Gyroscopic gunsights had been developed in the latter stages of WW2. A pilot could then quickly adjust his gunsight to the wingspan of an adversary and the new computing gunsight automatically set up the correct deflection before the pilot fired. The fighter pilot needed only to track the enemy aircraft in his gunsight, then open fire. It aided the naturally gifted marksman but by the same token helped the below-average pilot to score hits on a target at angles that until then had been beyond him.

The greater speeds and heights reached by jet fighters brought with them the need for new tactics and new thinking in combat. The pilot needed special clothing to protect himself against the pressures of G-forces that high speed turns placed upon his body. Compressibility problems had been encountered at high speeds during WW2 when buffeting affected both the aircraft's performance and the pilot's ability to shoot straight. Aerodynamic design gradually overcame these problems and the early high-speed jet fighters increasingly saw the light of day with swept-back wings. The two main adversaries of the Korean War, the US Sabre and the Soviet MIG, both had swept-back wings.

In June 1950 Communist North Korea invaded South Korea, the latter being aided by the United Nations, with US forces predominating. The American Far Eastern Air Force quickly swept the North Korean Air Force from the sky. The North Koreans flew Russian propeller-driven YAK-9s and Ilyushin Il-10s, the Americans flew a variety of propeller machines, including the F-82 – a sort of 'double Mustang' – and three of the first-generation jets, the F-80 Shooting Star, F-84 Thunderjet and F9F Panther.

The first combat victories of the Korean War came on June 27, 1950. Lieutenant Colonel J W Little (5 destroyed in WW2) and Lieutenant W G Hudson in F-82s shot down two YAKs while flying air cover. Shortly afterwards four F-80s fought a battle with Il-10s. Captain R. Schillereff shot down one, Lieutenant R Wayne two others while Lieutenant R Dewald scored a fourth.

Right: USS **Antietam** (CVA-36) operating with Task Force 77 off the east coast of Korea in October 1951. On deck are Corsairs, F9F-3 Panthers and Grumman Bearcats.

Left: The aircraft of the Korean War – the F-86 Sabre. This section of four on patrol are of the 51st Fighter Interceptor Wing.

The American Navy scored its first air-to-air victories of the Korean War on July 3, 1950. Propeller-driven Corsairs and Skyraiders flew from a Navy carrier while the British Royal Navy launched Seafires and Fireflies to attack the North Korean air base at Pyongyang. Panthers later went off as air cover in case the YAKs joined in. They did so, and Ensign E W Brown and Lieutenant L Plog each shot down one.

Generally, however, the American and British aircraft flew army support missions, using rockets and napalm. As 1950 progressed and the UN forces pushed the North Korean invaders back towards the Chinese border, China warned the UN that further advances into the North's territory would bring the Chinese into the conflict. On October 19, the Chinese carried out the threat and sent troops across the border – the Yalu River. They also sent six MIG-15 jets against some American Mustangs. These failed to shoot down any of the P51s but, now that the opposition had a powerful modern jet, the possibility of jet-versus-jet combat was imminent.

The Russian MIG-15 would easily dominate the air war in North Korea if allowed to do so and the only American fighter likely to be able to contend with it was the F-86A Sabre. America had only US-based Sabre Groups, and when the MIGs began to inflict losses and damage on American B29 bombers raiding North Korean targets, the 4th Fighter Group flew into Kimpo, north-west of the South Korean capital of Seoul, in December.

MIG-15 VERSUS SABRE
Both the Sabre and MIG had swept-back wings and were very much alike in a general view. However, the MIG had a better rate of climb and service ceiling than the Sabre. The Sabre (A) could reach 675 miles per hour, the MIG 684. The Sabre's armament was six 0.50 machine guns (with 14 seconds firing time), while the MIG's was much heavier with two 23-mm (80 rounds each) and one 37-mm cannon (40 rounds). In some ways the MIG-15 was like the Zero of WW2 – fairly basic with little sophisticated equipment, which helped it to climb faster than the Sabre, and above 20 000 feet it was faster in level flight. It could also out-turn the American aircraft at height, but the Sabre was a better gun platform when flying at high Mach speed; indeed, above

Mach 0.86 the MIG tended to 'snake' about.

With the power of these jet fighters, combats tended to be fought at much higher altitudes than in WW2. This brought its own problems for the pilots, because at such altitudes the thinner air affects lift. Thinner air also meant less oxygen, essential for jet-engine performance, so power declined. Hard turns, in consequence, were difficult if not impossible, for the pilot could easily black out and an enemy waiting for just such an occurrence had a sitting target.

In fact the war in Korea began to show how difficult modern air combat was becoming. Speed alone brought aircraft into action so much quicker. Coming out of an azure, cloudless sky at speeds around 600 mph, it took but split seconds for a speck to become a fighter closing in. In head-on action where speeds were combined aircraft were on each other before being aware of it.

The first jet-versus-jet combat victory occurred before the Sabre arrived, on November 8, 1950. B29s were bombing Sinuija, on the Yalu River, escorted by Mustangs and F-80 Shooting Stars. Six Chinese MIG-15s took off from their base at Antung, rapidly climbed to 30 000 ft before diving in pairs onto the F-80s 10 000 ft below. They made a fast attack as the F-80s turned to meet them and, as the MIGs zoomed away, one broke and dived. Lieutenant Russell Brown dived in pursuit, the heavier F-80 easily closing in before loosing a 5-second burst into the MIG. It spiralled down, crashing into the bank of

the river. The whole action lasted less than a minute.

With the arrival of the Sabre-equipped 4th Fighter Group, patrols were flown over a 100-mile-wide piece of airspace, to the south of the Yalu – which became known as MIG Alley – to prevent the MIGs attacking UN bombers and fighter-bombers from the safety of China. The Sabres had their first success on December 17.

Four F-86s, led by Lieutenant Colonel Bruce Hinton (336th Squadron), patrolled in the traditional Finger Four formation, throttled right back to fly at 400 mph. In this way it was hoped that the Chinese radar would assume the aircraft to be the slower F-80s. Shortly afterwards four MIGs came up from Antung at an 'astonishing speed'. Colonel Hinton radioed to his men to drop tanks but he found his radio not working. As the MIGs crossed ahead of him, Hinton banked to come in behind them, but in doing so became separated from his flight. The nearest MIG was the leader's wingman and it was at this that Hinton fired. He hit the MIG, taking several more bursts to send it down, and returning to Kimpo to perform a celebratory 'victory roll' over the base.

Hinton's tactic of flying at slow speed to entice the MIGs to come up could not be continued once the Chinese and North Korean pilots knew that the Sabre had arrived. Like most tactics it was effective only until the opposition had a counter to it. The Sabres, finding that MIG interceptions were almost always carried out at high speed,

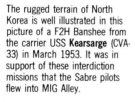

The rugged terrain of North Korea is well illustrated in this picture of a F2H Banshee from the carrier USS **Kearsarge** (CVA-33) in March 1953. It was in support of these interdiction missions that the Sabre pilots flew into MIG Alley.

also needed to fly fast while in the combat zone. Naturally this burnt more fuel, thus reducing patrol time from a little over half an hour down to only 20 minutes or so. To maximize the effective air cover, Sabres were routed into MIG Alley at five-minute intervals, enabling them to provide cover for an hour during periods when bombers or fighter-bombers were flying missions to the North.

In the next big combat using these tactics the Sabre pilots destroyed six MIGs for the loss of one F-86. The situation was reversed at the end of the year when a Chinese offensive pushed back UN forces as far as Seoul, forcing the Sabres to abandon Kimpo air base and return to Japan, from where they flew missions over the front lines. MIG Alley was beyond their range and patrols there were consequently suspended. It was not until March 1951 that Seoul was retaken, allowing the 4th Fighter Group to return to Korea, at Suwon, 20 miles south of Seoul. Whether at Kimpo or Suwon, it was still a 200-mile trip to MIG Alley. To help, the F-86s carried two 120-gal drop-tanks. Contrary to some artists' drawings of Sabres in combat, showing tanks gone but the support still attached, in fact the whole fitting came off when the tanks were jettisoned, to give the Sabre its 100% clean line for combat.

THE FIRST US JET ACES

Gradually the American pilots gained the upper hand over the MIGs, combating the superior Russian aircraft with better tactics, taking full advantage of the few problems that the Chinese pilots had with their MIGs, while building on a solid basis of better-trained fighter pilots.

America's first jet 'ace' – Captain James Jabara – had only four MIG victories by the time his squadron was due to be rotated back to Japan, so he was transferred to another squadron hoping to get his 5th. But weeks passed without a single MIG being sighted, and Jabara was nearing the completion of 100 missions, which would automatically end his tour.

Then, on May 20, the MIGs sought a fight. Fifty of them attacked 20 Sabres and Jabara with 14 more Sabres went up to help out. When the relief force arrived above the Yalu the battle still raged. Dropping his external tanks, Jabara found one tank had hung-up which ordinarily meant he should abort. But Jabara was too close to bagging his 5th, so, warning his wingman, he went after three MIGs. As he closed in three more came down on the two Sabres, who turned into them; two broke away. Jabara got onto the tail of the third, fired, stayed with it, fired again and the

MIG pilot baled out. Jabara then climbed and attacked another MIG in a formation of six. This went down in flames but then a MIG attacked him and he was unable to shake it off. He was saved by two Sabres who came to his rescue and shot the MIG from his tail. Jabara returned for another Korean tour in January 1953 and raised his total score to 15 MIGs (he had scored 3½ victories in WW2) – making him the second highest scoring US jet ace.

Another 'ace', Captain Ralph Duane Gibson of Mt Carmel, Illinois, gave his account of combat action with the 4th Fighter Group and of fleeting opportunity seized in lightning fashion: '*O*N *June 18 1951, a bright summer day, I was flying my thirty-fifth Sabre mission to the Yalu. The mission was routine, flying cover for F-80s and F-84s on a fighter bomber sweep. I was leading an element on my squadron commander's right.*

'*We were forty miles out of the Yalu when contrails were sighted ahead, moving toward us. We counted at least thirty-six MIGs. We were eight in number. Dropping tanks, we made a 270-degree turn to the left. During the turn, I flew high cover for the flight, where I met a flight of the MIGs – one of them passing within ten feet of my aircraft. At 600 mph ten feet is a paper-thin margin!*

'*As we completed the turn, my CO was on a MIG's tail, and the MIG's wingman was maneuvering to get behind the CO. I called and said that my wingman and I would get the second MIG. We turned in to the attack.*

'*Leading the turn, my wingman fired two long bursts into the MIG. The enemy jet burst into flames before I could fire on him, and spun off burning to crash a few seconds later. When my wingman and I rolled out on a southerly heading, I saw a MIG drop into position behind my friend. I shouted to him to "break left!" as I came in on the MIG's tail, firing bursts as I came.*

'*On the first burst, the enemy reversed his turn, but I easily out-turned him, closed to about five hundred feet and opened up on him again. He made evasive turns, and I fired again, getting numerous hits around the wing root and cockpit. Flames streamed from his speed brakes and he crashed to the ground.*

'*Rolling out of this fight, my wingman and I ran into yet another MIG. He was higher and in front of us, coming in from our ten o'clock position. We made a hard turn into his attack and closed to five hundred feet. I fired one burst into his right wing root, and the whole right wing flew off his aircraft. He went in immediately.*'

Four F-80 'Shooting Stars' of the 8th Fighter Bomber Wing. Before the Sabres arrived, it was the F-80s of the 51st Fighter Interceptor Wing (FIW) that were charged with keeping air superiority over Korea. Flying an F-80, Lt Russell Brown shot down the first MIG-15 gaining history's first jet-versus-jet victory.

The air battles over North Korea remained constant for the next year despite the start of protracted peace talks. The Chinese had an estimated 450 MIG-15s and would often attack the Americans with forces of between 30 and 50 aircraft. Sometimes they threw over 100 MIGs into big battles against B29 bombers. Against this the 4th Fighter Group had only 50 Sabres, so, before the end of 1951, the 51st Fighter Group arrived to reinforce the American Sabre force. Even so the Sabre pilots were often outnumbered 4 to 1. The Chinese pilots sometimes flew some of their MIGs south of a fight in the Alley at high altitude in order to pounce on the American pilots as they returned towards Kimpo or Suwon with empty guns and drying fuel-tanks.

During 1951 the MIG pilots usually gained height and formed up north of the Yalu in Chinese airspace where the Americans were unable to reach them before crossing the river border. The Red pilots knew that above 35 000 ft their MIGs had better flight performance than the heavier Sabre. Colonel Francis Gabreski, Deputy Commanding Officer of the 4th Fighter Group, credited the MIG-15 with 'excellent performance'. By August the Communists had an estimated 525 MIGs, with which they began an all-out offensive on September 1, 1951.

At the start of that month the MIG pilots began to introduce new fighter tactics. Some made attacks in trail formations, others used the Lufbery Circle to keep at height before diving down at an opportune moment. There was also an occasion when 16 MIGs swept into an attack in four sections of four aircraft in line abreast in head-on passes, similar to Luftwaffe tactics against B17s.

'BANDIT TRAINS'
They flew in fours in groups of seven, eight or even more, sometimes stepped up, sometimes down. The Americans called them 'bandit trains', and often two such 'trains' would cross the Yalu perhaps 40 miles apart. If these MIG formations spotted Sabre patrols the MIG leader would send sections down to engage while the others would fly south to a point above Pyongyang where they would re-form before heading back north. On this homeward track they would again engage any Sabres they found. As they neared the Yalu, a third group of MIGs would fly over to cover their returning friends. Invariably, however, these big MIG formations, sometimes totalling as many as 200 MIG-15s, were too large and too unwieldy.

In the spring of 1952 the Sabre pilots noticed that the 'bandit trains' began to be replaced by large gatherings of MIGs but in individual sections of four, each giving mutual support. This was far more flexible and gave the MIG pilots a better tactical advantage. They also used another tactic: often at the heights that the MIGs and Sabres flew they left contrails which obviously both sides could see. Aware of this, the Chinese would detach small units well below contrail height. They could thus perhaps steal in unseen towards a Sabre patrol while the American pilots were watching the higher trails. When the Sabre pilots realized this, they too kept low sections to counter the tactic.

Following tactic and counter-tactic, the MIGs began to put aircraft well above contrail height while two-man sections were sent below the main group which were making the trails. These small sections also maintained mutual support positions and for a while the Sabres were in trouble. They in turn began to put two-man elements into the same lower levels, where in fact their performance gave them the advantage over the MIGs.

The MIGs usually just stayed at height and used the old, well-tried tactic of dive-and-zoom. If they were pounced upon, the MIG pilots tried a sort of, 'defensive split' tactic where one would pull round in a tight turn while the other would use its superior climbing skill to pull up and over, ready to dive down on the two Sabres that had most probably pulled round after the lower MIG. The Americans began calling this the 'yo-yo' tactic and later copied it; it became the forerunner of modern jet-fighter tactics – the 'high-speed yo-yo' and the 'low-speed yo-yo'.

EVENING UP THE ODDS

Meanwhile, the MIG pilots in Korea retained many tactical advantages with aircraft of better performance, good radar and ground control and having a large section of sky (north of the Yalu) in which to deploy or to escape to, and where the Sabres could not follow. To combat this the Americans really had only two counters – good teamwork and a high state of morale. Great stress was laid on the two-plane element – leader and wingman. This pairing was always based on experience and skill rather than rank. A new pilot to Korea, irrespective of rank or position, would fly as wingman for at least his first dozen combat missions. At first Sabres flew in squadron strength but later this was reduced to eight – two sections of four. Later still, just four-plane sections went out at intervals unless there were specific escort missions. This interval tactic guaranteed a large number of Sabres in the combat zone, and they would not all begin to run short of fuel at the same time. Once in the combat zone, the Sabre pilots kept up a high speed – usually around Mach 0.9 – which made them less vulnerable to the MIGs' high attack. High speed was always maintained, especially in combat. If this tended to lose them height, the Sabre pilots had no need to worry, for it brought the MIGs down to an altitude where their performance was then below that of the Sabre. If attacked from above or behind, the Sabre pilot usually pulled over into a hard diving turn. The MIG pilot found it difficult to pull round hard enough to gain the necessary deflection.

Even when the MIGs managed to beat the Sabre patrols and get in amongst the UN fighter-bombers it was not easy. The Mustangs and Corsairs were so much slower, as were the F-80s in comparison to the MIG-15s, that they could simply turn away from an attack, cut throttles and the MIGs would go sailing past seeing just empty sky. If they were quick enough, the slower UN aircraft could turn inside the MIG and, if they got in a quick burst – as a number did – they could even damage or destroy a MIG. For instance, Captain Jesse Folmar, flying a Corsair on September 10, 1952, was part of a mission over North Korea which was attacked by two pairs of MIGs. Pulling into a sharp turn the MIGs overshot and Folmar turned inside them and fired a 5-second burst of 20-mm cannon into one. The MIG began smoking and its pilot jumped, only to have his parachute catch fire.

In the fall of 1951 the first F-86E models began to arrive in Korea, going to the 51st Group. These had an all-hydraulic flight-control system and a modified tail that simplified turns at high speed.

The Russian-built MIG-15. The Sabre's main opponent over Korea, it was flown by North Koreans, supported by Chinese and Russian pilots.

NORTH AMERICAN F-86E SABRE versus MIKOYAN/GUREVICH MIG-15

FIRST FLOWN IN 1947, THE F-86 was the first Western fighter with sweptback wings and tail to reach higher speeds. It also had hydraulically boosted controls, and altogether it soon became an outstanding combat aircraft, very reliable despite its complexity and limited only by its small guns. The MIG-15 was made possible by Britain's extraordinary decision to ship its newest turbojet to Moscow in March 1947. Much lighter and simpler than the F-86, the sweptwing MIG climbed much faster and higher and had devastating guns. In the Korean war, however, the advantage lay with the USAF fighter, largely because of the much greater skill and experience of US pilots.

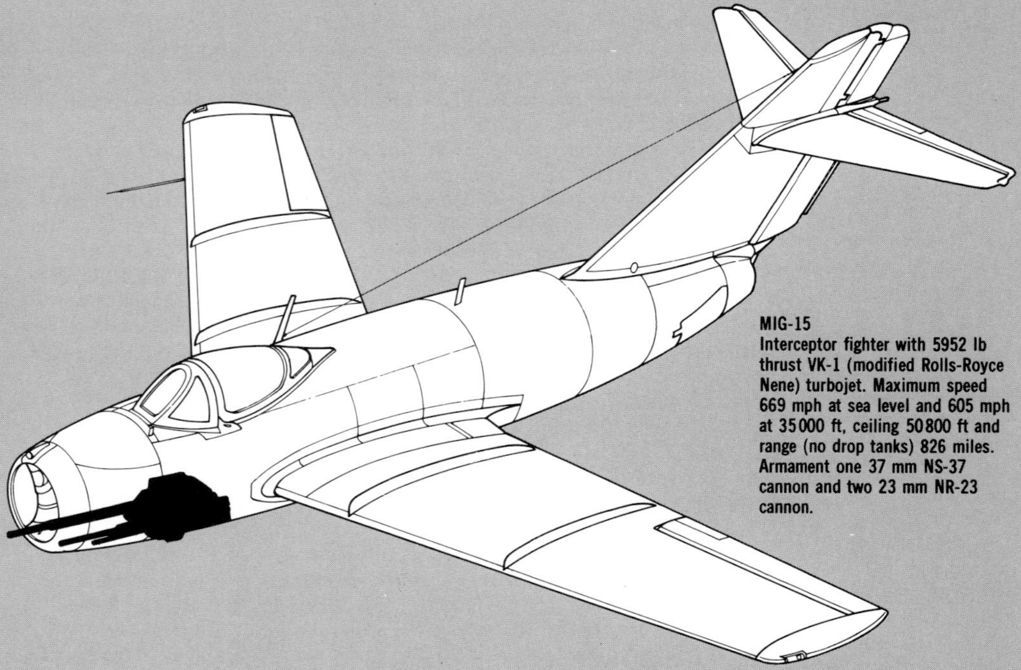

MIG-15
Interceptor fighter with 5952 lb thrust VK-1 (modified Rolls-Royce Nene) turbojet. Maximum speed 669 mph at sea level and 605 mph at 35000 ft, ceiling 50800 ft and range (no drop tanks) 826 miles. Armament one 37 mm NS-37 cannon and two 23 mm NR-23 cannon.

F-86E SABRE
Fighter-bomber with 5200 lb thrust General Electric J47-13 turbojet; maximum speed 679 mph at sea level, about 600 mph at 35000 ft; ceiling 47000 ft and range (no drop tanks) 650 miles. Armament six 0.5 in Browning heavy machine-guns, and two 1000 lb bombs or 16 rockets.

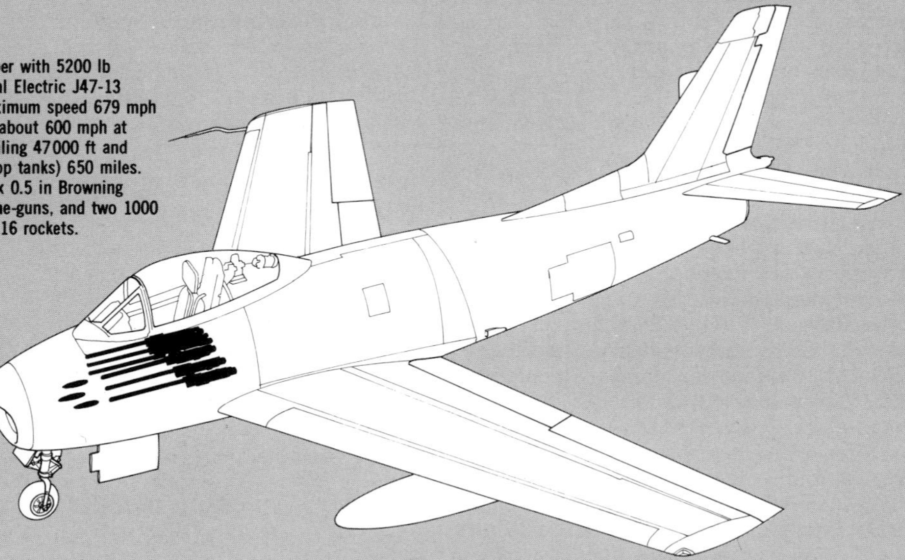

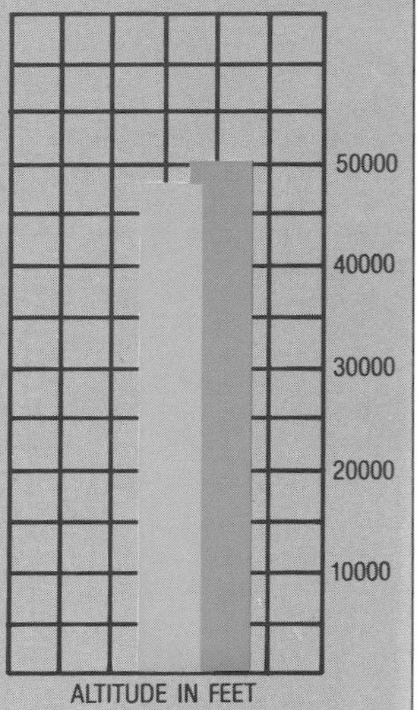

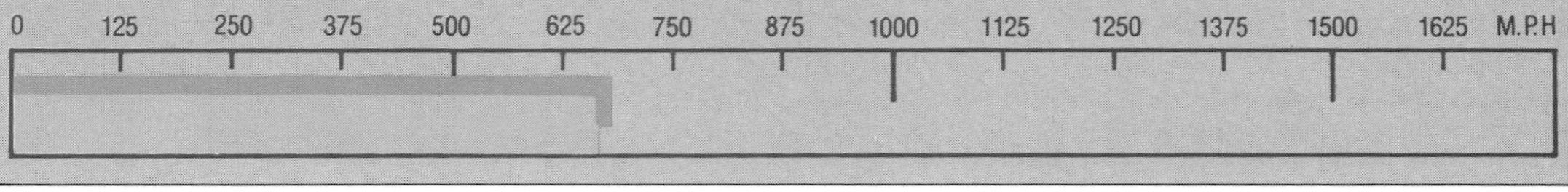

ALTITUDE IN FEET

50000
40000
30000
20000
10000

0   125   250   375   500   625   750   875   1000   1125   1250   1375   1500   1625   M.P.H

They started to arrive as the Communists were operating at 'high tide' over North Korea – seriously challenging the United Nations' air superiority. In October, for instance, UN pilots counted 2573 airborne MIGs of which 2166 engaged in combats. Although 32 MIGs were claimed shot down, 24 by Sabres, US losses were seven Sabres, five B29s, two F-84s and one RF-80. In addition MIGs were now operating at airfields below the Yalu, in North Korea itself.

The North Koreans also used a number of other aircraft types, including TU-2 bombers and La-9 fighters. In November and December 1951 a number of these propeller-driven aircraft were encountered. The 4th Group flew a mission on November 30 and nearing MIG Alley the Sabre pilots could see some familiar contrails high over the Yalu, while others could be seen very high up on the Korean side. With such activity the Sabre pilots began checking all over the sky for other suspected activity. They spotted a formation of aircraft flying out of Manchuria heading south along the Korean coast. On closer inspection they were identified as 12 TU-2s and 16 La-9s.

Colonel S B Preston led the attack, pulling round behind them in a vertical bank at terrific speed. Lieutenant Douglas K Evans picked out a bomber in the rear box making a quarter head-on pass. His fire raked the bomber and as he went past its wing and tail, Evans looked back to see flame erupt from its right engine. As Evans pulled round for another pass he saw the bomber's wing burst into flames before falling away to splash into the waters of the Yellow Sea. Evans, then dived at a La-9, but as he fired the fighter broke to the left and turned back as Evans and his wingman roared past it, the La-9 pilot even managing a quick burst at the second Sabre. After the battle the Sabre pilots claimed eight TU-2s, and three La-9s plus a MIG. It transpired that these aircraft were flying down to a new base at Taehwa-do. It was not a good day for the Red air force. Major George Davis got three of the TU-2s and the MIG, making him the 5th US ace in Korea. On December 13, in a battle with 145 MIGs, 13 MIGs were shot down, Davis getting four to make him the first double 'ace' with 10 victories.

After this the MIGs were reluctant to engage the Sabres, preferring to stay up at about 48 000 ft and cruise to and fro. Only occasionally would a section dive down in an attempt to surprise a Sabre element. It was a frustrating time for the Sabre pilots – even in the 'E' models they could not reach the MIGs. But in January 1952 some Sabres climbed to 45 000 ft and surprised a number of MIGs, claiming 25 shot down in that month.

The Communists also had an improved model of the MIG – the MIG-15 BIS – with a more powerful engine. As 1952 began, MIGs could be seen at height as far south as Seoul.

Colonel Richard Turner, last met in Chapter 9 as a Mustang pilot, flew 13 Sabre missions in Korea with the 4th Fighter Group, before a recurring WW2 back injury put him out of operational flying. He recalled: '*T*HE F86 responded to the slightest touch and it could hold its own with anything from the deck up to 25 000 feet. As I flew missions with the 4th, it was easy to divine their basic tactics. They flew up to the Yalu area at 45 000 feet, about 5000 feet below the lighter MIGs. (That was about as high as the F86 could fly in formation with enough positive control to make it safe.) There they cruised around until they could entice the MIGs to make an attack, bringing them to the lower altitudes. The length of my temporary duty only allowed me to get in 13 missions, and the lack of experience obliged me to fly wing on all but two missions.

'On February 5, 1952, I flew my first flight lead on a morning mission to the Yalu area. We took off in pairs, pulling back to 94% climb-out power, and turned right to climb-out heading. A few minutes later we reached 45 000 feet in group formation, and headed for the Yalu where the squadrons took up separate patrol area patterns. A few minutes later we heard one of the other squadrons get bounced, and we dropped tanks and started searching for MIGs. About this time I saw an F86 streak downward 500 yards ahead of me with a MIG hard after him. I dove to intercept the MIG with my 0.50-calibers firing way in front to distract him from the F86. As I began to line-up behind the MIG, he broke off of his attack to the left. Starting to follow him, I heard my wingman calling for a break right, which I quickly executed. The MIG's wingman had been following him far enough behind so that I hadn't seen him, and was now queuing up on me. As I broke, the second MIG overshot me and plunged straight on down, depriving my wingman of a shot at him. The flight had stayed with me through all this, and we continued to search for more MIGs. Oddly enough, we were unable to find a trace of any aircraft at all, friend or foe. The high jet speeds had scattered some 80 aircraft over a 300- to 400-mile radius. The only evidence of a fight was an open parachute at about 25 000 feet which was slowly descending through the crisp cold air.'

In mid-1952 the 'F' model F-86 began to arrive, its performance closing the gap between the MIG

The end of a MIG-15. Frame from an F-86's camera gun film showing the final moments of one of the 827 MIGs to be shot down over Korea.

'As we dove, four MIGs chandelled to the left, and three pulled up to the right. In short order, we were nicely boxed in. The four from the left came whipping in just as the flaming MIG pilot ejected. We broke hard into them. This set us up for the three MIGs on the right, who then came in firing.

'We continued our turn to the left, managing to keep this turn tight enough for the MIGs to fire and never hit us. The original four, however, now repositioned themselves and took up a firing position right where their three pals left off. Our turn carried us right to the deck. By this time, the MIGs were firing at us from head-on ninety degree angle-off, and from our six o'clock position.

'Just as our fuel reached the point of no return, the seven MIGs all broke off and pulled up into the overcast. With a new lease on life, we headed for our home base, 160 miles to the south. Minutes later we arrived, limp and exhausted, but with a story that would hold up any bar in the Air Force.'

Major Robert Love, Canadian-born, tells his story, just as grippingly but in language and jargon common to the pilots: '*T*HIS WAS ONE of those "max effort" days when we managed six aircraft up out of the squadron on a cover mission. These birds, F-86A and F-86E, were tired "A" models up through the middle of the "E" series. Our flight of four was to cover west to east, south of the "creek" from the Yellow Sea and meet my two-ship element working east to west from the Mizu area.

'I was flying a tired "A" with another on my wing, flown by a pilot who always aborted opposite Cho-do Island on the way in, and today was no exception. Lieutenant Ted Campbell was spare, and filled in on my wing with an "E" when my first boy dropped out. We held radio silence, driving to Mizu and turning west at 27 000 feet, just south of the creek. We were under an overcast, in haze, with about two miles' visibility.

'I punched off the tanks and watched Ted clean up. I checked Ted's area to the south and east (left wing) and then checked my own five o'clock position just in time to find seven MIGs breaking hard on us from the north and level. Had we been five seconds later, they would have passed in front of us ninety degrees off, north to south.

'Their drops (tanks) were already fluttering down, so I called a hard right break into them, and once I saw the lead MIG driver, an instructor type, was washing through badly in his turn, I called a hard reverse back into him. We met about ten degrees off. I am sure Ted didn't hear the

and the Sabre. It had a more powerful engine, resulting in higher top speeds and better altitude performance. The Sabres could now reach the MIGs. About this time, while the majority of MIGs still refused combat, some skilled and aggressive MIG pilots were encountered. These the American pilots called 'Honchos', and it was firmly held that these were not Koreans or Chinese, but Russians. It is now known that a Russian wing of 70 MIG pilots, led by Colonel Ivan Kojedub (who scored 62 kills in WW2), operated on the North Korean side.

JET PILOTS REMEMBER
Captain Leonard William Lilley of Washington DC, tells a gripping story of what jet combat was like over Korea: '*O*N 4 SEPTEMBER 1952 I was flying close support on fighter bombers, who were bombing the main supply route leading south from Sinuiju, North Korea. First Lieutenant Drury Callahan was my wingman. While heading north at 18 000 feet, just under an overcast, we passed eight MIGs in a staggered-V formation, heading south.

'We immediately swung south and fell in trail with this formation. The MIGs started to turn right, and this enabled us to close in to effective firing range. Still unobserved, we closed to within 1500 feet of the lead MIG. I opened fire, and the MIG burst into flames and started to dive straight ahead. We pursued, firing all the while.

reverse call, as his reverse was delayed just long enough for the MIG to latch on behind him.

'At this time, I noted the MIG instructor type's students were still in their turn to west, and rather wide in 'flock' formation. I reversed the third time and followed the MIG on Ted, turning my six o'clock to the students. I spent the next four minutes and several thousand feet of altitude trying to catch that full-power "E" Sabre and the MIG in some real rough crossed-needle 360-degree turns. At times, I felt Ted would have to shake the MIG without my help, as when I managed to trim on the inside, Ted would reverse and leave me again on the outside, running out of breath and strength.

'I fired short bursts of tracer, trying to scare the MIG off, but the range was letting the tracers burn out. Each few seconds we would meet The Students, in string, head-on, around these five-and six-G turns. We'd worked down to around 15 000 feet when Ted could no longer read me due to plugged ears, and pulled up to the west in a climbing turn. Ted at this time was convinced he'd lost the MIG, but broke down and to the east when he heard my call.

'During the entire rat race the MIG fired at Ted, but failed to score a single hit. Once I could fly the tired "A" under the first line, I caught the

MIG in close range with two bursts after his climbing turn. The canopy and engine doors left the MIG and the driver continued a slow turn from south to east.

'In his hard, fast break to the east, Ted received only part of my call to "reverse and pick us up at three o'clock." He reversed and disappeared under me to the south – toward "Long Dong." The MIG reversed in these few seconds, and with no canopy, engine doors gone, dumping fuel and belching smoke, he stuck the nose down and headed east. He fired the rest of his ammo, and simply pulled hard over the top.

'Following him, I was once again on the first line (no elevator deflection) and lost him as he pulled up into the sun. I managed to trim around somewhat of a pullup. I climbed into the sun until reading 170 knots, and being once again in the middle of The Students, I went out the bottom, joined with Ted farther south and back to home plate.

'I never saw the lame MIG after his break upward. A photo Joe with an 86-escort flight from 334th Fighter Interceptor Squadron witnessed the scrap and confirmed the MIG as splashed. I felt this MIG driver was one of the better types, and Mach-wise, his MIG could give an "A" model Sabrejet trouble. This was one of those scraps at low altitude and working downhill, where a few muscles, a G-suit and those hours of rat-racing with your buddies pays off.'

And again, of another encounter with MIGs:

'ONCE AIRBORNE AND ON COMBAT frequency we picked up the first flights calling MIGs out and shooting in general. Being off late, and to catch the MIGs before they turned north again, we maintained a flat, fast climb up the west coast, turning right (east) and paralleling The Creek on the south side. It sounded a little quiet over the horn, and it appeared the MIGs were about to leave the scraps east of us and go home.

'We dropped tanks. At about 30 000 feet we met the first two "early returns" almost head-on. These boys were going slightly more down and in a westerly direction. We broke left on to their tails, when we were bounced by two more from about three o'clock high. These latter two fired and broke up hard from west to south. Continuing on up, our element three and four latched on to these second two MIGs and chased them all the way up to where only a MIG would operate. Both these MIGs were damaged.

'"Jumpin' Bob" (Second Lieutenant Bob Straub) and I continued on a NNW heading after

THE HIGH SPEED YO-YO

With high-speed jet combat, it is very easy to overshoot a hard-turning opponent. Instead of turning, therefore, the attacking pilot pulls up, rolls and makes a diving turn to make a pass. Such a move takes precision to fly properly. If made too early, the opponent has a chance to dive and get away. If made too late, the opponent can pull up and catch the attacking aircraft in a scissors maneuver.

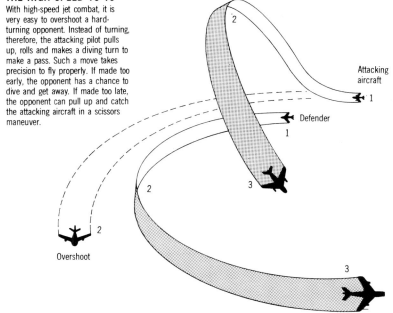

Attacking aircraft

1

Defender

1

2

3

2

Overshoot

2

3

'MIG ALLEY', NORTH KOREA OCTOBER 26, 1951
SABRE VERSUS MIG-15

12 F-86A SABRES,
336TH FIGHTER SQUADRON,
4TH FIGHTER GROUP
US FAR EAST AIR FORCE

1

Below: By the second half of 1951 the Chinese MIGs were operating in large numbers. Their favorite tactic was to cross the border in force and at high altitude where they comfortably outperformed the Sabres: as on October 26, small groups at low level were invariably accompanied by bigger formations higher up.

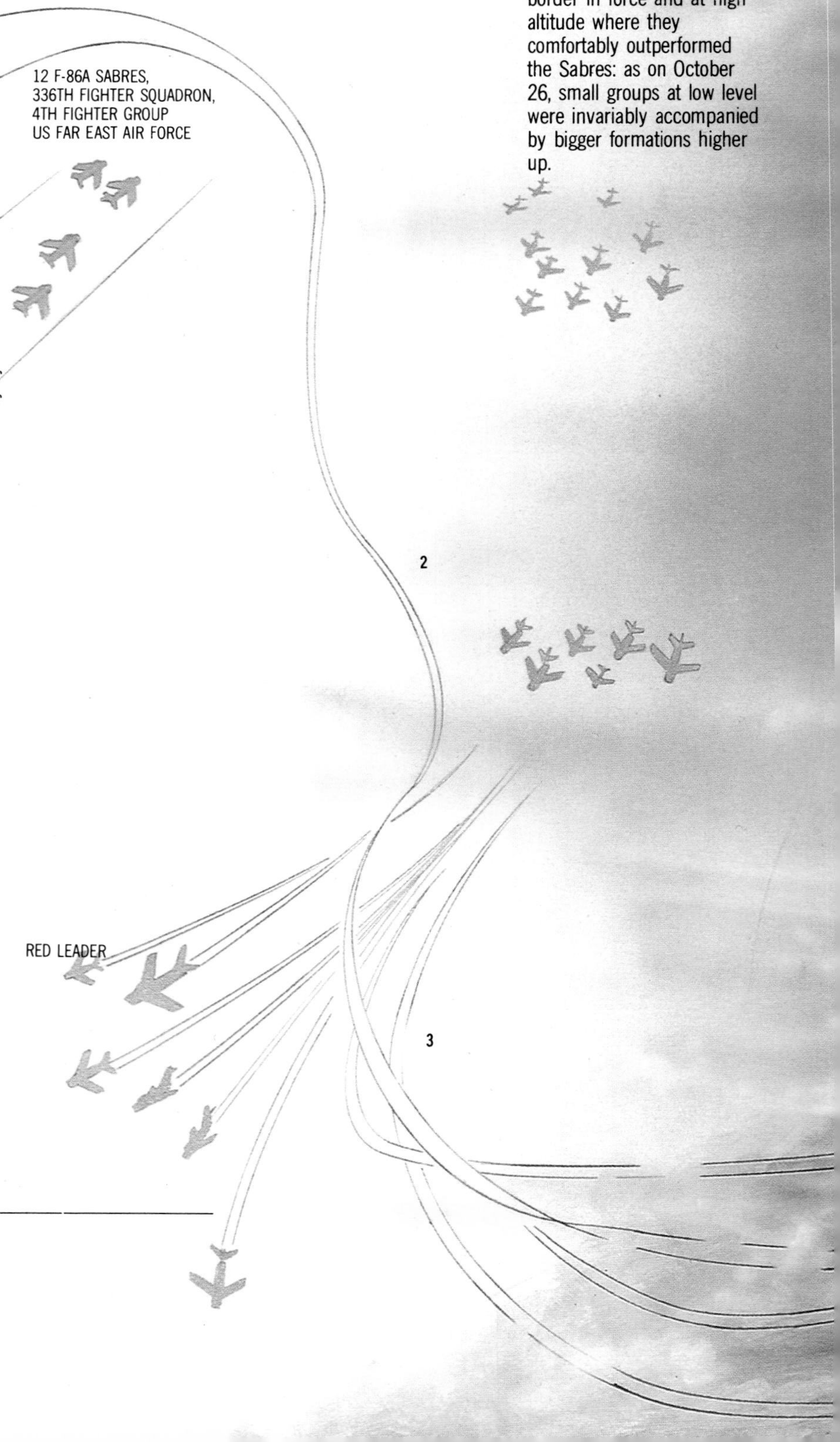

2

3

RED LEADER

When F-86A Sabres of the US Far East Air Force and Chinese MIG-15s first met over North Korea on 15 December 1950 it was less than six weeks since an F-80C Shooting Star had shot down a MIG-15 to claim the first recorded victory in jet on jet fighter combat. On their first sortie, four Sabres of the 336th Fighter Squadron encountered four of the Chinese fighters, shooting down one, and in early engagements the Sabres continued to hold their own, but largely because of the inexperience of the Chinese pilots.

By mid-1951 the Sabres in 'MIG Alley' over the Yalu River, which formed the border with China, were encountering more formidable opposition. The MIGs had taken to crossing the border in large numbers and at the high altitudes where they had a distinct performance advantage, before detaching flights to make fast passes at the fighter bombers operating in support of ground troops, or at the Sabres sent to intercept them, and then diving back across the border.

In the face of superior numbers, the Sabre pilots' survival depended on perfect teamwork between leader and wingman, and their kills on the aggressive pursuit of adversaries, whatever the cloud conditions.

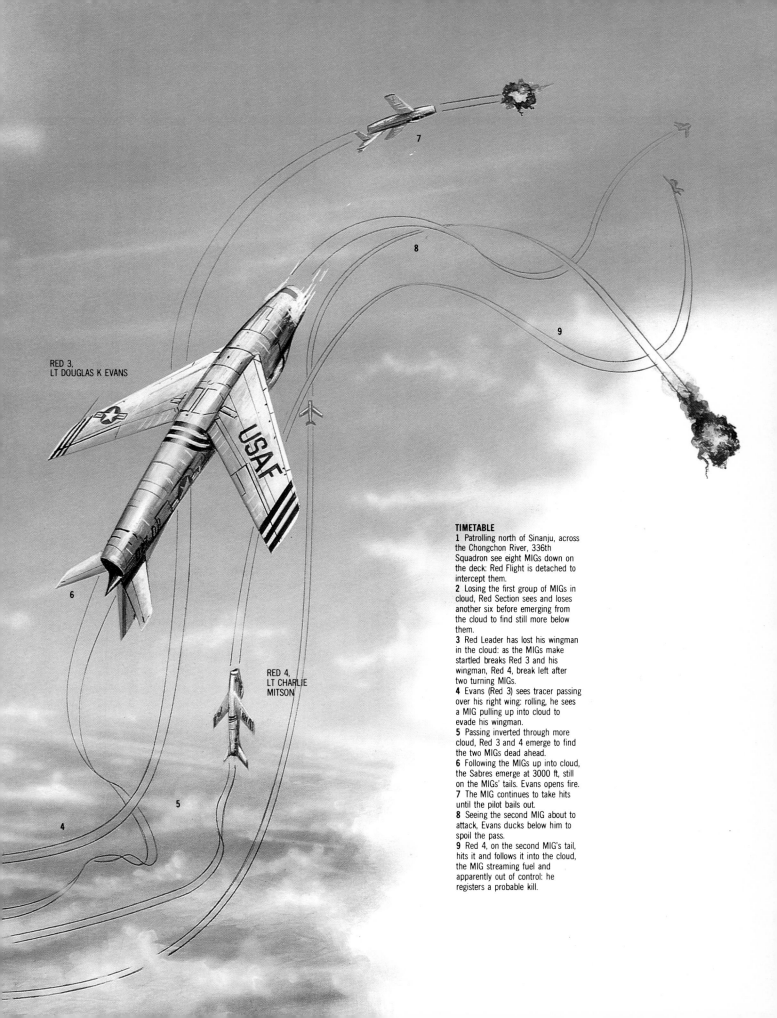

RED 3,
LT DOUGLAS K EVANS

RED 4,
LT CHARLIE
MITSON

TIMETABLE

1 Patrolling north of Sinanju, across the Chongchon River, 336th Squadron see eight MIGs down on the deck: Red Flight is detached to intercept them.

2 Losing the first group of MIGs in cloud, Red Section sees and loses another six before emerging from the cloud to find still more below them.

3 Red Leader has lost his wingman in the cloud: as the MIGs make startled breaks Red 3 and his wingman, Red 4, break left after two turning MIGs.

4 Evans (Red 3) sees tracer passing over his right wing: rolling, he sees a MIG pulling up into cloud to evade his wingman.

5 Passing inverted through more cloud, Red 3 and 4 emerge to find the two MIGs dead ahead.

6 Following the MIGs up into cloud, the Sabres emerge at 3000 ft, still on the MIGs' tails. Evans opens fire.

7 The MIG continues to take hits until the pilot bails out.

8 Seeing the second MIG about to attack, Evans ducks below him to spoil the pass.

9 Red 4, on the second MIG's tail, hits it and follows it into the cloud, the MIG streaming fuel and apparently out of control: he registers a probable kill.

Right: The F-86 Sabre (FU-266) flown by Lt Douglas K Evans in September 1951 – a Mark 86A of 4th Fighter Interceptor Wing.
Below right: First Lieutenant Douglas Evans with his Crew Chief, Sgt H L 'Frenchy' Richard after Evans had notched up his first kill, October 1951.

the first element of MIGs. We couldn't close enough to fire until the MIGs started a slow turn to the south. I threw in two short bursts and the wingman bailed, almost hitting Jumpin' Bob's bird. The element leader had broken hard up and to the north as we continued to turn south. Incidentally, the MIG wingman's hot seat functioned perfectly, as he separated from the seat on slipstream contact and his chute blossomed at once.

'"Junior Bob" (Lieutenant Bob Campbell) of our element three and four had moved to the inside of our turn south and called, "Break left and cover me, I've got one cold." We broke hard left, and three MIGs in an uneven string had passed under us to the east, ninety degrees off. As we completed the hard turn, I was able to tell Campbell he was covered and detect which of the string he intended to chop up.

'Campbell made a four o'clock pass on the number two MIG, cutting the enemy bird in half. Number three MIG slid on to Campbell's tail. I shook this MIG with a short burst and called a hard up and right break to Campbell. The number three MIG I'd hit finished in true Hollywood

fashion, looping east to west at 8000 feet. I flew slot man on this boy, hitting well through the first half of the loop, firing out inverted. Dumping fuel, parts and debris, and smoking badly, the MIG continued on through the first half of a Cuban eight, but neglected to pull out.

'During this acro show, Jumpin' Bob was in element, and as I completed firing he yelled, "Break left!" I had just rolled right side up. One MIG came in from four o'clock and almost rammed the element. Bob didn't waste time calling this left break again, as he had a flight of four MIGs firing from seven o'clock at him. He could hear the cannons in the pit.

'We continued our hard left break to the south, and were clear of MIGs in twenty seconds. Their top cover almost worked – almost got us. Low over the water we checked our birds for hits. There were none. Our damage was one jammed gun on each side of my aircraft due to G's and heat. We had knocked off three MIGs in less than two minutes.'

On this mission, as all three pilots with Bob Love were also named Bob they had to work out a radio call sign appropriate to each pilot. Bob Love became 'Old Bob.' His wingman Bob Straub, who was credited with two MIGs destroyed in Korea, was 'Jumpin' Bob,' while the number three, Lieutenant Bob Ferber became 'Ferb.' The number four pilot, Lieutenant Bob Campbell was called plain 'Bob' or 'Junior Bob'. Such names were used because with ears plugged and pulling 5-Gs call-signs like 'Able, Yellow and Purple' all sounded the same. A name like Jumpin' Bob could be understood under all but the worst conditions.'

Towards the end of 1952 the MIG pilots returned to flying similar tactics as used the previous year: large groups staying high and going fast. The Americans countered by using larger flight sizes – the 51st Group used six-plane elements, the 4th eight. They also began staggering their height in order to be ready to engage MIGs they found at any altitude, operating F-86Es at between 30–35 000 ft and the F-86Fs at 42–45 000 ft.

The MIGs tried to adopt similar tactics in November and December 1952, seeking to avoid all contact with the Sabres while endeavoring to engage only fighter-bombers if they could do so with a fair degree of safety. Also in December the MIG pilots seemed to be testing out a team tactic, having seen for a long time the Americans using teamwork with success. They certainly used wingmen to cover a leader, and that had not been really evident before. MIGs also tried again to use the tactic of attacking Sabres who had had to break off a patrol and head for home, low on fuel, by trying to 'box-in' the retiring aircraft. Luckily for the American pilots, radar warning saved them from many of these traps. However, this ploy caused several Sabre machines to run out of fuel and their pilots had to eject before they could reach Kimpo.

At the beginning of 1953 there was apparently a newer type of MIG pilot about – for their aircraft were painted differently, being tan above and sky-blue below instead of silver and red. These were far more aggressive and keen to initiate combat. However, in February MIG pilots increasingly made the mistake of coming down to lower altitudes and flying too far into UN territory. A number were shot down. They did this again in March while trying to cover the battle front – they lost 34 MIGs and shot down only two Sabres.

In the spring of 1953 the Americans began at last to try to install four 20-mm cannon in their Sabres. Despite the high kill-ratio of the Sabres, it was acknowledged that more MIGs would have been destroyed if the Sabres had a harder-hitting weapon than their 0.50s. At first the 20-mm-armed Sabres could carry enough ammunition for only a four-second burst. To extend the firing time the pilot was able to switch off two guns and fire only two at a time – a total of eight seconds.

US SUPERIORITY TELLS

As 1953 progressed there were now four Sabre wings operating in Korea (two fighter and two fighter-bomber) and, with the weather improving, the MIGs had to contend with larger numbers of hard-hitting, faster and high-flying Sabres. The MIG pilots became less and less eager to engage in air fights. When fights did take place in the final weeks of the war it seemed to the Americans that the 'Honchos' had gone. In June 1953 F-86 pilots shot down 77 MIGs, without loss.

The Korean war ended on July 27, 1953. The Reds had lost 954 aircraft, 827 being MIG-15s, of which Sabre pilots claimed 792. In air combat the Americans lost 78 Sabres, 14 Shooting Stars, 18 Thunderjets, 10 Mustangs, and 17 B29s, with many more so badly damaged that they never flew again. The big B29 bombers, that had been giants to Japanese pilots in WW2, were simply too slow to combat the MIGs and their computer gunsights just could not keep up with the rapid closure rates of the Russian aircraft. Despite superior numbers and better aircraft, the Russian and Chinese pilots had been outflown and outfought by the UN forces – not only Americans but also British, Australian and South Africans, in army, air force and navy planes.

Top-scoring Sabre pilot was Captain Joseph M McConnell Jr with 16 MIG victories, Major Jabara second with 15. Six others scored between 10–14, 31 others became 'aces', a number being WW2 veterans. This included Colonel Francis Gabreski, who got 6½ MIGs, Major Bill Whisner with 5½ and Lieutenant Colonel Vermont Garrison who scored 10 to add to his tally of 11 in WW2. It was a feature of this air war that many of the jet 'aces', and even those who scored fewer than five victories, were of the older generation. Being a successful jet pilot needed a wealth of experience. It was no longer a young man's game.

After Korea, Major Douglas K Evans discussed the lessons of the air war in his *Introduction to Advanced Fighter Tactics*. Among the guidelines he laid down were the following:

1. *Contrary to some opinions, the 'dogfight' is not obsolete. Speed, performance and weapons systems have changed considerably over the years but the ultimate objective remains the same – get the other man. How can the 'dogfight' be with us in our present day equipment? Let's define 'dogfight': it is the maneuvering solution to a positioning problem, the last stage of which is the tracking solution to the firing or kill zone. When two aircraft of relatively similar performance meet, pilot ability will probably be the deciding factor. If you think the maneuvering battle of 'dogfight' is unnecessary, wait until you find a hungry tiger at your six o'clock position about to ventilate you with 20 mikes or blast you with a missile. You'll either do some outstanding gyrations or be a piece of cake. Also, bear in mind that just sneaking into*

JOSEPH McCONNELL JR

JOE McCONNELL HAD FLOWN AS a navigator in B24 bombers in WW2, with the 8th Air Force, but managed to get himself assigned to pilot training at the end of the war. In so doing he was one of the first US pilots to be trained right through to the new P-80 Shooting Star jet. By this time the Korean War had started, but his first unit posting was to a squadron in Alaska. He applied for a posting to Korea but it was not until late 1952 that he was sent to the 51st Fighter Interceptor Wing, joining the 16th Squadron as a flight leader.

Learning his trade, he shot down his first MIG-15 on January 14, 1953, and his fifth on February 16, to become the 27th ace of the Korean War. On April 12, he destroyed his eighth MIG but was then himself shot down, ejecting from his stricken Sabre, and coming down into the Yellow Sea off the west coast of North Korea. He was rescued almost immediately by a helicopter of the 3rd Air Rescue Wing, none the worse for his dunking.

During the next month, McConnell added five more MIG victories to his score, and on May 18, he shot down no fewer than three MIGs – his best day – to raise his score to a record 16 kills, making him the top ace of the Korean War. Posted back to the United States on completion of his combat tour, he took a post as a service test pilot. On August 25, 1954, while testing an F-86H Sabre, he was killed in a crash at Edwards Air Force Base.

FRANCIS GABRESKI

A FLIGHT COMMANDER WITH the 56th Fighter Group, 'Gabby' Gabreski scored his first victory on August 24, 1943, flying the P47 Thunderbolt. He became an ace on November 26 by downing two Me110s and by the end of the year had raised his score to 8.

In 1944 he was given command of the 61st Fighter Squadron and scoring steadily, downed his 19th German aircraft on May 8 (the same day as Bob Johnson scored his 28th and last victory). On May 22 Gabby had his best day, shooting down three Focke-Wulf 190s, and to these he added five in June, his 28th kill coming on July 5, to equal Johnson's score.

He added one more victory to his name, but this was destroyed on the ground. As the 8th Air Force included ground kills in a pilot's score, this made a total of 31 for Gabreski, but only 28 air-to-air kills. On July 20, he was ground-strafing an airfield near Coblenz, Germany, and flew so low that his propeller hit a slight hump, forcing him to crash-land. His capture was quite a coup for the Germans. As fate would have it, his July 20 mission would have been his last in any event, for after it he was due to be rested.

Gabreski refused to use tracer in his guns lest the tracer shells give warning to his opponent. He also flew with half-empty guns since he believed that, with a full load, his aircraft's wings were too heavy to turn inside a 109. Like all successful fighter pilots, he believed in getting in close.

He left the USAAF in 1946 but returned to fly with the 4th Fighter Interceptor Wing in Korea. He quickly showed he had lost none of his fighting technique, downing 6½ MIG-15s between July 1951 and April 1952.

a man's six doesn't ensure a kill unless you can match his gyrations and keep him boresighted. It's very embarrasing to jump into the six o'clock position and after a flurry to find yourself at twelve o'clock. These maneuvering and positioning matters sound like old fashioned man-to-man stuff but with training and confidence they apply to the basic two-plane unit or element which means teamwork. It is in this field of maneuvering, head-work and mutual support of team mates that this brief is concerned.

2. In general, the day-fighter mission is supremacy in the air to allow operation of our ground forces and attack aviation with minimum or no enemy air opposition. This mission will be enhanced by the aid and direction of GCI. The ideal formation to initiate the typical 'fighter sweep' (termed counter air mission in Korea) is two elements working as a team in flight formation. When receiving or initiating a bounce, the flight should engage as a unit and remain so as long it is advantageous for concentrating attacking effort or mutual support. A split to separate elements may be ordered by the fighter direction (GCI) but a flight is the ideal patrol formation when expecting hot opposition. Each element is responsible for covering the other element. The wingman should be able to give his sector the necessary scrutiny at all times. It should never require his full attention to maintain his proper position. Figure it out while you are maneuvering. Can you maintain position? Are you covering yourself or could someone sneak up on your tail? The leader should call any large changes in power setting and the wingman should fly well up on his leader using maneuver to maintain position, not the go-handle. Remember, the leader may be the full bore. The wingman should fly far enough forward (35 degrees out from leader) and out to the side (500 ft) so that when either pilot is looking at the other his side vision will cover a close-in firing range·(1000–15 000 ft) behind the other's tail. Keep striving for this position on wing lookout. Coverage must be maintained not just in level flight but steep climbs and even vertical dives, etc.

3. Whenever you have engaged the enemy and it is not a hit-and-run affair, but a determined fight, the various flights will probably break down to element-versus-element combat. Anytime that an element is split or reduced to single aircraft, these singles must extricate to a rendezvous point for re-engagement or with-

drawal. Single aircraft are cold meat for an alert enemy element and any single plane making an attack is wide open at six o'clock while his eyeballs are glued on a gun sight. Many a single tiger, while licking his chops behind a flamer, has discovered (fatally) that the smoke attracted unfriendly snoopers that turned him into a victory. Of course, if you are defending friendly installations, anything goes. You want to save your own landing strip and at worst, if shot-up you can jump out and get a new bird.

4. At all times that the flight is together, the flight leader is the tactical commander and the other three aircraft will deploy at his direction and discretion, not on individual whims. Likewise for leadership of a separate or independent element. In an attack, the flight leader initiates and the element leader positions himself to support. The wingmen, number 2 and 4, accompany their respective leaders with the duty of lookout and cover. Observations within the flight should be called out as follows: 'Red 1, this is Red 2 (or 3 or 4), Bogies (type bandits if definitely enemy) ten o'clock low, closing.' The leader must acknowledge and take action. If at first observation the enemy is in the six o'clock zone in firing range and firing, the pilot sighting will call: 'Red flight, break (right or left – to advantage)'. A break does not require acknowledgment but it does imply maximum effort, max rate of turn. Be reasonable in voice transmissions, clear and precise – a shriek can cause more shakes and confusion than the enemy.

5. The leader is primarily concerned with the frontal zone, scanning for targets of opportunity. The wingman is the security 'eyes' of his element. As the leader will be the most experienced, the destruction of the enemy aircraft and the conduct of the mission is his responsibility – the responsibility of the wingman is to ensure the success of his leader, to warn him of a counterattack and to lend his firepower when requested. Every fighter pilot begins this business as a wingman and learns the way to leadership. The responsibility of the wingman cannot be overestimated. Be prepared for violent maneuvers – don't wait for them – be with them. The leader must be aware of his wingman's position and if necessary make sharp turns to enable his team to close up an extended interval, but cutting off the turns. If you are losing ground, tell your leader. A good speed rule in the combat patrol area is to keep the equivalent of a good climb mach for your altitude.

AMERICAN SABRE ACES OF KOREAN WAR

Name	Total	WW2 Score
Capt Joseph McConnell Jr	16	–
Lt Col James Jabara	15	3½
Capt Manuel J Fernandez	14½	–
Lt Col George A Davis Jr	14	7
Col Royal N Baker	13	3½
Maj Frederick C Blesse	10	–
Capt Harold E Fischer	10	–
Col James K Johnson	10	1
Lt Col Vermont Garrison	10	11
Maj Lonnie R Moore	10	–
Capt Ralph S Parr Jr	10	–
Lt James F Low	9	–
Lt Cecil G Foster	9	–
Lt Col James P Hagerstrom	8½	6
Maj Robinson Risner	8	–
Col George I Ruddell	8	–
Capt Clifford D Jolley	7	–
Capt Leonard W Lilley	7	–
Lt Henry Buttelmann	7	–
Lt Col Winton W Marshall	6½	–
Col Francis S Gabreski	6½	31
Maj Donald E Adams	6½	4
Col George L Jones	6½	–
Capt Robert J Love	6	–
Lt Col John F Bolt	6	6
Lt James H Kasler	6	–
Maj William T Whisner	5½	15½
Capt Richard S Becker	5	–
Capt Ralph D Gibson	5	–
Lt Col Richard D Creighton	5	2
Capt Robert H Moore	5	–
Capt Iven C Kinchloe Jr	5	–
Maj William H Wescott	5	–
Capt Robert T Latshaw Jr	5	–
Col Harrison R Thyng	5	8
Capt Dolphin D Overton III	5	–
Capt Clyde A Curtin	5	–
Maj Stephen L Bettinger	5	1
Col Robert P Baldwin	5	–

6. If, as in cases of a determined 'dog-fight', the flight becomes unwieldy, the element leader will notify his flight leader of his departure and press the engagement on his own. The wingmen will at all times remain with their leaders. When a flight or element is under attack, it is the responsibility of the leader to extricate the unit from the situation. Then it becomes the leader's turn to become the 'eyes' as he must keep close watch on the enemy to outmaneuver him and the wingman must depend on his leader and concentrate on his maneuvers. This is another time to use the radio to keep each other advised in solving maneuvering and positioning problems. Remember, when live ammunition is being used, you'd better know your tactics and teamwork but you must also expect and be willing to take risks.

7. In jet combat, you have no time to hesitate – if you do, you miss a kill or give the enemy that moment he's looking for. Let the enemy debate his tactics in the air – you debate yours on the ground (serious ready-room discussions of tactics are a big part of this). If you are outnumbered, attack the nearest enemy, the best maneuver in a bad situation is to attack. There are many cases where enemy forces have been disrupted and confused by inferior forces. If the enemy has the altitude advantage, and keeps it, climb up to him if you have the time and fuel, but maintain a good mach or your altitude will mean nothing. If the enemy is above and wants to engage, he'll come after you – then pilot ability counts. Even if the enemy has superior altitude and position on you to initiate his attack, you may salvage the show if you know your tactics and are complete master of your own aircraft. If you find the enemy below, you are (or should be) in the saddle with meat on the table. You will have superior speed, after your dive – if you haven't got him at the breakaway, zoom over his back and half roll on him. Wingman, be prepared – anticipate! Don't kill all your speed advantage with speed brakes unless you have the sky to yourself – remember – you can be bounced at the best of times. When you contact the enemy, be aggressive – attack first – it's far better than receiving and then figuring a defense. Shake the enemy up.

8. Combat readiness in tactics cannot and never will be achieved by a set number of hours or training missions. Some people learn slow, others get hot in a hurry but all take hours and hours of serious air work and serious concentration. You are getting the right edge when you feel you can hack almost anybody and have experienced hundreds of situations and maneuvering problems – and when (as they said in WW1) you feel you are the master of your machine. There are certain times when you must fly smooth and precise – close parade formation, landing patterns, on instruments, gun-sight tracking and shooting. The rest of your flying should be max performance to squeeze the last drop of capability from yourself and your plane.

Remember, tactics must be versatile – do change when the objective (offensive) requires and do change when forced to by obvious necessity (defensive). Do not expect the tactics of the last war to solve the next and do not discard or ignore old tactics as obsolete. Use your imagination – most new tactics are variations and/or combinations of old tactics.

CHAPTER TWELVE

VIETNAM, THE FALKLANDS AND BEYOND

SIMILAR VETERAN PILOTS TOOK a good share in America's next major war action — Vietnam. In the dozen or so years following the end of the Korean conflict, aircraft and air weaponry had advanced considerably. The aircraft involved had come a long way in the interim. The well-used 0.50 machine guns had departed from major aircraft types, replaced almost totally by 20-mm cannon. But the main armament of the fighters were now air-to-air missiles. Missile guidance systems, radar, in-flight refuelling; these were just part of the modern sophistication that the pilots engaged in air combat above Vietnam had to master. At the beginning of the jet age, experts predicted that dogfighting was no longer feasible. Korea disproved that, but when that war ended the same theory was being expounded: that dogfights were no longer possible with the increased speeds of the latest aircraft. In the Vietnam war, however, dogfighting still went on.

As Colonel (later General) Robin Olds wrote:

'*PERHAPS THE BIGGEST LESSON Clobber College over there taught us is that dogfighting today is surprisingly like our experiences in World War II and Korea. We found ourselves doing the things that people in the services swore would never be done again.*'

Vietnam was a different war from Korea in that it was not just two sides locked in ground battles and supported by air actions. The Communist North used guerrilla tactics with their Viet Cong forces against the conventional South Vietnamese Army and the Americans. The South's air war was mainly directed against Viet Cong supply lines and supply centers, or in direct support of any land actions that flared up long enough to be given air support. The American Air Force, Navy and Marine aircraft were among the best in the world.

THE COMBATANTS

The McDonnell F-4 Phantom II weighed 25 tons and carried a crew of two - pilot and Radar Intercept Officer (RIO). It was designed as an air superiority fighter as opposed to an interceptor which meant it sought its enemies over hostile territory, instead of flying over home territory to engage incoming raiders. It carried powerful radar equipment and its armament consisted of four Sparrow and four Sidewinder missiles, but no guns - at least, not in the early versions. The Sidewinder, when fired, homed in on infrared

Left: The Phantom was to Vietnam what the Sabre was to Korea. The rear McDonnell F-4J Phantom aboard the USS **Constellation** in the Gulf of Tonkin is from VF-96 Naval Squadron. Its crew is Lieutenant Randall H Cunningham and Lieutenant (jg) Willie Driscoll, first US aces in the Vietnam War – note five stars on side of fuselage. Nearest Phantom (5799) is of VF-92.
Above: Russian MIG-17 'Fresco' flown by the North Vietnamese Air Force. Fast in the turn, the MIGs were fought by the Americans using 'yo-yo' tactics.

emissions – heat – from the target airplane. Once it was activated in combat, the pilot would pick-up a growl sound in his earphones. Once the growl became strong enough – near the target – the missile was fired. The Sidewinder accelerated to Mach 2.5 in about 3 seconds and then sped towards the target. Its range was two miles and a proximity fuse detonated the warhead when within killing distance. Its reliability was not sound, as heat from the sun, or from a factory on the ground when flying at low level, could deflect it. For the best chance of success, the early Sidewinder was fired only in a tail-chase where it would home-in on the exhaust pipe of the enemy aircraft.

The Sparrow, on the other hand, was guided by radar. It was larger and more expensive than the Sidewinder and its initial speed on firing was Mach 3.7. Range was better – 25–28 miles – but a pilot needed to be absolutely certain that the distant aircraft was hostile.

The Republic F-105 Thunderchief was at the time the heaviest single-seat jet in service, weighing 50 000 lbs (22.3 tons) fully loaded. It carried one Sidewinder for defense and one internal 20-mm Vulcan cannon which had a formidable rate of fire – 6000 rounds a minute.

Both the 'Thud' and the Phantom had high wing-loading so were not suited to a turning air-fight.

The Chance-Vought F-8E Crusader carried four 20-mm cannon and later Sidewinder missiles as well. Together with the 'Thud' and the Phantom, these three aircraft took part in the bulk of the strike missions and air fighting that occurred over Vietnam. Their opponents in the jet battles were again Russian MIGs.

The North Vietnamese Air Force used MIG-17s, 19s and 21s. The MIG-17 ('Fresco') looked not unlike its older Korean sister (the MIG-15) with its distinctive high tailplane and similar armament, although it also carried air-to-air 'Atoll' missiles. With a far lower wing-loading than the American fighters, MIG-17s had a great advantage in a turn, therefore the US pilots always fought them in the vertical plane, using their superior speed and acceleration to outclimb them, using 'yo-yo' tactics. The Crusaders could out-turn MIGs only at high speed where the MIGs' control responses were not as effective as the F-8s. Most MIGs shot down over Vietnam were of the 17 type.

In contrast, the MIG-19 was not met in any quantity. Although its performance was generally better, it lacked the MIG-17's cut-and-thrust qualities and its main armament was only cannon.

The MIG-21 ('Fishbed'), which arrived later, had good supersonic maneuverability and low drag, capable of Mach 2 speeds. It was more than a match for the US fighters despite the fact that its delta-wing configuration gave it poor lift at subsonic speeds where the majority of combats took place. It carried two 30- or 37-mm cannon but like the MIG-17 its main armament was two 'Atoll' heat-seeking missiles, very similar to the Sidewinders.

With these main aircraft types the scene was set to begin innumerable high-speed combats above North Vietnam where the combatants fired missiles at each other instead of the hitherto customary close-up gun-actions.

MISSILES IN ACTION
These combats began on April 3, 1965 when the US carriers *Coral Sea* and *Hancock* launched 50 planes against an important bridge south of Hanoi. Two aircraft were shot down by ground fire, then some MIG-17s made a sudden single firing pass at the Americans but without inflicting any damage. However, on April 5 some MIGs stole in on some F-105 'Thuds' attacking the Than Hoa Bridge and shot down two. On April 9 four Phantoms from the carrier *Ranger* flying a

McDONNELL DOUGLAS F-4D PHANTOM II
versus
MIKOYAN/GUREVICH MIG-21PF

DESPITE ITS CLUMSY appearance, great size and weight, and original design for carrier operation, the F-4 Phantom II was the world's greatest all-round combat aircraft for 20 years from 1958. The F-4D, built for the USAF, was used in Vietnam in ways that negated its ability to use powerful radar and AIM-7 missiles to kill at a distance, in favor of the dogfight, the preference of the agile MIG-21. Despite this the Soviet-designed fighter made little impression, because its pilots mostly had extremely limited flying experience.

F-4D PHANTOM II
Two-seat all-weather fighter-bomber, powered by two 17 000 lb (full afterburner) thrust General Electric J79-15 turbojets. Maximum speed (clean, high altitude) 1400 mph or Mach 2.1; ceiling (clean) 62 000 ft and range 800 miles (attack mission) to 2300 miles (ferry). Four AIM-7 Sparrow AAMs recessed under fuselage, two more AIM-7 or four AIM-9 Sidewinder AAMs under wings, and varied attack loads.

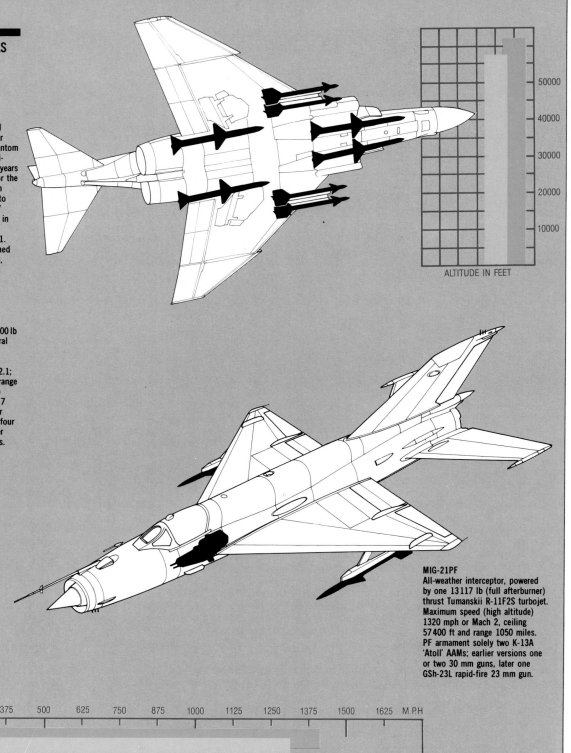

ALTITUDE IN FEET

50000

40000

30000

20000

10000

MIG-21PF
All-weather interceptor, powered by one 13 117 lb (full afterburner) thrust Tumanskii R-11F2S turbojet. Maximum speed (high altitude) 1320 mph or Mach 2, ceiling 57 400 ft and range 1050 miles. PF armament solely two K-13A 'Atoll' AAMs; earlier versions one or two 30 mm guns, later one GSh-23L rapid-fire 23 mm gun.

| 0 | 125 | 250 | 375 | 500 | 625 | 750 | 875 | 1000 | 1125 | 1250 | 1375 | 1500 | 1625 | M.P.H |

The 'Thud' – the Republic F-105 Thunderchief. Its 20-mm Vulcan cannon fired at a rate of 6000 rounds a minute.

patrol south of Hainan Island were engaged by four MIG-17s, using cannon. Being gunless, the F-4 pilots began to use their superior speed to gain enough distance to achieve a 'lock-on' with their missiles. Some were fired and a Sidewinder exploded next to one MIG, which was claimed as probably destroyed, but one Phantom failed to return. The North Vietnamese reported the American plane shot down by a Sidewinder!

By June 1965 the North Vietnamese had about 70 MIGs, mostly 17s – the MIG-21 did not arrive until the end of that year. The first American victories came in that month when, on June 17, two Navy Phantoms shot down two MIGs. These fell to Commander Louis C Page and his RIO Lieutenant John C Smith, Lieutenant Jack D Batson and Lieutenant Commander Robert B Doremus, of VF-21 from the USS Midway.

Page picked up approaching aircraft on radar when they were 35 miles away. Page and Batson closed head-on with the four MIG-17s at a combined speed of about 1100 knots and at 10 miles each Phantom fired a Sparrow missile. Both went home and two MIGs erupted in flames while the other two MIGs rapidly broke away.

The American and South Vietnamese aircraft flew with limitations similar to those of the Korean War. Just as Sabre pilots were not allowed to engage aircraft across the Chinese/Manchurian border, so too were the US and VNAF pilots not allowed to cross the North Vietnam border with China where MIGs gained height. Perhaps sensibly too, the MIGs took interest in attacking only aircraft actually engaged in strike or reconnaissance sorties, and rarely took on fighters flying MIGCAP missions (MIG Combat Air Patrols).

THE SAM THREAT

Anti-aircraft fire has always been a considerable factor to be coped with by all flyers in wartime. Many treated it with contempt, and indeed it usually was a case of 'hard luck' if you were hit. But by this stage in aerial warfare, guided missiles from the ground were not so easily ignored. As the Americans found in Vietnam, the Communists had surface-to-air missiles (SAMs) to complicate their lives. With this threat and the MIGs now in the war, a pilot really did need to be constantly on the alert. If you flew too low, ground fire was the danger; if too high, the MIGs waited; and if you flew straight and level for too long SAMs would be after you. If you were above cloud the SAMs would come through and give no time for a pilot to evade. Pilots needed to see the ground, actually needed to see the SAMs launched, then try to outmaneuver them. SAMs came straight up before turning onto a more level angle before the boosters disengaged. It needed steel nerves and good timing to dodge them. Dodge too quickly and the SAM could turn and catch the airplane, too late and it would detonate near enough for a hit. What was required was a dive hard at the right moment and, as the SAM followed down, pull the aircraft up equally as hard as possible, a tack which the SAM could not

Ready for launch – an F-6 Crusader aboard the carrier USS **Oriskany** in the Gulf of Tonkin, August 1967. Its Sidewinder missiles and 20-mm cannon can be clearly seen. The Navy Crusaders scored 19 air-to-air kills over Vietnam.

better at close range so Olds activated one. As the growl grew, the MIG was going into cloud and he fired, but this too missed. Seeing another MIG-21 ahead, Olds pulled to the left, barrel-rolled to the right, held his position above the MIG and as he came within range completed the roll and dropped behind and slightly to the left of the target.

Activating two Sidewinders, he sighted the MIG and, as the growl intensified, fired. The first missile hit the Russian aircraft, which dived, pulled up, then burst into flames. Five more MIGs fell on that day, after which the MIG pilots became ever more wary.

GUNS OR MISSILES?
Olds was very alert to the importance of armament: '*AIR-TO-AIR MISSILES GAVE our fighters a tremendous capability relative to the MIG-17, which carried only cannons and rockets. But fighting a MIG with a gunless F-4 is like fighting a guy with a dagger when he's got a sword, or maybe vice versa. A fighter without a gun, which is the most versatile air-to-air weapon, is like an airplane without a wing. Five or six times, when I had fired all my missiles, I might have been able to hit a MIG if I'd had cannon, because I was so close his motion was stopped in my gunsight.*

'*When we got the General Electric Vulcan M-61, which fires 6000 20-mm shells a minute, it turned out to be the greatest gun ever built for a fighter. It jammed very little. One of our exceptional pilots, Captain Darrel Simmons, shot down two MIGs with this Gatling in one day. He got them where he wanted them and just tapped the trigger twice for a total of 494 rounds. Of my 18 or more MIG scraps, the longest one was just 14 minutes. You have only a few seconds to fire in any MIG engagement, so I found our single Gatling's 6000 rounds per minute more than adequate...*'

As the war and the tactics and countertactics developed so too did MIG activity increase. To prolong their CAP missions the Phantoms flew at high subsonic speeds, which placed them at a disadvantage if attacked by MIGs, whose tactics were generally confined to single gun-firing passes. In this way, as the MIGs carried on down, the F-4 pilots had no chance to 'put their foot down' and accelerate to catch them. The Phantom pilots had been taught to fly and fight in the vertical plane, with dives and zooms which the MIG pilots could not emulate. The MIG pilots, however, confined their combat tactics to a

follow. Later the American tactic was to destroy either the SAM sites or the ground radar positions. It became very hazardous as the MIG menace increased, for to attack the ground sites the US aircraft needed to fly low, and below 20 000 ft the MIG-17s were more maneuverable and therefore more dangerous.

With the coming of the MIG-21, the Phantoms and Thunderchiefs could be outpaced and in a fight the MIG could out-turn both, although it could not out-climb the Phantom. The MIG pilots' tactics would be to wait at low altitudes where they were difficult to detect on the Americans' radar. As the US strike force made for their target area the MIGs would streak in to pick off any trailing aircraft with cannon or Atoll missiles.

By the end of 1966 the MIGs became such a menace that a big American fighter sweep was organized to try to trap some. Consequently on January 2, 1967 a force of 56 Phantoms led by Colonel Robin Olds flew towards Hanoi, in a typical strike formation. They had radar jamming and reconnaissance aircraft along too so as to confuse the North Vietnamese into thinking that they were a normal attack group.

The group headed towards Phuc Yen airfield, where most of the MIGs were located, then flew to and fro above a 7000 ft cloud layer, hoping to entice the MIGs up. This was successful and MIGs began quickly to pop up through the cloud. Olds' rearman Lieutenant Charles Clifton got his radar locked onto one and Olds fired two Sparrows, but both missed as they were too close for them to be used effectively. Sidewinders were limited altitude because of their power limitations, thus engaging in the horizontal plane. It was no longer an advantage either to have height above one's opponents, as heat-seeking missiles were not reliable when fired at targets below since 'ground returns' confused the missile's heat-seeking apparatus.

When the MIG-21s arrived, equipped with Atoll missiles, their tactics were to make supersonic attacks from astern, release their missiles, then turn away before escorting fighters could counter them. To combat this, Phantoms flew MIGCAP sorties to the rear of US strike or bomber groups. In this way five MIG-21s were shot down by Air Force F-4s.

In any war, it is always a big advantage to see the enemy first, and this was just as true in Vietnam. The Americans had respect for the MIG-21s but were thankful that the latter possessed no missile equivalent to their Sparrows. The North Vietnamese pilots had only tail-on missiles, so all that the American pilots had to do was see the MIGs first, then maneuver to stay out of the lethal range of their weaponry. Once the enemy was in a good position and within his missile's range, it was almost impossible to escape him, so the tactic was to begin evasion as soon as the MIG was spotted.

One of the MIG-21's good qualities was its small frontal area, which made it difficult to see if it was approaching head-on. It was good at high Mach above 25 000 ft, so the solution was to lure it

THE BARREL ROLL ATTACK
A Vietnam update on the WW2 P47's barrel roll maneuver. The Phantom pilot, unable to stay with a fast-turning MIG-21, cuts the corner by flying a high barrel roll away from the target, then pulls down and below in order to lock-on and fire a Sidewinder missile. The MIG, flying in the horizontal plane, is thus defeated by a three-dimensional maneuver often used successfully by American pilots.

down to 10000 ft where the Phantom in particular, with its tremendous thrust-to-weight advantage, was superior. Also the Phantom could maintain altitude even in an 8-'G' turn, whereas the MIG-21 in a high angle of attack situation bucked about almost uncontrollably. Because of its inlet design deficiencies the MIG's airspeed was limited to around 570 knots while the Phantom could reach 750, giving the American pilots enough speed to escape from an awkward situation.

To avoid being surprised by the MIGs, the Phantoms flew mutual support tactics, a flight flying into enemy territory in a combat spread 6000 to 10 000 ft apart, each pilot clearing the other's tail. To counter an attack from the side and abeam – the MIG's favorite position – the Phantoms turned into the attack. The sharpness of this turn would depend on when the MIG was seen. If it was picked up before beginning its attack, a defensive bank of 25–30 degrees forced the MIG to react. If the MIG was coming in fast, the bank angle was increased to 45–60 degrees, but if it was already close-in then the Phantom needed to go into a break turn at maximum performance, with a nose-down maneuver to throw the attacker off.

Whatever the tactic used, the object was to get the MIG to overshoot and, once it had been forced to the outside of the turn and became the target and not the attacker, the Phantom went for it. Because of the Phantom's higher thrust-to-weight ratio and superior high-angle attack performance it should be able to get on the MIG-21's tail in two turns. Usually the MIG tactics were to dive, attack, fire and get away fast. Nevertheless, this was usually sufficient to force the bomb-carrying Phantom to jettison its payload to defend itself – so the MIG at least achieved something.

In 1966 the F-8 Crusader pilots opened their scoring against the MIG-17s, three falling in June, a fourth in October. It was to be a year later, however, before a MIG-21 was brought down by a Navy Phantom.

Navy Phantoms from the carrier *Constellation* flew cover to a strike against Phu Ly on August 10, 1967. While they were watching the attack, MIG warnings were given but none seen. Then two MIG-21s came through cloud 6000 ft above and ahead of the two F-4s. They had not seen the Americans, who pulled round in a 360-degree turn to come in behind the MIGs. Each fired Sparrow and Sidewinder missiles, one exploding close enough to do the job, another actually going into the other MIG's tailpipe. By the end of that year the Air Force had shot down 17 MIG-21s, while a

ROBIN OLDS

BORN IN CALIFORNIA, THE SON of a Major General, Olds saw combat during the summer of 1944, flying P38 Lightnings with the 479th Fighter Group of the 8th Air Force in England. His first two victories came on August 14, and three more on August 25 to make him an ace in just two air battles. On February 14, 1945 he shot down his ninth aircraft, bringing him to top place among P38 pilots in the 8th Air Force.

The 479th then converted to single-engined P51 Mustangs. Olds shot down two German aircraft on March 19, and his 12th victory fell on April 7. In addition to his air-to-air kills, he was credited with the destruction of a further 11 on the ground, making 23 in all, and he ended the war as a Major.

He remained in the US Air Force after the war, and married movie star Ella Raines. As a full Colonel 20 years later, he commanded the 8th Tactical Fighter Wing in Vietnam, flying F-4C Phantoms. On January 7, 1967 he led his men into a battle which resulted in seven MIG-21s being shot down, Olds claiming one for himself. His second victory over a MIG-21 came on May 4, and on May 20, when his pilots destroyed four MIG-17s, Robin Olds got two of them. With a total of four MIGs shot down, he was top-scoring US pilot in Vietnam when his tour ended and he returned to the United States to take up a training post. His record stood until 1972 when Lieutenant Cunningham of the US Navy and Captain Ritchie of the USAF each gained five kills, also flying Phantom aircraft.

total of 42 MIG-17s had been shared by Phantoms, Crusaders and Thunderchiefs. The highest scorer was Robin Olds. After his first on January 2, 1967, he shot down three in May in company with Lieutenant Steve Croker as RIO. His record of four lasted until 1972.

However, it was far from one-sided. In a seven-month period from August 1967, MIG-21s shot down 18 US Air Force fighters and lost only five of their own. The North Vietnamese were almost always handled rigidly from the ground by a very efficient controlled interception organization: being told where to fly, when to attack and even when to fire.

With the opening of peace talks in 1968, the United States called a halt to the bombing of North Vietnam in November, which ended air combat too. This lasted until December 1971, when the air war began again, as by then it was obvious that the North had no intention of ending hostilities with the South.

PHANTOM ACES

By this time the American fighter pilots were flying a system they called Double Attack. Flying in two-plane elements, the first crew to gain a contact, radar or visual, took the lead, the other flying as wingman. This tactic was very similar to that used by Godfrey and Gentile in WW2 over Germany. It really worked only when aircraft operated in pairs instead of flight formations, but as Phantom pilots regularly operated in pairs in Vietnam it proved quite useful. Once they found a radar contact the Phantom crews usually turned the hostile aircraft for a head-on shot with a Sparrow. This tactic had the advantage of turning the radar scan towards the bandit. Once within five-mile range the RIO's job would be to protect the tail while the pilot concentrated on the attack.

And it was in the last year of the war that the Americans acquired their two 'ace' pilots of that conflict. Both were Phantom pilots – one Air Force, one Navy.

Navy Lieutenants Randy Cunningham and William Driscoll already had two MIG victories by May 10, 1972. On that day their squadron, VF-96, launched a raid from the USS *Constellation* against railyards in Haiphong. Pulling out of his bomb-run, Cunningham found a MIG-17 on his tail but his missile-armed wingman could not fire for fear that he would hit the lead Phantom. Cunningham pulled round sharply, too sharply for the diving MIG, who promptly overshot. Cunningham again pulled round after it and launching a Sidewinder blew the MIG apart. Seeing more MIGs attacking Phantoms below, he then saw three chasing a lone Phantom. He was now in a position similar to that in which his own wingman had been – unable to fire in case he hit the F-4. Closing in, Cunningham called the other F-4 pilot, telling him to break fast. While this went on, four MIGs curved down on Cunningham's tail. With Driscoll calling out the warnings, Cunningham changed course slightly to throw the MIG pilots' aim. Finally the lead Phantom pulled round and Cunningham loosed a Sidewinder which hit one MIG causing it to flame. Cunningham himself then sideslipped away and turned. Breaking off from a sky full of MIGs he headed back toward the carrier, but near the coast saw a lone MIG-17 coming head-on. Instead of zooming away as usual, the MIG pilot began firing, so it was the American who zoomed out of the way.

Ordinarily, the MIG would have kept on going but this one turned and flew right up to the Phantom. Both were climbing but, as the Phantom's speed pulled it ahead, the MIG slipped into

The McDonnell Phantom – deadly opponent in the air.

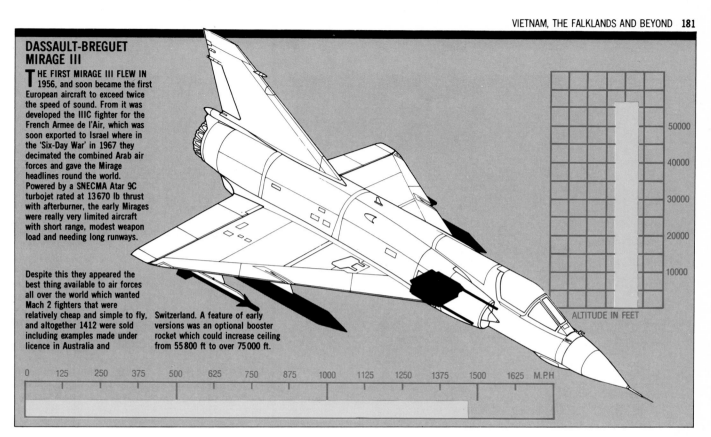

DASSAULT-BREGUET MIRAGE III

THE FIRST MIRAGE III FLEW IN 1956, and soon became the first European aircraft to exceed twice the speed of sound. From it was developed the IIIC fighter for the French Armee de l'Air, which was soon exported to Israel where in the 'Six-Day War' in 1967 they decimated the combined Arab air forces and gave the Mirage headlines round the world. Powered by a SNECMA Atar 9C turbojet rated at 13670 lb thrust with afterburner, the early Mirages were really very limited aircraft with short range, modest weapon load and needing long runways.

Despite this they appeared the best thing available to air forces all over the world which wanted Mach 2 fighters that were relatively cheap and simple to fly, and altogether 1412 were sold including examples made under licence in Australia and Switzerland. A feature of early versions was an optional booster rocket which could increase ceiling from 55800 ft to over 75000 ft.

ALTITUDE IN FEET

50000
40000
30000
20000
10000

0 125 250 375 500 625 750 875 1000 1125 1250 1375 1500 1625 M.P.H

a position behind and began firing. Cunningham rolled, then dived, turning to re-engage, as the MIG came at them again. The dogfight raged, neither pilot gaining an advantage. Finally, perhaps low on fuel, the MIG began to dive away, nearly straight. The Phantom went after it and Cunningham let go a Sidewinder. A flash and a puff of smoke resulted, and the MIG went into the ground.

More MIGs attacked and two SAMs also flashed past them, but they fought their way out despite damage from one of the exploding SAMs. With the hydraulics gone, the two men had to eject into the sea but were quickly rescued by Navy helicopters. They had not only shot down three MIGs, to become the first US 'aces' of the Vietnam War, but the last MIG had been flown by the leading Communist pilot, Colonel Nguyon Tomb, who flying MIG-17s and 21s had 13 US aircraft to his credit.

On the same day, May 10, Captain Steve Ritchie and Captain Charles 'Chuck' DeBellevue shot down a MIG-21, their first of five while with the 555th Tactical Fighter Squadron (TFS). DeBellevue was credited with four MIGs flying with Ritchie and went on to share a fifth and sixth, to become top US scorer of the war.

As if to emphasize the eventual superiority of the American fighter pilots over Vietnam, the case of the final F-8 Crusader victory in the war on April 22, 1972, makes the point. Two Crusaders were launched from the *Hancock* as TARCAP (Target CAP) and orbited the coast while the strike planes attacked targets in the Mekong Delta.

When bandits were reported they were eventually put on a course to meet them, but met nothing but ground fire. Lieutenant Jerry Tucker then saw the glint of sun on perspex low to the north. He told his leader and the two F-8s turned towards it; Tucker then saw a MIG-17, near the tree-tops. His leader could not see it, so turned the lead over to Tucker, who pulled up to the left, then rolled in behind the MIG ready for a Sidewinder shot. When Tucker was only half a mile from the enemy plane the MIG pilot baled out, having apparently seen the two Crusaders and decided to parachute rather than engage.

By the end of the war, US aircraft had shot down 192 MIGs and two propeller-driven machines, having themselves lost 92 planes in combat, 76 of which were fighters. Phantoms had claimed 75%, a total of 145; F-8 Crusaders had scored 19 for the loss of three, Thunderchiefs 30.

Jet combat in the Middle East. A MIG-21, flaps down, falls to the guns of a Mirage III armed with 30-mm cannon.

Only about 45 were shot down by gunfire, or partially by gunfire, the rest by missile attack. A good number of US aircraft were shot down by gunfire before and after the introduction of Atoll missiles by the North Vietnamese.

COMBAT IN THE MIDDLE EAST
While Phantoms and MIGs fought it out in Vietnam, these two aircraft, with others, were meeting in combat in the Middle East. Ever since the state of Israel was created in May 1948 there has been tension and action over the areas of Egypt, Israel, Palestine, Syria and other Arab countries. In the early air battles it was the aircraft of WW2 that battled over the deserts – Spitfires, Fiat G50s, Mustangs and Avia C.210s. The tactics mostly followed those of that war; indeed, a number of the pilots involved were ex-WW2 flyers.

In 1956 came the Suez Crisis and in the early 1960s there were a number of Israeli clashes against the PLO, Jordan, Syria and Egypt. The various warring factions used aircraft from three major nations, Russia, America and France.

Israel used Dassault Mirage, Mystère V and Ouragan fighters, while Syria and Egypt adopted MIG-19s and 21s, Egypt also using Tupulov TU-16 bombers and Sukhoi SU-7 fighter-bombers. In practice, Israel's Mirage III was able to outfly and outgun any of the aircraft flown by the Arab states, with its two 30-mm cannon and American Sidewinder missiles.

At the beginning of 1967 Israel had some 300 front-line aircraft, compared with the Arabs' 850. By this time a full-scale war seemed imminent and, despite peace talks, it was obvious that the situation would only worsen. Soon after dawn on June 5, 1967 – soon enough after this traditionally

dangerous hour for Egypt to have relaxed her early-morning vigil – the Israeli Air Force struck at Egypt's air bases. Vautours, Mystères, Ouragans, Magisters, Super-Mystères and Mirage IIIs all swept into a lightning attack, destroying 32 MIG-21s on the ground and cratering runways. Eight MIGs got off the ground, shooting down two attacking Israeli aircraft, but were themselves all shot down.

The assault continued for three hours, the Israelis knocking out Russian SA-2 missile sites in addition to 20 MIG-19s and 21s that flew into the battle from the south. All were shot down or crash-landed when their fuel gave out with no usable airfields to land on. At the end of the three hours, Egypt's air force no longer existed, and 300 of its 340 aircraft had been shot down or destroyed on the ground.

The Israeli pilots had to be well aware of how to fight the Russian MIGs for, apart from the Mirages, the MIG could beat their aircraft except at low level. Therefore they did not dogfight MIGs at high level; nor were they enticed up to fight them. They used the same tactics against the air forces of Syria, Jordan and Iraq. By day two of this conflict – which lasted but six days altogether – Israel had knocked out 393 Arab aircraft on the ground and 23 in air combat for the loss of only 26 of their own – mostly to ground fire.

An uneasy peace lasted until the late summer of 1968, escalating in March 1969. Israel had now begun to re-equip with American aircraft – Phantoms and McDonnell Douglas A-4 Skyhawk fighter-bombers. The Skyhawks were used to knock out SA-2 missile sites while the Mirage fighter pilots flew cover sorties. By 1970 the Phantoms too were striking deep into the area of the Nile Delta, attacking missile and radar installations, manned by Russian advisors. The Russians in turn supplied five MIG-21 squadrons with pilots to help to protect them and their personnel.

The first clash came on July 30, when a flight of Phantoms was attacked by 16 MIG-21s above the Gulf of Suez, but flying top cover were Israeli Mirage fighters. In the fight that followed the Phantom and Mirage pilots destroyed five MIGs for no loss. This dangerous escalation ended almost immediately and a cease-fire was reimposed.

Over the next few years Egypt and Syria augmented their air forces with MIG-17s, 19s and 21s and SU-7s and TU-16s, as well as more air-to-ground missile sites. Israel felt safe after her earlier victories, a position confirmed on an occasion such as September 13, 1973 when a

MIG-21 patrol attacked Israeli Mirages and Phantoms off the Syrian coast where the result was 13 MIGs lost against one Mirage.

Yet another big battle was being planned, but this time it was to be Egypt that opened the attack.

On October 6, 1973, an estimated 250 MIGs and SU-7s attacked Israeli air bases, radar and missile sites in the Sinai, supporting a heavy land offensive. Counterattacks by the Israelis cost them 40 aircraft shot down, mostly to ground defenses. But Israel fought back, held the Egyptians and outfought the Syrians. Only then did it turn fully on the Egyptian Army and once again MIGs fought it out with Phantoms as the Israelis regained lost ground, forcing yet another uneasy truce – a truce that remains unsteady with still the occasional clash of arms.

1982 – THE FALKLAND WAR
For Britain, a major clash of arms occurred far away from its shores and major bases. In the South Atlantic came a new enemy – Argentina – who tried to take by force the Falkland Islands situated 400 miles off her eastern coast and 8000 miles from Great Britain.

Although a brief conflict, the Falklands campaign not only tested Britain's ability to support a battle so far away and without any nearby land bases, but also blooded a significant front-line fighter – the Harrier jump-jet.

The Harrier was not a new aircraft. Developed from the Hawker P.1127 Kestrel, it was the first operational high-performance V/STOL (Vertical/Short Take-Off and Landing) fighter in the world, entering service with the RAF in 1969. Thirteen years were to pass before it was tested in an operational situation, and it triumphed despite the limitations of environment.

With the Falklands naval Task Force which sailed to the South Atlantic to retrieve the islands from the Argentinian forces went the Royal Navy's Sea Harrier FRS1, on board the aircraft-carriers *Hermes* and *Invincible*. Only 20 in number, the Harriers were to be used for Task Force defense and attack sorties against Falkland targets. The Argentine Air Force had 11 Mirage III fighters, 46 Skyhawks, 34 Dagger (copied from the Mirage V) fighter-bombers plus 6 Canberra bombers – a total of 97. All (except the Canberras) could carry missiles. The Mirage and Daggers had two 30-mm cannon, the Skyhawks two 20-mm cannon. The Argentinians also had a number of lesser combat aircraft available – Pucaras, Macchi 339s and Learjet 35As-L, but also five Dassault Super Etendards, and 11 Skyhawks of

the Argentinian Navy. To reinforce the Sea Harriers, the RAF sent 10 Harrier GR3s of No 1 Squadron RAF to operate from *Hermes* mostly on strike sorties. The Harriers carried two 30-mm cannon but their main weapons were two AIM-9L Sidewinder missiles for air-to-air combat, or a number of other weapons for ground-attack sorties.

HARRIER IN COMBAT
The front-line Argentinian aircraft could all fly faster than the British Harriers but the latter had two advantages over the South American flyers in air combat. One was its reputed ability to use VIFF (thrust Vectored In Forward Flight) which embraced the Harrier's ability to vary the direction of its engine thrust, – essentially what gave the Harrier the power to rise vertically, hover and move backwards or forwards. When used in forward flight, the pilot was able to vector engine thrust to push his airplane up or down. In a dive he could use the thrust capabilities to blast himself into a steeper dive or, by reversing the exhaust nozzles of his Rolls-Royce Pegasus engine, slow his descent, allowing an opponent to overshoot.

In reality, however, the operational use of VIFF had only limited use. No skilful Navy or RAF pilot would willingly allow an enemy aircraft to get into a position to attack him, so that he could then show how clever he was to be able to use VIFF to escape. And if surprised from behind, to engage VIFF would be too slow an operation merely to avoid on-coming missiles and aircraft. The mere fact that a pilot using VIFF slows his aircraft down negates the essential element of successful modern air combat – high speed. This same reality in actual combat showed the British pilots that VIFF was good in only a couple of instances, perhaps to point the Harrier's nose higher than would otherwise be possible so that the pilot could get a shot at a hostile aircraft, or, secondly, if under attack, it could be used in a violent deceleration but only if all else had failed.

The other advantage was the Harrier's AIM-9L version of the Sidewinder missile. This latest model could home-in on an aircraft from almost any position, even head-on to a degree. The earlier Sidewinder, such as those used in Vietnam, could home-in only from the rear. Although limited VIFF and the AIM-9L were listed as advantages, neither had been proved in a genuine situation.

Out of land-based radar range, the Task Force had to use shipboard radar, the Navy throwing a screen of ships about its main force to warn them of approaching aircraft. The Argentinian aircraft

SOUTH ATLANTIC MAY 1, 1982

SEA HARRIER VERSUS MIRAGE

The aircraft element of Task Force 317, which left Portsmouth for the Falkland Islands on April 5, 1982, included 20 Sea Harriers, 12 with 800 Sqn aboard *Hermes* and eight with 801 Sqn on *Invincible*. The Sea Harriers' tasks would include defending the force from attack by Argentinian aircraft, including Fuerza Aérea Argentina Mirage IIIs and Daggers, both capable of Mach 2, though distinctly subsonic at low levels, and operating at ranges from their mainland bases that would allow only minimal time for combat — 12 minutes at the high altitudes where they had the advantage in performance, or a bare five minutes lower

down. However, the task force would be standing well off the islands, so the Sea Harriers would also be limited in combat endurance, as well as being heavily outnumbered.

Combat air patrols were mounted with increasing frequency as the task force moved south, and the first contact came on April 25, when two of 801 Sqn's aircraft intercepted an FAA 707 on a reconnaissance mission, though being outside the declared total exclusion zone they did not attack it.

On May 1 the first combat missions were flown, 12 Sea Harriers from *Hermes* attacking Port Stanley airfield and Goose Green with top cover provided by aircraft from 801 Sqn. *Invincible*'s Sea Harriers made several further contacts, and that afternoon two of the fighters took off to intercept a high-altitude raid. Their armament included the standard pair of 30 mm Aden cannon, plus AIM-9L Sidewinder missiles.

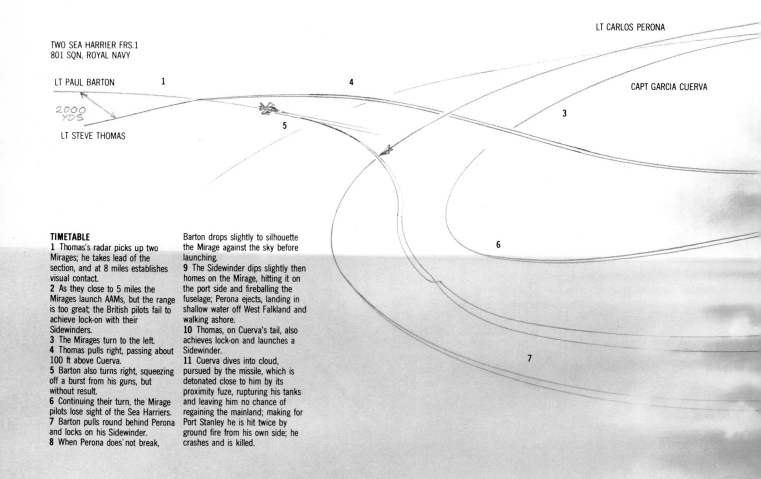

TWO SEA HARRIER FRS.1
801 SQN, ROYAL NAVY

LT CARLOS PERONA

LT PAUL BARTON   1

2000 YDS

LT STEVE THOMAS

CAPT GARCIA CUERVA

4

5

3

6

7

TIMETABLE
1 Thomas's radar picks up two Mirages; he takes lead of the section, and at 8 miles establishes visual contact.
2 As they close to 5 miles the Mirages launch AAMs, but the range is too great; the British pilots fail to achieve lock-on with their Sidewinders.
3 The Mirages turn to the left.
4 Thomas pulls right, passing about 100 ft above Cuerva.
5 Barton also turns right, squeezing off a burst from his guns, but without result.
6 Continuing their turn, the Mirage pilots lose sight of the Sea Harriers.
7 Barton pulls round behind Perona and locks on his Sidewinder.
8 When Perona does not break,

Barton drops slightly to silhouette the Mirage against the sky before launching.
9 The Sidewinder dips slightly then homes on the Mirage, hitting it on the port side and fireballing the fuselage; Perona ejects, landing in shallow water off West Falkland and walking ashore.
10 Thomas, on Cuerva's tail, also achieves lock-on and launches a Sidewinder.
11 Cuerva dives into cloud, pursued by the missile, which is detonated close to him by its proximity fuze, rupturing his tanks and leaving him no chance of regaining the mainland; making for Port Stanley he is hit twice by ground fire from his own side; he crashes and is killed.

Below: The echelon formation used by the Mirage pilots, with the two aircraft 1200 yards apart, leaves the rear aircraft to guard the leader's tail, but makes mutual support more difficult. The Sea Harriers in combat spread formation, 2000 yards apart in line abreast and one slightly below the other, have much greater tactical flexibility.

1200 YDS

2

TWO MIRAGE III
GRUPO 8, FUERZA AEREA
ARGENTINA

10

11

9

8

would be seeking the ships carrying the invasion force troops and support craft.

In the event the British Harriers destroyed a total of 22 Argentine aircraft – 9 Daggers, 8 Skyhawks, 2 Mirages, plus a Canberra, a C-130 Hercules and a Pucara, mostly by Sidewinders – for no loss in air combat. The Harrier was better than the Mirage in the turning-circle. But when attacking the Dagger, it was unable to catch the enemy once it had dropped its bombs and had accelerated to near-supersonic speed. Even in a dive the Harrier had no chance of gaining on the Dagger.

Air-to-air combat began on May 1, 1982 when Mirage III fighters attacked. Six were spotted on ships' radar when only two Harriers were up on Combat Air Patrol. They were at 15 000 ft and accelerated to fighting speed as they headed towards the incoming Mirages, the two British pilots in battle formation, line abreast, 2000 yards apart, each able therefore to watch the other's tail. They picked up the Mirages on their aircraft radar at 35 000 ft. Flying from the Argentinian mainland, the Mirages could remain in the Falkland combat area for only 12 minutes at high level or a mere five at low level. Knowing the Harriers were better at low level, the Mirage pilots remained at 35 000 ft. For the same reason, the Harrier pilots refused to be enticed to this

AIR COMBAT FIGHTER CLAIMS OVER THE FALKLANDS

ROYAL AIR FORCE AND FLEET AIR ARM

Date	Name	Aircraft Destroyed	Armament Used
May 1	F/Lt Paul Barton RAF	Mirage	Sidewinder
	Lt Steve Thomas	Mirage	Sidewinder
	F/Lt Tony Penfold	Dagger	Sidewinder
	Lt Al Curtiss	Canberra	Sidewinder
May 21	Lt Cdr Ward	Pucara	30mm Cannon
	Lt Cdr Mike Blissett	Skyhawk	Sidewinder
	Lt Cdr Neil Thomas	Skyhawk	Sidewinder
	Lt Cdr Fred Frederiksen	Dagger	Sidewinder
	Lt Steve Thomas	2 Daggers	Sidewinder
	Lt Cdr Ward	Dagger	Sidewinder
	Lt Clive Morell	Skyhawk	Sidewinder
	F/Lt John Leeming	Skyhawk	30mm Cannon
	Lt Clive Morell	Skyhawk	Sidewinder
May 23	Lt Martin Hale	Dagger	Sidewinder
May 24	Lt Cdr Andy Auld	2 Daggers	Sidewinder
	Lt David Smith	Dagger	Sidewinder
Jun 1	Lt Cdr Ward	Hercules	Sidewinder & 30mm
Jun 8	F/Lt David Morgan	2 Skyhawks	Sidewinder
	Lt David Smith	Skyhawk	Sidewinder

height. It was not long before their fuel state forced the Mirage pilots to turn for home.

That afternoon Canberras, Skyhawks and Daggers flew towards the islands, two Mirage fighters leading them in, to take on the Harriers. The defending Harriers were vectored by the ships' radar towards the Mirages, staying low. The Mirage pilots seemed bent on a fight, reducing height in order to engage them. When the Harrier pilots saw them the two Mirages were flying in echelon, 1200 yds apart. Tactically the Argentine formation was in disarray, for if the rear aircraft was attacked the leader would be unable to give assistance to him. The Harrier pilots, Flight Lieutenant Paul Barton RAF and Lieutenant Steve Thomas, RN, surprised both Mirages, Barton hitting one with a Sidewinder. It broke up and the pilot ejected. Thomas fired a Sidewinder at the other but both the Mirage and the missile were swallowed up in cloud. However, the missile struck the Mirage, severely damaging it. The luckless pilot tried to land at Port Stanley, only to be struck by gunfire from his own side (see pages 184–185).

After the action of this day the Mirage IIIs were pulled out of the fighting. This was because the RAF had bombed the airfield at Port Stanley, using a Vulcan bomber in a 15½-hour flight from Ascension Island, a round trip of 7860 miles. The Argentine government reasoned that if the RAF could bomb Port Stanley then it could bomb

Built by British Aerospace, the Harrier, with its VTOL capability was the ideal aircraft to operate from Royal Navy carriers off the Falklands. Far from land it proved a first-rate defensive fighter and ground-attack airplane.

targets in Argentina. The Mirage IIIs from then on were used for home defense, thereby reducing the Falklands' attack force and taking from it the only pure fighter that might have given the Harrier serious opposition.

The worst day for the Argentinian Air Force was May 21 when they lost 10 aircraft to the RAF and RN fighter pilots. Five Skyhawks, four Daggers, and one Pucara all went down that afternoon. Seven fell to Sidewinder missiles, the Pucara and a Skyhawk to 30-mm cannon and another Skyhawk damaged by ships' fire and a Sea Harrier's 30-mm cannon.

HARRIER PILOTS – AN ASSESSMENT

For many years the Harrier fighter had lived with an unproved reputation but the name it and its pilots gained during the Falklands war fully vindicated all those who knew that it would be an important aircraft especially as it was the only airplane that could be used in the unique circumstances that had to be faced.

It was unusual too in that the Royal Navy and RAF pilots had been trained to respond to radar contact and assistance. In the Falklands, the Harrier's interception tactics had to revert to almost pre-WW2 methods. Early warning radar coverage was just not available, and the pilots had, just as the Typhoon pilots of 1942–43 had, to revert to standing patrols in order to hope to combat fast low flying hit and run hostile aircraft.

However, once the Harrier pilots had the Argentinian aircraft in visual sight, they were usually able to pounce on them from above, and

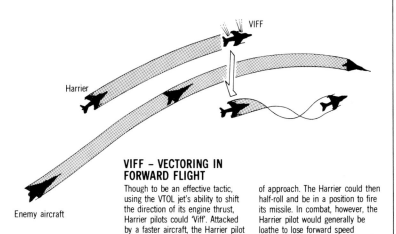

VIFF

Harrier

Enemy aircraft

VIFF – VECTORING IN FORWARD FLIGHT

Though to be an effective tactic, using the VTOL jet's ability to shift the direction of its engine thrust, Harrier pilots could 'Viff'. Attacked by a faster aircraft, the Harrier pilot changed his engine's directional thrust to vertical, and the aircraft is pushed away from the attacker's line of approach. The Harrier could then half-roll and be in a position to fire its missile. In combat, however, the Harrier pilot would generally be loathe to lose forward speed (necessary when 'viffing') rather than making a hard turn away from the attacker.

use their speed to close into missile range. There were very few Sidewinder failures in the Battle, and once fired, the Argentinian aircraft were doomed. They had little time to respond, and if ever a pilot saw an approaching missile it was too late to do anything about it. Invariably the only pilots to see them were those not being attacked, and a call to their endangered companions was all but a waste of time. Moments later the target aircraft would be an exploding mass of metal and burning petrol.

The British pilot's skill was proved beyond all doubt, their years of training finally paying off. The Harrier's small size too was an asset being less vulnerable to enemy gunfire than a larger one might be; and its engine is relatively smoke-free – yet another advantage in the 'who sees who first' battle.

The Harrier pilots' best day in air combat against the aircraft of a Argentinian Air Force was 21 May. In the early afternoon Lieutenant Commander Mike Blissett and his wingman, Lieutenant Commander Neil Thomas arrived over Goose Green at the commencing of their patrol. Blissett later recorded: '*W*E

headed west-south-west at 300 feet – there were some patches of low cloud and we wanted to be beneath them. We were flying in defensive battle formation, in line abreast about 2000 yards apart with Neil to the north and me to the south. When we were three miles east of Chartres Settlement I caught sight of four Skyhawks in front of me about three and a half miles away, flying across my nose from left to right; they had just crossed the coast on their way in. With the very high closing speed there was no time for me to do anything but call to Neil, "Break starboard!", because I really wanted him to come round hard. I pulled into a very hard turn to starboard. As we passed over the top of them they saw us, their nice arrow formation broke up and they began to jettison underwing tanks and bombs. Everything was happening very rapidly. They pulled round over some rising ground to the south-east of Chartres. By now I was in the lead with Neil to my left and about 400 yards astern, with all of us in a tight turn. The Skyhawks were in a long echelon, spread out over about a mile. I locked a Sidewinder on one of the guys in the middle and fired. My first impression was that the missile was going to strike the ground as it fell away – I was only about 200 feet above the ground. But suddenly it started to climb and rocketed towards the target. At that moment my attention was distracted somewhat as a Sidewinder came

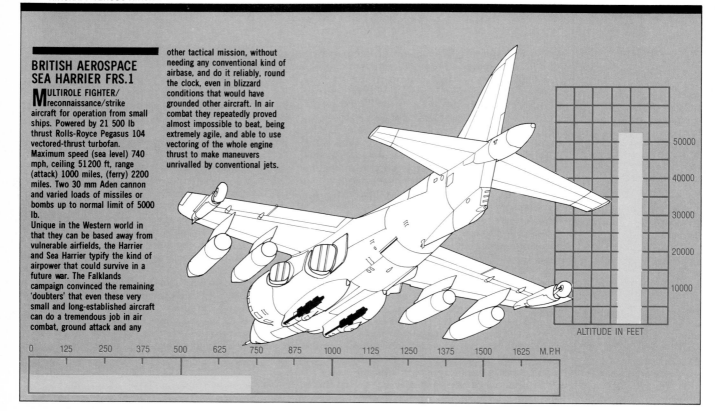

BRITISH AEROSPACE SEA HARRIER FRS.1

MULTIROLE FIGHTER/ reconnaissance/strike aircraft for operation from small ships. Powered by 21 500 lb thrust Rolls-Royce Pegasus 104 vectored-thrust turbofan. Maximum speed (sea level) 740 mph, ceiling 51200 ft, range (attack) 1000 miles, (ferry) 2200 miles. Two 30 mm Aden cannon and varied loads of missiles or bombs up to normal limit of 5000 lb.

Unique in the Western world in that they can be based away from vulnerable airfields, the Harrier and Sea Harrier typify the kind of airpower that could survive in a future war. The Falklands campaign convinced the remaining 'doubters' that even these very small and long-established aircraft can do a tremendous job in air combat, ground attack and any

other tactical mission, without needing any conventional kind of airbase, and do it reliably, round the clock, even in blizzard conditions that would have grounded other aircraft. In air combat they repeatedly proved almost impossible to beat, being extremely agile, and able to use vectoring of the whole engine thrust to make maneuvers unrivalled by conventional jets.

ALTITUDE IN FEET

50000
40000
30000
20000
10000

0   125   250   375   500   625   750   875   1000   1125   1250   1375   1500   1625   M.P.H

steaming past my left shoulder – Neil had fired past me, which I found very disconcerting at the time! I watched his "winder" chase after another of the Skyhawks, which started to climb for a patch of cloud, then the aircraft disappeared into the cloud with the missile gaining fast.

'Then I glanced back to the right and saw my missile impact on the Skyhawk I had aimed at. Suddenly, about 800 yards in front of me, there was a huge fireball as the aircraft blew up in the air; there was debris flying everywhere. As I started to lock on my second missile I caught sight of something flickering to my left, out of the corner of my eye; it was the Skyhawk Neil's Sidewinder had hit, tumbling out of the clouds with the back end well ablaze. It came down cartwheeling slowly past my aircraft about 100 yards away, looking like a slow-motion replay.'

These Skyhawks were from Grupo 4, their pilots, Lieutenants Lopez and Manzotti were both killed.

Two hours later Lieutenant Clive Morell and his number two, Flight Lieutenant John Leeming were also over Goose Green about to begin their patrol above Falkland Sound. Then he saw bombs exploding near to a RN frigate to the north of his position. Morell stated:

'**I** DEDUCED THAT the attackers would probably exit going south-west down the Sound. I looked to where I thought they would be and they appeared, lo and behold, below a hole in the clouds. They were easy to see from above, painted white. I said, "Christ, Leems, there they are!" We were in line abreast battle formation, I was on the left. I just rolled steeply down and he followed me. Once I had cleared the cloud I saw two of them and I slotted in behind the rear one. Leems went in behind the third man, who was back further still.

'I had some problems with my weapons system; by the time I fired my Sidewinder I was down at his altitude, about 100 feet, at a range of 800 to 1,000 yards. The missile streaked after him and exploded within a foot or so of his jet pipe, virtually a direct hit. His aircraft went into the sea in a big ball of fire.

'Initially, my other missile refused to fire at the second guy. So I opened up with my guns but I didn't see any of the rounds hit. Having exhausted my ammunition I switched back to the missile, it was locked on to him and it fired on its own accord. At first it looked as if it was guiding nicely, then it just seemed to lose interest. It got to

within a length or two behind him then stopped guiding and fell away into the sea.

'Now I had no more bullets or missiles, I looked round to see what was going on behind. To my left and behind I could see this large ball of fire going down into the sea. I thought, "I hope that's not my No. 2," But then John called up and said, "Spag (my nickname), are you OK?" I said, "Yes, how about you?"'

When they returned and landed on HMS *Hermes*, they each claimed one Skyhawk destroyed. However, it later transpired that Morell's 30 mm cannon had scored hits and damaged the Skyhawk's fuel tanks. With no hope of reaching Argentina, the pilot flew to Port Stanley and ejected. The three Skyhawks were from the 3rd Naval Fighter and Attack Escuadrilla. Two pilots in fact ejected, both from aircraft hit by Morell. Leeming's victim died. John Leeming too was to die a few months later in air-to-air combat training flight when his fighter collided with another Harrier.

What was apparent to the British was that the Argentine pilots had little idea of how members of a good flight formation could give each other mutual cover when attacked by the Harriers. Indeed, they were briefed to avoid air fights and, if attacked, to get down low where it would be every man for himself. They knew that they were outclassed by the Harriers and their Sidewinders, and felt that there was no point in even trying to combat them. Being engaged on attack sorties against the Royal Navy ships, they did not even carry air-to-air missiles and in any event the Argentinian missiles – the Shafrir, Matra-Magic and early model Sidewinders – could not equal the AIM-9L.

Although superior in numbers the Argentine pilots were seriously handicapped. They had a long way to fly to reach the combat zone, and faced an equally long flight home. Once the Mirage IIIs were pulled out they lost any chance of fighter cover and they knew they were outgunned and outflown. They did not lack courage, but the Harrier and the British pilots were just too good for them. Once again superior aircraft coupled with sound tactics and good training won the day.

And what of the future? Tomorrow's fighter pilot will rely more and more on computer generated head-up displays, feeding him all the essential information he will need to carry out his missions. Finger tip controls will give him instant checks on all flight data without the need to read the myriad of instruments in front of him. In

combat situations he will be able to bring into play any number of sensors, from radar, low level flight television, infra-red imaging for a clear picture of the target, air or ground. His head-up display (HUD) will give him instant pictures by computer produced graphics in order that he can fly through enemy defense systems – or rather that the computer can fly him through danger areas. Has the age of the dogfight, therefore, ended? The answer has to be no. Tactics, speeds, weapon systems and aircraft design and technology have improved and will continue to improve. But while there is a thinking man (or indeed woman) in the cockpit with the final control over his or her element, however sophisticated is the equipment about him, the air battle will continue. Only when the fighting is taken over completely by machines will it end, or will it just be, yet again, simply different?

BIBLIOGRAPHY

Robert Loraine - W Loraine Collins, 1938
Eagles of the Black Cross - W A Musciano I Oblensky, 1965
Von Richthofen & the Flying Circus - H J Nowarra & K S Brown Harleyford, 1958
Ace of Aces - R Fonck Doubleday, 1967
Fighting Airman - C J Biddle Doubleday, 1968
Max Immelmann, Eagle of Lille - F Immelmann J Hamilton Ltd,
Recollections of an Airman - L A Strange J Hamilton Ltd,
Fighting the Flying Circus - E V Rickenbacker Doubleday, 1965
Hostile Skies - J J Hudson Syracuse, 1968
Flying Fury - J B McCudden Aviation Book Club, 1930
No Parachute - A S G Lee Jarrolds, 1968
The Balloon Buster - N S Hall Corgi, 1967
Last Train over Rostov Bridge - M Aten Cassell, 1962
Albert Ball VC - R C Bowyer Wm Kimber, 1977
For Valour - The Air VCs - R C Bowyer Wm Kimber, 1978
Air Aces - C F Shores Bison, 1983
Combat over Spain - J Larios Spearman, 1970
Fighter over Finland - E Luukkanen Macdonald, 1963
First Kill - W Gnys Wm Kimber, 1982
History of the Polish Air Force - J Cynk Osprey, 1972
Nine Lives - A C Deere Hodder & Stoughton, 1959
Fight for the Sky - D Bader Sidgwick & Jackson, 1973
War Eagles - J S Childers Wm Heinemann, 1943
Battle over the Reich - A Price Ian Allen, 1973
Fighter Aces - R Toliver & T Constable Macmillan, 1965
The Blond Knight of Germany - Toliver & Constable Arthur Barker, 1970
Horrido - Toliver & Constable Arthur Barker, 1968
Pattle - Supreme Fighter in the Air - E C R Baker Wm Kimber, 1965
Wings God gave my Soul - J W Noah Charles Baptie, 1974
The Last Chance - J Steinhoff Hutchinson, 1977
The First and the Last - A Galland Methuen, 1955
The Wildcat in WW2 - B Tillman Nautical & Aviation Publishing Company of America, 1983
The Hellcat - B Tillman PSL, 1979
Samurai - S Sakai/M Caiden Wm Kimber, 1959
Five Down and Glory - G Gurney Putnam, 1958
Fighter Tactics & Strategy - E Sims Cassell, 1962
Fork-Tailed Devil: The P38 - M Caiden Ballantine, 1971
Duel Under the Stars - W Johnen Wm Kimber, 1957
Thunderbolt - R S Johnson/M Caiden Ballantine, 1971
Faith, Hope and Charity - K Poolman Wm Kimber, 1954
Zero - Okumiya, Horikoshi & Caiden Cassell, 1957
Fighting Squadron - R A Winston Zenger, 1982
Hell in the Heavens - J M Foster Zenger, 1981
Mustang Pilot - R E Turner Wm Kimber, 1970
Fighter Pilot Tactics - M Spick PSL, 1983
The Focke Wulf 190 - A Famous German Fighter - H Nowarra Harleyford, 1965
The Me109 - A Famous German Fighter - H Nowarra Harleyford, 1963
Mustang at War - R A Freeman Ian Allan, 1974
Aces of the Eighth - G B Stafford/W N Hess Squadron/Signal Pub, 1973
Munster: The Way it Was - I Hawkins Robinson Typographics, 1984
Mig Alley - L Davis Squadron/Signal Pub, 1978
Battle for the Falklands, Air Forces - R Braybrook Osprey, 1982
Fighting Jets - B Walker Time-Life, 1983
Air Warfare - C Campbell Hamlyn, 1984
Mig Master: F8 Crusader - B Tillman PSL, 1980
Air War South Atlantic - A Price/J Ethell Sidgwick & Jackson, 1984
Sabre Jets over Korea - D K Evans Tab Books Inc, 1984

The publishers would like to express their thanks to those of the above for use of extracted material in this book.

INDEX

CONCISE INDEX OF AIRCRAFT